Minorities: The New Europe's Old Issue

Minorities:
The New Europe's Old Issue

Edited by
IAN M. CUTHBERTSON and JANE LEIBOWITZ

With a Foreword by Joseph S. Nye, Jr.

INSTITUTE FOR EASTWEST STUDIES

PRAGUE · BUDAPEST · WARSAW
NEW YORK · ATLANTA

Distributed by:
    Westview Press
    5500 Central Ave.
    Boulder, Colorado 80301
    (800) 456–1995

Library of Congress Cataloging-in-Publication data

Minorities: the new Europe's old issue   /   edited by Ian M. Cuthbertson
and Jane Leibowitz
    p. cm.
    Includes bibliographical references and index.
    ISBN 0-913449-37-7 (IEWS). — ISBN 0-8133-2199-9 (Westview) :
$39.85
    1. Minorities—Europe, Eastern.   2. Europe, Eastern—Politics and
    government—1989-   3. Europe, Eastern—Ethnic relations.
I. Cuthbertson, Ian M., 1957-   .   II. Leibowitz, Jane, 1967-
DJK.M56   1993
305.8'00947—dc 20   93-38402
                                                               CIP

To our parents with the deepest gratitude for all of their support. This would not have been possible without you. If you hadn't brainwashed us into going to university we could have been very rich plumbers by now.

Contents

Foreword

Ignoring minority issues is like ignoring a volcano. Both in Europe and the United States, the tensions embedded in the political, cultural, and economic lives of minorities tend to be obscured until an explosion brings the camera crews rushing in, thrusting minorities and related issues into the limelight. The explosion may be one of rage, such as the Los Angeles riots, or it may take less dramatic, but just as heartfelt, forms, such as ostracism by classmates. But the pattern is well-established—a quick and superficial examination of the situation surrounding the "plight" of the minority. It begins with an impeachment of the careless, forgetful, discriminatory, or abusive behavior of the majority and its government representatives, followed by a series of glib "solutions" from a bevy of activists, advocates, and experts, all of whose approaches seem to require large amounts of political concessions on the part of the majority and large-scale economic support for the minority. Then it's on to the next eruption.

While such a news cycle may be inevitable in today's media age, it does little to address the real issues surrounding the situation of minorities either in North America or Europe, and especially in East Central Europe, today. The collapse of communism brought great joy to many minorities. For the first time since 1945, and in many cases long before that, individuals were free to express a group identity at odds with the label that the state and the party had assigned to all facets of life. This situation brought about the renaissance of many minorities who had long struggled to maintain their religious, ethnic, or cultural identities in the face of a system dedicated to the eradication of differences and the promotion of homogeneity. The result was a babble of voices calling for local and international recognition of the existence of certain distinct groups of people with a common identity and for "special" group rights that went beyond those codified in identity documents or passports.

But this plethora of groups demanding recognition and rights did little to help strengthen the cohesion of societies still struggling through the transition to democracy and trying to undo the legacies of communism. Indeed, the issues that surround minorities in much of East Central Europe have little to do with the consequences of the revolutions of 1989, or even the end of World War II. Many, if not most, date back to the collapse of the multiethnic empires, the

Ottoman and Austro-Hungarian, and the dismemberment of the German and Russian Empires after 1918.

The longevity and intractability of the minority question can be seen at its starkest in the former Yugoslavia, where the claims and counterclaims of injustices and atrocities date back far beyond this century. Participants often wind up citing events in the Middle Ages. The passions that such long-held grievances generate can be seen in the unrestrained violence of a war the likes of which Europe never thought to see again.

However, in some of the calls for minority recognition and the desire for special group rights to go along with this new consciousness, the idea of group *responsibilities* has been much slower in gaining acceptance. There is strong resistance on the part of many minorities, especially among their most visible and vocal advocates, to accept that there are responsibilities, in terms of behavior and allegiances, that go hand in hand with recognition of group identity and the rights of association.

Individual states and the international community as a whole must be careful not to endorse or support the granting of rights to one group at the expense of the same rights of another group. Moreover, in an atmosphere characterized by an international system under threat from destabilizing national, social, and economic tensions, the inviolability of international borders has become one of the cornerstones on which the current European international system is based. Thus, both national and supranational rules and regulations are needed to regularize the place of minorities in societies. At a time when there are strongly competing trends towards transnationalism, regionalism, and group identification, all taking place simultaneously in the same regions, countries, and societies, ways must be found to address the urgent and complex issues that surround minority rights and responsibilities.

With these pressing problems in mind, it was prescient of the Institute for EastWest Studies to address these issues at its Thirteenth Annual Conference, held appropriately in Slovenia, an oasis of calm in a corner of the world that is tearing itself apart in internecine battles. The conference set out to examine the many facets of the minority question, not just in Eastern Europe, but in the continent as a whole. This volume is a collection of the best papers from the conference. They are both timely and insightful. Their recommendations will not be palatable to everyone, but they should and must serve as the catalyst to a debate in which we in the international community must engage—and of which many individual states are already in the throes—if we are to avoid seeing issues of minority rights and responsibilities become an unstable powder keg setting off explosions across the continent.

It is a common responsibility, not the burden of any one group or society, to find solutions. I believe that the conference and this volume may help to bring about some tangible progress on issues that seem likely to preoccupy us for years to come. It hope that with good will and original thinking on all our parts, we can find prescriptions that are not only acceptable to all, but that receive the enthusiastic endorsement of everyone. We in the United States and other countries of the Western community have experiences, both good and bad, with minority rights and responsibilities to share. We stand ready to help find common solutions to these universal issues.

Joseph S. Nye, Jr.

Editors' Acknowledgments

This volume explores an issue that remains the most sensitive of political topics in East Central Europe and the Newly Independent States. Issues of ethnicity, political power, and discrimination excite strong passions in the well-established democracies of the West. They are doubly sensitive in a region where democracy and stability are still at a premium. To all of our colleagues in the region who worked with us on the IEWS project on "The Future of CSCE: Minority Rights and Responsibilities," of which this volume is the culmination, we thank you.

The staff of the IEWS also deserves a great deal of credit. Pride of place must go to Johanna Bjorken. Her passionate commitment to the region, especially her abiding interest in Slovenia and Croatia, is a source of constant wonder. Without her help, support and patience, working on this book would have been a much greater challenge. We are both deeply appreciative of all the support she has provided to us. Holli Bennett also bore the brunt of the stress as we edited the papers from Lake Bled, and she is to be congratulated for keeping her idealism intact. Dana Wallach should also be thanked for all of her hard work that made this book possible.

Richard Levitt, our Director of Publications, performed above and beyond the call of duty to produce this volume. Rosalie Morales Kearns did her usual excellent work in the challenging copy editing and in the production of the index. Amy Lew also performed her word processing to her usual high standards.

To all of the Institute staff who provided support to the Lake Bled Conference that this book is derived from, and in particular to Hollison Kaplan and Helena Ackerman, we owe a deep debt of thanks.

We also wish to thank all of our board members and friends who wrote papers and acted as speakers, chairs, respondents, and rapporteurs at the conference. They are the core of this work. The paper writers represented in this volume deserve special thanks for their discipline and diligence in producing high-quality work under tight deadlines. Richard Allan, Adam Albion, and Robert Mickey, whose papers appear in this book, deserve special thanks. As Institute staff, they were hit with particular force by the heavy hand of our editing.

Finally, without the support of the W. Alton Jones Foundation and the director of its Secure World Project, George Perkovich, and the Carnegie Corporation of New York, our project and this book would not have been possible. It was their support that allowed us to fully explore a difficult and at times highly technical topic, and illuminate the key issues that drive much of the security debate now preoccupying Europe in its search for viable solutions to what often seem intractable problems. We remain grateful for these foundations' vision and insight.

Introduction

IAN M. CUTHBERTSON
JANE LEIBOWITZ

A truism is no less valid for being true. We are all members of minorities. Left-handed people, opera lovers, ballroom dancers . . . we all belong to groups the membership in which makes us in some way different from the people who surround us. But this type of minority status rarely causes any difficulties or carries any penalties. It is the other types of minority identities—those based on race, religion, or national origin—that serve to excite passions.

These types of minorities, anxious to assert their group identities, have a mission to secure recognition of their separate identities in a way few opera lovers would consider either necessary or desirable. In asserting such identities, such minorities are often reacting to real or perceived oppression or discrimination on the part of the majority. In East Central Europe, such perceptions are age-old. Life and politics often play like a historical liturgy of expulsions, massacres and discrimination.

Yet the types of rights sought by minorities in East Central Europe, and the sometimes confrontational nature of their relationship with the majorities who hold political power, often seem to preclude the type of dialogue on which any accord must be based. In an unstable region with developing political structures, majorities many times feel threatened from without and besieged from within. This is because all too often the debate lacks a balance between the rights being sought by a given minority and the responsibilities that such groups and individuals must be willing to assume as part of the process of attaining recognition, especially with regard to the territorial integrity of the states of which they form a part. Responsibility cuts both ways. The majority, in recognition of the existence of a distinct minority population, assumes that the minority recognizes its own group and individual responsibilities. These are central to the success of any pact, because all too often where the rights of a minority are compromised, the rights of the majority soon follow the same route. As Pastor Martin Niemöller (a victim of the Nazis) said:

> First they came for the Jews and I did not speak out—because I was not a Jew. Then they came for the communists and I did not speak out—because I was not a communist. Then they

came for the trade unionists and I did not speak out—
because I was not a trade unionist. Then they came for
me—and there was no one left to speak out for me.

Such a situation was thought unrepeatable in today's Europe. Yet
in the former Yugoslavia, precisely this process is occurring. And
Yugoslavia is the locus of only the most violent and visible of a number
of ethnic disputes in East Central Europe. Throughout the region,
security risks have changed and multiplied during the post-Cold War
social and economic transition, resulting in unclear visions of the
future and a *terra incognita* of both domestic and international
relations.

In the past, the bipolar military and ideological confrontation
between East and West was clear-cut and relatively simple to manage.
Forty-five years of practice helped both parties, NATO and the
Warsaw Pact, perfect the complicated minuet that their security
relationship had produced. Now, newfound liberties amidst apparent
chaos have lent expression to rediscovered nationalism, ethnic grievances, and, in some cases, the disintegration of multiethnic states that
have proved unable to manage domestic tensions between the constituent nationalities, absent the imperatives of communist ideology and its
attendant police apparatus. Accompanying this turbulence has been a
deterioration of minority-majority relations throughout East Central
Europe, as both sides become more polarized over the issue of what
type of recognition minorities deserve in terms of their group
identities, and which obligations such rights in turn carry with them.
This dangerous trend is not contained within state borders. It also has
negative ramifications for interstate politics, as perceptions of irredentism on the part of not only national ethnic minorities, but of their
putative "mother-states" as well, exacerbate relations already marked
by a high degree of tension. Representing one of the major challenges
facing the continent, minority issues clearly play a crucial role in
relations both between and within states.

In communist Europe, minorities went unrecognized, as the
universality of Marxist ideology theoretically made everyone equal.
The reality, however, was very different. Many groups found the
weight of communist oppression especially heavy if they refused to
submerge their identity in some vision of the "communist person."
The collapse of communism unleashed pent-up emotions, leaving a
legacy of turmoil that Europe, both as a whole and as individual
nations, must come to understand and address.

The explosiveness of the situation assumes greater proportions
when woven into the tenuous fabric of nascent democracies. The

various wars going on simultaneously on the territory of the former Yugoslavia show only the most dramatic example of what might happen elsewhere when new democracies attempt to enfranchise and empower minorities and at the same time maintain cohesion and national sovereignty. In addition, it may also represent the final refutation of the view, held widely since World War I, that self-determination for Europe's ethnic minorities would tend to help stabilize countries rather than fragment them.

This is an issue that continues to resurface, with a consensus evolving that the concept of self-determination is too destabilizing to be applied broadly as a solution to ethnic grievances; and that the splintering of state entities into smaller and smaller ethnic enclaves is destroying both the political and economic cohesiveness of the European continent. Such a view would hold that President Woodrow Wilson's position on self-determination was therefore, in essence, wrong and Secretary of State Robert Lansing's was right. Simply put, there are dangers to wholesale acceptance of the concept of self-determination—that on the basis of language, the right to independence should be granted to minorities—because that would require recognition of over 6,000 countries, the number of languages existing in the world.

To give President Wilson credit, he did not envision the establishment of thousands of new nations; instead he expected a process of bonding to take place. He failed to foresee, however, that minorities would believe that the right to cultural autonomy extends also to the right to form a state. In some cases, Western Europe has successfully dealt with this issue: Belgium has a fractious yet successful system of coexistence based largely on economic interdependence between two antagonistic linguistic communities. Another example is Scotland, a state that, despite its people's long-standing wish for a political identity distinct from England, has recognized that economic realities make it an issue not worth forcing. Western Europe provides a good model for replication in some cases because many West European states have a deeper awareness of where the benefits of collectivity lie, a recognition that hoisting a flag over land is rarely worth the ensuing destabilization and economic duress. As of yet, however, Eastern Europe has not yet achieved the same type of well-developed political culture. For this to occur, Eastern Europe must be encouraged towards cooperation, and international organizations should create as conducive an atmosphere as possible for this to occur.

The eruption of dozens of examples of unanticipated ethnic friction in the wake of the recent collapse of the former Soviet Union and the end of the Cold War only foreshadows what is to come if the policy of self-determination continues to hold appeal for the minorities of the region. Already, conflicts in the name of ethnic pride have left tens of thousands dead and countless more homeless and caused the return of concentration camps and the use of mass rape as an instrument of ethnic policy. Ways of adeptly and peacefully managing ethnic and religious grievances must be found to allow emerging societies to function on a secure democratic basis. Otherwise, an unprecedented opportunity for democratization and the creation of free market economies in the new Europe will be lost for a generation, if not longer.

Accepting the premise of the inviolability of international borders, we can begin to look at policy prescriptions aimed at working within the established parameters of the current international system; favoring prescriptions focused on rebuilding rather than starting from scratch, we can stress confidence- and security-building measures that encompass local, regional, and international relations.

The chapters in this volume are based on papers presented at an Institute for EastWest Studies conference, "Minority Rights and Responsibilities: Challenges in a New Europe," held in Lake Bled, Slovenia on May 21–23, 1993. Bringing together world leaders and policy makers for full and frank discussion of the complex ethnic and religious issues that pertain to the conduct of states and peoples, we began with the premise that the problem is not a lack of ideas—the issue is not a new one, and international codes of conduct, standards, and rules abound—but rather the absence of clear, practical policy prescriptions and the means with which to implement them. Such prescriptions need to take account not only of the concerns of minorities themselves; they must also address majorities and the states that are often their representatives. A lack of objectivity in dealing with this critical issue is manifest on all sides, and rational discussion often seems absent, as many of the parties to various minority disputes rush to extreme positions based on long-standing misperceptions. Thus the focus of the international community must be to identify ways of rebuilding these ethnic relations, strained in the wake of the collapse of communism.

The authors' goal, from the outset, was to find the balance between the rights of minorities (if, in fact, such group rights should exist) and the responsibilities that such rights must also carry. This means that when the members of a group demand that their rights as a collective be recognized, they need to understand that such recognition also brings with it responsibilities in terms of their behavior towards fellow citizens who constitute the majority and their attitude towards the state of which they form a part. The book's treatment of this issue is an ambitious one due to the plethora of questions it raises: What level of autonomy is best for both sides? Are there new and workable models of federalism that make all parties feel more comfortable within existing state structures? What is the correct role for the CSCE High Commissioner on National Minorities? How do transnational minorities, such as the Roma and the Jews, fit into the emerging picture? When is international intervention in domestic disputes involving a minority both necessary and right? And what kind of enforcement provisions are necessary to ensure effective mediation and intervention by international bodies? The starting points for the deliberations were the nation-state, which has not, *pace* Marx, withered away; a realization that despite the emergence of transnational organizations violent minority conflicts persist; and the acknowledgment that efforts by the international community to defuse animosities and build cooperation have accomplished little.

The volume includes case studies of Macedonia, Bulgaria, Romania, the Russian Federation, Russians living in the NIS, and the particular issues of Jewish communities in East Central Europe. These and other chapters also discuss the need for different levels of solutions to the minority question—*local*, *national*, *bilateral*, and *international*. It is at the *local level* that most day-to-day interaction among people takes place, where the struggle for equality lies in maintaining what are often harmonious personal relationships in the face of group stereotyping and the concomitant pressure to support one's own ethnic or religious "side." At the *national level*, democracy building in ethnically diverse countries such as Macedonia, Bulgaria, and Romania, and the possibilities for a new type of Russian federalism (wherein ethnic enclaves might function as virtual states) show different routes nations can take toward the integration of minorities in political systems. Disappointment in international responses to minority questions both on paper and in practice has resulted in a new trend, discussed here, towards *bilateral* and regional-level treaties for minority protection. A number of East Central European states have negotiated bilateral treaties, a strategy that appears, more and more, to be overturning the universalist strategy of human rights protection embraced by the UN for the past 48 years and the CSCE for 18. This new trend is vaguely reminiscent of prewar practice, notably the League of Nations' intricate system of treaties aimed at minority protection. Finally at the *international level*, organizations such as the CSCE, the UN, and the Council of Europe have developed mechanisms for safeguarding the rights of minorities and preventing abuse that is based on ethnicity or religious affiliation. How well these mechanisms have been formulated and implemented is a major topic of the authors presented in this volume.

A prerequisite to any examination of the minority issue is an understanding of what is being discussed. Those who brandish terms assume that their definitions are self-evident, yet this is often far from the case. Finding no shortage of overlap and confusion, Iván Gyurcsík of the Hungarian Human Rights Foundation in New York provides an examination of the multiplicity of definitions and uses of such concepts as *state, nation, minority, sovereignty,* and *self-determination* in his chapter "New Legal Ramifications of the Question of National Minorities." In tracing their recent and historical uses in legal documents, as well as the philosophical perspectives taken on the concept of a minority, Gyurcsík examines approaches that have been available to states when formulating policies. The debate over whether to grant individual or group rights to minorities is informed greatly by the widely recognized right to identity. Granting autonomy is a plausible and acceptable means of upholding these rights, and other nations' experiences show that it has the potential to assume a great variety of guises, not all of them territorial.

Before approaching the drawing board with new ideas, the advantages and shortcomings of past experience need to be evaluated. "Responding to pressures to establish a new code of conduct for the protection of national minorities," Gyurcsík says, "the question might be asked: 'What was wrong with the old one? What should the new ones say?' " Reevaluation of terms cannot be the only step, however. One of the major shortcomings that Gyurcsík details in his analysis is the failure of the international community, despite this plethora of detailed elaboration of minority rights, to implement their conclusions. Without enforcement—perhaps available through encouraged cooperation, early warning mechanisms, preventive diplomacy, and, as a last resort, military intervention—hard-fought-for legal norms disintegrate to empty words.

Armed with a vocabulary for discussion, we can begin to understand the current state of affairs, examining various case studies of ethnic tension. Macedonia presents a particularly interesting case study, with political implications extending from the state to the region (the Balkans) to the international arena. In "Success in the Balkans? A Case Study of Ethnic Relations in the Republic of Macedonia," Robert W. Mickey and Adam Smith Albion, Research Associates at the IEWS European Studies Center in Prague, seek answers to these questions. Through extensive trips through the country and its neighbors, Mickey and Albion sought to identify possible solutions that have meaning both with regard to the present tragic situation in Bosnia and

Herzegovina and to the broader context of ethnic/religious conflicts generally.

Macedonia, a new republic whose status is disputed by Bulgarians, Greeks, and Albanians, is the only former Yugoslav republic to secede without violence—at least so far. Economically undeveloped, it has interpreted the 25%-30% ethnic Albanian constituency's demands for autonomy as a threat to the state's already tenuous identity. Mistrust on both sides has strained relations, and Mickey and Albion examine the influences that both exacerbate and relieve this tension, including the role of political parties, the looming presence of "mother country" Albania, the role of nationalism, and the connotation autonomy bears for both sides.

In Macedonia, other frustrations exacerbate ethnic tension, suggesting that alleviation of these other stresses would likewise take pressure off ethnic issues. In addition to economic rejuvenation, tackling these issues of regional relations requires stabilization with Greece and Kosovo and tightening the Albanian border. Albanians need to be wooed to remain faithful to the state; multiethnic cooperation, perhaps through ethnic party coalitions, could provide such incentives. In addition, education, anti-discrimination policies in employment, and a diverse media should be fostered to help curb negative stereotyping. There is cause for optimism, the authors conclude: "Given a renewed international commitment to Macedonia's future, this new state can survive, continue to surprise its detractors, and keep alive the possibility of multiethnic civil states in the Balkans."

The situation of a minority, such as the Jews or Roma, who have no geographical center in the region but who nonetheless exhibit a strong sense of common identity and a high level of group cohesion, has long presented Europe with unique problems. These groups seem to embody the idea of "apartness," being *in* rather than *of* the community. The result of such perceptions in the past are epitomized by pogroms and the Holocaust. In his chapter "Paradox of Freedom: The 'Jewish Question' in Postcommunist East Central Europe," André W. M. Gerrits, a professor at the University of Amsterdam's Institute for Russian and East European Studies, traces the role anti-Semitism has played in the 20th century, concluding that today in East Central Europe, it is based on historical influences of an authoritative political culture, historical prejudice, and insecurity in a state of flux, compounded by politicians who manipulate these influences to their own gain. Anti-Semitism is utilized in smear campaigns that use Jews or Jewishness as a metaphor to represent everything despicable in political life, or by emphasizing the opposite, that a candidate is a "true Pole" or a "Catholic Hungarian." Unlike traditional majority-minority relations, a quest for autonomy, real or otherwise, is not the reason behind the majority's discriminatory practices. Because of this, Gerrits believes that anti-Semitism *per se* is only part of a larger threat perception that links preoccupation with cultural decay and loss of national values with fears of a Western conspiracy.

Although anti-Semitism in the region is pervasive (despite being openly rejected, it is tacitly accepted as an unavoidable part of political culture), persecution of Jews does not exceed that of any other minority group. The difference lies, however, in the solution. Non-national minorities like the Jews promote universal human rights to combat intolerance, prejudice, and hatred and can also look to local- and national-level solutions; other groups can find answers in bilateral protection agreements between mother-states and host states.

In "Democracy Building in Ethnically Diverse Societies: The Cases of Bulgaria and Romania," Ivanka Nedeva, Senior Research Associate at the Free Initiative Foundation in Sofia, examines the case studies of Bulgaria and Romania, where sizeable ethnic minority populations repeatedly place minority issues at the forefront of the domestic agenda. In both countries, treatment of ethnic minorities has served as a bellwether for the transition to democracy: in Bulgaria, with its relations with indigenous Turks and Slavic Muslims, and in Romania, with ethnic Hungarians. Nedeva stresses the similarities between the two nations, such as popular feelings of nationalism and its manipulation by former communists in order to maintain power, idiosyncracies of legal mandates, the role of ethnic parties, and the conflicts of interest regarding minorities that each country faces. However, Nedeva chooses to focus on these two countries because of the differing approaches of the dominant ethnic parties. Both pro-mote issue-specific agendas primarily relative to their own interests, and with insight and thoroughness Nedeva traces and compares the paths the ethnic minority parties have taken, analyzes their impact, and offers country-specific solutions.

Russia presents a prime example of a country that has been the majority administration for centuries, and only now, due to the disintegration of multinational states, finds for the first time members of its community outside its borders. In "The Problem of Ethnic Minority Rights Protection in the Newly Independent States," Alex-ander A. Konovalov, Director of the Center for Military Policy and Systems Analysis, and Dmitri Evstafiev, Research Associate at the Institute for the USA and Canada, both of the Academy of Sciences in Moscow, speak of the sudden change of status, from majority to minority, of more than 20 million Russian or Russian-speaking citizens following the dissolution of the Soviet Union. As a result, both ongoing and potential ethnic conflicts in Russia and in other former Soviet republics represent serious threats to international security and stability. Konovalov and Evstafiev assert that massive and quick changes in the international strategic landscape eliminated bipolar confrontation and made obsolete and impotent practically all mechanisms, institutions, and principles that had been designed to ensure international security and stability. Huge nuclear potentials, military alliances, and sophisticated military strategic concepts have failed not only to be efficient, but even applicable means to deter ethnic and national conflicts.

In addition to calling upon the international community to create incentives for the ethnic Russians to stay in the republics where they have lived for several generations, Konovalov and Evstafiev propose some steps the international community can take to settle ethnic and national conflict and implement peacekeeping and peace enforcement provisions. They suggest that "international bodies and organizations should operate on the basis of true and full information about the processes unfolding in the former USSR. Independent sources of information are critical. Thus the idea of stationing permanent UN fact-finding missions in the former Soviet Union seems relevant. In addition, taking into consideration the importance of the problem, it seems sensible to establish within the organizational framework of the United Nations a special agency dealing with the rights of ethnic minorities in the former USSR."

In "Can Decentralization Solve Russia's Ethnic Problems?" Nicolai N. Petro, Assistant Professor of Political Science at the University of Rhode Island, discusses the impact federalism can have on maintaining harmonious ethnic relations. In his chapter, Petro asserts that the vast majority of people in the Russian Federation wish to preserve Russia's territorial and cultural unity but fear for the prospects for democracy in Moscow; moreover, the slow pace of economic revival has fueled speculation regarding Russia's disintegration. As the most important step taken to date to halt the fragmentation of the Russian Federation and its concomitant and inevitable ethnic upheaval, Petro cites the signing of the Federation Treaty on March 31, 1992. "[Its] triune treaty structure," he writes, "is based on a simple premise: only by encouraging the devolution of administrative authority from the center can the territorial integrity and historical unity of Russia be preserved. . . . The signatories . . . acknowledge that they are not constituting a new federation but redefining their membership in an existing one." The treaty also establishes "a framework within which to resolve future ethnic and administrative conflicts. . . . by emphasizing the priority of universal human and civic rights over territorial and ethnic sovereignty."

But the broader problem plaguing the Russian Federation, Petro asserts, is that "its cohesiveness is directly proportional to Moscow's ability to improve the quality of life in the country." Therefore he recommends that to prevent further disintegration, the Russian government must simultaneously strengthen democratic institutions, promote regional decentralization, and improve the economy. Petro terms this strategy of making Russia as desirable a partner politically and economically as it is culturally "guided decentralization." Prerequisites to this policy, he maintains, are a democratic government, a new constitution, and economic revitalization, not at the center but in each of Russia's already distinct economic regions.

Petro concludes with a warning that if the West rewards secession with economic investment and diplomatic recognition, attempts to federalize Russia will fail. However, the West must encourage economic rebirth through investment, not merely in the center but in regional and local projects; it will not be an easy balance to strike. But keeping this in mind, the West must be vocal and state a clear preference for a unified Russian Federation.

In "A Call for Confidence-Building Measures for Minorities in Eastern Europe," Andrzej Karkoszka, Director of the Department of Strategic Planning at the Ministry of Defense of Poland, states that security threats, real or imagined, are magnified by feelings of insecurity and—despite apparent stability in military structures—can develop into acute and actual threats, as witnessed in the internecine warfare in the Balkans, Georgia, Moldova, and Azerbaijan. Measures must be taken in areas where distrust between the majority and the minorities runs high *before* they reach this stage of open violence. Europe already has an extensive network of mechanisms to guide military endeavors characterized by a lack of trust between parties, and Karkoszka proposes they be restructured to be able to respond to nonmilitary instabilities.

Confidence- and security-building measures (CSBMs) need to be applied to promote mutual understanding, tolerance, and confidence between different ethnic groups. However, Karkoszka warns that these measures may be difficult to implement because it means influencing widespread and long-held social beliefs and stereotypes. CSBMs should, he therefore suggests, begin with direct contact at the grassroots level, between groups, involving exchange, interaction, and efforts to counteract the "enemy image." Finding ways to moderate the rhetoric of both sides will serve to slow or halt the drift to extreme positions. In addition, Karkoszka proposes establishing bilateral interstate arrangements that can act as a bridge of trust by codifying relations between minorities and their mother-state, as well as cross-frontier economic and cultural exchanges, which would serve to narrow the differences and help challenge perceptions that would normally divide states, alleviating suspicions of one another's motives vis-à-vis their national minorities. Lastly, improved methods of access for minority representatives to national legislatures and the provision of constitutional guarantees of equal rights and protection that will reflect the states' commitment to minorities, by ensuring a role in the workings of the state, are necessary steps towards building confidence.

Richard Allan, IEWS American Scholar-in-Residence and Professor of Law at Brooklyn Law School, warns in his chapter "The Failure to Recognize Minority Rights and Claims: Political Violence/Terrorism in the East and West," that if in the decision-making process the mistakes of the past are ignored, efforts to build confidence are not undertaken, and present trends continue, minorities will have fewer and fewer outlets through which to channel their efforts to participate in the political process; they will also have fewer opportunities to seek economic achievement; and will find themselves unable to attain social integration and acceptance. Allan believes history provides sufficient evidence that the protection of minorities is placed in great jeopardy when the consensus that is the basis for a movement toward a democratic form of government falters or fails. "Those who are truly oppressed, or who perceive themselves to be oppressed," will vent their frustration and seek to attain their individual rights and claims via political violence and terrorism. If individual rights in the East are denied or ignored, Allan maintains, a new form of violence—tribal terrorism—will move across the East and across the borders into the West.

In his chapter, Allan highlights both West European failures to resolve serious ethnic minority problems within their borders (France, Spain, and the United Kingdom), as well as successes (South Tyrol, Belgium). He places emphasis on the lessons to be learned from Western Europe—"that terrorism can and does become a way of life, a means of existence, or a method to retain the power realized through confrontation and terrorism"—and the necessity of making minority rights a priority in Eastern Europe now in order to help strengthen the chances for long-term social stability.

In "The International Community and Forms of Intervention in the Field of Minority Rights Protection," Koen Koch, Professor of Political Science at the University of Leiden, shows us the practical need for more bilateral agreements in his assessment of the international community's performance since the 1989 revolutions. Koch finds a growing contradiction between the normative commitments of the international community, embodied in universal and regional minority rights instruments on the one hand, and the level of implementation of these commitments and the reluctance of the international community to protect the rights when they are grossly violated on the other. His chapter analyzes the political causes of this contradiction, finding that faithful implementation of minority rights presupposes the specific rejection of nationalism by states—majorities as well as minorities—and the acceptance of pluralism, which acknowledges cultural and ethnic diversity and even fosters it. Normative commitments made by the international community have proven ineffective, lacking not only means but an international will to implement them.

In the face of sluggish international response, attention should be focused on regional solutions, specifically bilateral treaties. Third countries can be called upon to provide material assistance, if necessary, and can also draw up an official list of minorities, to protect those whose host countries deny their existence. Its weak record on actual commitment means that the international community must seriously consider its willingness to participate before issuing additional mandates. Instead, responsibility should be shifted to the players themselves, who can, with assistance and guidance, develop their own methods more suitable and flexible to actual situations.

István Íjgyártó, from the Office for Hungarians Living Abroad, also emphasizes flexibility as a priority for treating minority issues in his chapter "Codification of Minority Rights." He describes models various countries have used in their experiences with their own minorities, ranging from those that strongly emphasize individual rights to those that grant a generous amount of autonomy. Nations, especially emerging East European democracies who in general have shown a great deal of willingness and cooperation to confront the issue, need to develop flexible programs that will address the specific needs and grievances of the minorities in question. For this reason, Íjgyártó, like Koch, finds international agreements insufficient, since their broad prescriptions become legally meaningless, binding only as far as the willing participation of signatory states.

Íjgyártó cites the successful record some countries have had in forming bilateral treaties and agreements, which reflect a commitment on the part of nations who have a stake in the particular case. Hungary, especially, has played an active role in minority affairs, taking the initiative beyond international mandates and agreements. It has spelled out minority rights in its constitution and law (before Parliament, as this volume went to press). In addition to concern for minorities within its borders, the Hungarian government campaigns actively for the rights of Hungarians outside its borders. Rather than rely on the international community, however, Hungary has been negotiating on an individual basis with countries. A Hungarian-Ukrainian declaration of cooperation promises to respect and guarantee minority rights, and it has also been signed by Croatia and Slovenia.

The role of the CSCE High Commissioner on National Minorities (HCNM) is an important part of the discussion on the vagaries of international law as they relate to minority rights and the integrity of national borders. The CSCE's role is present in a number of different contexts, from its failure in the former Yugoslavia (a failure it shared with other European institutions) to the opportunities offered by the new office of the CSCE High Commissioner on National Minorities. Konrad J. Huber, Advisor to the CSCE High Commissioner on National Minorities, in his chapter entitled "Preventing Ethnic Conflict in the New Europe: The CSCE High Commissioner on National Minorities," provides a detailed background of the CSCE HCNM, how it came into being, and its mandate and functioning; and he offers policy prescriptions for strengthening its "ethnic conflict prevention capacity." Best characterized as an instrument of conflict prevention, the High Commissioner on National Minorities was recently established to identify and contribute to the possible resolution of inter-ethnic tensions at their earliest stages. Specifically, the High Commissioner (appointed in December 1992, former Dutch Foreign Minister Max van der Stoel began work as the first High Commissioner in January 1993) is to concentrate on analyzing and resolving tensions involving national minority issues that have the potential to develop into a conflict affecting peace, stability, or relations between states in the CSCE region (which encompasses the United States, Canada, all of the Newly Independent States on the territory of the former Soviet Union, and all other European states).

Although Huber states that it would be premature to offer definitive recommendations for strengthening the "ethnic conflict prevention capacity" of the CSCE and the High Commissioner, he identifies some broad needs, including more resources; clearer coordination of the CSCE's growing complex of decision-making bodies, consultative meetings, and executive institutions; continued development of its capacity to intervene constructively in nascent conflicts that have surpassed initial efforts at prevention by the High Commissioner; and further clarification of its relationship with other multilateral structures (e.g., the United Nations, NATO, the European Community, the Western European Union, and the Council of Europe). As in so many other areas and instances of the international community's response to the minorities issue, Huber concludes that the HCNM is a resource and a capability that has yet to be fully exploited. Huber is hopeful it soon will be.

Not all the recommendations suggested by the authors in this volume will be put into effect. Some are beyond the scope of political accommodation, and in some cases the various viewpoints contained in this book contradict one another. This is less important, however, than the general agreement shared by the authors that the minority issue is a pressing one, and we must do all that we can to ameliorate the problems at hand to stem further deterioration of an already unstable situation. The failure to do so, the authors realize, will result in an unprecedented proliferation of ethnic violence, creating a major setback for individual nations and the region as a whole in terms of progress made towards achieving market economies, establishing full-fledged democracies, and gaining entrance into European institutions. With this in mind, the authors endeavored to contribute, in a significant manner, to the difficult task of clarifying thinking on what may be practical solutions to minority problems and the methods whereby these solutions can be implemented.

Among the policy prescriptions formulated, discussed, and promoted in this volume are:

- Establishment of a much-needed independent center in East Central Europe that can provide factual information on what is actually going on in the postcommunist states of Europe with regard to minority rights and responsibilities. Such a center would fill a vacuum that presently exists, as there is no true and reliable information flow within the region.
- Creation of an inventory of the specific successes that can be identified in Eastern Europe in dealing with minority issues to promote positive perceptions. These successes exist, but they have simply not been collected and disseminated to the widest possible audience.
- Sponsorship by the CSCE of an intergovernmental conference on self-determination. It must be decided whether President Wilson's policy is still appropriate, or, if not, whether instead we should be striving for specific laws with realistic enforcement to guarantee international borders.
- Much more active participation in the lobbying of parliaments and governments, individually and collectively, to create the political momentum to create new constitutions in Eastern Europe, Russia, and the other Newly Independent States.

- Greater support of the CSCE, especially by Western nations. In particular, the office of its High Commissioner on National Minorities needs far greater resources placed at its disposal. The latter, with its crucial early action programs and rapporteur missions, must be revitalized, empowered, and provided with adequate funding for expansion.
- Greater involvement in supranational organizations, such as the European Community, the CSCE, and the Council of Europe, of countries in the region, especially those with significant ethnic minorities, by including them in all aspects of their deliberations and activities on these issues.
- Strengthening of good offices by third parties to pinpoint and report potential conflict points before they erupt.
- Pursuit of agreements that countries can negotiate on their own accord, bilaterally, to more flexibly accommodate and treat the real tensions and issues between groups.
- Support for policies within the borders of a state that emphasize the positive aspects of a minority constituency and curtail negative tendencies such as stereotyping. Economic incentives for cooperation and popular opinion shaped by the media are two extremely influential components that decision makers can employ towards increasing the confidence between groups.

No single solution exists to all the problems that East Central Europe faces. The minorities issue is only one of an extensive mosaic of overlapping and interconnected challenges, economic, social, and political, that face the region. However, it may be the most explosive. As Foreign Minister Kozyrev of Russia said in his speech to the UN General Assembly on September 28, 1993, "Developments in Yugoslavia, Abkhazia and Karabakh have shown also the real abyss of barbarism and the new major threat of aggressive nationalism. Outbursts of violence caused by xenophobia, even in traditionally prosperous countries, [demonstrate] the lack of guarantees against this threat. Today, it is no less serious than the threat of a nuclear war was yesterday."

These are words we should bear in mind as we tackle the minorities issue. The cost of not finding solutions is much higher than the price of any compromises we may all have to make.

Part I
Understanding the Issues

1

New Legal Ramifications of the Question of National Minorities

IVÁN GYURCSÍK

1. INTRODUCTION

The issue of national minorities has emerged as one of the most serious human rights and security problems facing Europe. Recent events have demonstrated that the lack of an effective system to guarantee the protection of minority rights can produce violent upheavals and major refugee problems. In this chapter, I will discuss some evolving legal concepts and practical dimensions of this question.

The protection of national minorities and the persons belonging to them is an especially urgent task in Central and Eastern Europe. A heritage of decades of totalitarianism, the weakness or complete absence of the rule of law, and the intolerance of the majority in many of these states place especially heavy burdens on minorities, in some cases threatening their very existence. It is against this pressing regional backdrop that I will address the prospects for developing a new legal framework to manage the problem of national minorities in this region and elsewhere in Europe.

The question of national minorities is often approached from the point of view of nation-states, with the minorities characterized as potential sources of instability. The view that national minorities have special "responsibilities" in addition to rights reflects this bias. But what special "responsibilities"—different from the responsibility of every citizen to accept the legal order of the democratic state—would it be reasonable and fair to apply before encroaching upon the principles of nondiscrimination and equality before the law?[1]

The focus has been on minorities as the *object* of a problem, with various forms of forced assimilation depicted, especially during the Cold War, as the solution rather than the problem. Discussion has centered on minorities' rights, at the expense of clarifying the policy of the state. In the first part of this chapter, I will reflect on both sides of the coin, that is, the rights of minorities and the policies of states.

A proper assessment requires some discussion of the concepts of *nation-state*, *sovereignty*, and *self-determination*, as well as the problems inherent in defining *minorities* and other basic terms. Next, it is important to review already existing provisions regarding minority rights, as contained, inter alia, in documents adopted by the United Nations, the Council of Europe, and the Conference on Security and Cooperation in Europe.

My basic argument is that the creation of any legal concept of minority rights depends less on technical formulations than on the political will of states. What is needed is to formulate standards for the rights of minorities and the policy of states toward minorities. New legal precepts need to be developed for the exercise of these rights at the local, state, and international levels.

Finally, I will suggest a possible direction to follow toward achieving the peaceful and constructive management of problems involving national minorities.

2. PROBLEMS OF DEFINITION

Until recently, the problem of defining such concepts as *state*, *nation*, *sovereignty*, *national minority*, and *self-determination* have dominated international legal discourse. There is no widely accepted definition of *nation*, *national minority*, or *self-determination*, and the concept of *sovereignty* is also changing.

For purposes of this paper it is important to distinguish between *state* and *nation*, terms often used interchangeably in the West.

In seeking to understand and manage the question of national minorities in Central and Eastern Europe, it is vital to recognize the differences in the way nations emerged in the Western versus the Eastern and Central parts of Europe. In Western usage, *nation* is practically synonymous with *state*, so much so that the term *international* law actually means law between *states*. Both terms, widely used in the West, refer to the people who constitute the citizens of a state.

In Central and Eastern Europe on the other hand, *nation* is defined mainly in ethnic terms. *Nation-state*, therefore, means a state dominated by the majority ethnic group, implicitly authorized to discriminate—using "democratic means"—against the national minority.[2] "The belief that every state is a nation, or that all sovereign states are national states, has done much to obfuscate human understanding of political realities. A state is a legal and political organization, with the power to require obedience and loyalty from its citizens. A nation is a community of people, whose members are bound together by a sense of solidarity, a common culture, a national consciousness."[3]

The state[4] is a recognized political entity that exercises the functions of government, while the nation is a cultural or social grouping with certain shared characteristics, such as language or ethnicity.[5]

In today's Europe, the process of interstate integration on the one hand, and the processes of the emergence of new states, the disintegration of states, and the need to guarantee minority rights through various forms of self-administration and regional autonomies on the other, argue for a reevaluation of the concept of sovereignty.

Sovereignty is a basic constitutional doctrine, the meaning of which is not universally agreed upon. Given the high level of interdependence in the contemporary world, it would be absurd to define sovereignty as the "supreme power" within a given state. Traditionally it was defined as a state's supreme and unlimited authority over the territory under its domain. More recently, it has been defined as "the authority or ability of a state to determine its relationship with outside powers."[6]

The fashioning of Western Europe into a common political, economic, and security entity is unimaginable without limiting to some degree the sovereignty of individual states. By the same token, the rights of national minorities cannot be guaranteed without some decentralization of power, invoking the principle of subsidiarity[7] and insuring democratic local self-government and self-administration to national minorities in the domain of their identity. "The time of absolute and exclusive sovereignty, however, is past; its theory was never matched by reality. It is the task of leaders of States today to understand this and to find a balance between the needs of good internal governance and the requirements of an even more interdependent world."[8]

The decades-old deliberations to find a proper definition for the term *minority* have often been invoked to justify the inability of international organizations to adopt and implement real and effective standards and measures for their protection. That a generally accepted definition failed to materialize is, of course, not the real reason for the absence of a system of international minority rights protection; the actual cause can be found more in the lack of political will on the part of some states to take effective steps in this direction. Where the political will is present, forward motion is possible. In the case of the term *people*, for example, the lack of a generally accepted definition has not prevented states from adopting covenants, protocols, and other instruments in which the term is left undefined. Regarding the problem of national minorities as well, some movement toward a more pragmatic direction is evident on the part of the international community.

As to the consequences of defining the term *minority*, it seems most appropriate to quote Francesco Capotorti: "Application of the principles set forth in Article 27 of the Covenant cannot, therefore, be made contingent upon a 'universal' definition of the term 'minority,' and it would be clouding the issue to claim the contrary."[9]

The most recent effort by the United Nations to define *minority* occurred at the 1985 meeting of the Sub-Commission on Prevention of Discrimination and Protection of Minorities. In its report, the definition reads:

> A group of citizens of a State, constituting a numerical minority and in a non-dominant position in that State, endowed with ethnic, religious or linguistic characteristics which differ from those of the majority of population, having a sense of solidarity with one another, motivated, if only implicitly, by a collective will to survive and whose aim it is to achieve equality with the majority in fact and in law.[10]

On February 1, 1993, the Council of Europe Parliamentary Assembly adopted Recommendation 1201 (1993) for an additional protocol on the rights of minorities to the European Convention for the Protection of Human Rights and Fundamental Freedoms. The proposal for an additional protocol to this Convention, concerning persons belonging to national minorities, defines national minorities in article 1 as follows:

> For the purpose of this convention the expression "national minority" refers to a group of persons in a state who
> a. reside on the territory on that state and are citizens thereof,
> b. maintain long standing, firm and lasting ties with that state,
> c. display distinctive ethnic, cultural, religious or linguistic characteristics,
> d. are sufficiently representative, although smaller in number than the rest of the population of that state or of a region of that state,
> e. are motivated by a concern to preserve together that which constitutes their common identity, including their culture, their traditions, their religion or their language.[11]

The difficulties surrounding the concept of *national minority* are closely connected with the different meanings of the term *nation* and the dissimilar formation of national minorities in Western as opposed to Central and Eastern Europe. "In Europe, particularly in Central and Eastern Europe, a major factor in the formation of minorities has been centuries of intermittent warfare accompanied by the drawing and redrawing of borders. Minority situations there are caused less by migration of peoples than by repeated changes in the political units within which settled populations found themselves."[12]

Starting in late 1989, as the process of democratic transformation began sweeping through Central and Eastern Europe, national minorities also organized their own political parties and began appearing as political communities. Apart from sharing a defined sense of cultural identity, national minorities began taking on the characteristics normally associated with actors in the political arena: group will and the capability to articulate their own political program. In several instances (e.g., Turks in Bulgaria; Hungarians in Slovakia, Romania, and Serbia), national minorities have attained parliamentary representation on behalf of their own political parties and have formulated their own programs for self-administration.

A problem associated with the term *national minority* is its suggestion of possessing fewer or lesser rights, and the assumption of some sort of non-equality. For this reason, demands have been formulated recently to use alternate terms such as *ethnic group* or *national community in a minority position*, or *partner-nation*, to try at least semantically to find the best expression for equality and nondiscrimination between the individuals belonging to communities in majority and minority positions. Nevertheless, we will use the expression *national minorities* in the meaning of the Council of Europe's definition, because certain groups living as minorities have their "mother nation"; therefore the term *national minority* more accurately describes the situation of these groups.

Self-determination is a right that is frequently discussed and invoked in international law and in the policy of states as well. Self-determination can mean:

1. the right of people to choose their own form of government within existing borders, for example by overturning a dictatorship or achieving independence from a colonial power;

2. the right of an ethnic, linguistic, or religious group to redefine existing national borders in order to achieve separate national sovereignty;

3. the right of a political unit within a federal system, such as Canada, former Czechoslovakia, the former Soviet Union or the former Yugoslavia, to secede from the federation and become an independent sovereign state;

4. the right of an ethnic, linguistic or religious group
within an existing sovereign state to a greater degree of
autonomy and linguistic or religious identity, but not to
a sovereign state of its own.[13]

The international organizations' concepts of the term *self-
determination* is in a state of flux. There is disagreement over whether
self-determination is a principle or a right. According to one author,
"Self-determination is a fundamental principle of international politics. At the same time it is also a right. In fact, it is a right that 'is a
prerequisite to the full enjoyment of all fundamental rights.' "[14]

Self-determination is seemingly at odds with other principles,
such as territorial integrity and non-interference in the internal affairs
of other states. One of the greatest problems surrounding the right to
self-determination is that there is no valid and generally applicable
definition of the concept of *people*, nor is it clear whether a minority in a
given state would qualify as a people. The confusion over who can be
the valid possessor or subject of this right, in the absence of clear
international standards, may often lead to its violation.

3. DIFFERENCES IN PHILOSOPHICAL APPROACH

For the purposes of this chapter, it is essential to touch on a number of
philosophical issues.

Minority rights can be examined from three different perspectives:

a. as rights of *individuals*, that is, the rights of *persons* belonging to
national, ethnic, religious, or linguistic minorities;
b. as rights exercised by individuals in *community with others*; or
c. as rights of *minorities*, that is, *group* rights.

Each of these concepts is based on fundamental differences in
philosophical and/or political tradition and approach. The various
traditions and approaches place differing degrees of emphasis on such
principles as freedom, equality, and nondiscrimination.

During a lengthy debate in the UN Commission on Human Rights
over the drafting of a declaration on the "Rights of Persons Belonging
to National or Ethnic, Religious and Linguistic Minorities," the
following views arose concerning the question of individual and
collective rights:

> *On the one hand*, it was stated that the collective dimension of
> the rights to be established would have to be recognized
> throughout the draft because of the very nature of the issues

under discussion, such as those relating to existence and identity. In this connection, reference was made to the group element in article 4 of the International Convention on the Elimination of All Forms of Racial Discrimination. *On the other hand*, a strong preference was expressed for the individual approach which was said to be based upon the general orientation of existing human rights instruments. *The third possibility*, namely the recognition or balancing of both dimensions, also received support by some delegations with express reference to the wording of article 27 of the International Covenant on Civil and Political Rights. One possible combination mentioned was the granting of certain group rights while the prevention of discrimination would be seen in the individual context.[15]

Regarding the question of individual or group rights, the UN Secretary-General, in a note presented to the Commission on Human Rights, observed that

> each individual has the right to identify himself or herself with a group of persons differing from the rest of society with distinct socio-cultural, religious, linguistic or ethnic character, and also that no person shall be obliged to identify himself or herself with any particular group. . . .
>
> It was pointed out that group rights can be accommodated in full respect of the territorial integrity of States, provided the parties make use of the wide range of options which can be derived from State practice in different parts of the world. The foundation should be in strict compliance with the principles of non-discrimination and equal political participation.[16]

The European Commission for Democracy Through Law, a consultative body of the Council of Europe, stated in its explanatory report on the proposal for a European Convention for the Protection of Minorities:

> it seems necessary to recognize rights as belonging not only to individual members of minorities but to the minorities as such, since minorities are not only the sum of a number of individuals but represent also a system of relations among them. Without the concept of collective rights, the protection of minorities would be somewhat limited.[17]

US senator and scholar Daniel Patrick Moynihan recently made the following remark on this subject:

The two dominant philosophical views of the century blinded officials into not recognizing that ethnic identity was going to be one of the most powerful historical forces of the century.

The first philosophical view was Marxism, which predicted that ethnic identity would give way to conflict over ownership and production among economic classes. The second view was . . . "liberal expectancy"—view of liberals from the time of Adam Smith in the 18th century that nations would get bigger for economic reasons and that the ethnic factor would fade in significance.

Both were wrong, and yet we have lived through the century seeing the world in these two perspectives.[18]

The basic purpose of international law should be the creation of effective respect for human dignity and the elimination of discrimination. Protection must be afforded to the individual (the person belonging to a national minority) as well as the group to which such individuals belong.

One essential axiom is the guarantee of the right to identity. In the case of the majority, this is guaranteed through the institutions of the state. The protection of the right to identity of national minorities can be realized through institutions and various forms of autonomy. Besides the guarantee of full equality before the law, it is important to guarantee also the protection of the right of national minorities to identity.

4. STATE POLICIES

Any effort to determine an international legal framework for the protection of national minorities should include an examination of the options available to states—the subjects of international law—in their policies toward minorities.

The question of state policy toward minorities usually becomes a subject of discussion at the international level if such policies lead to violence that threatens regional peace and stability and the security of other states. The subject is less apt to arise where the violation of human rights has no direct bearing or influence on other states.

Rights violations of the latter kind are commonly labeled *ethnic conflicts* or *inter-ethnic clashes*. To cite only two recent examples from the front pages of important US newspapers:

These simmering conflicts, rooted in the most basic forms of human identity, often do not command the headlines that rivet world attention on international wars and guerrilla insurgencies, but they frequently prove more vicious and intractable.[19]

The current ethnic conflicts are actually the third wave of this century, with the first two having taken place after World War I and the explosion of anti-colonial movements in Africa and Asia after World War II. But the newest wave is seen as even more complex, potentially more threatening to international peace and almost certain to grow in the years ahead.[20]

It is important to underline that in many cases the description of conflicts as ethnic warfare obfuscates the complexity of the problems, or overshadows the real conflict between powerful and powerless, central government and marginalized region, or majority and minority. Such characterizations frequently confuse more than they clarify.

As regards present-day Central and Eastern Europe, it is important to understand the presence of specific factors that contribute to the escalation of tensions and produce conflict situations. One such phenomenon is the emergence of several new states, which, in spite of a diversity of languages, national minorities, and ethnic groups, define themselves as ethnically pure "nation-states." For a clear understanding of this phenomenon, it is essential to recognize differences in the political culture and the principles of state building between Western and East Central European countries. The specific factors leading to the formation of a given state—whether resulting from the collapse of an empire, the disintegration of an artificially created multiethnic state, or the democratic expression of the right of self-determination—have great impact on the character of the government of the successor state. A key question is whether the creation of a new national identity in a given state is connected with democratization and with democratic values.[21]

Another factor specific to this region is the transformation of communists into nationalists, accomplished in order to maintain their hold on power—only this time using nation, not class, to justify their dominant position. Misusing the legitimate mass claim to a new national identity following decades of totalitarianism, such authoritarian rulers issue appeals to exclusivist nationalism with the aim of remaining in power. Under such circumstances, the protection of minority rights becomes the touchstone of democracy; the two are one and inseparable. Calls for postponing or ignoring the rights of minorities because the building of democracy is more important misconstrue the very essence of democracy. By artificially distinguishing the imperative to establish a democratic system from the need to introduce minority rights, such rationalizations can actually help to consolidate anti-democratic structures in these states.

Close international attention to the quality and consistency of democratization is extremely important at the early stages of the state-building process, for once the dominant power group has been successful in excluding another group or a particular class of rights from the basic principles of the new state, the exclusivist concept has prevailed, and the fuse on the time-bomb of intolerance has been lit.

Those political regimes where the new national identity is not based on democratic principles can hardly transform themselves into democratic ones. Here, it can be said, the leading forces falsely raised mass expectations on the basis of nationalism. In fact, such leaders have no intention of democratizing and modernizing, or decentralizing the state and guaranteeing minority rights, because each of these steps would threaten their ruling or dominant position and ultimately lead to their own demise.

What is needed on the part of Western democracies is a policy that clearly delineates and enforces the minimum standards for membership in the European organizations (the European Community, the Council of Europe, etc.).[22] Also important to such a policy would be to withhold any legitimization from anti-democratic methods of governance; to grant economic support on condition of progress in the implementation of democratic values and measures to protect human and minority rights; to support the creation of independent media, civil societies, local democracies, and regional trans-frontier cooperation; and to support those forces within these states that can harmonize democratic values and the protection of national minorities with the claims for new national identity.

The severe economic and social dislocations resulting from the shift to market economies, and the presence of nuclear weapons in the region, add to the complexity of the picture and the urgency of forging such a policy.

Hurst Hannum accurately pointed out the dangers of approaching this topic from an overly Western perspective:

> One difficulty in adopting a primarily legal approach to ethnic and other contemporary communal conflicts is that law, whether international or domestic, tends to assume a rational, egalitarian, individualistic structure. The sovereign equality of states—surely a fiction if ever there was one— reflects the Western conception of internal polity of a state as being composed of "free-floating" individuals, each of whom is endowed with a kit of basic rights and immunities and each

of whom is available for those tasks and associations that fit his talents and preferences. Ethnic conflicts, which are almost by definition based on ascriptive attributes, do not fit easily within the realm of a system of law which was created, in part, precisely to ignore those attributes.[23]

It is instructive here to briefly review the policy of states toward minorities in multiethnic societies according to two studies prepared at the United Nations.

According to Francesco Capotorti, the main options open to governments when formulating policy towards persons belonging to minority groups can be described in terms of *pluralism, integration, assimilation*, or *segregation*.

A policy of *pluralism* has the fundamental goal of preserving the identity of minority groups; it pursues this objective by granting them a large degree of freedom in the administration of their own affairs. Its application may thus entail the establishment of a special political and administrative structure or the granting of local autonomy on a wide range of matters to the regions where minorities live.

Integration has been described as a process which aims at the unity of the various groups of a given society while allowing them to maintain their own characteristics through the adoption of specific measures. Pluralism and integration are therefore two policies which can be followed simultaneously.

The objective of a policy of *assimilation* would be the establishment of a homogeneous society in which persons belonging to minority groups would have to abandon ... their traditions, their culture and the use of their language in favor of the traditions, the culture and the language of the dominant group. ...

The aim of a policy based on *segregation* would be to keep minority groups separate and maintain them in the position of inferiority.[24]

There is a certain degree of ambiguity in some of those terms, which the author also admitted. For example, in the case of assimilation there is no discussion of whether the process depends on the free will of persons or is forced by the state.

An ambiguity in the above-mentioned terms, and the categorization of policies pursued by states (majorities), is also evident in the report recently submitted by Asbjorn Eide to the UN Commission on

Human Rights (the final report will be presented in 1993). He evaluated existing policies on the basis of their location along two continuums:

Homogenization ——— Separation
Domination ——— Exclusion ——— Equalization

Neither homogenization nor separation is inherently bad or good seen from a human rights perspective, . . . it depends essentially on whether it is done for purposes or with the effect of domination, exclusion or equalization, and more importantly on whether or not it is based on informed consent by all parties concerned.

"Homogenization" (making everybody alike, i.e. conforming to one common culture, one language, one set of mores and behavior) can be pursued in two different ways: by assimilation or by fusion.

"Assimilation" is . . . a process by which homogeneity is obtained based on a dominant culture, to which other groups are expected to conform by shedding their own cultural characteristics. . . .

"Fusion" is, in theory, different from assimilation. It consists in combining two or more cultures, on an equal footing, producing a new and different culture. . . .

"Integration" is . . . a process by which different elements combine to form a unit; while each group retains its identity, it does not threaten the overarching unity. Practical key indicators of the difference between assimilation and integration are found in language and in educational policies.

At the opposite end we find the policies of separation, which can be territorial or non-territorial.

Territorial separation typically falls into two categories, one based on dominance, the other being egalitarian.

The extreme version of dominant separation is that of segregation, the prime example being apartheid, which aims at keeping the ethnic groups territorially separate, unmixed and ranked in a hierarchical position. . . .

Territorial separation can also be on an egalitarian basis. Different groups may voluntarily choose to live separately within the same sovereign State. The territorial separation helps to preserve their own particular lifestyles and cultures, while at the same time they may be equal partners in a larger entity . . . .

Policies of integration include some degree of separation

on a non-territorial basis. Members of dispersed groups may want to be given separate treatment in some aspects of their life, while living with others on common territory. There are many examples throughout the world, particularly with regard to religion, language and education. . . .

Striking the right balance between separateness and equality is a task of considerable complexity.[25]

In seeking to identify an effective legal framework for the protection of national minorities, a distinction must be made between states along the lines of their overall conceptual approach to the function and make-up of the state. On the one hand are multiethnic, pluralistic, economically developed states (mainly West European countries), with institutionalized guarantees of respect for human rights and freedoms, a balance of power system, and implementation of the rule of law and the principle of decentralization. On the other hand are the "pure nation-states" where the state is not an institution belonging to every citizen, but a tool in the hands of the dominant ethnic group, employing authoritarian methods of governance, and involving weak democratic institutions, the violation of human and minority rights, legal uncertainties, and government policies influenced or motivated by national exclusivism, authoritarianism, or etatism, in addition to suffering great social and economic problems.

The international legal protection of national minorities needs different approaches in these two cases. In the first case, the existing organizations (the Council of Europe, the EC, the CSCE) can provide the framework for the protection of national minorities, through binding standards, regionalization, and integration. In the second case, which may be the source of more dangerous conflicts and will have serious impact on the security of the whole of Europe, the managing of the problem needs wider and more resolute action to influence the policies of states toward national minorities.

The objectives of making the minority question manageable in this region should include

- a governmental system based on the balance and division of power;
- constitutional guarantees for minority rights, including their right to identity and self-administration;
- institutional guarantees for individual human rights and freedoms;
- rule of law;
- an independent judiciary;
- democratic local self-government;

- legal and institutional safeguards for the protection of freedom of expression, including the private and public media;
- legal guarantees for a free market economy.

The current policies of several states in Central and Eastern Europe toward national minorities demonstrate several common elements, which can be identified as follows:

- The definition of the state in the constitution as a "pure nation-state," with government policies influenced by national exclusivism and the regime using the state to antagonize national minorities.
- The retention of a high degree of centralized state control, etatism, and legal and practical limits on local self-government, producing obstacles to regional self-administration and trans-frontier cooperation (Slovakia's recent refusal, for example, to participate in the Carpathian Euroregion), together with anti-minority-oriented gerrymandering (altering the administrative and electoral division of the state with the purpose of minimizing or eliminating the political representation of national minorities).
- Vocal reference to the vocabulary of democracy, but the misuse of democratic means by the "majority" to discriminate against minorities; violation of minority rights through "legal" means; attacks in Parliament against representatives of minorities, where such state definitions and policies can be the sources of conflict, can result in confusion over legitimacy and legality, and can enable legally elected leaders to carry out actions that violate the constitution.
- The holding of technically "free and fair" elections, while restricting the right of free and equal access to the media, failing to prohibit xenophobic scapegoating campaigns against national minorities, and violating freedom of expression in other ways.
- During the nominal transition to a market economy, the creation through legislation of unequal opportunities and discriminatory conditions (through, for example, laws on privatization and restitution that exclude minorities, and tax and loan policies that place minorities at a disadvantage).
- Imposition of limits not only on the right to identity and self-administration but also on the traditional basic minority rights (such as the right to use minority languages, receive education in the native tongue, etc.).

5. MINORITY RIGHTS

Is it possible to achieve a peaceful and constructive coexistence among different ethnic groups, nations, and national minorities? Is it possible to manage ethnic conflicts in an institutionalized form through peaceful dialogue? Is it possible to guarantee the right of national minorities to protect their identity in a democratic framework, and, if so, how? Should we understand minority rights as part of the domain of human rights, or should we rather broaden the traditional Western concept of human rights to include the right to identity realized through—*inter alia*—self-administration? Are the concepts of minority rights and self-determination themselves of a destabilizing nature, or is it their suppression that threatens regional security?

These questions are often asked during discussions concerning the protection of minority rights. Due to the limited space available, the following discussion will focus on the most important features of each question.

To date, international organizations have treated the rights of national minorities within the framework of traditional human rights, focusing on the individual.

The foundation of that system is anchored in and dependent on the values stated in the Universal Declaration of Human Rights, article 1 of which states that "All human beings are born free and equal in dignity and rights. They are endowed with reason and conscience and should act toward one another in a spirit of brotherhood."

These are the basic values valid for every human being, irrespective of the individual's membership in a national community in majority or minority position within the state.

A. Difficulties in Defining Minorities and Minority Rights at the International Level

According to Hurst Hannum, there are four socio-political realities today that give rise to difficulties concerning minorities and minority rights at the international level:

> First, the concept of "minorities" does not fit easily within the theoretical paradigm of the state, whether that state is based on the individual social-contract theory of Western democracies or the class-based precepts of Marxism. The state is seen as a collection of shifting coalitions founded on self-interest or of economic classes, yet the reality is that ethnic or linguistic ties are often much more influential than considerations of

class or individual interest in provoking or dampening many conflicts. . . .

Second, the reality of minorities and largely heterogeneous states in the contemporary world is also at odds with the theory of the nation-state as it developed in the nineteenth century, and the rhetoric of one people-one state has carried over into the concept of self-determination in the post-1945 period. . . .

Third, there is a fundamental fear on the part of all countries, and especially newer states, that the recognition of minority rights will encourage fragmentation or separatism and undermine national unity and the requirements of national development. The "natural hypersensitivity of new states about their sovereignty and the imperfect implementation of the principle of national self-determination" noted in the post-Versailles period has been at least as problematic in the post-colonial era.

Finally, one also must recognize the unpleasant social reality of widespread discrimination and intolerance based on religion and ethnicity. Such intolerance is found in all regions of the world and in states at all stages of economic development; it is fanned by dictators and democrats alike to serve narrow political interests. . . . While the often violent conflicts that result from such psychological hatreds may well have strong political and economic components, it would be a mistake to conclude (as some analysts would prefer) that ethnic and religious discrimination is not often a major factor.[26]

To Hannum's general (and very relevant) observations, two specific difficulties facing Central and Eastern Europe can be added.

The first consists of the special set of problems posed by the transformation, presently taking place, from centralized planned economies and totalitarian regimes to free market systems and parliamentary democracies. Progress is uneven in these states, with some of them clearly exhibiting a lack of real change, including the failure to implement the rule of law, create democratic institutions, and guarantee human and minority rights. In several countries, the elite of the former communist regime has only changed hats and remained in power by openly embracing nationalism. Such authoritarian leaders often depict national or ethnic minorities as scapegoats, labeling them responsible for the country's social and economic problems.

Second, it is important in this region to recognize the problems stemming from the split, division, or breakup of different artificially created multinational states. New states emerged during this transformation period, with several defining themselves as "pure nation-states." Although they are in fact multinational states, these are cases where the dominant ethnic groups are struggling to find or regain their own identity. In these cases, the state is used as a tool for the oppression of nondominant ethnic groups in different forms. The resulting aggression occurs beneath the surface in some of the former socialist countries and has led to bloody combat in several others; the worst of the latter we can see in the territory of former Yugoslavia.

B. Current Minority Problems

The report to the UN submitted by Asbjorn Eide discussed five categories of present-day minority problems:

    a. *Problems of discrimination*. . . . Where some groups are subjected to social discrimination, exploitation, or intolerance and hatred. . . .

    b. *Denial of pluralism*. . . . Restriction on the preservation of religious, linguistic and cultural identity. These are the typical situations to which the International Covenant on Civil and Political Rights article 27 apply; so does the . . . Declaration on the rights of persons belonging to national or ethnic, religious and linguistic minorities adopted by them. A wide range of possibilities for constructive arrangements exist in different parts of the world. . . .

    c. *Numerical minority in dominant position*. . . . In some cases numerical minority has obtained for itself a dominant position and maintained it through non-democratic means or through effective marginalization of the members of the majority group. . . .

    d. *Request of autonomy*. . . . Efforts, by groups living compactly together, to obtain some degree of autonomy, where there is resistance to these efforts by the central government. . . .

    e. *Secessionist movement*. . . . Secessionist movements, seeking to break a part of the territory away from the state, to become an independent entity or to be incorporated into another state (the "mother country").[27]

The Eide report considers the conflicts discussed under points (d) and (e) to be the most dangerous ones, which often lead to extensive rights violations. Eide adds: "External encouragement and even support to drives for autonomy or secessionist activities, to the extent of open intervention, is deeply disturbing to the international legal order."[28]

The problem with Eide's statement is that it makes no distinction between autonomy and secession, or between the internal and external forms of the principle of self-determination; rather, it defends the territorial integrity of states under all circumstances. In 1970, the Secretary-General of the United Nations declared the following:

> The United Nations' attitude is unequivocable. As an international organization, the United Nations has never accepted and does not accept the principle of secession of a part of its Member State.[29]

If these words had been consistently applied since 1970, the UN membership roster would not have grown by more than a dozen, to the 180 states today. The post-Cold War period shows an increasing number of new states, signifying the need to rethink the new dimensions of self-determination.

C. SELF-DETERMINATION AND NATIONAL MINORITIES

Besides the promotion of democracy and the rule of law, the basis for the protection of national minorities lies in rethinking the concept of self-determination.

In the post-Cold War era, "As a first step toward a modern approach, governments must adopt a broader and less alarmist view of self-determination. The full exercise of self-determination need not result in the outcome predicted by those who would discredit the principle—independent statehood for every single ethnic group. Rather, the full exercise of self-determination can lead to a number of outcomes, ranging from minority-rights protection, to cultural or political autonomy, to independent statehood."[30]

The respect of individual freedom is the basis for the claim of self-determination. "The principle of self-determination is best viewed as entitling a people to choose its political allegiance, to influence the political order under which it lives, and to preserve its cultural, ethnic, historical, or territorial identity."[31] Of course, this explanation will not solve the problem concerning the definition of *people*.

> In identifying a "unit" that may have a claim to self-determination, . . . the international community should not focus on a single criterion, such as single ethnicity, but should weigh both *objective* and *subjective factors*. *Objectively*, whether a

group is a "people" for the purposes of self-determination depends on the extent to which the group making a claim shares ethnic, linguistic, religious, or cultural bonds, although the absence or weakness of one of these bonds need not invalidate a claim. The *subjective* standard should weigh the extent to which members within the group perceive the group's identity as distinct from the identities of other groups.[32]

The principle of self-determination during this century has distinguished between an external and an internal self-determination.

The external right to self-determination consists in the possibility for a people to determine its own status—to decide whether it should possess statehood by itself or be part of another state. . . .

[The right to internal self-determination] is the right of people living within an independent and sovereign state freely to choose its government. . . . This can be organized through a unitary state system, a federal system, or a system with arrangements for autonomy (home rule) or devolution of power.[33]

Recent publications have reevaluated the internal-external distinction, and found it inadequate to answer the wide range of challenges and dilemmas that have emerged in the post-Cold War era. The newer writing divides the forms of self-determination into six categories:

a. *Anti-colonial self-determination*: "A claim to anti-colonial self-determination refers to a territorial population under colonial rule or alien domination that seeks complete freedom or more political power."

b. *Sub-state self-determination*: " 'Sub-state' self-determination describes the attempt of a group within an existing state to break off and form a new state or to achieve a greater degree of political or cultural autonomy within the existing state."

c. *Trans-state self-determination*: "A self-determination claim involving the concentrated grouping of a people in more than one existing state may be called a 'trans-state' claim."

d. *Self-determination of dispersed people*: "The claims of peoples dispersed throughout one or more states are proposed as a separate category to distinguish them from claims involving a geographically concentrated people."

e. *Indigenous self-determination*: "The claims of indigenous communities—that is, groups characterized by a distinct ethnicity and long historical continuity with a pre-colonial or pre-invasion society—pose a special challenge."

f. *Representative self-determination*: "A claim to 'representative' self-determination results when the population of an existing state seeks to change its political structure in favor of a more representative (and preferably democratic) structure."[34]

In order to understand the claim of national minorities for autonomy, the most important variations are "internal" (as defined by Eide) or "sub-state" (as listed above) self-determination. These forms of self-determination can guarantee—by preserving the identity of national minorities—the stability of states on one hand and the protection of the rights of national minorities on the other.

If persons belonging to such minorities can protect and develop their identities and may exercise their rights—individually as well as in a community with other members of their group—then this can improve the stability of states. As the UN Declaration makes clear, "the promotion and protection of the rights of persons belonging to national or ethnic, religious and linguistic minorities contribute to the political and social stability of States in which they live."[35]

Generally, the right to self-determination is interpreted to mean an effort toward separatism. This unfortunate misunderstanding of the term *self-determination* obfuscates the basic idea—the democratic expression of the freedom of the individual and the national community. If this freedom is violated, or selectively guaranteed, it can ultimately lead to secession:

> The nation-state initiates various nationalisms precisely when it partially or completely breaks with the principle of self-determination . . . the principle of self-determination not only is not the cause of nationalism, but—taken seriously and applied effectively—it is also the only realistic remedy for those conditions of power, subjugation and fear from which nationalisms are born.[36]

With the movement toward democracy in Central and Eastern Europe, national minorities have new opportunities to express their aspirations for self-determination and autonomy through their democratically elected, legitimate representatives. Unfortunately, however, representatives of the majority can—by manipulating in a "democratic manner" the concept of majority rule—deny the minorities' right to identity. Under such circumstances, national minorities are barred from attaining any results; through institutions based solely on the protection of the rights of individuals, it becomes impossible to guarantee effectively the minorities' right to identity. Majority representatives frequently portray the positive proposals for autonomy as threats to the nation-state; any consequent efforts to achieve the legal protection of "traditional" minority rights (to language, culture, education, and media) are also for the most part denied—in a "democratic manner." "The real mistake occurs when a government is so fearful of self-determination—even when it is not aimed at secession—that it denies minority groups the protection of their traditional rights. Such negativist actions can easily trigger minority discontent and upheaval and create the surge toward self-determination that the government so fears."[37]

The principle of self-determination does not *de jure* mean independent statehood or secession. Whether it de facto leads to secession depends not only on the aims of the national community, but also on the reaction and policies of the state: "The goal [of involvement in a self-determination dispute where a minority's rights are being violated] must initially be to press a government to see that its self-interest lies in accommodating the interests of a minority group, rather than in triggering more extreme self-determination claims—even secessionist demands—by alienating it."[38]

What should be the response to such challenges? Why would it be important to the international community to support those claims for self-determination that are expressed in a peaceful and democratic manner?

The rights of minorities can be basically protected through federalism, different forms of autonomy, constitutional guarantees, and the safeguarding of language rights. These forms of protection within states can be implemented according to the needs and historical, cultural, regional, linguistic, and/or religious traditions of a given group.

Where national minorities are concerned, especially in Central and Eastern Europe, the importance of internal self-determination claims must be underlined. If internal self-determination is not granted, it can lead to further violations of minority rights and thus to greater instability. Western democracies have an interest in averting such situations. Basically, the international community faces two options: either to implicitly accept the "Serbian solution" (by retroactively condoning the acquisition of territories through ethnic cleansing and the use of force), or to establish an international system that guarantees the acceptance of peacefully and democratically proposed plans for autonomy.

D. THE CONTENT OF AUTONOMY

Today's aspirations for self-determination that find expression through various forms of autonomy—based on the personal or territorial principle—represent a unique, highly innovative approach by national minorities to the problem of how best to promote and protect their rights to identity and their freedom within the state. Where peacefully and democratically presented within the confines of "pure nation-states," the various proposals of autonomy have failed.

In Central and Eastern Europe, the challenge to protect national minorities is the challenge of democracy. The creation of international protective mechanisms support the promotion of democracy and stability.

The principle of autonomy can be generally stated as follows:

> Persons should enjoy equal rights (and, accordingly, equal obligations) in the framework which generates and limits the opportunities available to them; that is, they should be free and equal in the determination of the conditions of their own lives, so long as they do not deploy this framework to negate the rights of others.[39]

According to this definition—under simple majority rule—individuals who share such common features as ethnicity, language, culture, and history can enjoy autonomy in a political sense. The question arises when there are individuals belonging to national minorities with different common features than individuals belonging to the majorities—how does the state guarantee their right to identity in a democratic manner?

There are positive examples in different West European countries (e.g., Italy, Belgium, Finland, and Switzerland). Positive elements of these models can support the creation of autonomies in Central and Eastern Europe, without mechanically copying the West European examples.

Within the framework of the CSCE, participating states have expressed appreciation for efforts to create and protect the different forms of autonomy.

> The participating States note the efforts undertaken to protect and create conditions for the promotion of the . . . identity of certain national minorities by establishing, as one of the possible means to achieve these aims, appropriate forms of local or autonomous administration.[40]
>
> The participating States note with interest that positive results have been obtained by some of them . . . by, *inter alia,*

... local and autonomous administration, as well as autonomy on territorial basis, including the existence of consultative, legislative and executive bodies chosen through free and periodic elections.[41]

The basic conditions for autonomy are, briefly, democracy, the rule of law, division of power, economic stability, and the acceptance of a pluralistic, multiethnic society. Autonomy may be created through (a) governmental decision; (b) legislation; (c) constitutional provisions; (d) international treaties; or (e) compliance with a guarantee provided by international organizations.[42]

The methods mentioned under points (a), (b), and (c) above can be achieved within the state, with the remainder involving the international level. In Central and Eastern Europe currently, the most effective way to create autonomies seems to be through international guarantees that would promote and protect the identity of national minorities and at the same time guarantee the stability of the region.

An important, highly political question presents itself: Who are the parties to the creation of autonomies? The parties can be (a) the states and national minorities themselves; (b) affected neighboring states; and (c) important states and international organizations.

The right to autonomy has to be assured, but there is no general prescription regarding its exact form. The minorities themselves have to decide what it takes to preserve their identity, since each minority has different needs and aspirations (historical, cultural, linguistic, educational, etc.), which have to be taken into consideration. It is essential to create a legal and institutional framework—i.e., autonomy—in which national minorities can realize their right to self-determination and the ability to protect and promote their identity within the state.

There is some recent literature discussing what minority rights are, and which rights create the content of autonomy. Below are a few of the different views on this question.

The Draft Convention on the Fundamental Rights of Ethnic Groups in Europe prepared by the Federal Union of European Nationalities lists the following ethnic group rights:

- *as general fundamental rights*: the right of existence, non-discrimination and equality of treatment, group protection, special protection;
- *as special fundamental rights*: compensatory rights—the right of language, education, association and organization, unimpeded contacts, information, employment in public service, political representation, autonomy, co-determination.[43]

The Committee of Experts for the Protection of Minorities in the
Council of Europe also prepared a list outlining the various minority
rights in effect within the member and nonmember states of the
Council of Europe at the end of 1992.[44]

Concerning autonomy, Hurst Hannum in his recent book states:

> While each situation is unique, the conflicts in which au-
> tonomy is viewed by one party as essential to the guarantee of
> its survival concern some or all of the following basic issues:
> *language*; *education*; *access to governmental civil service*, including
> *police and security forces*, and *social services*; *land* and *natural
> resources*; *representative local government structures*.[45]

The complexity of the question of autonomy does not allow a
further discussion of details within the limited space available. What is
of critical importance is that national minorities have the ability to
create bodies through which they can decide basic questions concerning the promotion and protection of their identity (education, culture,
language, media—cultural autonomy) and concerning the region(s)
where they form a majority (territorial autonomy). Given the circumstances of the newly emerging states of Central and Eastern Europe,
which are struggling with the difficulties of transition and in several
cases aiming to create pure nation-states in spite of their multiethnic
reality, an internationally recognized and guaranteed right to autonomy can be an effective form of minority rights protection.

6. LEGALLY CODIFYING MINORITY
RIGHTS, AND POSSIBLE NEW DIRECTIONS

Before turning to the problems of legally codifying minority rights and
possible new directions for further development, it is important to
touch on the frequently expressed view that the codification of new
laws is useless if no enforcement exists to implement already existing
ones.

This view is obviously correct—any legal system is only as credible
as its enforcement is sound—yet thus far it has not been applicable to
the area of minority rights protection.

There are a variety of declarations, recommendations, political
documents, and charters that provide a good basis for the creation of a
system of minority rights protection.[46] But few internationally binding
norms exist in this field, and there are even fewer mechanisms to
effectively monitor the implementation of the few existing standards.

Positive steps have been taken recently toward the creation of
such a system. But a European Convention for the Rights of National

Minorities has yet to be adopted, and there are no binding standards or mechanisms to implement any such set of rules. The paucity of such legal instruments becomes striking in light of the recent tragic events in the realm of minority rights. Given the very small number of existing laws, we are far from asking for a moratorium on the creation of new ones.

At the same time, if a new, legally binding set of international norms for the protection of national minorities is unable to respond in time to the challenges of recent tragic events, this failure will produce a severe loss of credibility on the part of the international community and will raise serious moral questions.

Responding to pressures to establish a new code of conduct for the protection of national minorities, the questions might be asked: "What was wrong with the old one? What should the new one say?"

The problem with the old one was that since World War II there simply has been no comprehensive and structured international code of conduct for the protection of national minorities. Instead, "the concept of minority rights was neglected [because] it was widely believed that by securing individual human rights, the protection of minority rights would become superfluous. . . . The fallacy of this view is painfully obvious from the events of the last 45 years and the tragedies unfolding today."[47]

The League of Nations' minority protection system was rejected, and the protection of minorities "receded as both a political concern and a legal right. There is no mention of minority rights in the UN Charter (1945) or the Universal Declaration of Human Rights (1948). International law is evolving to provide greater protection for minority rights, in part because such protection has the potential to prevent the dismemberment of a multiethnic state. But during the Cold War, the concept of minority rights was narrowly construed and rarely applied."[48]

This situation changed after the end of the Cold War, in 1989 and 1990, when for the first time the international community began adopting provisions protecting the rights of national minorities.[49] But a codified system still needs to be created.[50]

What should the new code of conduct say? Fundamentally, it should provide for the protection of the identity of national minorities and for their right to self-administration.

In terms of policy recommendations, the protection of minority rights throughout Europe can be developed through the further promotion of democracy and the rule of law. Steps in this direction can be taken at the local, state, bilateral, and international levels.

Due to differing political, economic, and security circumstances,

Central and Eastern Europe must be distinguished from Western Europe when discussing the practical steps to be taken for the protection of minority rights.

In Central and Eastern Europe, through the promotion of democracy and the rule of law, and through conditioned economic cooperation, conditions should be created for the elimination of authoritarian regimes. These regimes are based on an old-new kind of totality, an ethnocracy with the aim of creating a "pure nation-state" (through "ethnic cleansing," forced assimilation, forcing minority groups to flee the state, and other devices). States applying such policies create for the whole of Europe a basic human rights and security problem, and negatively influence the process of integration into the Western part of Europe.

The steps needed at the various levels are as follows.

At the local level, the close connection between democracy and the protection of the rights of national minorities is evident in the former communist countries. The basic issue of how to decentralize highly centralized, authoritarian states is deeply intertwined with the problem of minority rights protection. For this reason, it is critical to create the conditions for genuine local democracy and local self-administration bearing all the requisite rights and means, thereby enabling the diversity of local society to be reflected and guaranteeing the protection of minority identities. A pivotal development on the part of states in Central and Eastern Europe would be the adoption of the European Charter for Local Self-Administration and the implementation of its principles in their domestic legal systems and practical policies.

Legal and practical conditions must be created for persons belonging to national minorities to participate effectively in decisions at the local and regional level concerning the minority to which they belong or regions in which they live.[51] Concrete steps in this direction could be "to protect and create conditions for the promotion of the . . . identity of certain national minorities by establishing, as one of the possible means to achieve these aims, appropriate local or autonomous administrations."[52]

Other important provisions are to guarantee through financial means at the local level the protection of national minorities' right to identity and self-administration in the fields important to their identity (language, education, culture, and media); to guarantee national minorities the right to political representation at the local and regional levels; and to employ in public service persons belonging to national minorities in communities inhabited by them.

At the state level, constitutional provisions should be adopted guaranteeing the protection of the identity of national minorities and the right to different forms of autonomy (cultural, educational, personal, and territorial). States should be founded on the principle of pluralistic democracy, discarding the use of the "pure nation-state" concept as weapons for the dominant ethnic group to force the assimilation of minority cultures. The building of democratic institutions, power-sharing devices, the rule of law, civil society, and human rights guarantees all contribute to enhanced minority rights protection.

At the bilateral level, provisions securing the rights of national minorities should be included in bilateral or multilateral treaties. Support should be given to regional trans-frontier cooperation involving the national minorities.

At the international level, a system of legally binding standards and control mechanisms must be adopted for the effective protection of the rights of national minorities.

7. CONCLUSION

If we are looking for the real reasons for the paralysis and inability of international organizations to prevent conflicts in such tragic cases as the war in former Yugoslavia, we can see among others the differing interests of the major European and transatlantic powers, the lack of strategic interest, the lack of concepts on how to manage such conflicts in the post-Cold War situation, and a more or less latent commitment to protect the status quo in every case.

The problem of the protection of national minorities in international law is a political question rather than a legal one. Principles and norms of international law alone cannot manage or solve the legal protection of national minorities if there is a lack of political will on the part of states, mainly the more powerful ones. When thousands of people are being killed or become refugees in today's Europe simply because they belong to a certain national minority or ethnic group, international law must be only one of the tools in a multifaceted effort to protect national minorities. The political reaction of the international community to these crises surely will have a major impact on the future situation of national minorities in Central and Eastern Europe.

Due to the situation that we face after the Cold War, we need to reevaluate such concepts as *nation-state*, *sovereignty*, and *self-determination*. The reason for this is the pressure of great challenges of political and economic interdependence and regional integration on the one hand and the need to guarantee the rights of national minorities to safeguard their identity on the other.

Taking into account the difficulties posed by the transformation of societies in Central and Eastern Europe, international organizations must support in a clear and unequivocal manner the democratic forces in these states, the values of pluralistic societies, and the protection of human and minority rights and the rule of law. The period of transformation causes deep uncertainty for national minorities, who are often used as scapegoats and blamed for the problems. The challenge for democratic states is to maximize the chances for democracy in the whole of Europe. It is important to influence the governments' policies in this direction and at the same time to support the democratic demand of the legitimate representatives of the minorities for the protection of their identity and the establishment of autonomous structures for self-administration.

A significant task is to create international standards in the framework of the human rights system for the protection of the rights of persons belonging to national minorities. Standards must also recognize rights of these communities as such, including the right to take part in decisions affecting them, as well as the right to identity through self-administration, self-government, or appropriate forms of cultural, personal, or territorial autonomy. Additionally, an effective monitoring mechanism is needed to measure the implementation of these standards. In these efforts it is important to harmonize the standard-setting and monitoring work of international institutions (the United Nations, the Council of Europe, the CSCE), and then to harmonize these standards with the respective domestic legal systems. The right to legal remedy of persons belonging to national minorities and their communities has to be a part of the mechanism for the implementation of internationally binding standards for the protection of national minorities. Regional or bilateral standards, treaties, and cooperation exert a positive influence on this process.

The importance of early warning and preventive diplomacy in the case of the protection of national minorities cannot be overemphasized. To prevent massive rights violations and the escalation of disputes into more serious conflicts, long-term human rights monitoring, fact-finding missions, and effective response by international organizations are needed.

Finally, it should be emphasized that violations of minority rights constitute a legitimate concern of the international community. Systematic and gross violations of human and minority rights can threaten international peace and security, and must therefore be met with a firm response, which might include the imposition of sanctions or other forms of coercive measures in accordance with international law. Effective international response to violations is an essential element in the quest for creating stable frameworks for the protection of minority rights.

Today's unmanaged or disregarded issues, and the lack of effective protection of national minorities, may well produce tomorrow's security and refugee problems. It is therefore important to establish the necessary framework for taking effective action against those who violate minority rights, not excluding the option of military intervention in accordance with the Charter of the UN in cases of serious violations of human and minority rights.

The ultimate aim is the peaceful coexistence of different ethnic groups on the basis of democracy, rule of law, human dignity, and equality.

NOTES

The author gratefully acknowledges the consulting and editorial assistance of László Hámos in the preparation of this paper. Valuable technical resources and time taken from my Fellowship with the Hungarian Human Rights Foundation (New York) were generously afforded by that organization.

1. On this question of responsibilities, compare Article 14 of Recommendation 1201 (1993) of the Parliamentary Assembly of the Council of Europe on an additional protocol on the rights of minorities to the European Convention on Human Rights, which stated: "The exercise of the rights and freedoms set forth in this protocol are not meant to restrict the duties and responsibilities of the citizens of the state. However, this exercise may only be made subject to such formalities, conditions, restrictions or penalties as are prescribed by law and necessary in a democratic society in the interests of national security, territorial integrity or public safety, for the prevention of disorder or crime, for the protection of health and morals and for the protection of the rights and freedoms of others."

2. István Bibó, *The Distress of the East European Small States*, in *Democracy, Revolution, Self-Determination* (New York: Atlantic Research and Publications, 1991); UN ECOSOC, Commission on Human Rights, Second Progress Report: *Protection of Minorities, Possible Ways and Means of Facilitating the Peaceful and Constructive Solution of Problems Involving Minorities* [draft], E/CN.4/Sub. 2/1992/37, 1 July 1992 (hereinafter referred to as *Eide Report*).

3. Hugh Seton-Watson, *Nations and States* (London: Methuen, 1977).

4. The classic definition of "state" is found in the 1933 Montevideo Convention on Rights and Duties of States, article I of which provides: "The State as a person of international law should possess the following qualifications: a) permanent population; b) a defined territory; c) government; and d) capacity to enter into relations with other States."

5. Hurst Hannum, *Autonomy, Sovereignty and Self-Determination* (Philadelphia: U. of Pennsylvania Press, 1990), p. 3.

6. Ibid., p. 15.

7. As defined in the European Charter of Local-Self-Government, October 15, 1985, article 4, para. 3: "Public responsibilities shall generally be exercised, in preference, by those authorities which are closest to the citizen. Allocation of responsibility to another authority should weigh up the extent and nature of the task and requirements of efficiency and economy."

8. *An Agenda for Peace. Preventive Diplomacy, Peace-Making and Peace-Keeping*. Report of the Secretary-General Pursuant to the Statement Adopted by the Summit Meeting of the Security Council on January 31, 1992, para. 17.

9. Francesco Capotorti, *Study on the Rights of Persons Belonging to Ethnic, Religious and Linguistic Minorities* (New York: United Nations, 1991), p. 564.

10. E/CN.4/Sub.2/1985/31, para. 181.

11. Council of Europe, Parliamentary Assembly, EREC1201.WP, 1403–1/2/93–17-E, p.3.

12. *Eide Report*, p. 26, para. 133.

13. From Morton H. Halperin and David J. Scheffer with Patricia L. Small, *Self-Determination in the New World Order* (Washington, DC: Carnegie Endowment for International Peace, 1992), p. xi.

14. Biro Gaspar: *The right to internal self-determination of national or ethnic, religious and linguistic communities living in minority*, in *Dunataji Figyelo*, Budapest 1993/3, p. 3.

15. E/CN.4/1987/WG.5/CRP.1, 4 March 1987, pp. 4–5.

16. E/CN.4/1993/85, 10 February 1993, pp. 19–20.

17. CDL(91) 8–11 March 1991.

18. Quoted in "As Ethnic Wars Multiply, U.S. Strives for a Policy," *The New York Times*, Feb. 7, 1993.

19. "Ethnic Conflicts: Toll Mounts," *Washington Post*, May 26, 1987, p. A1.

20. "As Ethnic Wars Multiply, U.S. Strives for a Policy."

21. The curtailment of democracy can produce double standards in the approach to the question of national minorities. Leaders of Serbia, for example, demand autonomy for Serbs living abroad, while refusing to grant autonomy to Albanians in Kosovo and Hungarians in Vojvodina. Likewise, Slovak leaders claimed sovereignty and independence for Slovakia, at the same time rejecting all proposals by Hungarians for their autonomy in Slovakia.

22. A consistently supervised policy would also find appropriate response to such incidents as the recent failure by the Slovak government to live up to the human rights commitments it undertook toward the Council of Europe in return for its admission to that body. After agreeing to implement a number of ameliorative measures in the area of minority rights, on May 21, 1993 members of the Slovak Parliament belonging to the governing party obstructed a vote on a resolution containing the provisions that would have complied with the promises made.

23. Hannum, *Autonomy, Sovereignty and Self-Determination*, p. 5.

24. Capotorti, *Study on Rights of Minorities*, p. 50, para. 293.

25. *Eide Report*, pp. 15–17, para. 74–89.

26. Hannum, *Autonomy, Sovereignty and Self-Determination*, pp. 71–72.

27. *Eide Report*, pp. 7–8, para. 38, and also according to UN—A/CONF.157,LACRM/6, 15 December 1992, report by Eide, pp. 4–5.

28. *Eide Report*, p. 38.

29. UN Secretary-General U Thant, Jan. 4, 1970 -15.

30. Halperin et al., *Self-Determination in the New World Order*, p. 46.

31. Ibid., p. 47.

32. Ibid., p. 49.

33. UN A/CONF.157/LACRM/9, Dec. 15, 1992; World Conference on Human Rights, San José, Costa Rica, Jan. 18–22, 1993; *Ethno-nationalism and*

Minority Protection: The Need for Institutional Reform, a report by Asbjorn Eide to the First International Colloquium on Human Rights in La Laguna (Tenerife), Nov. 1–4, 1992, pp. 35–36.

34. Halperin et al., *Self Determination in the New World Order*, pp. 49–52.

35. UN Declaration on the Rights of Persons Belonging to National or Ethnic, Religious and Linguistic Minorities, December 1992.

36. Bibó, "The Paralysis of International Institutions."

37. Halperin et al., *Self-Determination in the New World Order*, p. 60.

38. Ibid.

39. David Held, ed., *Political Theory Today* (Stanford, CA: Stanford University Press, 1991), p. 228.

40. CSCE/Copenhagen 1990, art. 35, para. 2.

41. CSCE/Geneva 1991, IV, para. 8, hyphen 3.

42. Bibó, "The Paralysis of International Institutions."

43. See FUEN—Rorth version, May 28, 1992, Bozen/Bolzano, Europa Institute.

44. In this list—DH-MIN(92)5 prov. restricted, Strasbourg, Nov. 18, 1992—the basic points were the following:

1. Recognition by state;
2. Equality between citizens;
3. Language (official; in education; in official relations with administration; right to create and maintain associations to promote languages);
4. Religion (freedom of religious belief, practice and affiliation; freedom to create religious associations; financial support);
5. Cultural freedom (surname; names of cities; road signs; cultural associations and financial support);
6. Information (TV and radio programs; newspapers in foreign languages; state financial support);
7. Freedom of movement and settlement (right to enter and leave the country; freedom of movement and settlement within the country);
8. Participation in public affairs (existence of minority parties; financing; proportional representation; participation in the state organs);
9. Local autonomy (degree; financing);
10. Economic and social rights (fair employment in the private and public sectors; economic development of regions; safeguarding the environment of minority groups);
11. Other rights and practices (right of recourse before a specialized court; loss of nationality);
12. Enforcement of the protection.

45. Hannum, *Autonomy, Sovereignty and Self-Determination*, p. 458.

46. European Charter for Regional or Minority Languages, adopted on June 22, 1992; UN Declaration on the Rights of Persons Belonging to National or Ethnic, Religious and Linguistic Minorities, adopted on Dec. 18, 1992.

47. Memorandum of Frank Koszorus, Esq., Washington, DC, April 13, 1993, p. 2.

48. Halperin et al., *Self-Determination in the New World Order*, p. 54.

49. CSCE Document on Copenhagen Meeting on Human Dimension, June 1990; Charter of Paris for a New Europe, November 1990; Council of Europe Recommendation 1134/(1990) on the Rights of Minorities.

50. The following are the main standards that have provisions on minorities at the United Nations, at the Council of Europe, and within the framework of CSCE. *United Nations*: the International Covenant on Civil and Political Rights (article 27); the Convention on the Prevention and Punishment of the Crime of Genocide (1948, art. 2); the UNESCO Convention against Discrimination in Education (1960, art. 2, 5); the International Convention on the Elimination of All Forms of Racial Discrimination (1965, art. 1, 2, 3, 5); the UNESCO Declaration on Race and Racial Prejudice (1978, art. 1, 2, 5); the Declaration on the Elimination of All Forms of Intolerance and of Discrimination Based Upon Religion or Belief (1981, art. 1, 6); and the Declaration on the Rights of Persons belonging to National or Ethnic, Religious and Linguistic Minorities (1992). *Council of Europe*: the European Convention for the Protection of Human Rights and Fundamental Freedoms (1950, art. 14); the European Charter of Regional or Minority Languages (1992); Recommendation 1134 (1990) on the Rights of Minorities adopted by the Parliamentary Assembly of the Council of Europe; Recommendation 1177 (1992) on the Rights of Minorities adopted by the Parliamentary Assembly of Council of Europe; and Recommendation 1201 (1993) on an additional protocol on the rights of minorities to the European Convention on Human Rights (provisional edition). *The CSCE*: the Helsinki Final Act (1975); the Concluding Document of the Vienna Meeting (1989); the Charter of Paris for a New Europe (1990); the Report of the CSCE Meeting of Experts on National Minorities (Geneva, 1991); the Document of the Moscow Meeting (1991); the Document on the Copenhagen Meeting on the Human Dimension (1990); and the Document of the Helsinki Meeting (1992).

51. Referring to UN Declaration on the Rights of Persons Belonging to National or Ethnic, Religious and Linguistic Minorities, article 2, para. 3.

52. CSCE Document on Human Dimension, Copenhagen, 1990, art. 35, para. 2.

Part II
The Problems at Hand: Case Studies

2

Success in the Balkans?
A Case Study of Ethnic Relations
in the Republic of Macedonia

ROBERT W. MICKEY
ADAM SMITH ALBION

Ethnic conflict, the series of zero-sum relations between ethnic groups, is at present the most dangerous and poorly understood phenomenon in postcommunist Europe. Along with undermining regional stability and compromising the rights of several million people, it places at risk the political and economic transitions from communism.

The wars of Yugoslav secession and their ensuing media coverage highlight the nature of an ethnic conflict without making its causes and processes more understandable. However, Macedonia, the poorest and southernmost ex-republic of Yugoslavia, provides an excellent case study of the causes and consequences of ethnic conflict. Its central ethnic relationship, between Slav Macedonians (about 55%–60%) and ethnic Albanians (about 25%–30%), may place the future of this new state at risk.[1] Macedonia faces a number of other massive problems, but this ethnic relationship is the most important variable in the calculus of the country's survival. At present, ethnic tensions are growing day by day.

Macedonia should be highlighted for two other reasons. On the one hand, its potential collapse (or implosion) virtually guarantees a new Balkan conflagration, which would match the current war in Bosnia in its ferocity. On the other hand, despite a number of disadvantages, Macedonia has performed better than most Balkan states in managing its ethnic conflict.[2] In this chapter, special attention will be paid to the processes of ethnic politics, the specific grievances of Albanians, Slav Macedonian insecurities, and the question of the status of ethnic minorities within newly emerging states. Finally, recommendations will be outlined with a view to uncovering some effective policies to manage ethnic conflicts generally. First, some historical background should be provided.

1. HISTORICAL INTRODUCTION

A. THE SETTING

The Republic of Macedonia is situated south of Serbia, west of
Bulgaria, east of Albania, and north of Greece, in the region known
historically as "Macedonia." This term has been used to denote
territory that is now part of Bulgaria, Greece, and Serbia, as well as the
newly recognized Republic of Macedonia.[3] Under Philip II of Mace-
don, Macedonia included what is now the republic, Kosovo, Albania,
and Thrace (which extended across southern Bulgaria to European
Turkey).[4] Beginning in the fourth century AD, slews of invaders
dominated the area in succession. The Slavs had settled Macedonia by
the seventh century AD. Macedonia served as the seat to Bulgarian
and Serbian empires until it was overrun by the Ottoman Turks in the
15th century. For the past millennium, geographic Macedonia has
been highly valued as a strategic point of transit between West and
East.

Under Ottoman rule, what is now the Republic of Macedonia was
populated by Slavs, Albanians, Greeks, Turks, Vlachs, Jews, and Roma
(Gypsies), who often lived together in multiethnic communities.
Throughout the 18th and 19th centuries, as the Ottoman Empire
slowly unravelled, national awakenings occurred across the Balkans.
As they began to reassert their nationhood and form modern states,
Greeks, Serbs, and Bulgarians argued on historical, ethnic, and
linguistic grounds that various parts of Macedonia were rightfully
theirs. Macedonia, increasingly under dispute among newly emerging
states as well as the Great Powers, remained a very poor, rural, and
underdeveloped region populated largely by illiterate peasants, virtually devoid of democratic tradition.

B. THE MACEDONIAN NATION

By the beginning of the 20th century, there still did not exist a
"Macedonian" national identity. On the whole, Christian Slavs border-
ing Serbia considered themselves to be Serbs, while those on the
Bulgarian border usually identified themselves as Bulgarians. Differences between these Slavs' self-identification as Bulgarian, Greek, or
Serb were largely due to religious affiliation rather than some notion
of ethnic identity. Before and after the Balkan Wars of 1912–1913,
Bulgaria, Greece, and Serbia each attempted to assimilate the Slavic
population of the region. These efforts were made largely through the
establishment of schools in particular languages, as well as by the
spread of Greek Orthodox, Serb Orthodox, and Bulgarian Orthodox
churches.

At the conclusion of World War II, Bulgaria, Greece, and (what came to be) Yugoslavia carved up the region of Macedonia in a tripartite agreement.[5] Yugoslavia took control of "Vardar" Macedonia (named for this region's Vardar river valley). As the Socialist Federal Republic of Yugoslavia (SFRY) took shape, Josip Broz Tito encouraged the establishment of a Slavic Macedonian nation. The Socialist Republic of Macedonia was formed, and there followed an intensive period of nation building.[6] The SFRY encouraged the refinement of a Macedonian language and alphabet (which became the republic's official language),[7] revised state-approved versions of history, and introduced other policies to instill and make permanent among the citizens of the Macedonian Republic an attachment to the Macedonian "nation" quite set apart from a Serb or Bulgarian identity.[8] This national identity remains a bit tenuous, given its short history. Slav Macedonian insecurities related to demands from ethnic minorities, as will be shown below, stem partially from this self-identity problem. Now, as an independent state, Macedonia is surrounded by those disputants who endanger this fragile process of nation building. But whatever threats it may face, "the Macedonian nationality within the Republic of Macedonia, engineered by Tito or not, is an established fact."[9]

C. THE ALBANIANS IN MACEDONIA

The Albanians are the descendants of the ancient Illyrian tribes who inhabited present-day Albania as well as Kosovo. Albanians claim that their ancestors lived there centuries before the arrival of the Slavs.[10] Albanians began moving east into the geographic territory of Macedonia early in the 19th century, and by displacing local Slavs they settled mostly along the western rim of what is now the Republic of Macedonia. During Ottoman control of Macedonia, these Albanians (most of whom over time converted to Islam) often held privileged positions in society.[11] Many Albanians lived in multiethnic communities such as Debar, but the majority lived in tightly-knit Albanian villages.

During World War II, most of this area was absorbed by the Italian protectorate of Albania. After the war, most Albanians in Yugoslavia were grouped in the autonomous province of Kosovo (in the southern part of the Yugoslav republic of Serbia). However, northwestern and western Macedonia, though predominantly Albanian, were not added to this province when it was drawn because these areas were considered "traditional" Macedonian territory. Importantly, "there was some feeling that the Albanians might be more effectively controlled if they were administratively separated."[12] In sum, the Albanians were ultimately divided into three major areas: Albania proper, Kosovo, and Macedonia. This political and territorial division of 6 million Albanians living in a compact and contiguous area embodies the "Albanian Question." While not as well known, this question dominates the Balkans in the same way as the "Hungarian Question" dominates East Central Europe.[13]

Highly concentrated in western and northwestern Macedonia along the Albanian and Kosovo borders, the Albanians always have been set apart from Slavs and others: "Their language, customs, social organizations, and traditions have very little if anything in common with those of their Slav and Greek neighbors."[14] Organized in tightly-knit clans and following their own centuries-old "custom" law, the Albanians have had little meaningful social interaction with others. While most Albanians speak Macedonian, members of other ethnic groups do not speak Albanian. Like the Turks in Macedonia, Albanians are predominantly Muslim. Unlike the Turks, however, who are largely assimilated into the mainstream of Macedonian society, Albanians have remained fairly isolated socially.[15]

While relations between Albanians and Slav Macedonians historically were not tense on a day-to-day basis, there was and continues to be a great deal of ignorance about and mistrust of the other.[16] Albanians are generally poorer than Macedonians, segregated from them by employment sector, and less well-educated. To the extent that ethnic conflict is rooted in ethnic groups' perceived standing relative to other groups, relations between Albanians and Macedonians are likely to remain tense.[17]

D. ALBANIAN RELATIONS WITH THE STATE

Since the founding of the Yugoslav Socialist Republic of Macedonia in 1944, Albanians there have been disadvantaged by government policies. Like other communist regimes in the Balkans, Yugoslav Macedonia allowed no governmental or nongovernmental institutions that might effectively represent minority interests. Naturally, political parties, including those organized to advocate minority views, were not allowed. Albanians were represented only symbolically in Communist Party organs or in republic-level bureaucracies.[18] Religious, linguistic, educational, and cultural rights for Albanians were neither enshrined in constitutions or laws nor enforced by effective judicial systems.[19]

Besides these systemic problems, Albanians suffered from other forms of discrimination and neglect. Religious persecution against

Muslim leaders, laws against the wearing of veils, and propaganda campaigns against the dangers of "Islamization" in Macedonia occurred with regularity in this period.[20] Educational opportunities, particularly at the secondary and higher education levels, were scarce, as the state was slow to provide for schooling in the Albanian language. Less-developed regions in Macedonia populated largely by Albanians were often neglected by republic-level and federal-level economic development initiatives. Moreover, there was considerable discrimination against Albanians in the hiring and promotion practices of firm managers and state institutions. Organs of the Communist Party and other government institutions did not combat this problem.[21]

The new Yugoslav federal constitution of 1974 brought the Albanians expanded educational and language rights, as Albanians were now recognized as a "nationality" of the Yugoslav federation. In 1980–1981, however, the situation worsened. Riots in Kosovo, sparked by demands that Kosovo be made a republic of Yugoslavia (and therefore gain for the Albanians the status of "constituent people" in Yugoslavia), led to a new Belgrade-inspired campaign to stamp out all possible nationalist elements in the Albanian communities of Yugoslavia. The Macedonian government endorsed and implemented these measures against its Albanian citizens.

Advancements in opportunities for Albanian-language education were curtailed or abolished. The use of Albanian national names (including the names of newborn children and the Albanian names of towns) and symbols was banned. Those Albanians who clamored for the rights to use such symbols were labeled "nationalists" and were imprisoned. During the 1980s, penal policy against Albanian nationalists became even more stringent in Macedonia than in Kosovo.[22] Skopje- and Belgrade-based media launched campaigns to increase Macedonian fears of and antipathy toward Albanians.[23] In 1989, an amendment to the Macedonian constitution redefined the republic's statehood as the "national state of the Macedonian nation," where previously it read "state of the Macedonian people *and* the Albanian and Turkish minorities."[24] On the eve of Yugoslavia's collapse in 1991, policies toward Albanians in Macedonia were abysmal and contributed to a worsening of day-to-day social relations between Albanians and Macedonians.

The historical legacy of Albanian-Macedonian relations continues to have a great impact on these relations today, as will be seen in the discussion below. A few elements of this legacy can be summed up here: continuous international disputes over the control of geographic Macedonia; the area's mixed ethnic heritage and traditional backwardness; the relative newness of the Macedonian nation, and its constituents' relative insecurity; and the communist era.[25] Since there have been moments of Albanian-Macedonian solidarity in the past, and given the fact that the two groups have never been at war with one another, Macedonia's historical legacy perhaps provides more space for the attenuation of ethnic conflict than others in the Balkans.[26] But while the past provides the contours marking ethnic relations, the "resumption" of history over the past three years sets the quickly moving contemporary context of these relations.

2. INDEPENDENCE AND THE RECOGNITION CRISIS

Like other postcommunist states in Europe, Macedonia has undertaken a series of rapid transformations over the past three years. As in all multiethnic states, this time of transition exacerbates ethnic tensions, for "when it looks as if the shape of the polity is being settled once and for all, apprehensions are likely to grow."[27] For Macedonia, difficulties related to the transitions from authoritarian rule and from a command economy have been compounded by the republic's withdrawal from the Yugoslav federation. In the face of all these problems, Macedonia failed for 18 months to secure widespread international recognition.[28] Independence and the ensuing recognition crisis have had profound economic, political, and social effects, and frame the present context of Albanian-Macedonian relations.

Having declared itself independent on September 17, 1991, Macedonia, the only ex-Yugoslav republic to secede nonviolently, has been considered one of the bright spots in the former Yugoslavia. The European Community's influential Badinter Commission recommended Slovenia and Macedonia as most deserving of EC recognition.[29] On January 15, 1992, however, Croatia and Slovenia, but not Macedonia, were recognized.

The negative Greek response to the name "Macedonia" was enough to stall EC recognition. The Greeks argued that this name, used since 1989 to designate territory in northern Greece, can belong to no one state. To use it to signify a state is, they claim, tantamount to holding revanchist claims on the whole of geographic Macedonia.[30] The roots of Greek apprehensions are not easily understood, but there seem to be at least three sources: first, and most important, Greece fears the growing influence of Turkey in encircling Greece with the help of what may become a "Muslimized Macedonia";[31] second, recognition of Macedonia will increase pressure on Greece to recognize the existence of ethnic Macedonians in Greece as minorities, thereby opening up a Pandora's box of international delegations that would evaluate Greece's treatment of them;[32] third, domestic political gains can be made by feeding on Greece's plentiful chauvinist senti-ments.[33]

A. The Economy

Long considered one of Yugoslav's "underdeveloped" areas, the Yugoslav Republic of Macedonia's economy always lagged behind the rest of the federation. The 1980s brought on even worse economic difficulties for Macedonia, as Yugoslavia's interdependent economy sputtered and stalled. In 1987, the unemployment rate stood at 26.7%, the second highest in Yugoslavia (after Kosovo).[34]

Economic consequences of the failure to secure recognition have been massive. Privatization plans were stalled. As a non-entity, Macedo-nia was unable to join international financial institutions that could supply it with aid, credits, and loans. Compliance with United Nations-sponsored economic sanctions against Serbia and Montene-gro, Macedonia's main trading partners, has cost Macedonia an estimated $1.3 billion.[35] (Romania and Bulgaria have also suffered heavily due to the embargo of rump Yugoslavia.[36]) Greece's blockade of oil shipments from Thessaloniki to Macedonia was completely debilitating.[37] Fuel shortages have forced the closure of hundreds of firms. By December 1992, unemployment had reached 39.6%.[38]

Meanwhile, economic losses due to the collapse of markets in Croatia and in Bosnia and Herzegovina have taken a heavy toll. The Macedonian denar has been devalued several times in order to stave off hyperinflation. Macedonia owes more than $1 billion to foreign banks, but national banks hold foreign reserves of only $20 million. Eighty-five percent of GDP remains nationalized, and annual per capita income is less than $900 and shrinking.[39] In this context, with more unemployment to follow as Macedonia enacts a privatization program, it is not difficult to imagine social discontent rising to even greater levels. Macedonia's economy has reached a point of near-collapse, and there is no guarantee that such a collapse can be avoided in the coming months.

Many multiethnic societies in Eastern Europe and the Balkans have already demonstrated the dangerous effects of a shrinking economic pie on ethnic relations.[40] As Janusz Bugajski notes, "if wrenching economic reforms fail to bring visible and rapid benefits to the populace, radical forces will seek to exploit popular frustrations and apply pressure on the fragile government."[41] In multiethnic societies, these forces are divided along ethnic lines. Recent develop-ments throughout the Balkans bear this point out.[42]

B. POLITICS

Like other newly emerging multiethnic states in Europe, independent Macedonia has greatly altered its political landscape through the adoption of a multiparty system, free elections, a new constitution, and the public's increased political participation. In the peculiar context of Macedonia's independence and subsequent recognition crisis, four developments in particular have both ameliorated and exacerbated ethnic conflict in Macedonia.

First, like other states ushering in political pluralism, Macedonia has experienced a marked rise in chauvinist political forces. These forces are led by VMRO-DMPNE,[43] a right-wing, xenophobic, and Slavophile nationalist party.[44] In Macedonia's first multiparty elections (November and December 1990), it won the largest number of parliamentary seats and now holds 35 out of 120. Unable to form a government, VMRO is the leading opposition party in Parliament, where it opposes the governing coalition on almost every issue. It has strongly attacked President Kiro Gligorov for his compromises on negotiations with Greece over the "name" issue and is vociferously anti-Albanian, inciting public fears of the impending "Islamization" of Macedonia. VMRO is, like other nationalist forces throughout the region, characterized by both "political immaturity and [an] exaggerated defensiveness based on fears of domination, absorption, or extinction."[45] While currently unpopular among the voting public, VMRO has the capacity to quickly expand its public support and to increase the power of right-wing forces in Macedonia by taking advantage of Slav Macedonian insecurities vis-à-vis Albanian motives, general anxiety regarding the external environment, and social unrest in the face of economic dislocation.[46]

Second, through the collapse of communist institutions and the new freedom to organize politically, the Albanian community has formed political parties and nongovernmental organizations, and has made great strides in articulating its interests and grievances to the polity as a whole.[47] The chief Albanian political parties, the Party for Democratic Prosperity (PDP) and the National Democratic Party (NDP), control 23 out of 120 parliamentary seats, and are members of the present ruling coalition, which is led by the ex-communist Social Democractic Union of Macedonia (SDUM).[48]

Third, Macedonia's multiethnic governing coalition owes its existence and continued cohesion to the country's crisis. A nonpartisan "government of experts" fell in July 1992, due to its failure to secure widespread recognition for Macedonia and to halt the economic slowdown. VMRO, unwilling to form a government with Albanian and ex-communist parties, thus allowed the leading SDUM, in partnership with the Reform-Liberal Party and the Albanian parties, to form a coalition in the fall of 1992. The SDUM, whatever its intentions, has been forced to rely on the participation of the PDP and NDP, given VMRO's tactic of voting reflexively against the ex-communists.[49]

This inducement from the right to build a multiethnic coalition is joined by the pressure to secure recognition. Indeed, influential observers who argue in favor of recognition cite SDUM's inclusion of five Albanian ministers in the current government as evidence of the stable, multiethnic character of the new state. The Albanians, meanwhile, have participated in the coalition both in order to gain influence and to preclude a VMRO-led regime; as one PDP politician has noted, the Albanians "agreed to take part in a weak coalition to prevent war."[50] As an arrangement built almost solely on convenience, not on ideological solidarity, the coalition is weak. Without the struggle to attain recognition and opposition from the far right, it is unlikely that the governing coalition would have been created, let alone survived up until the present. However, as will be argued below, its survival (or its replacement with another multiethnic coalition) is paramount for stable ethnic relations in Macedonia.

Fourth, Macedonia's new constitution, ratified in December 1991, has been heavily influenced by the recognition crisis. A hodgepodge of different systems of power-sharing and checks and balances, the constitution was drafted in large part to suit the tastes of the international community, which clearly signalled that recognition would be contingent upon a multiparty parliamentary system that respected minority rights. On the whole, these rights are enshrined in the constitution. In fact, the constitution provides for more sweeping educational rights for ethnic minorities and rights of political association than those established in either the Albanian, Bulgarian, or Romanian constitutions.[51]

However, in a compromise with nationalist parties, the framers drafted the preamble to declare that Macedonia is a "national state of the Macedonian people." This clause, implying a lesser status for non-Slav Macedonian citizens, drives the Albanians' chief grievance— their status in the state. The Albanian parties have remarked publicly on many occasions that because of this failure to be recognized as a constituent partner of the Macedonian state, the international community should withhold recognition until the constitution is amended. Here, the constitution's mixed effects on ethnic relations are clear— while seeming to guarantee a pluralistic, multiethnic state, it leaves unsettled perhaps the most explosive issue in Albanian-Macedonian relations.

C. THE INTERNATIONAL CONTEXT

Ethnic conflicts are heavily influenced (and sometimes even determined) by external influences. This is of course doubly true in the Balkans, where international actors have played over multiethnic areas for centuries. Macedonia's uniquely precarious status in Southeastern Europe makes it especially vulnerable to events beyond its control.

External actors are motivated to worsen destabilizing forces within Macedonia. Forces in and out of power in Bulgaria, Serbia, and Greece continue to articulate revanchist claims on the new state. Bulgaria, the first to recognize Macedonia, still does not officially acknowledge the existence of a Macedonian nationality and considers most Slavs in Macedonia to be "Macedonian Bulgarians."[52] Relations with Bulgaria are stable at the moment, but traditional suspicions on both sides give these relations a somewhat tenuous character.[53]

Serbs view Macedonia as "South Serbia," and Serbian President Slobodan Milošević has pointedly refused to recognize the permanence of the Macedonian-Serb border. Other Serb politicians speak openly of invading Macedonia when the time is ripe.[54] The ethnic Serbs in Macedonia (about 2% of the population, but thought by Serbs to be as high as 15%)[55] could serve as a convenient pretext for Serb intervention if Milošević or a like-minded successor requires one. Suspicions of Serb plots to destabilize Macedonia are frequently voiced by government officials and journalists.[56] Meanwhile, Milošević has asked Greek Prime Minister Konstantinos Mitsotakis to consider the idea of their dividing and sharing Macedonia after an armed conflict.

Although Milošević has been rebuffed, the Greek position is not without danger to Macedonia.[57] Like the Bulgarians, the Greeks do not recognize the existence of a Macedonian nation; moreover, they consider the large Macedonian ethnic minority in northern Greece to be Slavic-speaking Greeks, but "pure" Greeks nevertheless.[58] The Greek oil blockade, as well as its substantial economic and diplomatic assistance to Serbia, one of its closest allies, demonstrates this danger. Macedonian defenses are comprised of only 10,000 active troops who lack armor, artillery, radar, and combat aircraft. They are supported by about 700 lightly armed UN peacekeepers. All in all, scenarios of Macedonia's dissection are not far-fetched.[59]

Macedonia also fears Russia's ties to Serbia as potentially deadly to their new state. And the existence of a small, relatively content, and well-assimilated Turkish minority in Macedonia leaves open the question of Turkish intervention in Macedonian matters. While Macedonia has signed various trade agreements and is promised significant economic and military aid by Turkey,[60] heightened Turkish interest in Balkan affairs is often perceived by Slav Macedonians as potentially destabilizing.[61]

Macedonia's precarious surroundings are similar to those of other states in the Balkans. Lacking any security guarantees or alliances with Western or regional powers, and troubled by ethnic conflict within their own borders, Albania, Bulgaria, and Romania share Macedonia's insecurities. The objective adverse effects on ethnic conflict include border tensions, the possibility of outside intervention in support of one or more ethnic group, and a worsening regional economic climate, among others. But these objective elements are joined by similarly important subjective elements. Slav Macedonians perceive an international environment that threatens their very identity—in this context, demands by ethnic minorities are easily viewed as additional threats to the survival of the Macedonian nation.[62] Faced with especially harrowing economic difficulties and the many dimensions of the Albanian Question, Macedonia is plagued by an international context that provides an even more treacherous setting for the conduct of Albanian-Macedonian relations.

D. The Albanian Question

The most dangerous threats to Macedonia from without and within are components of the Albanian Question. Here, the prospects of a "Greater Albania," the stability of Macedonia's borders with Albania and Kosovo, the possibility of armed conflict in Kosovo, and the quest of Albanians in Macedonia for territorial autonomy come together to exacerbate ethnic conflict in Macedonia.

The argument for a Greater Albania is based on the claim that this contiguous region has been settled by Albanians for over a millennium and by the more contemporary argument that Albanians form a numerical majority in Kosovo and in western Macedonia (which as a compact whole shares borders with both Albania and Kosovo).[63] Albania proper, as well as Albanians in Kosovo and Macedonia, understands that the formation of a Greater Albania is not an option over the near term, for it could only result from a war that they could not win. However, in both Kosovo and western Macedonia, most Albanians view a Greater Albania as an explicit goal for the long term.

Although Albania did not recognize Macedonia until April 10, 1993, it has over the past two years become gradually more cautious in its policies toward Kosovo and western Macedonia.[64] Through Kosovo's Albanian leader, Ibrahim Rugova, Albania's President Sali Berisha has pressured his compatriots in Macedonia to quiet their demands for autonomy.[65] He has also declared recently that Macedonia's borders should remain unchanged, on the grounds that Albanians there have made great progress politically (especially through their participation in the ruling coalition): "Independent Macedonia is a guarantee for the stability of both the Albanian people and of the entire Balkan region."[66] Despite sentiments expressed in Kosovo or Macedonia, therefore, the Albanian government is not considering the adoption of those surely destabilizing policies necessary to precipitate a Greater Albania.

Although this policy has defused short-term attempts to effect a Greater Albania, the problem of the Albanian-Macedonian border remains. This border is quite porous—neither state has the resources to patrol it sufficiently, and it seems that Tirana is content to allow its citizens to pass back and forth at will.[67] Such border crossings are alleged to be the source of criminal activities, including the supplying of weapons to Albanian Macedonians who are preparing to defend their brothers in Kosovo.[68] The shooting deaths at the border of several Albanians attempting to enter Macedonia and the ensuing flare-up in Albanian-Macedonian relations point to the inherent dangers in this border's continuing instability.[69]

Kosovo functions as the most dangerous external aspect of the Albanian question for Macedonia. Since 1990, Serbia has ruled formerly autonomous Kosovo as a police state. In the event of a violent Serb crackdown on the 90% Albanian majority in Kosovo, it is likely that Albanians will flee across the border into Macedonia. The Macedonian government has already stated that it would seal its border and repulse any waves of refugees from such a conflict.[70] (Already, as many as 150,000 Kosovar Albanians have fled Kosovo and now live illegally in Macedonia.)[71] On the other hand, it is also likely that Albanians from Macedonia would flood into Kosovo to join the fray.[72] The introduction of forces from the Republic of Albania, organized or not, may lead to attempts to alter the Albanian-Macedonian border. In any case, this much is clear: armed conflict in Kosovo presents several scenarios for the collapse of Macedonia.

Finally, the most dangerous aspect of the Albanian Question over the long term is an Albanian push for territorial autonomy in western Macedonia. There is simply no way of achieving such autonomy without bloodshed. Slav Macedonians will not tolerate this move, because in their view it would lead inevitably to the partition of their already small and vulnerable state. Calls for autonomous arrangements for Albanians have been made in the past, usually in the context of similar demands by Kosovar Albanians. But as Macedonia's international context remains so precarious and ethnic tensions remain high, autonomy is not considered an option by Slav Macedonians.

In January 1992, soon after the ratification of the constitution, the Albanian political parties in Macedonia organized a referendum on the territorial-political autonomy of Albanians in the western part of the country. This was in response, party representatives claimed, to the (Slav) Macedonian parties' "narrow-mindedness and egotism as far as the rights of the Albanian people in Macedonia are concerned."[73] The timing of the referendum, however, only four days before the EC was to announce its decisions regarding the recognition of the ex-Yugoslav republics, suggests that the Albanians were hoping to dissuade the international community from recognizing Macedonia, which would then make recognition contingent upon Macedonian concessions to Albanians.[74]

As a method of changing the status of Albanians in Macedonia, the referendum was not a serious effort. Besides its dubious legal standing, the idea of "autonomy" was never spelled out.[75] Moreover, polling stations were open not only throughout Macedonia, but in Slovenia, Croatia, Bosnia and Herzegovina, and 24 other European countries. While Albanian groups claimed 99.9% of those who voted approved the referendum, the referendum was boycotted by Turkish groups, as well as by a number of Albanians.[76] Many Macedonians considered the referendum "primarily a survey of [the Albanian] mood without any kind of legal basis that would bind the republican government or international human rights organizations."[77]

But others treated the referendum with deadly seriousness: "Unilateral acts of minorities, which do not take into account the opinion of the majority, lead to violence," proclaimed a government spokesperson after announcing that the referendum was unconstitutional. Macedonian parliamentary deputies warned of the large possibilities of open inter-ethnic conflict.[78] While no violence occurred, there was and remains the potential for violence merely in raising the possibility of autonomous arrangements.[79] Moreover, many Macedonians feel "left in the lurch" by the Albanians on the most important issue of all: international recognition.[80]

The logic of simultaneous Albanian demands for autonomy in Macedonia and for Macedonian recognition of the independence of a sovereign Kosovo could lead, one might conclude, to an eventual call for Albanian unification.[81] Although demands for autonomy are less visible of late, there is still talk of the need for autonomy of some kind.[82]

The drive for territorial, political, or cultural autonomy, and its effects on ethnic relations, are common elsewhere in the region. For example, when radical elements of the ethnic Hungarian HDFR umbrella group in Transylvania demanded autonomy, Romanian-

Hungarian relations immediately worsened on the parliamentary and local levels.[83] This is not to argue against territorial autonomy as a method of decreasing ethnic conflict, but only to demonstrate the high level of fear and hostility among majorities that becomes evident (and that is thought to be justified) as minorities demand changes in the shape of the state.

In sum, the drive for independence, political and economic reform, and the ensuing recognition crisis completely altered the playing field of ethnic relations in Macedonia. Economic troubles worsened, new political forces arose, there began an open (and increasingly hostile) dialogue among ethnic groups, the international context became threatening, and the Albanian Question was posed again on the Balkan stage. Slav Macedonian insecurities and Albanian demands for an improved position in Macedonia, the two chief variables in their relations, can be understood only within this context.

3. THE POLITICS OF ALBANIAN-MACEDONIAN RELATIONS[84]

"An upsurge of ethnic-based politics has been evident alongside the burgeoning of political pluralism and the erosion of central control" throughout Eastern Europe and the Balkans.[85] This brand of politics exacerbates ethnic conflict in the Balkans, where democratic institutions are either nonexistent or very weak. It also damages democratization processes by heightening tensions and often by convincing minorities that democracy may not provide a useful framework within which to achieve their aims.[86] The region's communist legacy worsens these trends. The collapse of these regimes has encouraged the politically ambitious to fill the new political vacuums by capitalizing on chauvinist sentiments.[87] Moreover, old styles of dispute resolution hinder the reduction of ethnic tensions,[88] as does the overall amateurism of the current regimes.[89]

An atmosphere of mutual distrust and antipathy between ethnic groups causes these groups to organize themselves politically along ethnic lines. The mere existence of organized parties that serve the interests of ethnic minorities sparks a majority backlash; majorities in all Balkan states call for the banning of such parties, and inter-ethnic tensions increase.[90] Since ethnic parties of majorities and minorities do not compete with one another for voters, these parties have no incentives to moderate their demands. Electoral incentives are thus centrifugal, not centripetal. Turnout is increased by incitement of ethnic hatreds or by the exaggeration of threats faced by an ethnic group.

The issues at stake in ethnic-based politics are often zero-sum in nature and thus contribute to the intractability of ethnic disputes. Language issues, the regulation of the use of ethnic symbols, and the question of an ethnic group's status within the state, for example, "are not readily amenable to compromise. In this, they differ from claims deriving wholly from material interest. Whereas material advancement can be measured both relatively and absolutely, the status advancement of one ethnic group is entirely relative to the status of others."[91] It is perceived that political symbols are so important because "claims concerning [them] usually connote something about future treatment: who will be discriminated against and who will be preferred."[92] Meanwhile, non-ethnic issues are often not sources of political capital and are thus given less attention than they may deserve.[93]

Moreover, ethnic minority communities and their parties are often organized hierarchically.[94] They are successful in suppressing a diversity of opinions from being expressed politically, except when factions within these communities attempt to "outbid" one another by making more and more stringent demands of the majority.[95] These parties' virtual monopoly over political expression allows them to generate very high and almost unanimous turnouts. Therefore, political parties of ethnic minority groups gain political participation and influence in Parliament and local elective bodies at levels disproportionate to their size, thereby often heightening majority fears.[96] In sum, this brand of politics can worsen already strained relations between ethnic groups.

The fledgling Republic of Macedonia is not immune from these trends. Slav Macedonians are represented by a range of parties located along both left-right and cosmopolitan-nationalist spectrums.[97] Turks, Serbs, Roma, and Vlachs all have formed their own political parties, which are active in publicizing their grievances and concerns. But concerning ethnic conflict, the most important manifestation of ethnic politics can be found among the Albanians.

Albanian concerns in Macedonia are articulated largely by the two leading Albanian parties already mentioned, the Party of Democratic Prosperity and the National Democratic Party.[98] Their membership is almost exclusively Albanian, and they have failed to recruit across ethnic lines in order to earn their "multiethnic" labels.[99] Among ethnic Albanian political parties, only the PDP and NDP hold seats in Parliament and therefore have unique access to Macedonian, Albanian, and international media. This access allows these parties to dominate the Albanian community's political landscape and to marginalize the formation or growth of rival parties. The PDP and the NDP are very well organized in party structures, on the local level, and in Parliament. They are funded by a radical diaspora that pressures them to adopt increasingly stringent positions.[100] They are adept at mobilizing constituencies quickly, owing partly to the Albanian community's social cohesiveness.[101]

However, there is growing discontent among the Albanian populace over the quality of its representation. Many Albanians feel that the PDP and NDP party leaderships focus on issues of lesser importance, and often do so to satisfy their own personal interests. Prospects for more pluralistic representation of Albanian concerns are growing. Whether an increase in the number of Albanian parties will lead to ethnic "outbidding" and the further radicalization of Albanian demands or to a broader spectrum of political positions remains to be seen.

Three primary characteristics of Albanian party behavior are crucial for an understanding of the nature of ethnic conflict in Macedonia. First, the role of the Albanians in Parliament is of great importance. Without the votes of the 23 Albanian MPs, the moderate-left governing coalition would collapse, given VMRO's tactic of reflexively opposing almost every step taken by what it calls the "Albanian-communist" alliance. But rather than lose important votes on issues affecting Albanian interests, the PDP and NDP tend to walk out of Parliament before the votes are held. They have also bolted from coalition positions on a number of issues, including ratification of the constitution in December 1991, and many votes concerning the endorsement of the government's negotiations with Greece on the "name" issue. These tendencies demonstrate the weakness of the present coalition, and may point to its collapse when a new set of political incentives for the Albanians appears.

Second, the Albanian parties focus on a narrow band of issues directly related to Albanian grievances and interests. As they themselves admit, Albanian MPs make little contribution to parliamentary debates or legislative discussions unrelated to explicitly "ethnic" issues (these non-ethnic issues include the privatization plan, foreign policy issues, etc.). The Macedonian Parliament, however, commits an inordinate amount of its time precisely to "ethnic" issues.[102] As elsewhere in the Balkans, a large proportion of these ethnic issues involve the use of political symbols. Battles over the appearance of the Albanian flag, the national anthem, and the composition of bank notes and other symbols dominate political discourse. As will be shown below, Albanians and Macedonians have not reached agreements on most of these issues, and these stalemates lower the possibilities of resolving other issues of material interest to both sides.

Third, the PDP and the NDP have capitalized on the willingness of the Macedonian government's leadership (President Gligorov as well as Prime Minister Branko Crvenkovski) to keep open an important backchannel of communication. President Gligorov, especially, has proven quite adept at balancing Albanian concerns with the demands of nationalist forces and the needs of the governing coalition. It is reported that this backchannel serves as a crisis prevention and resolution tool.[103] Such backchannels have played key roles in Bulgaria and Albania as well, where ethnic minority leaders have employed close ties with the presidents and others in efforts to reach agreements over previously intractable issues.[104]

Ethnic politics as conceived here is a dangerous phenomenon new to postcommunist Europe. Born out of an explosive growth in political expression and a rise in ethnic tensions, ethnic politics can be mitigated only through careful, modest steps aimed at encouraging cooperation across ethnic lines. Such steps will be reviewed as policy recommendations are considered.

4. ALBANIAN GRIEVANCES

A. THE NUMBERS GAME

The question of the size of a minority relative to a state's population is a crucial issue in all ethnic conflicts, and affects all debates between ethnic groups. Ethnic conflicts center around relative comparison— what matters is the relative, not absolute, size of an ethnic group's population. These numbers are thought by disputants in ethnic conflicts to determine "whose country it is."[105] In the Balkans, wildly divergent estimates of the sizes of ethnic groups both reflect ethnic tensions and worsen them. Estimates of ethnic Greeks in Albania, Roma and Hungarians in Romania, and Roma and Turks in Bulgaria made by the state, ethnic minority groups, media, and majority groups often differ from one another by a factor of ten, and the ensuing arguments divert attention from other issues, heightening mutual mistrust and suspicions.[106]

Currently, most Albanian leaders claim that their people comprise about 40% of Macedonia's population. The last census, which the Albanian community boycotted on orders from the PDP and NDP, estimates about 22%.[107] Emigre groups in the United States (as well as some Albanian politicians in Macedonia) argue that there is a clear majority of Albanians in Macedonia.[108] Macedonians, on the other hand, estimate that Albanians number about 25%.

Regardless of what the "true" numbers are, it is clear that this issue has tremendous impact on most political disagreements between

Slav Macedonians and Albanians. Debates over government expenditures on education, the number of hours of minority-language radio programming, employment in the state sector, the use of nationalist symbols, and a host of other issues are articulated in terms of what an ethnic group is thought to deserve in terms of its relative size. The general tenor of relations changes with the numbers—Albanians at 40% feel emboldened to make a number of demands that they might not consider as politically viable at 22%.[109]

B. EDUCATION

Education is one of the most hotly contested issues between majorities and minorities in Eastern Europe. Throughout the Balkans, levels of education have often been quite low, especially in the poorer areas that minorities often inhabit. As the postcommunist era commences, these minorities focus much of their political energies on the reform of previously discriminatory educational policies, for they view education as their primary avenue for social and economic advancement, the "great equalizer" that can raise their standing relative to other ethnic groups. Moreover, education embodies the key issue through which debates over the use of minority languages occur. In the face of various assimilationist pressures, ethnic minorities strive to maintain cultural solidarity, and the preservation of their native tongue is at the heart of this effort. Therefore, minorities demand the opportunity to educate themselves in their own language.[110]

Majorities, on the other hand, often interpret efforts to maintain cultural solidarity as the refusal to integrate, to form one society, and (in the more extreme articulations) to remain loyal to the state. The use of the majority language is, it is thought, paramount to effective integration. Thus, demands for minority-language education can seem to be the first step toward ethnic separatism. They also can intimidate insecure majorities about the eventual loss of their status as owners of the state at the hands of better-educated and wealthier minorities. Education as a policy issue, like most issues driving ethnic conflict, is so divisive because it is considered by all sides to be, at root, about the future.

Albanian- and Macedonian-language secondary education in western Macedonia has historically been poor in quality and not readily available. Soon after the conclusion of World War II, the Macedonian government successfully established a large number of Albanian-language primary schools. There remained, however, very few opportunities for Albanian schoolchildren to study at the secondary or higher-education levels in the Albanian language.[111] As part of the Belgrade-led campaign against Albanian nationalism in the 1980s, new laws were passed in Macedonia that made it more difficult for Albanian pupils to attend secondary school classes in their own language (a right bestowed to all nationalities in the 1974 Yugoslav federal constitution), and enrollment plummeted. While officials claimed that many schools had to be closed due to a lack of qualified Albanian teachers, at least 150 such teachers were fired in 1988 for "allegedly indoctrinating their pupils with Albanian nationalism."[112]

With the onset of political reforms and independence, the state's approach to minority education has been greatly liberalized. Today, Macedonia's constitution contains an expanded set of education rights for minorities. Articles 44 and 48 make the following provisions: "Everyone has a right to education"; "Education is accessible to everyone under equal conditions"; "Primary education is compulsory and free"; and "Members of the nationalities have the right to instruction in their language in primary and secondary education, *as determined by law*"[113] (italics in original).

But implementation of these provisions has been less than successful. Albanians continue to voice complaints about the availability of secondary-level schooling. The conditions necessary to fulfill the right to secondary-level education, as stipulated by the Education Ministry (staffed entirely by Slav Macedonians), include sufficient numbers of Albanian parents in a local community interested in their children receiving Albanian-language instruction; the availability of appropriately skilled teachers; classroom space; and the maintenance of national curricular standards.[114] If these conditions are not met, Albanians (as well as Turks, Vlachs, Serbs, Roma, and others) must continue with their education at a Macedonian-language school.

In fact, Albanians claim that of the 8,000 Albanian children who finished primary school in the past year, there were spaces available for only 23% of them to continue studies in their native language.[115] Macedonian educational administrators argue that the chief problem is a shortage of qualified Albanian-language teachers, coupled with the more difficult issue of maintaining a minimum standard of quality in these schools. These administrators note that the quality of teaching, students, and materials in Albanian schools (as well as in Turkish schools) is lower than the national average.[116] And given the country's economic crisis, the argument goes, the government cannot afford to open more schools.[117]

Albanians respond that the real barrier to improvements is a Slav Macedonian resistance to a better-educated Albanian community. They argue that there is a surplus of Macedonian primary and secondary school teachers in the country, and rather than put these teachers out of work, the government refuses to offer many classes in Albanian. In this way, the government forces Albanians to study in Macedonian, to withdraw from school, or to enroll in a private school.[118]

Since only primary education is compulsory, many Albanian parents withdraw their children from school rather than have them continue in a Macedonian-language school. Therefore, many children quit school at grade eight. Even if students complete secondary schools, the lower quality of Albanian-language schools means that many of these students are unable to gain admittance to faculties of higher learning, where almost all instruction is in Macedonian. In the 1991–1992 school year, only 386 of 23,000 university students were Albanian.[119] (There have been no opportunities in former Yugoslavia to study at the college level in Albanian since 1990, when Albanian-language classes were outlawed at the University of Priština in Kosovo by the Serb authorities.[120])

Deputy Minister of Education Vladimir Mostrov and other education officials claim that the ministry is doing everything within its powers to improve this situation. They note that an Albanian deputy minister is being hired to help draft education guidelines. Moreover, the ministry has begun to take decisive steps to decentralize educational decisions down to the local level so that Albanian communities have more control over financial and administrative issues. Regarding higher education, at the University of Skopje and at other faculties, there is a new 10% quota to increase Albanian applications.[121]

There is much at stake in this debate over educational policy. Albanians are seeking to overcome traditional backwardness through education, but demand to do so in a manner that preserves their cultural solidarity. Macedonians are striving to reduce spending and to maintain their own spending priorities. Budgetary limitations do indeed play a major role in the shortage of secondary schools.[122] But many Macedonians and their nationalist party representatives are opposed to bilingual education on the grounds that it is one step on the slippery slope to separatism and civil war. A less stringent Macedonian objection is that such a system would "ghettoize" the various nationalities, including the Albanians, and further divide an already poorly integrated society.[123] But as long as secondary schools are not widely available in Albanian, Albanians will continue to abstain from attending Macedonian-language secondary schools, and will remain economically disadvantaged and socially disenfranchised.[124] The lack of Albanian-language higher education perpetuates this status.

However, when compared with the rest of the region, Macedonia's educational policies are quite progressive. No other Balkan state, save Slovenia, has established and begun implementing such sweeping constitutional rights concerning education. In southern Albania, Greeks have very few schools in the Greek language, and these rarely exceed ages 6–9 years.[125] In Bulgaria, Turks have secured the right only to optional classes in the Turkish language for a few days per week. Hungarians in Romania are still struggling to reinstate secondary schools that teach only in Hungarian, rather than both Hungarian and Romanian.[126]

Despite its current problems, Macedonia's education policy has outperformed those of its neighbors. But the issue will remain a focal point of Albanian-Macedonian relations as long as mutual distrust marks these relations. In other words, education policy will reflect and exacerbate ethnic conflict in Macedonia as long as either group is insecure about its future standing.

C. The Media

The media across postcommunist Europe are in a state of flux. New freedoms have ushered in a confusing period in which newly established private media outlets compete with those controlled or heavily subsidized by the state (which is usually controlled by the ethnic majority). Television, by far the most important medium, is still primarily in state hands.

The media play a crucial role in ethnic conflicts throughout Eastern Europe and the Balkans. The tenor of these media can quite easily exacerbate already fragile ethnic tensions. In extreme cases, regimes have survived through their overwhelming control of television and radio.[127] In many situations, the media have worsened ethnic relations and reduced the political space available for compromise and reasoned debate. But the possibility exists that the media can, in those cases where social interaction between ethnic groups is very limited, act responsibly as a force for social stability and contribute to a reduction of ethnic tensions.

Additionally, there is the matter of access to media outlets for ethnic minorities. Ethnic minorities currently clamor for the right (and the financial support) to broadcast radio and television and to publish newspapers and magazines in their own languages. Such policies were implemented by most states during socialist times as a method of depoliticizing ethnic relations through "cultural programming"; many of these privileges, however, have been curtailed in the postcommunist period in the face of budget troubles and the rise of nationalist forces opposed to special rights for minorities.

These two issues are very much alive in Macedonia. Albanians, like other ethnic groups, complain about the dearth of radio, television, and newspaper coverage in their own language.[128] Their arguments are rooted almost solely in their perceived share of the state's population.[129] Thus, they demand one-third of broadcasting time on the three national radio stations, as well as an increase in their current allotment of television air time; some have proposed exclusive Albanian use of one of Macedonia's three national television channels. Currently, Albanians are allotted six hours per day of air time on state radio.[130] When asked by Macedonian Radio to compose a workable nine-hour programming chart, they were unable to do so. Macedonian officials report that there are not enough trained technicians or professionals among the groups who could staff 12-hour, or 24-hour, programming in line with their demands.[131]

There is one Albanian newspaper, *Flaka e Vëllazërimit*, which is largely state-subsidized and appears three times a week. Albanians are asking for greater subsidies in order to allow it to be published daily, as are two Macedonian-language newspapers.[132] This request is unlikely to be fulfilled, given the country's economic difficulties. Newspapers have become unprofitable in Macedonia as production costs and prices have risen while personal income has dropped steadily.[133] The main Macedonian newspaper, *Nova Makedonija*, is able to flourish due to its monopoly on printing and distribution throughout Macedonia. The paper is also closely linked to the SDUM, the leading partner in the ruling coalition.

Opportunities for the establishment of private media outlets have been few and unsuccessful. There are a number of local radio stations and television stations, but none provides the news and cultural programming that Albanian parties are demanding. Meanwhile, the state media apparatus is crumbling and almost bankrupt. Financed overwhelmingly through subscription fees, state radio and television are greatly endangered by the fact that as much as 70% of a dissatisfied public refuses to pay these fees.[134]

The state's media bureaucracy is staffed almost solely by Slav Macedonians, and 95% of journalists from communist days still hold their jobs.[135] These twin facts bode ill for responsible media, but overall the Macedonia media performance has been good. Unlike Romania, Serbia, Albania, and Greece, where ethnic relations have worsened as both state media and a number of privately funded, extreme nationalist outlets have contributed to heightening tensions, Macedonian radio and television have generally acted responsibly.[136] This is more surprising given the anti-Albanian media campaigns of the 1980s. While there has been anti-Albanian reporting at some moments,[137] Macedonia has been able to avoid the vicious media attacks and poisonous atmosphere that have plagued other Balkan countries.[138] Here, Macedonia undoubtedly benefits from the absence of many of the recent and very severe historical rifts between ethnic groups that are drawn on by actors in other ethnic conflicts.[139] Indeed, when interviewed, Albanian politicians and others targeted all of their complaints about the media on what they considered to be paltry broadcast time; they did not discuss ethnic or political bias.[140]

Thus far, as confirmed in Mazowiecki's report to the UN, most problems regarding minority-language media are related to Macedonia's financial difficulties.[141] Unfortunately, there is no guarantee that the media will remain in the hands of those seeking to attenuate ethnic conflict. If, for instance, VMRO were to assume power, state media (and especially television) would probably change its tone a great deal, and ethnic relations would surely suffer. Additionally, Albanian reaction and subsequent demands for independent media space would play into the hands of the nationalists as moves toward separatism. As long as media are tied to the state, media will remain especially vulnerable to political winds.

D. EMPLOYMENT

Drastic economic slowdowns in Eastern Europe and the Balkans are partially responsible for the increase of ethnic tensions in the region. Majority fears and prejudices, especially, are amplified by a shrinking economic pie, as exemplified by clashes in Germany. Policy makers, in order to avoid responsibility for economic problems, are able to play the "ethnic card" and blame ethnic minorities for these slowdowns. Meanwhile, ethnic minorities are increasingly vocal about the state's responsibility, primarily through job growth and quotas, to help them reach the socioeconomic levels of majorities.

Over the past half-century, Albanians have worked primarily in the agricultural sector. However, they are now also concentrated in the construction industry, local educational administration, blue-collar maintenance work, and in light industry.[142] Historically, Albanian families have relied on their sons to work abroad for a few years for foreign wages. Given painfully high unemployment rates in Albania proper, Kosovo, and Macedonia (where it is estimated to be over 40%), this custom is now even more common. In Macedonia, Albanians are prominent in a very well-organized "unofficial" economy, in which they are thought to draw on their considerable entrepreneurial skills.[143] In sum, this relative ethnic stratification by employment sector as well as the Albanians' geographical compactness has led to feelings among both Albanians and Macedonians that Albanians live in a parallel society, not part of an integrated whole.

Albanians in Macedonia have traditionally suffered from discrimination at the workplace. Today, they complain of discrimination across the board, whether at state-owned firms, republic- and local-level governmental institutions, or private firms. For instance, Servet Avziu, Minister Without Portfolio (who is from the Albanian coalition PDP-NDP), notes that Albanians are basically nonexistent in government service. He claims that there are no more than three Albanians in each ministry, and their presence in these low posts is usually symbolic.[144] Unlike Kosovar Albanians, those in Macedonia never had the opportunity to serve in party and government offices.[145] Additionally, there are continued complaints of discrimination against Albanians for blue-collar positions with factories and other firms. Many Albanian businesspeople argue that Macedonian firm directors are unlikely to hire Albanian workers. Even in Tetovo, the predominantly Albanian community north of Skopje, one well-known Macedonian factory refuses to hire Albanians.[146]

Traditional discrimination against Albanians, the paucity of high-skilled and well-educated Albanians, and the current economic crisis all converge to paint a bleak picture of Albanian employment in Macedonia. Some Albanian leaders, including Ilijaz Halimi (president of the very radical NDP), have demanded that "proportional representation" be arranged for Albanian participation not only in government offices, but also in "social institutions."[147] Similarly, the Hungarian HDFR in Romania has called for proportional minority representation at all levels of administration.[148] Partially in response, the Ministry of the Interior has introduced quotas for Albanians at the police high schools and faculties in Skopje, arguing that ethnic integration of the police force is crucial to the future stability of ethnic relations.[149] Thus far, results have been unimpressive.[150]

Currently, however, most demands of Albanians concerning employment have dealt with individual cases of discrimination, both petty and severe. Public statements of Albanian political leaders omit broader demands for provisions barring discrimination at the workplace. The grievances they voice are heavily influenced by the socialist past, as they focus on Albanians as state employees, not on the quantity and quality of jobs for all Albanians across employment sectors. As privatization looms larger, this emphasis may change. But it is likely that in the near term Albanian responses to low employment levels will be pitched to the state. Such demands must be viewed in the context of the battered Macedonian economy. As mentioned above, the effects of the shrinking economic pie on ethnic conflict can be severe, and demands for proportional employment at all levels of government and business are sure to inflame what is from the Macedonian perspective an increasingly zero-sum situation.[151]

E. LOCAL GOVERNANCE

Ethnic conflicts are reflected in and affected by such matters as parliamentary activity, government ministry policies, and television, but they occur on a day-to-day basis at the local level, where frustrations accumulate and tempers flare. Ethnic conflicts that are successfully managed politically at the state level may still spiral into violence if local-level problems continue to fester. In postcommunist Europe, the governance of ethnically mixed communities exacerbates these day-to-day contacts. Ethnic minorities often equal or outnumber the majority ethnic group on the local level and clamor for commensurate local political representation. Albania, Bulgaria, and Romania, like Macedonia, have experienced heightened tensions and even outbreaks of violence emanating from such problems.[152]

In the communist period, local municipalities had very free rein over their own affairs. Oversight from Skopje was lacking and usually ineffective. Predominantly Albanian villages and towns were controlled by Macedonian functionaries. Electoral and financial abuses were common. Some of the most dangerous confrontations between Albanians and the state during the late 1980s occurred due to flare-ups involving municipal governments in which Albanians had little or no political influence. Since independence, the situation has worsened. The Parliament and state ministries in Skopje have exercised tight control over municipalities while legislation reconfiguring state-local relations is pending. This control has been especially problematic in Tetovo and Gostivar, two predominantly Albanian cities. In both cities, the PDP and NDP won local elections in 1990. However, Macedonian officials refused to allow the newly elected representatives to assume their positions. The Parliament's mediation efforts failed, and eventually the Albanians formed their own municipal assembly and elected their own mayor.[153]

Both sides claim the other is acting illegally. Albanians object, of course, to the Macedonian officials' refusal to step down after having been defeated. Macedonian nationalist parties argue that a national minority cannot simultaneously fill offices locally and in Parliament.[154] More recently, Macedonians claim that Albanian politicians have attempted to dominate all administrative offices in Tetovo, have illegally assumed control of local property, and have harassed local Macedonian residents in order to force them from Tetovo.[155] Much of the municipality's power has been assumed by Skopje during this imbroglio. Meanwhile, most taxes go uncollected in Tetovo, and rudimentary municipal services such as public sanitation are super-vised—poorly—by the state government.[156] Among Albanians and Macedonians rage persistent rumors that the other side is arming itself for a possible conflict.[157]

Minister Without Portfolio Gordana Siljanovska argues that draft legislation on local governance that returns a good deal of power to the municipalities will contribute to improving ethnic relations by giving the Albanians the responsibilities they demand. However, in territorial units in Tetovo, they will be responsible for Slav Macedo-nians as ethnic minorities. This responsibility, she argues, is what is needed to increase a mutual sense of accountability between ethnic groups.[158] Unless solutions to the problems of majorities-as-minorities are reached, local-level politics will remain charged with the potential to sour interpersonal relations, heighten majority fears, paralyze governance, and spark ever-worsening spirals of violence.

5. ALBANIAN GRIEVANCES IN CONTEXT: THE QUESTION OF STATUS WITHIN THE STATE

The question of the Albanians' status in the new state of Macedonia provides the lens through which all facets of the Macedonian-Albanian conflict must be examined. All Albanian grievances reflect and are fueled by their dissatisfaction with their present status as a "nationality" in Macedonia. Indeed, status is of the greatest interest to combatants in ethnic conflict: concern over status supersedes "conflicts over needs and interests."[159] Regionally, the issue of constitutional status for ethnic minorities is a matter of great importance as they search for guarantees of present treatment and future standing. Majorities, on the other hand, fearful of their loss of ownership of the state, foreign intervention, and incessant minority demands based on ever-elastic notions of equality, attempt to provide themselves with a constitutional firebreak that secures their own future.

The background of this dispute is complex. After the ratification of the 1974 Yugoslav federal constitution, Albanians in Yugoslavia held the status of a "nationality." Nationalities were granted expanded educational and cultural rights. However, they held a status secondary to the Macedonians, who were recognized as one of the six "Nations of Yugoslavia." These nations were the constituent elements of the federation, and held special powers in federal representative bodies; each had to be consulted over decisions involving the future of the republic, and each held the right to secede. Meanwhile, until 1989, when a Serb-led crackdown on minorities began, the Macedonian republic-level constitution in its preamble gave special recognition to its Albanians and Turks as minorities who shared the state with Macedonians.[160]

The preamble to the new constitution of Macedonia, which was passed on November 21, 1991, declares that "Macedonia is established as a national state of the Macedonian people, in which full equality as citizens and permanent coexistence with the Macedonian people is provided for Albanians, Turks, Vlachs, Romanies and other nationalities living in the Republic of Macedonia."[161] Albanian MPs refused to vote on the constitution's ratification, and still recommend against the international recognition of Macedonia because of the phrase "national state of the Macedonian people."[162]

This formulation is recognized by Macedonians and Albanians alike as placing the "ownership" of the country in Macedonian hands. Macedonians argue that they are entitled to hold the highest status in the constitution, because, unlike minorities, they have no "host" state to whom they can appeal for help, no land of their own to which they can return. Their argument here corresponds with that of other majorities in Europe.[163] Moreover, they argue, the constitution, both in the preamble and in all other articles, provides for the equality of all citizens as well as an extensive array of minority rights.

Albanian objections to this formulation are several.[164] They argue that their possession of lesser status precludes their ability to prevent the government from fundamentally altering the nature of the state to the Albanians' detriment. Here, they mention most often the example of a VMRO-led government that might seek to form a federation with Bulgaria.[165] Conversely, equal status in the state gives its possessor the right to continuous consultations, both formally and informally, on the most urgent issues facing the state. A second benefit of "nation" status Albanians perceive is the right to proportional representation in Parliament and other political and social institutions based on share of population.[166] Finally, Albanians argue that their own characteristics as an ethnic group qualify them for the status of co-owner of the land.[167]

There are some clear benefits to "nation" status. The preamble of the 1989 republic-level constitution was used to justify the government's refusal to make improvements in minority-language education.[168] Macedonian politicians have relied on the current preamble's formulation to defeat Albanian arguments on draft laws concerning citizenship, a new citizen identity card, and the composition of new Macedonian banknotes. Further, the preamble is available to reinforce other constitutional provisions, such as the qualifications to the right to secondary-school education.

Perhaps more important than these implications of the preamble are its subjective powers. Albanian dissatisfaction with their status in the new state hinders their ability to believe in the impartiality of state institutions.[169] Lacking faith during the fragile transition period, armed with a host of grievances described above, and presuming that they cannot obtain political and civil service representation without a constitutional guarantee, it is difficult for them to hold any "stake" in the state. Lacking a powerful shared notion of citizenship in Macedonia, Albanians are much more likely to seek political and territorial autonomy or even secession.

Hungarians, the other major ethnic minority in Eastern Europe, articulate similar demands in Slovakia and Romania. For instance, the Romanian constitution declares Romania "a unitary . . . national state." In response, the HDFR argues for "state-creating" status, which would recognize that they are "equal partners" in a "common homeland" with Romanians.[170] A high-ranking Hungarian official advocates for minorities in both countries the status of "partner nation" when Hungarians are of a significant number in a certain area. This status would grant them rights above and beyond those of other minorities.[171] Such arguments have been cited by moderate and extremist Romanians as dangerous statements that could lead to violence.

The legal status of present constitutions and these proposals, and their possible utility in managing ethnic conflicts, are less clear than the deep and abiding insecurities that motivate them, and the majority fears that they themselves engender. Macedonians argue that Albanians cannot have such a status because they would "aspire to have their own state and [the right to] secede."[172] In the minds of most Macedonians, alterations of the present preamble are no different from calls for autonomy in their potential danger to the stability of the country. Here, Macedonian perspectives hold the key to understanding the boundaries of viable political arrangements for managing ethnic conflict in Macedonia.

6. MACEDONIAN PERSPECTIVES

In Eastern Europe, majorities often feel beleaguered in their own states. Dual economic and political transitions, combined with international problems, take their toll on these groups' faith in their future as "owners" of viable states. And anxieties about their nations' future standing amidst a slew of ethnic minorities contribute to a siege mentality that further worsens prospects for inter-ethnic relations.

Macedonians face prospects as difficult as anywhere in the region (save Bosnia). They are citizens of a young nation in an insecure international environment that doubts their claims to nationhood. They perceive threats from Kosovo and Serbia, are alarmed by the treatment of fellow Macedonians in Bulgaria and Greece, and lament their inability to defend themselves. They can also perceive real prospects of economic collapse and the subsequent introduction of an international protectorate (in which the first UN Protection Force [UNPROFOR] deployments are feared to be only a scouting force).

Meanwhile, the Albanian problem only intensifies these other anxieties, since threats from within make threats from without more likely. Here, an important source of anxiety is the Albanian birthrate, which is the highest in Europe and considerably higher than that of Macedonians.[173] Macedonians consider this a "survival issue."[174] This fear of being supplanted in their own land is further heightened by the presence of more than 50,000 Bosnian Muslim refugees who passed through or have continued to dwell in Macedonia since early 1992.[175] The specter of a Muslim conspiracy overwhelming its Slav opponents by sheer numbers is found in Serbian media and resonates with many Macedonians.[176]

Recent legislation demonstrates the impact of this fear. First, a new law stipulates that each family with more than two children must itself cover the medical and social insurance costs of every child after the second. Macedonians speak publicly about the necessity of the law to prevent great strains on the budget; privately, they speak of the need to curb the Albanian birthrate. Meanwhile, Albanians see the law as discriminatory and openly combative.[177] Second, in the new citizenship law, foreign nationals face a residency requirement of 15 years, a length of time seen by Albanians and other groups as meant to discourage non-Slavs (e.g., Kosovar Albanians) likely to emigrate from former Yugoslavia from doing so.[178]

Next, the lack of social interaction between Albanians and Macedonians feeds anxieties about Albanians. Macedonians feel threatened by Albanians, seen by many as a strange people who have their own customs, law, and traditions.[179] Macedonian lack of understanding of Albanian language, culture, and history quickly transforms itself into fear. Here, social stratification exacerbates ethnic conflict, because it plays into the hands of extremists on both sides.[180]

The political behavior of Albanians is another source of dissatisfaction among Macedonians. They perceive a radical Albanian leadership that articulates a litany of complaints and excessive demands that cannot be met. This feeds into real doubts about the present and future loyalty of Albanians as Macedonian citizens. The frequency with which Albanian MPs walk out of Parliament before votes are held; their urging of foreign governments not to recognize Macedonia; and their talk of autonomy only exacerbate real fears that western Macedonia will eventually pass on to Albania. Were this to occur, Macedonia would find itself so small and vulnerable that its existence would be well-nigh impossible. Thus, civil war would be the only remaining alternative.

All in all, Macedonian public opinion and political behavior is relatively moderate considering its context. There is relatively little violence in the country, and when it occurs, it remains localized; there is a dearth of chauvinist media, either public or private; and support for nationalist politicians in Macedonia remains low. As demonstrated above, ethnic relations could worsen quite quickly, but it is remarkable in this context how moderate Macedonian public opinion has been.

7. POLICY RECOMMENDATIONS

It is worth noting that in attempting to mitigate ethnic conflict, ethnic conflict itself needs to be the subject of treatment. Ethnic conflict is heavily influenced by, but not reducible to, international developments, economic performance, constitutional reform, and modernization, among other factors.[181] Ethnic conflict in the region has many roots, not one; one method of conflict reduction employed alone will not greatly improve the situation.

A. THE INTERNATIONAL CONTEXT

The international context greatly increases Macedonia's internal instabilities. A number of steps must be taken to reduce pressures on Macedonia. First, the United States and the EC must immediately recognize Macedonia. The situation of US troop deployments to supplement UNPROFOR in Macedonia without the US having recognized Macedonia is ridiculous and must be corrected. Second, the number of UN peacekeepers should be bolstered tenfold and deployed on the Macedonian borders with Kosovo and Albania. The Macedonian-Albanian border must be regulated to halt the illegal passage of weapons and people. On the border with Serbia at Kosovo, UN peacekeepers must seal the border between Kosovo and Macedonia, even if this means that Kosovars cannot travel into Macedonia.

At this point, the tradeoff between Kosovo and Macedonia becomes clear. Short of a UN-sponsored invasion, the situation in

Kosovo will not improve without a significant and lasting regime change in Belgrade. Although this situation is terrible, the stability of Macedonia must be prioritized over the improvement of the plight of the Kosovars. Given its surroundings, and the long-time interests of its neighbors, Macedonia's collapse would usher in a new Balkan conflagration. Macedonia can remain stable even if Kosovo does not, but only through the introduction of much larger ground forces under UN command.

Third, economic assistance must be introduced into Macedonia. The IMF should negotiate a standby loan with Macedonia to help institute viable macro-stabilization policies, Macedonia's highest economic priority.

Fourth, Macedonia should begin to establish better bilateral relations with Albania. New UN deployments will problematize relations with Albania, but both sides would be well served by new border agreements, economic trade agreements, and cooperation on the Albanian Question. President Berisha remains influential with Macedonia's Albanian elites, and he should be given economic and political incentives to dampen expectations of a Greater Albania and provide stability to the region.

Fifth, relations with Greece must finally be normalized, with or without international mediation. Macedonians will never feel secure bordered by a hostile Greece. Additionally, Macedonia and Greece would both benefit greatly from resumed economic activity across the border. Trans-frontier cooperation, especially concerning the travel of Greece's ethnic Macedonians, should be encouraged by all influential parties, most especially the EC Twelve.

Sixth, the West should encourage regional economic cooperation in Southeastern Europe. Such cooperation will have numerous political benefits so long as these states can be convinced that this cooperation will not delay their entrance into West European economic zones. Of particular importance and potential benefit is the reestablishment of the Via Ignatia, an ancient trade route running from the port of Durres in Albania to Skopje, Ohrid, and Sofia, and on to Istanbul. The EBRD is already funding the reconstruction of highways in parts of the route and should consider deepening or leveraging this investment to help locate other investors. In sum, the improvement of Macedonia's international context can lower risks of further problems and reduce Slav Macedonian insecurities—thereby weakening the political influence of nationalist forces and dampening Albanian Macedonian aspirations for a Greater Albania, all of which should increase the opportunities for inter-ethnic cooperation.

B. Macedonia's Domestic Scene

Ethnic conflict in Macedonia can be mitigated and controlled by focusing on two broad goals: encouraging multiethnic cooperation across party lines and providing Albanians with political and economic incentives to have a "stake" in the state. These goals are understood in light of the imperative that Macedonia's borders not be changed.

Encouraging multiethnic cooperation will not be accomplished through the advocacy of multiethnic parties. Such parties are not likely to survive a single election cycle; the realities of ethnic politics do not permit them at this stage. Instead, efforts should be focused on increasing the political incentives for each side to take part in multiethnic governing coalitions. To remain stable, and to cement the process of providing electoral incentives to ethnic parties, such a coalition must eventually cooperate on running a single slate of candidates. For example, the PDP/NDP and the SDUM can assist one another by delivering votes for each other's candidates in multiethnic communities. Incentives for multiethnic coalitions should be targeted at the most realistic level—party elites' incentives to remain in power. Here, the Council of Europe will be of assistance in redrawing its electoral districts. But the Albanian parties need to understand the costs to the coalition, and the adverse effects on Macedonian public opinion, of bolting from the coalition when they are not satisfied with individual parliamentary votes. In the long run, this behavior will cost more than it gains.

Along these lines, Macedonia should be persuaded to activate its largely dormant council on inter-ethnic relations, which is provided for in the constitution. Romania's recent experiences with its new minorities council are not without signs of hope. Regardless of its official products, such a council may serve as an additional backchannel of mediation between Albanians and Macedonians. This is especially important considering the present overreliance of both sides on 76-year-old President Gligorov.

Also crucial is the reform of state-local lines of authority. The situations in Tetovo and other multiethnic communities are recipes for disaster. Macedonia should consider, with the help of the Council of Europe, methods of minority representation (whether Macedonian or Albanian) in municipal assemblies and other local offices. The Council of Europe should also review the draft law on local governance and recommend guidelines for Albanians to follow in guaranteeing rights of Macedonians in predominantly Albanian communities. And NGOs such as the Helsinki Citizens' Assembly are, if properly funded, presently equipped to make real progress in establishing effective local-level inter-ethnic dialogues.

By the same token, the international community should, with President Berisha's help, recommend against political and territorial autonomy for western Macedonia. Like most minority enclaves, western Macedonia is actually ethnically heterogeneous; Slav Macedonians and Turks live in these communities as well as Albanians. Drives for autonomy will only lead to violence; the plight of Croatian Serbs should serve as a warning.

Here, Albanian Macedonians require incentives to take a "stake" in the state. Put another way, the costs of autonomy, in the form of benefits to be lost were the autonomy path taken, should be placed too high. Directly addressing Albanian grievances is the best method. First, Macedonia must quickly expand its secondary-school offerings in Albanian. It should also begin the establishment of college-level faculties in the Albanian language. If Romanians can eventually tolerate an assimilated Hungarian minority in Transylvania with its own higher education, Macedonians can do the same. Funding should be available from a gradually more realistic Albanian emigre community.

Second, the Council of Europe and nongovernmental organizations such as the International Media Fund have significant roles to play in helping establish private media outlets. The Fund has already played a very important role in the diversification of media in Albania in this regard.

Third, employment issues need to be tackled through strong employment discrimination regulations, and, perhaps more importantly, through targeted regional economic investment. This investment will be all the more necessary as privatization begins. The EBRD, agricultural development foundations, and others can make investments to lessen these shocks to Macedonia's economy. Preferential policies, either economic or educational, should be employed sparingly and should not be relied on—the benefits are unclear at this point, but the costs, in terms of both raised expectations and Macedonian resentments, are clear and high. Inflexible programs of proportional representation in civil service positions with fixed targets and deadlines are also not wise. Albanians clamor for representation on the basis of their share of the population, but level of education—not population—is the proper criterion. Ministries should not be staffed by secondary-school graduates. Recognizing the importance of Albanian representation in government offices, this point underscores again the need for massive improvements in the education field.

Fourth, the question of constitutional status will have to be dealt with at some point. At present, there is not the political space available to alter the constitution. The ruling coalition could not survive such a move, and VMRO would stand only to benefit. Moreover, moderate Macedonians are probably not willing to alter the constitution. At this point, the question of alternatives and compromises is tied to Macedonian public opinion. Given the government's handling of other grievances, it can buy time on this issue. It is possible that the Albanian demand for constituent people status will be defused as its political community diversifies, as some grievances are addressed, and after the census in April 1994 helps solve the numbers game. But if after two or more years this issue remains controversial, international pressure will have to be brought to bear on Macedonians to reach a compromise with the Albanians.

8. CONCLUSION

Thus far, despite all its problems, Macedonia is a Balkan success story. The only ex-Yugoslav republic to avoid a war, and the most politically astute by governing itself through a multiethnic coalition, Macedonia has so far defied all predictions of its immediate destruction (due to ethnic conflict, spillover from wars to the north, economic collapse, etc.), and it has done so in the face of an international community that has only exacerbated its problems. Given a renewed international commitment to Macedonia's future, this new state can survive, continue to surprise its detractors, and keep alive the possibility of multiethnic civil states in the Balkans.

NOTES

The authors wish to express their gratitude to the following people for their kind assistance, without which this paper could not have been written: Slobodanka Markovska, Emilija Simoska, Trajko Slaveski, and Duncan M. Perry.

1. Other minorities, namely Serbs, Turks, Vlachs, and Roma, comprise about 15% of the country's population of 2.1 million.

2. For the sake of comparison, we will be mentioning Albania, Bulgaria, Croatia, Greece, Romania, and Serbia.

3. For the sake of brevity, the authors will refer to the "Republic of Macedonia" rather than the clumsier "Former Yugoslav Republic of Macedonia," the temporary designation with which the Republic of Macedonia was admitted to the United Nations General Assembly on April 9, 1993.

4. This discussion relies on Duncan M. Perry, *The Politics of Terror: The Macedonian Liberation Movements 1893–1903* (Durham: Duke University Press, 1988), chap. 1.

5. Duncan M. Perry, "The Current Situation of Macedonians in Bulgaria and Greece," paper presented at the IEWS Conference at Štiřín, Czechoslovakia, "European Institutions and the Protection of National Minorities in East Central Europe and the Balkans," Oct. 10–13, 1991, p. 3.

6. From this point on, unless otherwise noted, "Macedonia" will be used to denote the Republic of Macedonia, not the geographical region discussed above.

7. Great debates continue over whether Macedonian is a unique language or merely a dialect of Bulgarian. In ethnic conflicts, such apparently harmless and academic controversies take on great importance, since language is considered a major determinant in judging whether a "people" actually constitutes a "people" deserving of its own state.

8. Stephen E. Palmer and Robert R. King, *Yugoslav Communism and the Macedonian Question* (Hamden, CT: Archon Books, 1971), chap. 10.

9. Perry, "Current Situation of Macedonians in Bulgaria and Greece," p. 26. Unless otherwise noted, "Macedonians" will henceforth be used to denote ethnically Slav citizens of the Republic of Macedonia.

10. Peter Prifti, *Socialist Albania Since 1944* (Cambridge: MIT Press, 1978), p. 224.

11. Perry, *The Politics of Terror*, p. 18.

12. Palmer and King, *Yugoslav Communism*, p. 175.

13. This division is considered by most analysts as inherently unstable. See for instance Patrick Moore, "The Albanian Question in the Former Yugoslavia," *RFE/RL Research Report* 1, no. 14 (April 3, 1992), pp. 7–15.

14. T. Zavalani, "Albanian Nationalism," in *Nationalism in Eastern Europe*, ed. Peter F. Sugar and Ivo J. Lederer (Seattle: University of Washington Press, 1969).

15. Albanian cultural traditions concerning the role of women exacerbate these differences. It was and remains unlikely for women to be encouraged to receive any significant amount of schooling given their subservient function within the Albanian family. In general, social and economic advancement opportunities for Albanian women have been scarce. Interview with Teuta Arifi, member of the executive committee of the League of Albanian Women, Tetovo, Macedonia, March 27, 1993. The status of Albanian women is in striking contrast to that of Slav Macedonian women, who have begun to play important roles in Macedonian politics.

16. Interview with Vladimir Milčin, Director, Open Society Fund— Macedonia, Skopje, March 26, 1993. A fairly reliable indicator of social interaction between ethnic groups is the tolerance of parents to inter-ethnic marriages for their children. A 1974 report shows that "95% of the Albanian and Macedonian and 84% of the Turkish heads of individual households would not let their sons marry a girl of different nationality while for daughters the figures were even higher." Quoted in *Minorities in the Balkans* (London: Minority Rights Group, 1989), p. 28.

17. Donald Horowitz, *Ethnic Groups in Conflict* (Berkeley: University of California Press, 1985), p. 197.

18. Palmer and King, *Yugoslav Communism*, pp. 179–80.

19. Ibid.

20. *Minorities in the Balkans*, pp. 27–28; Palmer and King, *Yugoslav Communism*, pp. 177–78.

21. Palmer and King, *Yugoslav Communism*, p. 179. Interviews conducted in Tetovo and Skopje, March, 1993.

22. *Minorities in the Balkans*, pp. 25–27.

23. Ibid; interviews in Tetovo, March, 1993.

24. Emphasis added. Milan Andrejovich, "Resurgent Nationalism in Macedonia: A Challenge to Pluralism," *RFE Report on Eastern Europe*, May 17, 1991, p. 27. The significant political and social consequences of an ethnic group's status will be explored at length below.

25. Many of these characteristics are shared by Albania, Bulgaria, Romania, and the other former Yugoslav republics. However, Macedonia's regional context is perhaps more severe than any other Balkan state save Bosnia.

26. Muhammed Halili, head of the Albanian Macedonian parties' parliamentary group, notes that Albanians joined Slav Macedonians in the fight for independence against the Turks in 1903 (in Foreign Broadcast Information Service, *Daily Report: Eastern Europe* [hereinafter referred to as FBIS], Dec. 10, 1992). The veracity of this claim is less important than its demonstration that Albanians and Macedonians (for Stojan Andov, the Macedonian parliamentary speaker, makes the same point) can draw on history to encourage, as well as limit, inter-ethnic cooperation and dialogue. In the same way, Macedonian-Albanian relations have been spared the vicious historical disputes that dominate other ethnic relations in the region.

27. Horowitz, *Ethnic Groups in Conflict*, p. 190.

28. The UN General Assembly admitted Macedonia as a member on April 9, 1993. Prior to this date, Macedonia was recognized by, among others, Bulgaria, Russia, Turkey, Croatia, and Slovenia.

29. Macedonia twice amended its constitution in order to reassure the international community of its intentions vis-à-vis Greece. The amendments swore off any pretensions whatsoever in changing Macedonia's borders. The commission's report, released on January 14, 1992, emphasized as criteria a state's human rights record and its treatment of ethnic minorities. UN Human Rights Commission Special Rapporteur Tadeusz Mazowiecki notes in his report that recognition of Macedonia would actually help to accelerate the improvement of the human rights situation there by allowing international assistance to encourage compliance with international standards. *Situation of Human Rights in the Territory of the Former Yugoslavia*, Feb. 10, 1993, section 248.

30. The right-wing Macedonian party did not help to ease Greek fears of Macedonian revanchism by announcing at the end of its first party congress that the next meeting would be held in Thessaloniki.

31. An official in the Greek Foreign Ministry expressed the fear that a part-Muslim Macedonia would become "a pawn on the Turkish chessboard." Quoted in Jens Reuter, "Policy and Economy in Macedonia," *Balkan Forum* 1, no. 3 (June 1993), p. 169.

32. The treatment of ethnic Macedonians at the hands of Greece is, by all accounts, deplorable. This evaluation is borne out by evidence collected by DIGNITY, the Association for Protecting the Human Rights of Macedonians Discriminated By the Republic of Greece (interview with Kole Mangov, president of DIGNITY, Skopje, March 24, 1993).

33. "Mr. Mitsotakis faces such stiff opposition from his New Democracy party over the government's economic policy that his one-seat parliamentary majority could be overturned if he agreed to 'Nova Makedonija,' the name proposed by Mr. Cyrus Vance, the former UN mediator." "Macedonia Wins Time to Resolve Row Over Name," *Financial Times*, June 21, 1993.

34. Sabrina P. Ramet, *Nationalism and Federalism in Yugoslavia: 1962–1991*, 2nd ed. (Bloomington: Indiana University Press, 1992), p. 143.

35. This estimate comes from Macedonian President Kiro Gligorov, and appears also in Belgrade's *Politika*. See FBIS, Dec. 10, 1992, p. 53. Also in Vasil Mitskovski, "An International Stranglehold," *War Report* (October 1992), p. 6.

36. *RFE/RL Daily Report*, April 25, 1993, pp. 3–4 (Romania); and June 16, 1993, p. 4 (Bulgaria).

37. The blockade began immediately after the Macedonian declaration of independence and was lifted entirely by December 1992; it reportedly caused Macedonia to lose $1.6 billion in income. Mitskovski, "An International Stranglehold." Also see Mihail Petkovski, Goce Petreski, and Trajko Slaveski, "Stabilization Efforts in the Republic of Macedonia," *RFE/RL Research Report* 2, no. 3 (Jan. 15, 1993), p. 34.

38. *Macedonia: Basic Economic Data* (Skopje: Republic of Macedonia Statistical Office, 1993), p. 30.

39. Mitskovski, "An International Stranglehold," p. 6.

40. This shrinking pie impacts adversely in a number of ways. For example, Bulgarian-Turkish relations have suffered appreciably in those areas where Slav Bulgarians fear economic dislocations due to their status as minorities within Turkish communities in southeastern and northeastern Bulgaria. Ivan Ilchev and Duncan M. Perry, "Bulgarian Ethnic Groups: Politics and Perceptions," *RFE/RL Research Report* 2, no. 12 (March 19, 1993), p. 39.

41. Janusz Bugajski, "The Contours of Ethnic Politics in Eastern Europe," *Balkan Forum* 1, no. 3 (June 1993), p. 29.

42. See Ivanka Nedeva's contribution to this volume for examples from Romania and Bulgaria.

43. VMRO-DMPNE stands for Internal Macedonian Revolutionary Organization—Democratic Party for National Unity.

44. It is often accompanied by a less radical counterpart, the Movement for All-Macedonian Action (MAAK). MAAK is also an influential Macedonian nationalist party, but does not at present hold any parliamentary seats. Duncan M. Perry, "Macedonia and the Odds for Survival," *RFE/RL Research Report* 1, no. 46 (Nov. 20, 1992), p. 18.

45. Bugajski, "Contours of Ethnic Politics in Eastern Europe," p. 23. VMRO shares these traits with, among others, Romania's Greater Romania Party and Bulgaria's Committee for the Defense of National Interests. See, for example, Michael Shafir, "The Greater Romania Party," *RFE/RL Research Report* (Nov. 15, 1991), pp. 25–30.

46. Duncan M. Perry, "Politics in the Republic of Macedonia: Issues and Parties," *RFE/RL Research Report* 2, no. 23 (June 4, 1993), p. 35. In March 1993, only about 6% of the potential voters indicated their intention to vote for VMRO in the next elections.

47. Of course, their political mobilization encourages the chauvinist forces mentioned above. As VMRO's leader, Ljubo Georgievski, noted, "The first interethnic conflicts came from the Albanian side when they formed their parties." Interview published in Zagreb's *Vjesnik* daily, and reprinted in FBIS, Aug. 27, 1991.

48. Other minority groups in Macedonia have also mobilized themselves politically. The Serbs, Turks, Vlachs, and Roma have all formed political parties and NGOs to advocate their interests.

49. This motivation has similarly propelled both the Union of Demo-

cratic Forces and the Bulgarian Socialist Party to participate in coalitions with the Turkish party in Bulgaria, the Movement for Rights and Freedoms.

50. Muhammed Halili, PDP/NDP parliamentary group leader, quoted in Veronique Soule, "Macedonia: The High Price of Recognition," *Liberation* (Paris), reprinted in FBIS, Dec. 18, 1992, pp. 42–43.

51. The Albanian and Bulgarian constitutions prohibit the formation of political parties along ethnic lines (including the United Macedonian Organization, which advocates the interests of ethnic Macedonians in Bulgaria). The Romanian constitution forbids political parties from advocating secessionism. Indeed, speech of "territorial separatism" is criminalized. See Jon Elster and Stephen Holmes, "New Constitutions Adopted in Bulgaria and Romania," *East European Constitutional Review* (Spring 1992), pp. 11–12.

52. Nor does it recognize the existence of Macedonian ethnic minorities within Bulgaria, an omission that raises fears among some Macedonians that Bulgaria still maintains a pretext to move its border westward. If, it is thought, a Macedonian nation were recognized by Bulgaria, then Bulgaria would be compelled to respect Macedonia's sovereignty as a nation-state among equals.

53. These suspicions were illuminated in a recent scandal in which Bulgarian Prime Minister Filip Dimitrov dispatched an adviser to Skopje to discuss the possibility of large arms sales to Macedonia. This decision helped fell the Bulgarian government in October 1992, and was a source of great controversy between various pro- and anti-Bulgarian political forces in Macedonia.

54. Reuter, "Policy and Economy in Macedonia," p. 153.

55. Quoted in Yugoslav News Agency (TANJUG), and printed in FBIS, March 22, 1993, pp. 72–73.

56. This charge has been levelled at the Serbs most intensively in regard to the Bit Pazaar incident, in which a confrontation in Skopje between police officers and Albanian black marketeers in November 1992 led to a gunfight resulting in four deaths and 30 injuries. It is claimed that agents of the Serb counterintelligence service (KOS) infiltrated the ranks of the Albanians and fomented the gun battle in an attempt to spur greater violence and ethnic instability in Macedonia. For example, see "Frckovski Accuses FRY of Fomenting Trouble," reprinted in FBIS, Nov. 16, 1992, p. 44.

57. Saso Ordanoski, "What's In a Name?" *East European Reporter* July/August 1992, p. 33.

58. Interview with Caterine Loupas, Political Counselor, Embassy of Greece, Prague, the Czech Republic, March 12, 1993.

59. Paul Beaver, "Neighboring States Up in Arms," *War Report*, January 1993, p. 23.

60. Hugh Poulton, "The Republic of Macedonia After UN Recognition," *RFE/RL Research Report* 2, no. 23 (June 4, 1993), pp. 27–28.

61. These concerns fuel (and are fueled by) more common fears of the gradual "Islamization" of Macedonia. These fears will be discussed below in section 6.

62. See below for a discussion of Macedonian perspectives on ethnic relations with Albanians.

63. Moore, "The Albanian Question," p. 8.

64. See Louis Zanga, "Albania Afraid of War Over Kosovo," *RFE/RL Research Report* 1, no. 46 (Nov. 20, 1992), pp. 20–23. Beleaguered Albania

recognizes more clearly that the prospects of an all-out Balkan war sparked by a drive toward unification would likely result in the country's own collapse.

65. Rugova is coordinator of all Albanian political parties outside of Albania proper (this includes parties in Serbia, Montenegro, Kosovo, and Macedonia). FBIS, April 9, 1993.

66. Quoted in the Macedonian Information and Liaison Service daily bulletin, May 17, 1993.

67. *Report of the CSCE Spillover Monitor Mission to Skopje*, Sept. 10–14, 1993, p. 8 (hereafter CSCE Spillover Mission Report).

68. "For Our Own Good: Interview with Ljubomir Danailov-Frckovski, Minister of Interior," *East European Reporter* (September/October 1992), p. 50.

69. AP wire reports, April 5, 1992; June 18, 1992; and Feb. 28, 1993.

70. This declaration was made by Minister Frckovski and quoted on the AP wire, Dec. 24, 1992.

71. Estimate found in Andrejovich, "Resurgent Nationalism in Macedonia," p. 26.

72. PDP leader Nevzat Halili declared that the PDP recognizes an independent Kosovo (see note 77), and has remarked that "a Kosovo war is an all-Albanian war." Quoted in an interview reprinted in FBIS, April 9, 1993.

73. FBIS, Jan. 3, 1992, p. 45.

74. This view is corroborated by statements by PDP party chief Nevzat Halili, as pointed out in Reuter, "Policy and Economy in Macedonia," p. 162.

75. The ballot asked whether "you are in favor of political and territorial autonomy of the Albanians in Macedonia." FBIS, Jan. 13, 1992, p. 57.

76. Ibid.; Xhafer Krasniqi and Sinan Kamberaj, "400,000 Albanians in Macedonia Vote on Autonomy Plan," *Illyria*, Jan. 13, 1992.

77. FBIS, Jan. 14, 1992, p. 57.

78. FBIS, Jan. 13, 1992, pp. 57–58.

79. There were reports that Albanians in villages around Tetovo and Gostivar (both primarily Albanian cities) were taking up arms. Such claims, however, should be treated skeptically. FBIS, Jan. 13, 1992, p. 57.

80. Reuter, "Policy and Economy in Macedonia," p. 162.

81. At the PDP Party Congress in February, 1992, Nevzat Halili stated that the PDP recognizes an independent Kosovo, and the PDP will recognize *Macedonia* if Macedonia first recognizes Kosovo (quoted in Skopje's *Flaka e Vëllazërimit*, reprinted in FBIS, Feb. 21, 1992, p. 22). The logic of this strategy is pointed out by Reuter, "Policy and Economy in Macedonia," p. 163.

82. Albanian politicians in Tetovo were unable to define specifically what they meant by "autonomy" (interviews, April 1993). Nor could the radical American-Albanian emigre community report what it was the Albanians were (or are still) specifically demanding (personal communication with journalists at *Illyria*, an English-language newspaper of Albanian affairs published in New York, May 5, 1993).

83. Michael Shafir and Dan Ionescu, "Romania—The Minorities in 1991: Mutual Distrust, Social Problems, and Disillusion," *RFE/RL Research Report* 1, no. 50 (Dec. 30, 1991), pp. 24–28.

84. This section draws on the pioneering work of Horowitz, *Ethnic Groups in Conflict.*

85. Bugajski, "Contours of Ethnic Politics in the Balkans," p. 19.

86. Macedonian Interior Minister Frckovski admitted that when Alba-

nians are outvoted along ethnic lines in the Parliament on most issues, "this is not democracy." CSCE Spillover Mission Report, p. 18.

87. Janusz Bugajski, writing about Eastern Europe after 1989, remarks that "in the midst of a destabilizing and uncertain period of capitalist restoration and widening pluralism, ethnic politics began to occupy an important role not only for minority groupings seeking greater self-determination, but also for some majority populations fearful of losing influence, power, or their access to important resources." "The Contours of Ethnic Politics in Eastern Europe," p. 30.

88. "In Western democracies, parties and political organizations are structured on the basis of interests. In [Eastern Europe, parties] are structured on the lines of fears, desires, and passions. Under the communist system [we] had to resolve our problems not by striking a deal and finding a . . . compromise, but by 'eliminating' the adversary. . . . This mentality survived and . . . must be changed." Gyorgy Tokay, the parliamentary leader of HDFR in the Romanian Parliament, quoted in Michael Shafir and Alfred A. Reisch, ed., "Roundtable: Transylvania's Past and Future," *RFE/RL Research Report* 2, no. 24 (June 11, 1993), p. 33.

89. For example, Romania: "The successive postcommunist governments in Bucharest have all . . . been prone to amateurism, ill-will, and a propensity to seek short-term political advantage by exploiting the mutual suspicion, mutual ignorance, and mutual oversensitivity that have traditionally marred interethnic relations in Romania." Michael Shafir, "Minorities Council Raises Questions," *RFE/RL Research Report* 2, no. 24 (June 11, 1993), p. 35.

90. See Ivanka Nedeva's chapter in this volume.

91. Horowitz, *Ethnic Groups in Conflict*, p. 223.

92. Ibid., p. 216.

93. In Macedonia, as in Romania, economic policy has fallen victim to a lack of informed, sustained debate largely because, unlike ethnic issues, it is not considered a "safe" source of votes. See Aleksandr Soljakowski, "Many Political Parties But Few Results," printed in Skopje's *Nova Makedonija*, Dec. 26, 1992, reprinted in FBIS, Feb. 4, 1993, pp. 57–60.

94. Ivanka Nedeva notes that the Movement for Rights and Freedoms (MRF), a Turkish party in Bulgaria, has become increasingly authoritarian in its organization as its constituency has grown increasingly dissatisfied with its performance.

95. Ethnic outbidding appears to be common in the politics of Northern Ireland. David Welsh, "Domestic Politics and Ethnic Conflict," *Survival* 35, no. 1 (Spring 1993), p. 68.

96. This has been true for Hungarians in Romania, Turks in Bulgaria, and Albanians in Macedonia.

97. However, even avowedly non-nationalist parties are forced by the electoral constraints of ethnic politics to play on nationalist prejudices and fears, and to identify their ethnic "angle" on what are not normally considered ethnic issues. Soljakowski, "Many Political Parties," pp. 57–58.

98. The following discussion is based predominantly on a series of interviews with journalists, politicians, and businesspeople in Skopje and Tetovo, March and April, 1993.

99. Like most ethnic parties, the PDP and NDP declare themselves to be multiethnic. Macedonian Information and Liaison Service, "Profile of the

Major Political Parties in Macedonia," 1993; Interview with NDP President Ilijaz Halimi, March 27, 1993.

100. Saso Ordanoski, "A Fragile Peace?" *Eastern European Reporter* November/December 1992, pp. 10–12. Ordanoski discusses the attempt by radical Albanians in Chicago to assassinate PDP leader Nevzat Halili, whom they considered too weak in his demands for the eventual creation of a Greater Albania.

101. This skill was apparent in the organization of the boycott of the national census in 1991, and in the referendum on territorial and political autonomy, held in January 1992.

102. The Parliament has held 52 sessions, and concluded only four of them. The most recent sessions were halted after debates broke down over the shape of the state's coat of arms, and the makeup of the proposed citizen identity card. Cited in Macedonian Information and Liaison Service, daily bulletin, May 26, 1993.

103. Interview with Saso Ordanoski, Skopje, April 21, 1993. An example of this backchannel may be the prevention of the spread of violence after the Bit Pazaar incident. Indeed, after incidents of inter-ethnic violence in Macedonia (including border incidents in which Albanians were shot attempting to enter Macedonia), the violence remained localized and did not spread.

104. The Turkish Movement for Rights and Freedoms in Bulgaria has maintained through its leadership a highly important relationship with President Zhelev. Ethnic Greeks in Albania had close contacts with advisors of former President Ramiz Alia, a fact that inspired the Parliament's ban on the political party activities of the Greek minority's cultural association, OMONIA.

105. Horowitz, *Ethnic Groups in Conflict*, p. 194.

106. Andre Liebich, "Minorities in Eastern Europe: Obstacles to a Reliable Count," *RFE/RL Research Report* 1, no. 20 (May 15, 1992), pp. 34–40.

107. Albanians claimed that the census was unfair because instructions explaining how to fill out census forms in the Albanian language were written in Macedonian. Moreover, they argued that no one on the census board was Albanian. They have agreed, however, to participate in a special census to be held in April 1994, under the watchful eyes of international observers. The census will be funded by the European Community through the auspices of the Council of Europe.

108. Krasniqi and Kamberaj's article in *Illyria* stated that the Albanian demands for autonomy were reasonable because of this majority.

109. In situations where ethnic identity is blurred, where ethnicity is dynamic, not static, the numbers game adversely affects ethnic relations in another way. In both Bulgaria and Macedonia, Turks and Albanians have been accused of attempting to coerce Muslim Slavs and Roma into identifying themselves in censuses as Turkish or Albanian, respectively, by drawing on their common religious affiliation (Islam). These charges, which seem to hold some truth, provide rhetorical ammunition for majority nationalist parties, increase majority fears of losing their superior status as owners of the land, and heighten ethnic tensions. *RFE/RL Daily Report*, April 29, 1993, p. 6 (Bulgaria); Andrejovich, "Resurgent Nationalism in Macedonia," p. 27.

110. The Hungarian Democratic Federation of Romania (HDFR) "affirmed that the reestablishment of Hungarian-language instruction at all educational levels was the cornerstone of maintaining the Hungarians' ethnic identity." Edith Oltay, "The Hungarian Democratic Federation of Romania:

Structure, Agenda, Alliances," *RFE Report on Eastern Europe*, July 19, 1991, p. 33.

111. Palmer and King, *Yugoslav Communism*, p. 178; *Minorities in the Balkans*, p. 25.

112. In 1981, there were 8,200 Albanian pupils in secondary schools; at the end of 1988, there were only 4,221. *Minorities in the Balkans*, p. 27.

113. *Constitution of the Republic of Macedonia* (Skopje: NIP Magazin 21, 1991), pp. 16–17 (emphasis added). Moreover, citizens have the right to "establish private schools at all levels of education, with the exception of primary education, under conditions determined by law." Note that "in schools where education is carried out in the language of a nationality, the Macedonian language is also studied."

114. Interview with Vladimir Mostrov, Deputy Education Minister, March 25, 1993.

115. In Tetovo (the largest Albanian community in Macedonia and over 70% Albanian), only 18% of primary school graduates have been eligible to attend secondary school. Interview with Minister Servet Avziu, March 28, 1993.

116. Ibid. Teaching materials in Albanian are available, but only from Tirana. There is a clear need for the development of Macedonia-oriented Albanian-language materials, especially to encourage an attachment as citizens to the state of Macedonia.

117. Mostrov interview.

118. At present, the laws concerning the establishment of private schools are rather vague, and many of the private schools now established by Albanian communities are operating illegally. Here, Macedonians opposed to educational reforms that benefit Albanians have exploited a common historical stereotype of Albanians as "lawless."

119. Aleksandr Soljakovski, "An Education in Complexity," *War Report*, October 1992, p. 5.

120. The problem of educational policies for non-Slav Macedonians is certainly not limited to the Albanians. All ethnic-based parties and associations complain of lack of space in secondary schools and of extremely limited opportunities for pursuing studies at universities. Indeed, the secretary-general of the Turkish Democratic Party of Macedonia, Erdoğan Saraç, calls education "the most painful question for the Turkish people in Macedonia." In eastern Macedonia, for instance, some schools provide Turkish schooling only for grades 1–4, in violation of the constitution. Only 5% of these students continue with grade five, and most of the remainder drop out. Similar to the Albanians, Saraç argues that an increase in the number of Turkish schools would mean firing Macedonian teachers, and this is a decision that Macedonian bureaucrats are loathe to make. Interview with Turkish Democratic Party secretary-general Erdoğan Saraç, March 27, 1993.

121. Mazowiecki report, p. 50, no. 235.

122. Ibid.

123. Vladimir Mostrov, deputy Education Minister, articulated this position.

124. As the secretary-general of the Turkish Democratic Party argues, "non-educated masses are potential enemies of the state because they can hold it back." Saraç interview.

125. *Minorities in the Balkans*, p. 36.

126. Shafir, "Minorities Council Raises Questions," p. 38.

127. For example, Milan Andrejovich, "Rump Yugoslavia" in "The Media in Eastern Europe," *RFE/RL Research Report* 2, no. 19 (May 7, 1993), p. 34.

128. Serbs, Turks, and Vlachs all demand greater broadcasting time in state media outlets.

129. Avziu and Halimi interviews.

130. There are four hours per day in the Turkish language, and one-half hour per day in each of the Vlach and Romany languages.

131. Nevertheless, Albanian programming time could be doubled or tripled and a regional network across western Macedonia consolidated if Macedonian Radio could afford to purchase three relatively inexpensive FM transmitters. Interview with Slobodan Čašule, Director, Radio Skopje, March 23, 1993.

132. Interview with Daut Dauti, March 25, 1993.

133. Duncan M. Perry, "Republic of Macedonia," in RFE/RL Media Survey, *RFE/RL Research Report* 1, no. 39 (Oct. 2, 1992), p. 46.

134. Duncan M. Perry, "Macedonia," in "The Media in Eastern Europe," p. 29.

135. Perry, "Republic of Macedonia," p. 45.

136. Ibid., p. 46.

137. Dr. Stefan Troebst, a Balkanist serving at the CSCE Spillover Mission based in Skopje, noted that Macedonian-language media coverage of the Bit Pazaar incident was fairly homogeneous and more often than not clearly anti-Albanian.

138. There is a conspicuous lack of privately funded ethnically chauvinist newspapers and magazines. Mazowiecki's verdict on Macedonia's media compares favorably with all ex-Yugoslav republics except Slovenia (p. 52). Concerning Romania, on the other hand, where Hungarian-language television broadcasting hours have been cut and local and national media used to heighten fear of Hungarians, see Michael Shafir, "Extreme Nationalist Brinksmanship in Romania," *RFE/RL Research Report* 2, no. 21 (May 21, 1993), pp. 31–36; and Dan Ionescu, "Romania," in "The Media in Eastern Europe," p. 31.

139. As discussed in the introduction, Macedonian-Albanian relations are fortunately spared the high level of animosities fueled by past betrayals and atrocities as those that plague Croat-Serb, Hungarian-Romanian, Greek-Albanian, and Albanian-Serb relations.

140. The lack of a "media war" is confirmed in Mazowiecki, no. 245, p. 52. However, such complaints are made. Turkish Democratic Party chief Erdoğan Saraç argues that over the past three years, his party has been able to appear on television only twice. Moreover, he charges that party statements are distorted by Macedonian editors. Saraç interview, March 27, 1993.

141. Mazowiecki report, sections 241 and 244, p. 52.

142. After World War II, about 70% of the Albanian working population was in the agricultural sector. Now, after urbanization and other developments, that share has dropped to under 20%. Interview with Trajko Slaveski, Faculty of Economics, Cyril and Methodius University, Skopje, April 21, 1993.

143. To the extent that official employment rolls show Albanians to be completely without work, they are misleading. Interviews with Trajko Slaveski and Vladimir Milčin.

144. Saraç makes the same complaint regarding ethnic Turks in government service.

145. Avziu interview.

146. Discussions with Albanian businesspeople in Tetovo, March 28, 1993; Mazowiecki report, p. 50. Tetovo is about 75% Macedonian and is, after Skopje, the largest municipality in Macedonia.

147. Interview with Ilijaz Halimi, President, National Democratic Party, Tetovo, March 28, 1993.

148. Oltay, "The Hungarian Democratic Federation of Romania," p. 32.

149. Mazowiecki, *Situation of Human Rights in the Territory of the Former Yugoslavia*, section 234.

150. Interview with Sašo Ordanoski, April 21, 1993.

151. This is evidenced by the effort to keep Macedonian schoolteachers employed at the cost of the availability of minority-language secondary schools. However, the relative ethnic stratification in employment sectors has thus far mitigated the adverse effects of economic decline on ethnic tensions in Macedonia. Ethnic clashes over economic issues such as employment, like those in Germany and Transylvania, have not occurred in Macedonia. Donald Horowitz demonstrates quite clearly that ethnic groups in conflict often better manage their relations when groups are divided by employment sector (*Ethnic Groups in Conflict*, pp. 108–113). This division limits excessive and often violent economic competition.

152. In Romania, riots in Tirgu-Mures and in Cluj resulted in several deaths. Ethnic Bulgarians, minorities in some Turk-dominated municipalities, exhibit fears about dislocation and an increased hostility toward Turks in an analogous manner to those of Macedonians (see below). See Ilchev and Perry, "Bulgarian Ethnic Groups," pp. 35–41.

153. Andrejovich, "Resurgent Nationalism in Macedonia," p. 28. Gostivar faces a similar situation.

154. Ibid.

155. "Macedonian Houses for Sale," *Nova Makedonija*, reprinted in FBIS, Sept. 29, 1992, pp. 26–28.

156. Interviews with analysts at the Center for Ethnic Relations, Skopje, March and April, 1993.

157. Andrejovich, "Resurgent Nationalism in Macedonia," p. 28; interviews in Tetovo, March, 1993.

158. Interview, April 23, 1993.

159. Horowitz, *Ethnic Groups in Conflict*, p. 187.

160. See section 1.D, above.

161. Constitution (1991).

162. The phrasing was a late compromise reached after VMRO members of the drafting committee demanded that Macedonia be referred to simply as a national state of the Macedonian people.

163. These states share an assumption that a state "belongs" to and serves the dominant ethnic group, that it is one ethnic group's vehicle to power and its place in the sun. Such a principle follows from Gellner's definition of nationalism as "the political principle . . . which holds that the political and the national unit should be congruent." Ernest Gellner, *Nations and Nationalism* (Oxford: Basil Blackwell, 1983), p. 1.

164. Their dissatisfaction is shared by the Serbs, the Turks, and the Vlachs.

165. Muhammed Halili, quoted in *Borba* (Belgrade), Nov. 19, 1992, reprinted in FBIS, Dec. 10, 1992, p. 51. Ilijaz Halimi suggested that Albanians have been denied nation status deliberately so that Macedonians will have a free hand to enter into such arrangements. Interview, March 28, 1993.

166. Ilijaz Halimi interview.

167. The question whether the Turks, for example, also deserve constituent people status draws mixed responses from the Albanians, who base their own case on the following complex of perceived attributes: their substantial share of the population (40%–50+%); their geographical compactness; autochthony; and the Albanians' positive historical contribution to Macedonia. Halimi, Avziu, Aliu interviews.

168. Andrejovich, "Resurgent Nationalism in Macedonia," p. 27.

169. Currently, Albanians hold very little regard for either the judiciary or the police.

170. Oltay, "The Hungarian Democratic Federation of Romania," p. 33.

171. Ivan Baba, deputy minister for foreign affairs, quoted in Stephen Engelberg and Judith Ingram, "Now Hungary Adds Its Voice to the Ethnic Tumult," *The New York Times*, Jan. 25, 1993.

172. Interview with Vladimir Mostrov, Deputy Minister for Education.

173. See *Minorities in the Balkans*, p. 25. Census statistics show that from 1971 to 1981, the number of Albanians increased more than 36%. This report repeats the claim that the birthrate in Tetovo (the largest predominantly Albanian city in Macedonia) was more than three times the national average.

174. Simoska interview. Zlatko Blajer, editor of *Vecer* and one of 27 remaining Jews in Skopje, remarked, "And don't forget that we [Slav Macedonians] are like a quiet Kosovo. . . . We face the same fate as the Serbs in their historic homeland." In Robert D. Kaplan, *Balkan Ghosts: A Journey Through History* (New York: St. Martin's Press, 1993), p. 70. Albanians are now more than 90% of Kosovo's population.

175. The CSCE Spillover Mission Report estimates that 65,000 refugees have entered Macedonia in this period. Riots occurred in a Skopje suburb over the construction of housing for refugees—a citizens' committee leading the protest cited its "fear of the Islamicization of the suburb." FBIS, Feb. 22, 1993.

176. New data from the Center for Ethnic Relations in Skopje suggests that ethnic intolerance is being supplemented rather quickly with heightened religious intolerance. More than 70% of both Muslim and Orthodox Slav populations in Macedonia think that marriages should occur only between people of the same religion. However, only 45%–47% of both populations believe that only *ethnically* homogeneous marriages are proper. Only a year before, merely 20% of the Orthodox population disapproved of interfaith marriages. Emilija Simoska, "Macedonia Between the Myths About the 'Muslim Conspiracy' and the 'Endangered Orthodoxy,'" forthcoming paper, p. 7.

177. Actually, a law of this type has been considered since the late 1980s, when the Macedonian government fell in line with Belgrade's anti-Albanian policies. See *Minorities in the Balkans*, p. 28.

178. Moreover, persons of Macedonian descent who have never lived in Macedonia have preference for gaining citizenship over those non-Macedonians who have lived for a time in Macedonia but who carry passports from other ex-Yugoslav republics.

179. Interviews with analysts at the Center for Ethnic Relations, Skopje, March 23, 1993.

180. Less moderate Albanians use these perceptions to bolster their claims that they form, in fact, their own nation and therefore deserve commensurate territorial and political autonomy. Macedonian nationalists, on the other hand, draw on these perceptions to argue that the Albanians have no intention to integrate themselves into mainstream society and to live in Macedonia as loyal citizens.

181. For example, "international conditions cannot create a conflict where one does not exist—for contagion is not the source of ethnic conflict." Horowitz, *Ethnic Groups in Conflict*, p. 5.

3

Paradox of Freedom:
The "Jewish Question"
in Postcommunist East Central Europe

ANDRÉ W.M. GERRITS

The Jews are an exceptional minority in East Central Europe today—
they have a rich and dramatic history but a bleak future. For centuries,
East European Jewry was the most important community of the
Diaspora. At the end of the last century, four out of every five Jews
lived in this part of the world. This community formed the center and
in some respects the origin of modern Jewish religious, cultural, and
political life; today it no longer exists. Jewish life was destroyed by the
Nazis during World War II, and it had no chance to recover during
the first postwar decade of Stalinism. However, the numerical strength
of the surviving Jews has never been indicative of their political
significance. In other words, the fact that only a relatively small
number of Jews remained in the communist countries of East Central
Europe after the war has not diminished the urgency of the "Jewish
issue" or the virulence of anti-Semitism in the region. The question
then is: do developments in postcommunist Europe (leaving the
former Soviet Union largely aside) corroborate this general observation? What is the position of the Jewish minority in East Central
Europe today, and what role do the "Jewish question" and anti-
Semitism play in postcommunist politics and society? These questions
demand some introductory remarks.

First, they can only be answered when the Jewish issue is put in
the context of historic relations between Jews and non-Jews (and the
state) in the region and in the context of nationalism. The nature, the
virulence, and the persistence of anti-Semitism and the specific
character of the Jewish communities in East Central Europe cannot be
understood when the historic dimension or continuity of the Jewish
question is not taken into account. Actually, there are two "continuities":
with communism and with pre-communism (especially during the
interwar period of authoritarian rule). These experiences have left
their tracks in the postcommunist period, strongly influencing the

nature of the region's dominant forms of nationalism and anti-Semitism.

The renaissance of nationalism in East Central Europe after the fall of communism has often been explained by the "freezer" metaphor. Traditional nationalist controversies and resentments were covered for more than 50 years by a layer of ice (the *Pax Sovietica*), reviving only when the ice began to melt and the political conformity enforced by the Soviet Union collapsed. This metaphor is only partly true. First of all, nationalism was never put in a freezer; indeed, it was frequently used and manipulated by the communist regimes. Second, it did not remain unchanged under communism. The metaphor underestimates the continued relevance of nationalism during communist rule. Nationalism, in its particular "communist" form, was a constituent part of the postwar experience. All communist regimes attempted to legitimize their rule by placing it in the framework of national history and tradition. The fact that these endeavors largely failed does not in itself diminish the relevance of nationalism. It is worth mentioning here that anti-Semitism was, and to some extent still is, an important component of radical nationalism in the area—before, during, and after the communist period.

A second introductory remark refers to a problem of definition: what is understood by Jews, and how to define the Jewish question in East Central Europe? East European Jews have always been a heterogeneous part of the population in political, cultural, and socioeconomic respects. Their "communality" was never based on self-definition only; it was determined by a combination of self-definition and the judgement of non-Jews. In (post)communist East Central Europe, the main thing was not whether one regarded oneself as a Jew but rather whether one was seen and treated as such by others. The Jewish question was basically a political issue, that is, an issue of political power and morality. It included everything related to "Jews" or "Jewishness" that was regarded by the state or by parts of society as a specific political problem, with or without a real economic, religious, or cultural dimension. One did not need Jews to have a Jewish problem. The Jewish question might as well refer to Jews as a concrete group of persons as to an imaginary phenomenon, a chimera, a fantasy. In other words: Jews as a metaphor. Anti-Semitism without Jews.

NATIONALISM AND STATE FORMATION

Jewish history in the eastern part of Europe is almost 1,000 years old. Jews came here from all directions, though most of them arrived from medieval Western and Central Europe, where they fled anti-Jewish restrictions and repression. In the course of the centuries, a large part of East European Jewry (the so-called *Ostjuden*[1] or eastern Jews) developed their own specific, religiously inspired life-style and culture, with which they gradually distinguished themselves from the Jewish communities in the rest of Europe. The East European Jews formed a much larger share of society than the Jews in Central and Western Europe. They lived mainly in compact communities in the big cities or in smaller Jewish towns scattered over the countryside, the *shtetls.* (More than 300,000 Jews lived in Warsaw alone during the interwar years, which is considerably more than the total number of Jews in the whole area of East Central Europe today.) The social and occupational structure of Jewish society not only differed fundamentally from that of the predominantly agrarian non-Jewish population, but it was also highly unequal. The Jewish community was divided into a small upper class of wealthy merchants and manufacturers and an overwhelming majority of poor lower-middle-class people. There was no Jewish bourgeoisie comparable to the one in Western and parts of Central Europe.

However, the most significant difference between East European Jewry and the Jewish communities in Western and Central Europe became the level of assimilation. In spite of the fact that Jewish emancipation and assimilation in West Central Europe since the end of the 18th century remained subject to certain restrictions, and that Jewish traditions and anti-Jewish sentiments persisted, both Jewish life and relations between Jews and non-Jews and the state changed considerably. The situation of the Jews in Eastern Europe contrasted sharply with the position of West European Jewry: at the beginning of this century the majority of East European Jews were still far from a status of full emancipation and the tempo of their assimilation into Christian society was much lower. This difference cannot be explained by the alleged hostility of the non-Jewish population only. The isolated position of the Jewish communities was, to some extent at least, the result of a free choice, inspired by the force and rigidity of their traditions. Jewish assimilation remained a minority movement. On the whole, the East European Jews, the most numerous, the poorest and the most sealed off part of European Jewry, made little effort "to breach the invisible walls of isolation and discrimination surrounding them."[2]

How was this Jewish community affected by the rise of nationalism and the process of state formation that occurred in the region since the second half of the last century? In Eastern Europe, nationalism lost both its initial political (or liberal) nature and its integrative function.

Even though there has never been a strict geographic division between different sorts of nationalism in Europe, it is undoubtedly true that a romantic idea of the nation dominated in the eastern part of the continent. This romantic or organic concept of the nation stressed the relevance of ethnicity, descent, language, religion, and other cultural criteria. Moreover, national consciousness displayed itself not "within" the existing state, but against it—"*nicht im und am Staat, sondern gegen den Staat*," as the German historian Schieder wrote.[3] Nationalist agitation was primarily aimed against the prevailing international order. Nationalist arguments were not only used to legitimize the idea of national self-determination, but also to propagate the conviction that ethnicity would be the most suitable principle of state-formation.

Nationalism lost only little of its vigor after the so-called nation-states were established in East Central Europe after World War I. Still, 23.6 million of the 94.5 million people living in the area during the interwar years belonged to ethnic minority groups, including more than 5 million Jews.[4] Their position in society had actually deteriorated since the disintegration and collapse of the region's multinational empires. National minorities lost a great deal of their political relevance and economic power. They could no longer count on the possible benevolence or shifting preferences on the part of the former royal or aristocratic elites (like the Jews as "Magyarizers" in the Kingdom of Hungary during the second part of the 19th century). Ethnic minorities frustrated the supreme objective of the new regimes: the creation of nation-states in the real sense of the word—states of one nation. As a rule, in independent East Central Europe, political power was exercised by the dominant ethnic group in society and legitimized by the specific nationalism of this group. The nationalism of only one nation, the dominant nation, became the basis of legitimacy of de facto multinational states.[5]

Anti-Semitism became an almost integral part of this dominant variant of nationalism. It was based on a combination of age-old, principally religiously inspired anti-Jewish sentiments, and modern political prejudices, of which the most important was the idea of "Jewish internationalism." Both the nation-state—perceived as a historic subject of the highest moral and political value—and its absolute opposite, Jewish internationalism—the supposed embodiment of degeneracy and subversion—were artificial, political constructs. Of course, these were modern myths, which found receptive ground in large parts of East Central Europe, which after all was a real patchwork of different ethnic groups, with a history of "foreign" domination and mutual conflicts. The most powerful, effective and ultimately destructive variant of this myth of Jewish internationalism became the equation of Jews and communism: Jews = communism = Russia. The image of Jewish communism arose out of the prominent role revolutionaries of Jewish origin had played in the years of political turbulence during and immediately after World War I. Jews indeed played a disproportionate and conspicuous role within the European labor movement, both within its communist and its social-democratic branches. However, the majority of these revolutionaries were in reality "non-Jewish Jews," who had gone beyond the boundaries of traditional Jewish life, who were looking for universal solutions to the challenges of modernity and to the Jewish predicament. They had found these in socialism. It is still a bitter paradox that, although this myth of "Jewish communism" was based on a general identification of Jews with communism, for most communists of Jewish origin their Jewish identity was unknown or irrelevant.

STALINISM

The traditional Jewish communities of East Central Europe were destroyed during World War II and the first decade of communist rule. While the Germans and their local auxiliaries physically eliminated the majority of the Jews, the Stalinist rulers would subsequently destroy the socioeconomic basis and the independent cultural life of those who had survived the genocide and stayed in the region. Many survivors (probably more than 300,000; exact figures are lacking) left East Central Europe immediately after the war. Most of those who did stay suffered serious deprivation—from illness, exhaustion, and hunger, to, again, hostility and violence. Pogroms took place in Hungary (Kunmadaras, Miskolc), in Slovakia (Svinná, Velké Topol'cany), and in Poland (Rzeszów, Kraków, Kielce).[6]

The specific postwar conditions perpetuated and even stimulated anti-Jewish sentiments among large parts of society. The massive repression and killing of Jews during the war strengthened feelings of aversion or guilt rather than compassion or remorse. The survivors were infected, so to speak, with their dreadful experiences. "They are somehow soiled, marked with suffering, branded with tragedy," Janina Bauman writes in her memoirs. "It is better to keep away from them and not to let the evil taint one's own tidy life."[7] The Jews who came back were resented for more trivial reasons as well. They claimed the properties, houses, and businesses that had been stolen years earlier and were now occupied by non-Jewish fellow-countrymen, who were not really inclined to give up their recently acquired possessions. A report from the Delegate's Office, the wartime representative in occupied Poland of the Polish government-in-exile, stated in August 1943:

> In the Homeland as a whole—regardless of the general psychological situation at any given moment—the position is such that the return of the Jews to their jobs and workshops is quite out of the question, even if the number of Jews were greatly reduced. The non-Jewish population has filled their places in the towns and cities; in much of Poland this is a fundamental change and final in character. The return of masses of Jews would be perceived by the population not as an act of restitution but as an invasion against which they would have to defend themselves, even by physical means."[8]

Finally, and most important perhaps, anti-Semitic feelings after the war were encouraged by the prominent role of a number of Jews (or actually non-Jewish Jews) in the communist regimes. Immediately after the Jews had suffered their greatest catastrophe, the *Shoah*, they were more prominent and more powerful than ever before. For the first time in history, Jews wielded political power in East Central Europe. The myth of Jewish communism received an enormous impetus. The region was in ruins, and subjected to a foreign power, the Soviet Union. And the Jews seemed to be ruling. The equation of Jews and communism (or Stalinism) became the most crucial ingredient of popular anti-Semitism in the area.[9]

Initially, during the first postwar years, the policies of the communist-dominated coalition governments vis-à-vis the Jewish communities remained rather ambivalent. On the one hand, the rebuilding of an autonomous Jewish community life was stimulated and sometimes even financially supported, and discriminatory prewar provisions were ignored or lifted. On the other hand, full Jewish assimilation was presented as the sole solution to the Jewish problem. Soon, however, ambivalence gave way to outright enmity. Independent Jewish community life did not fit into a monopolistic communist political system. 1948 was the turning-point. Within a year, cultural life was made practically *Judenfrei*. All references to "Jews" or "Jewishness" disappeared—except as arguments in the struggle against real or imagined political opponents. The *Shoah* became a taboo subject. All relations with Jews abroad, within or without the communist bloc, were severed. The American Joint Distribution Committee and other international Jewish organizations, which had played a vital role in enabling the decimated and destitute East Central European Jews to survive during the first postwar years, had to suspend their activities. Independent Jewish political organizations, the Zionists in particular, were suppressed, their leaders prosecuted and forced to emigrate. The Jewish communist movement was purged of "rightist deviationists." Every specific Jewish approach to Jewish problems was categorically rejected. Full and if necessary forced assimilation into socialist society was the only option now. Jewish autonomy was considered unnecessary; Jewish nationalism was regarded as criminal. Activists of Jewish origin figured prominently among the many communist zealots who destroyed the remnants of authentic Jewish life in the region in these few years. The same process of subversion, suppression, and enforced assimilation that took almost three decades in the Soviet Union after 1917 was accomplished in East Central Europe within only a couple of years.

When Stalin died in March 1953, there was no longer an authentic Jewish community life in the area. During the Stalinist decade, Jews had suffered because they were Jews. They were victims of both popular anti-Jewish violence and of discrimination and persecution by the communist state, especially in the dark years of 1948–1953. However, Jews had gained from the new political order as well. Communism had offered them unprecedented opportunities for social mobility, economic development, and political emancipation. Jews shared this somewhat ambivalent experience with most national or ethnic minorities. The policies of the communist regimes with regard to these minorities was a product of the dynamic relationship between nationalism and communism in the postwar period.[10] The communist rulers considered traditional nationalism, like most other values and institutions of prewar society, an important and dangerous ideological rival, which they suppressed and attempted to eradicate, but with which they were ultimately forced to come to terms. The nature of the compromise was determined by the varying national conditions the communist regimes had to take into account, and by their willingness and ability to exploit and manipulate these conditions for reasons of legitimacy and regime stability. All communism was to some extent "national," at least in terms of policy content or decision making (i.e., the degree to which local leaderships were able to set their own political priorities vis-à-vis the Soviet Union).

Also in the communist period, state nationalism was the national-ism of the dominant ethnic group in society. And even though the new rulers treated the issue of ethnic minorities in different ways, their strategies were largely based on similar political and ideological principles. The communist leaderships tried to combine a certain measure of ethnic and cultural diversity with political and ideological uniformity. Ethnic groups sometimes enjoyed the privilege of basic education and publishing in their own language, but they lacked political autonomy. They were able to join together in social and cultural organizations, but these were led by loyal communist appointees. Representatives of ethnic minorities could even be elected or nominated, often *qualitate qua*, to prominent political positions, but they were expected to represent general or national interests, not to defend any specific group rights. The position of ethnic minorities was basically determined by the failure of democratic rights and political pluralism that characterized the communist system. Traditional cultural and religious Jewish life was destroyed by the communist authorities, not primarily because it was Jewish, but because it was traditional and autonomous, and therefore incompatible with communist doctrine and practice. Jewish institutions, in other words, met with the same fate as most other noncommunist organizations. The same is true of the traditional Jewish economy. This was a capitalist economy, which could not possibly be reconciled with the new rulers' determination to fully plan and control their countries' households.

The fact, however, that ethnic groups were subjected to the same terror and conformity as the dominant nationality does not imply that minorities were never specially targeted or treated differently from other groups in society. They were—the Jews especially. In a number of respects, the Jewish question in communist East Central Europe was unique, and it remained so until the revolutionary upheavals of 1989. The Jewish question (anti-Semitism) played a far more prominent and lasting role in political fights and propaganda than most other minority-related matters. Moreover, it was an international problem par excellence, an issue in foreign relations, especially with the Western world. And finally, the Jewish question in East Central Europe seemed to be finite, to become a thing of the past—not because the communist rulers had found the definitive answer to the Jewish problem, but because the Jewish communities were slowly dying out. They simply ceased to exist.

ANTI-SEMITISM, COMMUNISM, NATIONALISM

Anti-Semitism manifested itself in the communist countries of Europe first of all as subject matter in the struggle for power and legitimacy within the communist elites and as an argument against the opposition and the capitalist world. In the first postwar years, parts of the anti-communist opposition pointed at the Jews within the Stalinist leaderships to stress the "non-national" character of these regimes. In later years, these regimes themselves would blame the Jews (the "Jewish Stalinists") for the problems and shortcomings with which the socialist societies had to contend. Already by the beginning of the

1950s, in most countries the party leaderships (which still included quite a number of people of Jewish origin) tried to minimize the presence and conspicuousness of Jewish comrades. This certainly played a role in the purges and show trials that took place in the years 1949–1953, although ordinary lust for power, envy, or fear, and, particularly, pressure by the Kremlin, were probably more important. The purging of Jewish communists continued after the death of Stalin. Now, however, a real political issue was at stake: whether to follow the Stalinist mode of politics or to reform. And although communists of Jewish background fought on both sides of the barricades, the new post-Stalinist leaders took the opportunity to further "nationalize" the party cadres. In all East Central European countries, with the partial exception of Hungary, Jewish communists were now gradually removed from power. In some socialist states, however, the Jewish question lost only a little of its vigor. One of the most important consequences of de-Stalinization was a growing diversity within the communist bloc in regard to the role that the Jewish question played in domestic and foreign policies. Here we concentrate on two specific cases: Romania, where the Jewish issue became primarily a matter of foreign relations; and Poland, where it generally remained an issue in domestic politics.

The ghost of anti-Semitism reappeared again and again in Polish politics (in 1956, in 1968, and in 1980–1982), basically as a result of the manipulation of anti-Semitic feelings by the communist party elites. All functions of the Jewish question as a political instrument and as a diversionary tactic were combined here: to decide disputes within the party, to obtain legitimacy, and to fight the anti-communist opposition. After 1968, the majority of the remaining Polish Jews were compelled to leave the country. These were mainly "Jews by force, not by choice," as Paul Lendvai rightly states.[11] They were fully assimilated into Polish society, and perhaps most of them were not even conscious of their Jewish origins. This did not protect them against discrimination and oppression. After all, it is the anti-Semite who decides who is Jewish and who is not. Even though the anti-Jewish campaign of 1967–1968 seriously damaged Poland's image abroad, it did not directly harm the country's international interests (as perceived by its rulers). Western governments and private banks were willing to advance the Gierek regime (1970-1980) the loans and credits that it was looking for, and for some time at the end of the 1970s Warsaw was even able to act as a broker in East-West relations.

In Romania, the attitude of the communist leaders vis-à-vis the Jewish population was primarily shaped by foreign policy deliberations. Their strategy was threefold. Bucharest maintained diplomatic relations with Israel; it gave the Jewish community a remarkable cultural and religious latitude (including the possibility of emigration); and it tolerated or even encouraged anti-Semitism in the official press. This particular policy mix served the regime's basic and interrelated interest, namely to strengthen its legitimacy at home (for which it manipulated traditional Romanian nationalism) and its autonomy abroad (for which it needed good relations with the Western world). The Jewish community, led by Rabbi Mozes Rosen, functioned as a pawn in the country's foreign relations. Rosen fully participated in official political life, and was always willing to defend Romania's case in exchange for concessions to his Jewish congregation. The communist leaders for their part were very pleased with the image of Romania that Rosen presented abroad. Ceauşescu's predecessor, Gheorghe Gheorghiu-Dej, once remarked to him: "We have had 14 ambassadors and 300 diplomats in the United States since 1945, but all of them together did not do as good a job for us as you did, Chief Rabbi."[12] Rosen took advantage of the fact that the interests of the Jewish community (as he defined them) and those of the party leadership were to some degree identical. Yet, it was an opportunistic alliance. Rosen's strategy was controversial not because he collaborated with the communist regime in his country (under the given circumstances he probably had no other choice), but because he was inclined to ignore those criminal activities by the regime that did not directly affect Romanian Jews. By that he incriminated himself and the Jewish community, and he fed the prejudice of "Jewish communism."

In the interwar period, Jews were primarily a socioeconomic and cultural problem in East Central Europe; after the war they were perceived as a political problem; now that there are not very many Jews left,[13] they are basically a moral problem.[14] The Jewish issue has survived the Jews. The classic question is of course: why Jews again? Why were Jews the object of political machinations in the communist countries of Europe? Often, the motivation of anti-Semitism had little to do with Jews as a reality, as a living community. First and foremost, the "Jew" was an image—an image and an ideal scapegoat. Anti-Jewish demagoguery offered the unique opportunity to combine traditional prejudices with the ideological premises of the communist order. And in spite of the fact that society was certainly not immune to this rhetoric, the use of anti-Semitism did not come up to the expectations of the communist elites. Anti-Semitism could have been an important basis of political legitimacy (for example in Poland), had it not been inevitably linked to those who openly used it: the communist leaderships. Anti-Semitism and communist state national-ism in general were a product of the official political culture, carefully prescribed in form and content. They had to correspond with the specific interests of the communist leaders and their international obligations. In this respect, they were unlikely to be fully responsive to the sentiments and aspirations of society. People were neither expected nor allowed to participate freely in anti-Semitic, or for that matter nationalist, manifestations. This probably explains why the communist anti-Semitic campaigns evoked only limited response in societies where anti-Jewish feelings were traditionally rather strong. Enthusiastic participation was broadly regarded as a service to a despised regime (if there was no private lucre involved, of course).

POSTCOMMUNISM

The collapse of communism in East Central Europe came unexpectedly and had enormous consequences—in and outside the region. In a number of respects, however, it affected the Jewish communities less dramatically than it did some other national or ethnic minority groups.[15] First of all, even before the fall of the communist regimes, Jewish nationalism often had a legal outlet or safety valve: emigration to Israel. Second, in a number of communist countries (especially Poland, Hungary, and the Soviet Union) during the 1980s, the Jewish question had already lost part of its political significance, the Jewish communities had gained some more room to maneuver, and different taboos had been broken.[16] But still, what goes for the population of East Central Europe in general goes for the Jews as well: postcommunist reality is ambivalent. It offers not only unforeseen opportunities and challenges, but also dangers. The collapse of communism brought the Jewish communities an unprecedented measure of political and cultural freedom. The whole of society could profit from political democratization, of course, but for the small and vulnerable Jewish part of the population it was absolutely essential. Democracy creates the necessary conditions for a revival of Jewish community life in East Central Europe. It is the basic requirement for the preservation of a collective Jewish identity that goes beyond the consciousness of a mere *Schicksalsgemeinschaft* (a community of fate).

In most countries, different kinds of Jewish grassroots organizations were established, especially in the cultural field, and they were free to engage in contacts with international Jewish institutions. These organizations competed with the radicalized existing establishment associations, which had been loyal to the communist authorities until the very last moment but whose official and conformist leaderships were now generally dismissed. These leaders of the official Jewish community had undoubtedly overexaggerated their allegiance to the communist rulers, and some had deliberately (out of fear or conviction) harmed the interests of their community and its members. "The leaders of the community are more afraid of change than the government is," as a Jewish activist in Czechoslovakia complained.[17] However, most of these leaders were only little apparatchiks, largely impotent and sometimes tragic puppets in the hands of others. But in their own way, they contributed to the preservation of what was left of the Jewish communities in the eastern part of Europe.

Most of the Jewish themes that had been banned by the communist authorities could now be openly addressed. The Jewish past, anti-Semitism, and the often painful historic relations between Jews and non-Jews were finally released from the ideological bonds, the written and unwritten rules that had prevented any meaningful discussion. The relevance and topicality of anti-Semitism could be freely debated. The *Shoah* was no longer taboo. The memorials and monuments dedicated to the victims of anti-Jewish violence that have been recently unveiled in a number of countries symbolize a unique achievement: for the first time ever, the Jews in East Central Europe are able to honor the memory of the victims of war and genocide in a way they themselves regard as proper.

However, Jews also suffered adverse consequences of the collapse of the communist regimes. The disintegration of the authoritarian party-state and the rise of political pluralism gave a radically different dimension to anti-Semitism. This is the paradoxical side of freedom: while political liberalization put an end to discrimination by the state, it also created ample opportunity for individuals and groups to openly manifest their anti-Jewish sentiments. And while state anti-Semitism was to some extent anonymous and largely nonviolent, grassroots xenophobia is mostly very personal and direct, face-to-face.[18]

The significance of anti-Semitism in postcommunist Europe today is largely based on the same combination of historical and actual circumstances that is behind the rather unexpected virulence of extreme nationalism in the area: the continuity of authoritarian political culture and practice; the force of history and the persistence of historical prejudices, resentments, and national mythologies; feelings of insecurity and alienation in societies in a state of flux; and, last but not least, the radicalization, politicization, and mobilization of these feelings by politicians and ideologues (after all, nationalism has a function).[19] However, neither nationalism nor anti-Semitism is a simple, one-dimensional phenomenon. To estimate the current political relevance of anti-Semitism in East Central Europe, one needs to distinguish between three different levels: society, politics, and the state.

SOCIETY

Many of the anti-Semitic events that took place in East Central Europe after the fall of the communist regimes did nor really differ from those that happen in other parts of the world as well, Western Europe and the United States included: desecration of tombstones and of places of worship, vandalism of other Jewish property or places of commemoration, disturbance of meetings, circulation of anti-Semitic leaflets and literature, anti-Jewish remarks made by minor political and intellectual figures—much more serious—defamation or harassment of individual Jews or of people regarded as such. This does not imply, however, that these events are equally significant in established democracies as in the postcommunist world, where the democratic order is still rather fragile. Moreover, anti-Semitic incidents in East Central Europe express the continuity of a strongly negative social definition of Jews, and the persistence of a sort of anti-Jewish paranoia, an obsession with Jewish omnipresence and omnipotence (the myth of the "hidden Jews").[20] As a Polish joke in the summer of 1990 put it: "There are almost no Jews in Poland, but why do all of them have to be in the government?"[21] This attitude implies, as the Polish publicist Konstanty Gebert rightly observes, the classic anti-Jewish prejudice that the way Jews obtain or exercise power is directly connected to their Jewishness and not to any other criteria, independent of their nationality, political views and opinions, professional status, or socio-economic position.[22] Gebert makes a distinction between holding anti-Semitic opinions and implementing these in personal and political behavior. "What we currently encounter in Poland," he concludes, "is not mass anti-Semitism but mass tolerance of anti-Semitism."[23] This differentiation seems useful—not to play down the significance of anti-Jewish sentiments in Poland, but to explain the discrepancy between the considerable degree of anti-Jewish prejudices in society and the relatively marginal position of most anti-Semitic political groups and parties. However, before we focus on anti-Semitism at the "political" level, the question needs to be answered, why are these anti-Jewish stereotypes and prejudices so persistent? The Polish historian Andrzej Bryk once aptly remarked that in Poland anti-Semitism is a matter of opinion and not a moral crime.[24] Polish society, and mutatis mutandis the same goes for most other former communist countries, has never been able to finish with its anti-Semitic past. First of all, Jews and non-Jews have traditionally lived in largely different worlds—without knowing much about each other and without much interest in each other. As such, this basic lack of mutual contacts in any other than the economic sphere perpetuated all kinds of traditional stereotypes and prejudices. Second, the *Shoah* in East Central Europe (and especially in Poland) never was a "watershed" in relations between Jews and Christians; it never functioned as the ultimate "disqualification" of political anti-Semitism.[25] Third, postwar political circumstances not only strengthened specific anti-Semitic ideas (like the myth of "Jewish communism"), but they also ruled out the possibility of public debate (which would be a precondition for overcoming these traditional antipathies). Fourth, for a very long time, authoritative institutions like the Roman Catholic Church refused to unequivocally condemn anti-Semitism, which in itself legitimized this sort of idea.

POLITICS

The line between society and politics as far as the relevance and significance of anti-Semitism is concerned is rather thin and in some respects even artificial. Anti-Semitism in politics is the coupling of anti-Jewish ideas and political activism for reasons of political profit (to gain support or legitimacy). Again, anti-Semitism in this respect is not a one-dimensional phenomenon. One should distinguish between at least two different manifestations of anti-Semitism in postcommunist politics: the display of anti-Jewish ideas or attitudes, either intentionally or unconsciously, by politicians who cannot really be considered anti-Semites; and, second, anti-Semitism as a basic ingredient of the political *Weltanschauung* of extreme nationalist forces. Both kinds of manifestations of anti-Semitism are based on the same circumstance: popular anti-Semitism is still a factor that can be exploited in public life.

We are largely familiar with the anti-Semitic incidents in postcommunist politics, because most of these events often reach the Western press. Election posters were plastered with swastikas and anti-Jewish slogans; candidates were "forced" to reveal their "true identity." Some of them were victimized by anti-Semitic whisper campaigns; others were too weak (or too opportunistic) to protest. Even though there is no reason to believe that in any of the recently held elections these events were part of an orchestrated campaign, anti-Semitism seems an almost intrinsic element of the postcommunist polity. However, this conclusion demands two additional comments. First, the words *Jews* and *Jewishness* are frequently used as epithets, aimed against persons or organizations (often politicians and political parties)[26] that have nothing in common with anything Jewish, but that are classified as such to express disagreement or disapproval.[27] They are the "political" Jews—a classic form of anti-Semitism and absolutely indispensable in a region where relatively few "real" Jews are left. Second, anti-Semitic arguments are mostly used implicitly. Politicians declare themselves to be "true Poles" or "Christian Hungarians." They are used implicitly, mainly because by now publicly expressed direct anti-Semitism has practically been delegitimized in mainstream East Central European politics.

This change for the better, which implies an enormous difference from the interwar period, is also one of the reasons why openly anti-Semitic political groups are still mostly marginal and politically irrelevant. Anti-Semitic ideas are propagated by a heterogeneous coalition of extreme nationalist forces, from members of the *anciens regimes* to former dissidents and right-wing reactionaries. Their anti-Semitism is a motley collection of traditional and new-fashioned prejudices. Jews are everywhere and they are mostly "hidden." Jews dominate international elite positions. Jews represent foreign and threatening outside influences, capitalist exploitation, Stalinist repression, powerless democracy, unrestrained freedom, cosmopolitan diversity, and, most of all, national disloyalty. The traditional myth of Jewish communism is still very much alive (though not as widespread as it used to be).[28] In *Romania Mare*, an extremely chauvinistic but popular weekly, prominent members of the opposition are being confronted with the Stalinist past of their fathers. It is a familiar theme, "fathers and sons," already used against Polish oppositionists during the 1960s. Political opponents are exposed as Jews or anyway as agents of international Jewry and therefore as traitors. Even the Romanian president Ion Iliescu was allegedly brought to power by Jews. The following passage from *Europa*, a weekly edited by a prominent member of the Greater Romania Party, Ilie Neacsu, seems rather typical of the anti-Semitic hodgepodge these groups present: it says that

> immediately after the coup d'état of December 1989, our dear kikes, who had rightly been removed from the fundamental structures of Romanian society by Dej and Ceausescu, again installed themselves at Romania's head. . . . Having been brought to power by a stupid combination of historical circumstances, Ion Iliescu finds himself today strangled by those people who had put him there. . . . The president has isolated himself from the electorate and has become close to the synagogue in the hope of improving his image abroad. Educated as he is at the school of Judeo-Stalinism and raised among Jews, Mr. Iliescu has become their prisoner.[29]

For most of the political organizations that openly disseminate anti-Jewish ideas, anti-Semitism is only a part of their ideological outlook, and generally not the most important one. These groups have diverging political roots and objectives, but they share an identical closed, authoritarian, and collectivist world view. They usually hold vague and inconsistent views on political and economic change, but most of them reject rapid or drastic reforms (including privatization). They all regard the role of the state in the process of change as crucial and dominant. These anti-Semitic groups suffer from xenophobia, and some are typical products of the romantic and intolerant tradition of nationalism in the area. The "question" of ethnic or national minorities is of supreme interest to all of these groups, in that they derive their political identity from it; it is their *raison d'être*. They are preoccupied with cultural decay and loss of national values and identity—part of their strongly anti-Western standpoints. These parties and politicians are obsessed with international conspiracies, with national suffering and martyrdom, and, of course, with the "image of the omnipotent and ubiquitous Jew."[30]

It is easy to perceive that a continual political and socioeconomic malaise offers an excellent opportunity for political manipulation, including the use of anti-Semitism. Radical nationalist organizations are among the first to do so. What is their support in society, and what is their political influence? It should be mentioned that not all nationalist parties and groups are explicitly anti-Semitic. Less extreme organizations, such as the Slovak National Party or the Confederation for an Independent Poland, nationalist groups in countries with no anti-Semitic tradition (as in Bulgaria), and parties that operate in a situation of open ethnic conflicts in parts of former Yugoslavia and the Soviet Union generally ignore anti-Semitic rhetoric. Moreover, most of the extreme nationalist political groups that openly propagate anti-Semitic ideas (for example, the Polish National Party, led by Boleslaw Tejkowski, which claims 4,000 members, and the small Republican Party in the Czech Republic) are still rather weak. They still have no mass following, a limited number—if any—of representatives in legislative bodies, and no direct government responsibility. But, it should be added, the situation seems to be changing. In an earlier publication, I concluded that extreme nationalist organizations (including anti-Semitic ones) do not primarily derive their political influence from formal positions of political power, but from their sometimes considerable support in ethnically mixed regions, from their association with much larger political-cultural organizations and their widely circulating periodicals (like *Romania Mare* and Vatra Romaneasca's publication in Romania, or the Committee for the Defense of National Interests in Bulgaria) and from the radicalizing effect they have on other, major political parties.[31] Although this conclusion still holds, in the meantime some radical nationalists and anti-Semites have considerably strengthened their political position—especially in Romania. Three parties of "radical continuity" (with the regime of Nicolae Ceaușescu) have been represented in the Romanian Parliament since the elections of September 1992: the Party of Romanian National Unity (8.12% of the votes), the Greater Romania Party (3.85%), and the Socialist Labor Party (3.18%). And what is even more disturbing, the government of the democratic National Salvation Front depends on the support of these groups for survival.[32] At the same time, Prime Minister Vladimir Meciar's Movement for a Democratic Slovakia has formed an informal coalition with the Slovak National Party (15 seats in Parliament).

THE STATE

Prominent politicians may not always have the courage (or will) to unequivocally distance themselves from the political use of anti-Semitism, and some even allow the use of anti-Semitic arguments against their opponents; governments occasionally depend on the support of anti-Semitic parties, but there are no anti-Jewish state policies in postcommunist Europe today.

CONCLUSIONS AND RECOMMENDATIONS

What policy conclusions and recommendations could be drawn from this analysis?

First, anti-Jewish ideas play a salient but not a crucial role in East Central European politics. Anti-Semitism is used to discredit political opponents, evoke an atmosphere of threat and instability, express feelings of guilt, and deny or shirk responsibility for decades of mismanagement and collaboration. Obviously, some politicians still regard anti-Semitism as an ideal outlet for popular frustration and anger. Political anti-Semitism is a twofold phenomenon: on the one hand, it is part of the ideology of a relatively small number of mostly extra-parliamentary political organizations; on the other, it is a component of the political discourse in most postcommunist countries. And even though a majority of politicians openly reject anti-Semitism (and therefore one should conclude that it has been politically delegitimized), they sometimes seem to accept it as an apparently unavoidable part of their country's political culture. Such ambivalence and the susceptibility to anti-Jewish emotions by still rather large segments of society make anti-Semitism a political factor to be reckoned with—although not to be overexaggerated. Any comparison between the interwar period and postcommunism as far as the virulence of anti-Semitism is concerned, either in society or in the political arena, falls short. One should distinguish between anti-Jewish trends and incidents, as Charles Hoffman rightly observes—not "every anti-Semitic incident is a harbinger of pogroms or fascism."[33]

Second, the "Jewish question" essentially differs from most other minority issues in East Central Europe. As a matter of fact, it cannot simply be regarded as a minority issue—it is first of all a question of political culture and social mentality. How to cope with ethnic, cultural, religious, and national diversity? Even though this general observation applies to all "minority problems" in East Central Europe, it specifically bears on the case of the Jews. After all, the Jewish question is a political construct par excellence. It primarily refers to "political" instead of "real" Jews. Anti-Semitism, therefore, is not aimed against Jews per se, but against everything in politics that one strongly disapproves of or hates. The "Jews" are a metaphor. Anti-Semitism is a byproduct of instability, alienation, or dissatisfaction in society, nourished by traditional prejudices, and manipulated by unscrupulous ideologues and politicians. As the Marxist-Polish-Jewish historian Isaac Deutscher once characterized it, anti-Semitism is the barometer of the political and moral health of society.[34]

The conclusion is as simple as it is disturbing: even if all possible formal minority rights for Jews were realized, even if all Jews would be fully assimilated into society, and even if there would be no Jews anymore, there could still be anti-Semitism. The "Jewish question" in East Central Europe supports the more general idea that the actual position of minorities is basically a political issue, rather than a legal one. It is not so much determined by legal concepts and other technical formulations as by the political and psychological climate in society and by the functioning of the state.

Third, many "Jews" in East Central Europe today, perhaps even a majority, do not primarily regard themselves as Jews, but as Hungarians, Poles, or Czechs, whether of Jewish origin or not. Their "national" self-identity is the identity of the majority of the population. What sometimes goes for other ethnic minority groups goes for the Jews in particular: they are difficult to define as a minority, because most of them do not perceive themselves as such.[35] They neither try to gain the status of a minority group, nor do they seek the specific "rights" often linked to this status. In fact, most Jews are fully integrated into society. There are no Jewish political parties (the fact that some political parties are considered to be Jewish is, again, a matter of political culture); nor are there political organizations that exclusively represent the interests of Jews. This does not mean, however, that "minority rights" are not of importance to Jews. They are, of course. These rights are relevant for all individuals in society, regardless of their ethnic or national background, and moreover, there are Jews in the postcommunist world who do explicitly regard themselves as members of a minority group (in this respect, they are a minority within a minority), and their community life is dependent on the fulfillment of these rights. Apart, though, from these formal minority rights, one should stress the relevance of "human rights education," because this affects all Jews (and other "minorities"), whether assimilated or not. The documents of both the Copenhagen and Moscow meetings of the CSCE explicitly mention this human rights education as a contribution to "combating intolerance, religious, racial and ethnic prejudice and hatred."[36]

Fourth, the Jewish issue differs from most other minority problems because Jews are a "transnational" or "nonterritorial" population group. This implies that the Jewish question (except for a relatively small number of people who believe in an international Jewish conspiracy) usually lacks the most sensitive and explosive dimension of the minorities issue: the security and integrity of the national state. There is no irredentism involved in the Jewish question, no separatism, no secessionism, not even geographical autonomy or self-determination. It is not very likely, therefore, that aggressive anti-Semitism will escalate into international conflicts within the region or that it will provide a serious threat to international peace or security.

This does not mean, however, that the Jewish question lacks any international dimension. During the communist period, there was no minority issue that played a more prominent role in East-West relations than did the Jewish question. One of the more well-known cases was the problem of Jewish emigration from the Soviet Union in Soviet-US relations since the early 1970s. Washington tried to link trade concessions to emigration policies (the Jackson-Vanik Amendment). But even in the interwar period and before, the treatment of the Jews was an issue in international political negotiations: there was a system of treaties to protect national minorities (including Jews) within the framework of the League of Nations. In any event, after the collapse of communism, the Jewish issue seems to have lost some relevance in international relations. There are other and more pressing minority issues now. Moreover, state anti-Semitism has largely disappeared (which does not say that it could not come back again). And recent possibilities of emigration have further reduced the number of Jews in the region.

Fifth, the Jewish question will (and should) remain a topic in relations between the United States/Western Europe and East Central

Europe, and most of the politicians in the region are very well aware of this. However, there is no (longer) reason for the West to single out the Jews as a special category in foreign policy. This does not refer of course to the Jewish state of Israel or to international Jewish organizations. They have their own priorities and obligations. For the Jewish communities in East Central Europe, the right to unimpeded contacts with Jews abroad seems of vital importance for their further development. The restoration of this right is only one of the positive achievements of the postcommunist period.

In the postwar period, "Western" commitment to the case of the Jews in East Central Europe has given these generally small and vulnerable communities a measure of protection. The West seems helpless, however, in the face of the greatest threat to the Jewish communities today, which is not physical or political harm but "cultural extinction." In other words: not the Jews but Jewish life in East Central Europe is in serious danger.

Sixth, from what has been stated above, it should be clear that I do not believe in any sweeping Western policies vis-à-vis the Jewish question in East Central Europe. This would not do justice to the divergent situation of the Jewish communities in the different postcommunist societies; moreover, it would ignore the fact that the Jewish issue is first and foremost a challenge or a problem for the East Europeans themselves to address and to solve. In the current uncertain and volatile situation in East Central Europe, any adequate approach towards this Jewish question can be realized only within the framework of a democratic policy. It demands both a principal espousal of the fundamentals of democracy, which are pluralism and tolerance, and a great deal of personal courage. In practical terms, three moral policy choices seem to be crucially relevant here. First of all, there must be a consequent and fundamental rejection by authoritative institutions and personalities in society of any form of popular anti-Semitism (or, for that matter, xenophobia), whether based on traditional prejudices or actual frustrations and fears. It speaks for itself that the role of churches is crucially important here, and recent events (like the pastoral letter issued by the Catholic Church in Poland last year) seem rather encouraging. This is the only way to "disqualify" or delegitimize mass tolerance of anti-Semitism in society and to convince people that anti-Semitism is not a simple matter of opinion but a moral crime indeed. Second, those who are politically active must have the courage and determination to abstain from playing the "Jewish card" in politics. It is, after all, extremely difficult for politicians who are being victimized by anti-Semitic insinuations to defend themselves. No matter what the reaction is (to deny or to confirm one's "Jewishness"), one gets mixed up in the dirty games of others; therefore, most personal anti-Semitic insinuations are ignored. Third, there must be openness—openness with regard to the often painful and "suppressed" history of Jewish-Christian relations. Postcommunist politicians and other authorities should be prepared to accept their own responsibility in this field. They should summon the courage to challenge taboos, to initiate debate, and to make possible a more objective assessment of the role of the Jews in their countries' past. It seems to me that the policy choices suggested here offer the ingredients of the best approach towards the Jewish communities in East Central Europe. After all, the Jewish question will be solved only if Jews feel at home in their own countries.

NOTES

1. Nathan Birnbaum, *Was sind Ostjuden?* (Vienna, 1916), p. 15.

2. Arno Mayer, *Why Did the Heavens Not Darken? The "Final Solution" in History* (New York, 1988), p. 42.

3. Otto Dann and Hans-Ulrich Wehler, eds., *Theodor Schieder: Nationalismus and Nationalstaat: Studien zum nationalen Problem im modernen Europa* (Göttingen, 1991), p. 350.

4. Stephan M. Horak, "Eastern European National Minorities, 1918-1980," in *Eastern European National Minorities 1919–1980: A Handbook*, Stephan M. Horak et al. (Littleton, Colorado, 1985), p. 5.

5. Cf. Hugh Seton-Watson, *Nationalism and Communism: Essays 1946-1963* (New York, 1964), p. 23.

6. Traditional anti-Jewish prejudices played a role in these riots, but so did still largely unresolved political circumstances (provocations). See Peter Meyer et al., *The Jews in the Soviet Satellites* (Syracuse, 1953); Krystyna Kersten, *Polacy Zydzi Komunizm: Anatomia pólprawd 1939–68* (Warsaw, 1992), pp. 89-142; Bozena Szaynok, *Pogrom zydow w Kielcach: 4 lipca 1946* (Warsaw, 1992).

7. Janina Bauman, *A Dream of Belonging: My Years in Postwar Poland* (London, 1988), pp. 13–14.

8. Quoted in Yisrael Gutman, "Polish and Jewish Historiography on the Question of Polish-Jewish Relations During World War II," in *The Jews in Poland*, ed. Chimen Abramsky et al. (Oxford, 1986), p. 182.

9. So far, not much research has been done on the role of "Jews" in the communist regimes in East Central Europe. See especially Jaff Schatz, *The Generation: The Rise and Fall of the Jewish Communists of Poland* (Berkeley: University of California Press, 1991); and Jerry Z. Muller, "Communism, Anti-Semitism & the Jews," *Commentary* 86, no. 2 (August 1988), pp. 28–39.

10. See André W.M. Gerrits, *Nationalism and Political Change in Postcommunist Europe* (The Hague: Netherlands Institute of International Relations "Clingendael," 1992), pp. 9–14.

11. Paul Lendvai, *Anti-Semitism Without Jews: Communism in Eastern Europe* (New York, 1971), p. 3.

12. *Dangers, Tests and Miracles: The Remarkable Life Story of Chief Rabbi Rosen of Romania as Told to Joseph Finklestone* (London, 1990), p. 205.

13. Jews in East-Central Europe numbered as follows during the 1980s:

Albania: 200; Bulgaria: 5,000; Czechoslovakia: 12,000; GDR: 400; Hungary: 80,000; Poland: 6,000; Romania: 23,000; Soviet Union: 1,810,876; Yugoslavia: 5,500. *The Jewish Communities of the World*, ed. Antony Lerman et al. (London, 1989).

14. Adapted from Aleksander Smolar, "Jews as a Polish Problem," *Daedalus* 116, no. 2 (Spring 1987), p. 58.

15. My assessment is partly based on Zvi Gitelman's analysis of the position of the Jewish community in the Soviet Union after Gorbachev. "Soviet Jewry in Transition," *Soviet Jewish Affairs* 19, no. 2 (1989) pp. 3–13.

16. The discussions in Poland are especially well documented. See Antony Polonsky, ed., *My Brother's Keeper? Recent Polish Debates on the Holocaust* (London, 1990); and "Ressentiments und Annäherungsversuche: Das polnisch-Jüdische Verhältnis in der polnischen Publizistik 1987–1992," *Dokumentation Ostmitteleuropa* 18, no. 5/6 (December 1992), pp. 217–362.

17. Charles Hoffman, *Gray Dawn: The Jews of Eastern Europe in the Post-Communist Era* (New York, 1992), p. 39.

18. Zvi Gitelman, "Glasnost, Perestroika and Anti-Semitism," *Foreign Affairs* 70, no. 2 (Spring 1991), p. 158.

19. Gerrits, *Nationalism and Political Change in Post-Communist Europe*, pp. 15–23.

20. Recent public opinion research showed that the "behavior" of Jews arouses "negative" reactions among 6% of the Hungarian respondents (Poles: 19%); 40% of the Poles would not like Jews to live in their neighborhood (Hungarians: 17%, Czechoslovaks: 23%); 75% of all Hungarians consider the Jews to be well integrated into society (Poles: 44%, Czechoslovaks: 52%); and 5% of the Hungarian respondents (Poles: 16%) believe the Jews constitute a danger to the development of their country in the postcommunist period. Some 26% of all Poles are of the opinion that Jews have too much influence in their country. (*Attitudes towards Jews in Poland, Hungary and Czechoslovakia: A Comparative Survey*, conducted for the American Jewish Committee and Freedom House [January 1991]; see also Ildikó Szabó and Paul Wald, "Hongrie: antisémitisme ou anti-assimilationnisme?" *La Nouvelle Alternative*, no. 6 [June 1992] p. 47).

21. Hoffman, *Gray Dawn*, p. 300.

22. Konstanty Gebert, "Anti-Semitism in the 1990 Polish Presidential Election," *Social Research* 58, no. 4 (Winter 1991), pp. 726–27. Gebert also quotes from public opinion research conducted in Poland during the presidential elections of 1990, which demonstrated that at least 30% of Polish citizens share these traditional anti-Jewish ideas. The poll also shows that almost 50% of those who supported Walesa and nearly 25% of Mazowiecki's electorate were of the opinion that indeed "Jews had too much influence in Poland."

23. Ibid., p. 727.

24. Andrzej Bryk, "The Hidden Complex of the Polish Mind: Polish-Jewish Relations During the Holocaust," in *My Brother's Keeper?*, ed. Polansky, p. 175.

25. For Polish-Jewish relations during World War II and the attitude of many Poles vis-à-vis the genocide of the Jews, see, among many other studies, Polonsky, ed., *My Brother's Keeper?*, and Smolar, "Jews as a Polish Problem."

26. The most well-known examples are the Democratic Union in Poland and its leader, former prime minister Tadeusz Mazowiecki, and the Hungarian opposition party Alliance of Free Democrats.

27. Gebert, "Anti-Semitism in the 1990 Polish Presidential Election," p. 729.

28. A classic example of political anti-Semitism is the tract ("Setting the Record Straight," in *Magyar Forum*, Aug. 20, 1992) by the Hungarian writer and politician Istvan Csurka, one of the vice-presidents of the government party Hungarian Democratic Forum. The article caused great turmoil in Hungary (and outside). Csurka had to resign as vice-president and later he was expelled from his party. This illustrates the fact that open anti-Semitism is indeed regarded as a transgression of political norms.

29. *Europa*, May 4–11, 1992, p. 124. Quoted in Michael Shafir, "Extreme Nationalist Brinkmanship in Romania," *RFE/RL Research Report* 2, no. 21 (May 21, 1993), p. 35.

30. Robert S. Wistrich, *Anti-Semitism: The Longest Hatred* (London, 1991), p. 187.

31. Gerrits, *Nationalism and Political Change in Post-Communist Europe*, p. 27.

32. Michael Shafir, "Growing Political Extremism in Romania," *RFE/RL Research Report* 2, no. 14 (April 2, 1993), pp. 18–25.

33. Hoffman, *Gray Dawn*, p. 326.

34. Isaac Deutscher, *The Non-Jewish Jews and Other Essays* (London, 1968), p. 86.

35. Article 32 of the Document of the Copenhagen Meeting of the Conference on the Human Dimension of the CSCE reads: "To belong to a national minority is a matter of a person's individual choice." Persons belonging to these national minorities should have the following rights in particular (according to the same document): to use freely their mother tongue; to establish and maintain their own cultural and religious institutions; to profess and practice their religion; to establish and maintain unimpeded contacts among themselves within their own country and across borders; to freely exchange information in their mother tongue; and to participate in decision-making procedures with regard to minority issues.

36. Document of the Moscow Meeting of the Conference on the Human Dimension of the CSCE (1991), art. 42.2; Document of the Copenhagen Meeting of the Conference on the Human Dimension of the CSCE (1990), art. 40.

4

Democracy Building
in Ethnically Diverse Societies:
The Cases of Bulgaria and Romania

IVANKA NEDEVA

1. INTRODUCTION

The collapse of communism and the consequent disintegration of such multinational states as the Soviet Union, Yugoslavia, and Czechoslovakia reestablished the nation-state as a separate entity in the area. Most of these states, however, are still confronted with ethnic and minority problems.[1] To some extent, only Albania, the Czech Republic, Hungary, and Poland can be regarded as ethnically homogeneous.

For the purpose of this paper, the examples of Bulgaria and Romania are taken as case studies. There are a number of similarities between these two countries regarding the complexities in the relationships between the ethnic majority and the different ethnic, religious, and linguistic minorities. Behind apparent similarities, however, there are deep differences rooted in history, political culture, and level of democratization.

Common to both countries is their situation in the most unstable region in Europe—the Balkans. The wars in Yugoslavia are close to them and each faces deep domestic crises, making them extremely vulnerable at the moment. The peaceful divorce in Czechoslovakia and the savagery in Bosnia signal the decomposition not only of the Yalta and Helsinki agreements but the demise of the whole geopolitical settlement in Europe arranged by the Great Powers in Paris after World War I. Things are thus back to where they were at the beginning of the century. While Western Europe is moving quickly toward the 21st century, the Balkans are falling back to the 19th. This is a profound contradiction in contemporary Europe.

Another similarity is that each country has among a variety of ethnic groups one minority—Hungarians in Romania and Turks in Bulgaria, respectively—that is sizable and determines to a large extent important interstate relations, specifically Bulgaria's with Turkey and Romania's with Hungary. Moreover, the potential for involvement of these minorities in serious, at some points even violent, ethnic conflicts is a real threat; they have already shown a strong capacity for organizing themselves politically and for formulating a particular defense of the rights of minorities; and last but not least they are able to mobilize support for achieving their demands vis-à-vis the majority-controlled state.[2]

Statistics play an important role in evaluating and analyzing ethnic problems. Serious obstacles exist to obtaining accurate statistics, not only in Eastern Europe but also in some democratic countries in the West. These obstacles can be a result of state policy or of claims of different interested parties. Thus, Andre Liebich's approach is taken here for estimating the most sizable of the minority populations in Bulgaria and Romania[3] (see population table at the end of this chapter).

Looking further for similarities between Romania and Bulgaria, it is quite clear from today's perspective that the treatment of minorities and the problem of civil rights became some of the strongest factors driving the 1989 revolutions in both countries.

In Romania, the strong dissatisfaction with Ceauşescu's dictatorial regime burst into mass protests in Timisoara. They were spurred by Hungarian Reformed Church pastor Laszlo Tőkes, who challenged the authorities with a series of statements in defense of human and nationality rights and played a leading role in efforts to defend the rights of the Hungarian ethnic minority. His criticism was especially sharp on the issue of the Ceauşescu regime's rural resettlement project, described by Tőkes as a threat to the values and the heritage of all communities and as an attempt by the regime to eliminate the peasantry as a social class. The National Salvation Front (NSF) was quick to promise a radical change of the former policy of assimilation and aggressive nationalism. In a declaration issued on January 5, 1990, within two weeks of its assumption to power, the NSF announced that it was necessary "to elaborate constitutional guarantees for the individual and collective rights of ethnic minorities," that it intended to establish a Ministry for Ethnic Minorities, and that the Hungarian cultural and educational institutions abolished by Ceauşescu would be reinstated.[4] However, Romanian fears that the demands of the Hungarian minority for more cultural autonomy, and especially education in its native language, were part of Budapest's design to revive territorial claims on Transylvania were used by nationalists to raise the level of inter-ethnic tension. As a result came the clashes in March 1990 in Tirgu Mureş, in which several people were killed and hundreds were injured.

In Bulgaria, a decision of the Central Committee of the Communist Party on December 29, 1989, which condemned the previous policy of forcible assimilation and restored the civil rights of Turks and

Muslims, provoked two weeks of protests mainly among Bulgarians in areas of mixed population. A serious effort was needed to restore peace and order. For this purpose, a provisional body representing organizations from the entire political spectrum was created (the Social Council of Citizens), which, after three days of heated discussions, worked out a compromise on future policies toward minorities. The main points in this compromise were that it restated the rights of Muslims "to choose their own names, practice Islam, observe traditional customs, and speak Turkish in everyday life." In addition, however, it recommended that any separatist or autonomist organizations among the minorities be banned and that the status of Bulgarian as the official language should be preserved. On January 15, 1990, the National Assembly approved a declaration reiterating the main points agreed by the Council. It also established a 30-member commission to study the problem of nationalities in detail.[5]

The brief outline of these "opening acts" of the revolutions in Romania and Bulgaria gives enough evidence that nationalism became firmly established in the political scene of both countries. The force and violence of nationalism's resurgence all over Eastern Europe, but especially in the Balkans, showed that the task of taming it is critical to surmounting the damage of the communist legacy and for building liberal democracy.

There is a serious amount of perplexity in the West when it comes to grasping the contents and the motives of Balkan nationalism, a nationalism that is draining resources and energies needed to resolve other issues. In his effort to sort out and explain reviving nationalism in Eastern Europe, J.F. Brown suggested the following classification of nationalisms: ethnic, protective, territorial, separatist, emotive, religious, and—finally—economic (in the sense that deteriorating economic factors are exacerbating ethnic and minority problems).[6] All these manifestations of nationalism have their place in Southeastern Europe, because Balkan nationalism has many faces and springs from different, usually contradictory, sources.

Its first major characteristic is that Balkan peoples are "belated nations," in that they were only able to establish their nation-states in the 19th century or even in the early 20th century, which is one of the reasons for the delayed ethnic self-identification. Apart from this, the long coexistence in multiethnic formations such as the Habsburg and Ottoman Empires created conditions for great ethnic diversity, making the drawing of state boundaries extremely difficult. This encouraged the territorial expansionism of the young, highly nationalistic Balkan states.

Another factor in the persistent presence of nationalism in the area is that the historical development of the young Balkan states was strongly dependent on the interests and the designs of the Great Powers. The present political map of Southeastern Europe is a product of the Congress of Berlin in 1878, of the Treaties of London and Bucharest after the Balkan Wars in 1913, and of the system of peace treaties devised in Paris after World War I. According to the existing diplomatic practice at that time, small Balkan states were reduced to objects in a great geostrategic game. Within this historical context, the states in the Balkans are a product of a clash of geopolitical interests and a gross violation of the principle of self-determination proclaimed by US President Woodrow Wilson. Today, history is presenting a list of bills for settlement, but there is a reluctance from some in the West to accept a share of responsibility.

Historical developments have combined the social, economic, and cultural underdevelopment of the region with a high level of inter-ethnic and religious tension, interstate mistrust, and hypersensitivity concerning sovereignty and territorial integrity. In the Balkans more than anywhere else in Europe, the problem of ethnic groups or minorities is openly or covertly connected with geostrategic concerns, such as territories, boundaries, and communications, among others.

In postcommunist Balkan societies, two parallel processes are taking place. The first is the very natural desire of ethnic groups to redefine their position within the state; the second is the susceptibility of the majority to the appeals of nationalism, explained partly by "the discrepancy between the immensity of the reconstruction tasks facing the East Europeans and their political, economic, and moral capacity to cope with them."[7] To this should be added the strong temptation of former communists "to use or rather abuse nationalism in unfavorable situations"—a problem that will receive special attention later in this chapter.

For Bulgarians and Romanians, the last two to three years have been a time when they realized that on the long cherished road to Europe there is one peculiar barrier: the substantial discrepancy between their strong feelings of renewed national identification and the ideas circulating in the West that the concept of the nation-state is obsolete, having lost both of its original meanings—the melting pot and the ethnic state. Thus both countries were confronted with the complex problem of the role of ethnic minorities in a nation-state, a problem that involves the most sensitive elements of international law, national legislation, and political practice. The dilemma is how to strike a balance between granting all rights to ethnic minorities— meeting West European standards in the organization of civil and political life—on the one hand, and maintaining national cohesion and sovereignty on the other.

Since the solution of this dramatic dilemma draws much of the attention and the energies of both the Bulgarian and Romanian societies, it seems relevant to explore those aspects of the problem that in our opinion touch the heart of the matter. They include popular feelings defined as nationalism; the forms in which the former communists misuse these feelings; the idiosyncrasy of the parliamentary and legislative acts on ethnic and minority matters; the role of ethnic parties in both countries; and the most decisive problems on which there is a conflict of interests between the majority and the minority of the population.

2. THE ROLE OF NATIONALISM

A. NATIONALISM IN BULGARIA

As was already mentioned, Balkan nationalism has various meanings and manifestations. The most important characteristic of Bulgarian nationalism today is that it is still oriented inwards, that is, public attention in the last three years has been engaged mainly with the problem of Turks and other Muslims in Bulgaria (and not with the problem of Macedonia, for example, which used to be a priority concern until World War II). From this perspective, certain anti-Turkish sentiments and prejudices, which have their origins in the period of Ottoman rule lasting from the 14th to the 19th century, play a dominant role. Towards the end of that period, Bulgarian nationalism constituted a powerful political force that established the notion of a distinct Bulgarian identity, including a Bulgarian Orthodox Church separate from that of the Greek Orthodox Church. Nationalism was in large part responsible for the April Uprising of 1876, which led to the revival of Bulgarian sovereignty and the creation of the modern Bulgarian national state after the Russo-Turkish war of 1877–1878. As a political force, Bulgarian nationalism grows from the strong conviction that the Ottoman conquest greatly impeded Bulgaria's political, economic, and cultural development and separated it from the European mainstream by introducing an alien, Asiatic culture and religion into the Balkan peninsula. As a result, Bulgarian nationalism has incorporated strong anti-Turkish stereotypes, which are most visible in history textbooks and scholarly research, where the role of the Turkish minority is quite hidden among the anti-Turkish exploits of Bulgarian national heroes.

Bulgarian fears and concerns connected with the Turkish minority today also have demographic and political dimensions. The Muslim population in Bulgaria—which consists of ethnic Turks, Roma,[8] and Bulgarian Muslims (Pomaks)—has quite a high birth rate, while that of the ethnic Bulgarian population is in fact decreasing. This has encouraged fears of gradual "Turkification" and "Islamization" of Bulgaria, especially among Bulgarians from certain parts of northeastern and southeastern Bulgaria, where the majority of Turks are situated, particularly in the countryside. Being a local minority in some areas, ethnic Bulgarians fear that they will be economically disadvantaged or even that they will be forced at some point to abandon their homes and property.

Even stronger concerns among wider groups of ethnic Bulgarians are connected with the role Turkey can play in inter-ethnic relations inside Bulgaria. Turkey's growing role as a new regional center of power since the collapse of the USSR, and its rapidly growing population (70 million persons by the year 2000), are viewed by many in Bulgaria as a threat. Besides, the traditional Bulgarian opinion that Bulgaria is more civilized and European than Turkey combines with the conservative belief that Turkey will not be able to reach West European standards in democracy, civic culture, and market economy. Because of this, most Bulgarians are unwilling to accept it as a developmental model or as an ally. At the same time, there exists a genuine fear among the majority of the ethnic Bulgarian population that granting collective rights to ethnic Turks would be the first step towards cultural and political autonomy and to a powerful increase in Ankara's influence on Bulgarian domestic affairs. Many Bulgarians still suspect Turkey of harboring territorial designs on Bulgaria, and a constant source of Bulgarian concern has been the large number of troops Turkey keeps stationed near the Bulgarian border. It should be noted, however, that apart from the forcible assimilation campaign in 1984–1989, Turks and Bulgarians have lived peacefully together, although they had separate and unequal lives. Nationalism is not a product of the social environment in the regions with mixed populations, but rather has been introduced from outside for political reasons. Recent research has shown that individuals from one group usually respond positively to individuals from the other; on this level there is no confrontation.[9]

Besides, Bulgarians have given evidence of a more tolerant attitude toward their ethnic and religious minorities than have other Balkan nations. During World War II, the Bulgarian government did not allow some 50,000 Bulgarian Jews to be deported to concentration camps. Minorities like Jews and Armenians are well incorporated in political and public life and as a rule there are no strong xenophobic sentiments or anti-Semitism.

Against this background, the Bulgarian Communist Party, re-named the Bulgarian Socialist Party (BSP), devised a diversified strategy of using nationalism for its own political ends. It relied strongly on local party nomenklatura who were trying to escape responsibility for the forcible assimilation of Bulgarian Turks and Muslims, and sought ways to defend their survival and privileges. Another group susceptible to nationalistic rhetoric were ethnic Bulgarians in predominantly Muslim areas. Along with the understandable concerns about maintaining their own rights, there also existed a group among them who profiteered unscrupulously during the Turkish exodus in mid-1989 and who were afraid of losing their gains. The BSP supported, created, and actively encouraged different nationalist formations. It is indicative that the most influential nationalist organization, the Committee for the Defense of National Interests, and its political wing, the Fatherland Party of Labor, joined ranks with the BSP in the October 1991 elections and managed to get representation within the BSP parliamentary group. Of the other two nationalist parties, the Bulgarian National Radical Party received 1.13% of the total in the October 1991 elections and the Bulgarian National Democratic Party 0.28%.[10] These are small numbers, but the relatively higher political influence of the latter lies in its nationalist weekly, *Zora*, although it does not have even one-tenth of the circulation of its closest Romanian counterpart, *Romania Mare*.[11]

As can be seen from the figures, the influence and the role of the nationalistic parties are quite limited. In reality, the main champion of nationalism remained the BSP. In its fight for votes, it revived archaic notions and mutual distrust, and increased the alienation between different segments of the Bulgarian population. During the October 1991 elections, the BSP became the major rival of the predominantly Turkish party, the Movement for Rights and Freedoms (MRF), in areas with mixed population, leaving the Union of Democratic Forces (UDF) on the sidelines.

BSP tactics of manipulating notions of Bulgarian national interests and the "Turkish threat," however, are only part of a flexible, Machiavellian policy for survival and for securing a decisive role on the political scene. The other side of the coin is the mobilization of "popular fronts," mirroring the frequently successful communist tactics of the 1930s. The BSP was the force behind the registration of the MRF for the June 1990 elections, in order to divert votes from the UDF. Some time later, in the changed political circumstances, these former antagonists on explosive ethnic and minority issues became allies and the "unholy coalition" between the BSP and the MRF voted out Bulgaria's first noncommunist government of Filip Dimitrov, standing behind the formation of Lyuben Berov's cabinet of technocrats in the closing months of 1992.

All in all, nationalism in Bulgaria does not have the same intensity that it does in other neighboring countries. It is a constant undercurrent in politics, yet it is a somewhat elusive political force. There are almost no representatives in the National Assembly who would publicly describe themselves as nationalists. While there are still strong controversies on particular political issues dealing with minorities, all major parties are convinced that rights of minorities must be safeguarded by law. The slow but steady process of rebuilding ethnic relations, together with the widespread dislike of shady maneuvers in the name of national ideals or of frequent invocation of the name of Bulgaria for political purposes, will effectively circumscribe the field and the potential for further manipulations.

B. NATIONALISM IN ROMANIA

Romanian nationalism is a more powerful and destructive force. It is intricately connected with anti-Hungarian feelings, which have deep historical and psychological roots. At a Romanian-American symposium on inter-ethnic relations, along with the "fundamentally different interpretations of the nature of the problem," it also became clear that the national majority is showing "hypersensitivity concerning national identity and ethnic Romanian (majority) rights." The peculiar siege mentality and the perception that Romanians are "one ethnic group in the midst of a struggle for basic rights with other ethnic groups"[12] indicates a level of national insecurity reminiscent of that which existed in 1918. This impression proves Wagner's thesis that contemporary nationalist feelings in the public debate are returning the country to a dilemma recurrently faced by the modern Romanian state since its foundation in 1919.[13]

By the Treaties of Saint Germain and Trianon, Romania annexed the territories of Bukovina, Transylvania, Maramureş, Eastern Banat, and others, doubling its size and population.[14] In this way, Romania became a conglomeration of regions differing substantially in their ethnic and cultural characteristics, with minorities accounting for 25% of the population. In spite of this, the modern Romanian state, according to the constitution of 1923, was conceived as a centralized nation-state, that is, the state of the Romanians. The political and legislative line aimed at building an ethnically homogeneous nation-state has been applied uninterruptedly until the present and has created in the mind of the majority a deep-seated notion that the "Romanian land" historically belongs to Romanians, while all the rest of the ethnic groups are only guests.[15] This notion is in contrast with ethnic realities, especially in Transylvania, where Hungarians, Romanians, and Germans have lived together for centuries.

A most sensitive aspect of Romanian-Hungarian relations is the fact that the Treaty of Paris of 1947 endorsed Romanian frontiers of January 1, 1941, with the exception of the Romanian-Hungarian frontier. The Vienna Award of August 30, 1940, was annulled and Romania once again annexed the whole of Transylvania.[16] The insoluble problem of dividing Transylvania historically, ethnically, or otherwise, and the fact of its incorporation within the Romanian state, explain why almost every demand of the Hungarian minority is regarded by Romanians as a territorial question and a sign of Hungarian irredentism. For its part, Hungary has accorded the issue of the rights of the Hungarian minority in Romania a central role in bilateral relations. Because of its concern mainly about Hungarians in Transylvania, Hungary has turned to international forums for support, seeking to have the concept of collective rights codified in international documents. This official political line is strongly opposed by Romania, which maintains that there are no problems in its treatment of minorities and that the minority issue is a purely internal affair.

Another reason for Romanian hypersensitivity is the fact that immediately after World War II broad minority rights were granted to the Hungarian minority in Transylvania in order to ease ethnic tension and avoid sharp controversies between Romania and Hungary. From this perspective, contemporary demands of the Hungarian minority have their justification in the recent historical past. In July 1950, a Hungarian Autonomous District was established in Transylvania with Tirgu Mureş as the district center. A system of schools and universities, financed by the Romanian state, was created to educate students in Hungarian. A network of Hungarian cultural institutions was functioning, and the Hungarian language was put on a par with the official Romanian language in the district. In 1960, however, the Hungarian Autonomous Region was renamed the Mureş Autonomous Region, its autonomy was minimalized, and, through partial redistricting, the Hungarian ethnic presence was reduced. After a general territorial reorganization in 1968, the Mureş Autonomous Region ceased to exist, and the state-organized process of increasing the number of ethnic Romanians in areas where the Hungarian ethnic element prevailed intensified. A further step in this direction was the rural resettlement project of 1988, the goal of which was to alter regional structures, considerably reduce the number of villages, and ultimately effect a comparatively painless assimilation of minority populations, in the first place Hungarians.[17]

While during the first stages of the Romanian revolution there were some manifestations of solidarity between citizens of different ethnic backgrounds, it soon became obvious that the nationalism of the ethnic majority was the prevailing popular sentiment. Romanian nationalism concentrated on minorities and distorted the substance of the public debate. Minorities found themselves again in a defensive position, and the totalitarian establishment, with the connivance of the National Salvation Front, gradually returned to positions comparable to those of the former regime. The NSF began to frequently use the "Hungarian threat" in order to divert attention from pressing issues of democratization. Nationalism became part of what the democratic opposition and many in the West perceived "as simulated democratization, behind which the NSF intended to perpetuate its domination over Romania's political structures."[18]

In May 1990, the NSF scored an overwhelming victory in the general elections, primarily because of the skillful manipulation of anti-communist and nationalist symbols. It openly sided with the extreme nationalist and anti-Hungarian positions of Vatra Romaneasca (Romanian Cradle), an organization of Romanians living in Transylvania that was backed by former members of the Securitate and that played a definite role in the ethnic clashes in Tirgu Mureş. Several prominent sympathizers of this organization were coopted by the NSF and elected on its lists in May 1990.[19] Part of the NSF tactics of strong reliance on chauvinism was the publishing of the weekly *Romania Mare*. Matei Calinescu and Vladimir Tismaneanu describe it in the following way: "With its anti-Semitic and anti-Hungarian outbursts, as well as unmitigated nostalgia for the times of dictatorial 'law and order' as opposed to the ongoing 'democratic cacophony,' *Romania Mare* represents an extreme version of the populist, chauvinistic ideology favored by the NSF leaders."[20] The nationalist line of *Romania Mare* is highly popular, and its circulation (estimated at around 600,000) is by far the largest among the hundreds of weeklies that sprang up after the revolution.

Nationalist sentiments, and the perceived Hungarian threat to the national integrity of Romania, formed the background from which a variety of political parties emerged. These parties have more relative weight than in any other East European country. One peculiarity is that nationalistic parties and movements represent groups of voters connected both with the legacy of the former dictatorial regime of Ceauşescu and with the new democratic opposition.

Among such nationalistic parties are the Party of Romanian

National Unity (PRNU), which is the political branch of Vatra Romaneasca, and the Greater Romania Party (GRP), which was formed around the weekly of the same name, *Romania Mare* (Greater Romania).[21] Both parties seek to restore "national communism." They openly show great admiration of Ceauşescu's discriminatory policies toward the Hungarian ethnic minority in Transylvania. Their xenophobic attitudes are very strong and they are known to have close links to the former Securitate and its successor, the Romanian Information Service. In the local elections on February 23, 1992, the ultranationalist PRNU won a decisive victory in Cluj, the capital of Transylvania.[22] While the immediate reason for PRNU's victory was the severe communal tension over educational provisions for the Hungarian minority, the results in Cluj are quite indicative of NSF efforts to promote nationalism as a means of disabling the mainstream opposition and of ultranationalists' chances in an atmosphere of economic uncertainty and low-level ethnic suspicions.

On the other side of the political spectrum are parties with nationalistic orientations that fully reject the communist era and are part of the democratic mainstream. Indicative of the level of the Romanian-Hungarian inter-ethnic tension was the decision of Radu Campeanu (leader of the National Liberal Party and a candidate for the presidency, the person for whom the Hungarian electorate in Transylvania voted en masse in the presidential elections) to take his party out of the opposition umbrella Democratic Convention in order to exploit for electoral purposes the anti-Hungarian sentiments, which could hardly be used within an organization that included the party of ethnic Hungarians, the Hungarian Democratic Federation of Romania (HDFR).[23]

Another alarming fact was the foundation of the Movement for Romania in December 1991, whose advocates return "to the genuine roots of Romanian right-wing activism" and which is accused by its adversaries of aiming to revive the interwar fascist Iron Guard.[24] The danger here is that its leader, Marian Munteanu, a prominent victim of the miners' raid on Bucharest in June 1990, has much greater credibility than the leader of the GRP, Corneliu Tudor, one of the most compromised of Ceauşescu's former worshippers.

Further gains by nationalists in Romania in the September 1992 elections, together with the temptation for any party to play the nationalist card, has created a dangerous situation in this country and made the protection of the rights of the Hungarian minority problematic. Some observers believe that things are at rock bottom in Transylvania: "Hungarian language kindergartens and universities remain closed, the number of schools is declining and even basic

cultural activities are proscribed."[25] Recently, the Romanian government appointed ethnic Romanian prefects in the predominantly
Hungarian regions of Harghita and Covasna, which is a new cause for
confrontation and a matter of serious concern for the Hungarians
there.

3. CODIFICATION OF MINORITY
RIGHTS AND THE ROLE OF ETHNIC PARTIES

The serious violations of the rights of minorities in Romania and
Bulgaria before 1989, and the need to incorporate ethnic groups into
the new political systems of both countries while developing their
cultural identities, brought to the political scene ethnic parties whose
mere existence was strongly questioned and opposed by nationalists.
Ethnic parties' agendas were originally limited to the area of minority
rights protection, and little attention was paid to economic and social
problems. Furthermore, the emergence of ethnic parties and their
narrow political agendas further stimulated certain negative processes
of ethnocentrism, the closing-off of minority communities, and inter-
ethnic alienation. The activism of ethnic parties, pressure both from
West European states and institutions and from neighboring countries
like Turkey and Hungary, and conflicting views within the internal
political spectrum have produced in the last few years idiosyncratic
national legislation concerning ethnic problems.

A. MINORITY RIGHTS AND ETHNIC PARTIES IN BULGARIA

In Bulgaria, the desire of the first several governments after November 1989 to distance themselves from the legacy of Zhivkov's Bulgarization campaign was combined with the realization that the degree of
Western political and economic support was likely to depend on
Bulgarian policies toward the country's ethnic minorities. Thus, the
first legislative steps were connected with the restoration of the rights
of ethnic Turks and other Muslims. A law on the restoration of Turkish
names was passed in March 1990;[26] several months later it was
amended to allow Muslims further freedoms in their choice of names.
By March 1991, 600,000 Bulgarian Turks, Pomaks, Roma, Tatars, and
other Turkish-speaking ethnic groups restored their previous names.[27]
Another law (June 1991) amnestied all persons sued in connection
with the assimilation campaign of 1984–1989. Two decrees approved
by the Council of Ministers (no. 29, 1990; no. 170, 1991) and the
so-called Dogan Act (1992) constituted an indemnity package dealing
with housing, property, and employment of Bulgarian citizens who

emigrated to Turkey in 1989 and later returned. In conformity with these acts, no less than 3,000 houses were returned to their previous owners. This required "enormous efforts" but it led more or less to the settlement of this explosive issue.[28] By the end of 1990, an Islamic Institute to teach Muslim culture was founded in Sofia, and several Muslim high schools were opened in the country. Soon after, the first re-established Turkish-language newspaper began appearing, followed by several others.

The process of granting human and civil rights to ethnic groups and minorities has been, however, uneven. The Bulgarian government had to stick to a step-by-step approach because of serious difficulties and strong controversies. In judicial practice, the accepted principle is that Bulgaria is a unitary nation-state. There is also a conviction that national security would be challenged if the existence of minorities were officially declared. Thus in political practices and in national legislation the term *national minority* is not used. The main arguments for avoiding its usage are: (1) this term has not been defined by international law, the leading principle of which after World War II has been the defense of individual human rights; (2) if the specific characteristics of each and every ethnic group in Bulgaria are not taken into consideration, there is a danger of an artificial unification of such groups on the basis of one feature, which will lead to the violation of the principles of equality and nondiscrimination; and (3) the official recognition of the term would create grounds for claims that go beyond the sphere of human rights and touch the political aspects of interstate relations.

A significant number of Bulgarian political activists point out that the term *national minority* does not exist in the bilateral and multilateral treaties that Bulgaria has signed with other countries. For them, the idea that affiliation of persons with different minorities should be a matter of individual choice is unacceptable because that could encourage Roma, Pomaks, and Tatars to identify themselves as Turks. Therefore, they suggest that the criteria for minority identification should not be the self-consciousness of individuals but objective historical circumstances. The Bulgarian government and most of the political parties so far rely on individual rights as the basis for dealing with the issue of ethnic groups and exclude the possibility of recognizing collective rights for minorities.[29]

This way of thinking, backed mainly by the BSP, has found expression in the new Bulgarian constitution, which was approved on July 12, 1991.[30] Though the rights and freedoms listed are extensive, all provisions still refer to the rights of individuals, and the word *minority* has been carefully omitted. Moreover, political parties based on ethnicity, race, or religion, as well as associations or religious societies that have "political aims" or engage in "political activities," are prohibited by the constitution. Parallel to this, in an attempt to accommodate human rights demands, the constitution explicitly bans persecution and assimilation, guarantees cultural and religious freedoms, and recognizes the rights of citizens for whom the Bulgarian language is not a mother tongue to study in their own language.

Though still dominant, this way of thinking is not the only one. The presidency and some representatives of the Union of Democratic Forces are suggesting some corrections to allow further liberalization of minority rights. In their opinion, the article in the constitution banning ethnic parties is discriminatory. Besides, it is formulated in a way that puts its applicability in question because it is in contradiction with the International Covenant on Civil and Political Rights and with the constitution itself, where conformity with international law is required.[31]

The differences in approach can be well illustrated by the teaching of Turkish in Bulgarian schools, which has been a source of serious tension among the three main political forces, the BSP, the UDF, and the MRF. On October 1, 1991, the predominantly BSP Parliament passed a Law on Public Education, legislating that Turkish can be taught only outside of state schools.[32] One month later, after the October 13 elections, the newly appointed Minister of Science and Education in the UDF government, finding out that most schools in Bulgaria are controlled by the municipalities and not by the state, instituted Turkish instruction in Bulgaria's public schools on an extracurricular basis. The MRF, for its part, insists that Turkish should be introduced as part of the regular curriculum in all Bulgarian schools.

A significant role for the promotion of human rights policies toward minorities was played by the Movement for Rights and Freedoms, whose political platform is based on strong defense of the rights of Bulgaria's Turkish and Muslim population. The MRF demanded legal protection for minorities in conformity with international law, political rights, active participation at all levels of local and government structures, and guarantees for their cultural and linguistic identity. In this way, the MRF successfully mobilized the nearly unanimous support of ethnic Turks and some groups of the other Muslims. In the course of time, thanks to the patient and flexible approach of its leadership, it has managed to become a decisive force in the Bulgarian political arena.

The movement started its activities openly on January 4, 1990,[33] although its leaders claim that their underground organization functioned since 1985 and that they organized the antigovernment protests in parts of eastern Bulgaria in May 1989. The MRF is a secular organization, rejecting the fundamentalist idea that Islam is incompatible with democracy and strongly defending the principle that the solution of minority problems and the development of democracy are intertwined. According to the MRF, the rights of the different ethnic groups will be better guaranteed if they acquire official status as minorities and if the collective rights of minorities are set out in national legislation. In this way, minorities can more successfully promote and achieve their group demands. From this perspective, the MRF sharply criticized the Bulgarian constitution for insufficiently protecting minority rights, especially the part of it that bans political parties on grounds of ethnicity. A target of strong criticism and dissatisfaction among the Turkish minority group has also been the problem of Turkish-language instruction.

While insisting on collective rights and fighting for cultural autonomy, the MRF has explicitly declared that it is categorically against the idea of political autonomy, considering it harmful for the integration of the Bulgarian nation and for the struggle of Muslims to preserve their ethnic and religious identity.[34] In a recently published book, the leader of MRF, Ahmed Dogan, went further to explain that the right of minorities can be safeguarded only if the rights of all Bulgarian citizens are guaranteed. Thus the MRF's priority of defending human rights is not in contradiction but rather in harmony with the principle of guaranteeing national integrity and sovereignty.[35]

The MRF's organizational structure consists of a Central Council, district administrative bureaus, and local committees. By March 31, 1993, the MRF had some 95,000 members organized in 800 to 900 branches and 22 regional offices throughout the country. The MRF weekly *Prava i Svobodi* (Rights and Freedoms) also has an edition in Turkish, but is mainly distributed by MRF members.[36]

In the June 1990 elections, the MRF won 23 of the 400 parliamentary seats and became the third largest force in a Parliament strongly polarized between the BSP and the UDF. In the next national elections, however, a very specific situation arose. According to the new constitution and the election law, the MRF was not recognized legally, on the grounds that it represented ethnic and religious interests. It sought to gain recognition as a political party but was refused this status by the Sofia City Court. Some time later, the Central Electoral Commission and the Bulgarian Supreme Court sanctioned the participation of the MRF in the national and local elections in October 1991. This created a peculiar contradiction between the provisions of the constitution and concrete political practice, a possible explanation of which is as follows. On one hand, the Supreme Court yielded to international pressure in "an attempt to please the Western world"[37] and to gain support for Bulgaria's integration with Western institutions, mainly the Council of Europe. On the other hand, it became clear even to conservative and nationalistic forces in Bulgaria that prohibiting a party with authority and well-established connections among the Muslim population would immediately increase ethnic tension and revive memories and stereotypes from the recent past.[38]

After its legal reestablishment on the Bulgarian political scene, the MRF continued slowly but steadily to increase its relative weight and influence. With 24 parliamentary deputies (out of 240 seats in the National Assembly) after the October 1991 elections and with more than 1,000 local councillors, 650 village mayors, and 20 district mayors, the MRF was established firmly as the third largest political force in the country and managed to add another percentage point to its 1990 vote.[39] The election results, according to which the UDF did not win an absolute majority in the Parliament, created a situation where the UDF had to depend strongly on the MRF support. The UDF and the MRF managed in the beginning to agree on basic policy issues, and decided that no MRF representatives would be included in the UDF cabinet in order to avoid stirring up anti-Turkish nationalism.

In the presidential elections in January 1992, the MRF supported the UDF candidate Zhelev. The very narrow margin with which Zhelev won against his BSP opponent (52.85% to 47.15%) speaks in support of the thesis that Zhelev won thanks to the support of Turks and Muslims in Bulgaria.

The strong polarization of Bulgarian society, and the absence of a well-defined center, produced as a result a simple two-party model, with the BSP and the UDF confronting each other on most of the issues arising in the process of democratization. Under these circumstances, the MRF acquired the very delicate but responsible position of holding the balance of power. At first, the movement gave little reason to suspect that it would exhibit independent behavior, and this perception created a false security among UDF leaders that the balance of power was unshakable. In the course of time, however, the MRF clearly showed its desire to play a more important role and to participate more actively in policy making on all levels of the administration and government. As a result mainly of the shift in the MRF's political behavior, the elected chairman of the Parliament, Stefan Savov, and the first noncommunist cabinet of Filip Dimitrov, had to resign.

The explanations for this shift of behavior are several. According to Mihail Ivanov, President Zhelev's adviser on ethnic and religious matters, many MRF voters had become increasingly dissatisfied with the party's earlier, more passive policy. Many of them are inhabitants of the underdeveloped mountainous and semi-mountainous regions in southern Bulgaria where unemployment is very high. As a result of this, during the last year there has been a mass emigration of Bulgarian Turks to Turkey. In Ivanov's opinion, the necessity of adjusting its policies to the needs of its voters is the way to understand the MRF's behavior in the last months of 1992, while the governmental crisis was a proof that the multiparty system in Bulgaria is functioning normally.[40]

Another explanation is that Turkey, which has economic problems of its own, has an interest in keeping ethnic Turks inside Bulgaria and strongly opposes any developments encouraging this ethnic group to leave Bulgaria and settle in Turkey. In a statement in October 1992, Turkish Prime Minister Demirel said that since the beginning of the year his country had received 160,000 Bulgarian Turks.[41] Turkey's negative stand, motivated by the fact that this would cause increasing troubles for its economy, currently in turmoil, and by the concern that this could also reduce Turkey's influence in Bulgarian politics, most probably influenced the MRF's assessment of this problem.

A very different explanation of the MRF's change of orientation has been suggested by the UDF. Its deputies claim that the key figures from the BSP maintained control over the actions of the MRF leadership mainly through the use of police files from the former state security service.[42] The fact that President Zhelev maintained close contact with the MRF's leader Dogan throughout the governmental crisis, and that the appointed head of the new nonparty "government of experts," Lyuben Berov, was a former adviser of the president, strengthen the UDF view that Zhelev was the chief instigator behind the fall of the UDF government in late October.

The most recent developments, which led to a high degree of political fragmentation and to the slowing down of the pace of reform, make the assessment of the role of the MRF more difficult. It is true that "the ethnic Turks have reacted to all the ordeals inflicted upon them with extreme forebearance," that the MRF "has acted very prudently by neutralizing extremist elements in its own camp,"[43] and that "the MRF has in the main struck firmly to the line of reasonable action and calmness in the face of all provocation, thus acting as a powerful stabilizing factor."[44] There are signs, however, that the MRF has introduced authoritarian discipline within its own ranks, that it played some role in the further alienation of certain groups of Pomaks from the Bulgarian ethnos, and that its policies are nontransparent and quite unpredictable.

The MRF's role and influence come mainly as a result of the monolithic support of the Turkish community. The current political developments in Bulgaria made it a more powerful force than its own electorate, and because of this the MRF became the most interested party in the postponement of new elections as long as possible. It also began to strive for acceptance as a non-ethnic political force. Whether it can achieve this aim is quite dubious. Within this context, however, it successfully circumscribed the occasional acts of embryonic Islamic fundamentalism, and its policies are evolving from the single issue of minority rights to a broader platform addressing a wider range of concerns.

MRF leader Dogan claims that his party "has shifted the balance of power in the Balkans," having in mind mainly Bulgaria's foreign policy orientation and its relations with Turkey.[45] A more realistic interpretation, however, is that the substantial influence that the MRF wields on Bulgaria's political scene now is the result of the specific dispositions of political forces and most probably will change in future elections. The case of the MRF does not support the thesis that, wherever there are high concentrations of the Turkish and Muslim population, Turkey has ripe opportunities to expand its influence.[46]

B. Minority Rights and Ethnic Parties in Romania

In Romania, the role of the Hungarian party, the Hungarian Democratic Federation of Romania, has been more limited due to the idiosyncracy of the political processes there. The HDFR's political activity is developing within the new legal framework of rights for national minorities.

The new Romanian constitution "recognizes and guarantees the right of conservation, development, and expression of ethnic, cultural, linguistic and religious identity for persons belonging to national minorities," but denies national minorities collective rights and stipulates that "the official language is the Romanian language."[47] Romania's draft constitution became one of the elements of the strong controversy between the HDFR on the one hand and the National Salvation Front and nationalist parties like the Party of Romanian National Unity on the other. The HDFR tried to prevent the passage of articles that could easily be interpreted as discriminatory against minorities. The article that defines Romania as a state that is "national, sovereign and independent, unitary and indivisible" was strongly objected to by

HDFR deputies because of the term "unitary state." It existed in the constitutions of 1923 and 1965 and usually was used as part of an official policy line that held that national minorities did not really exist in Romania.

In the so-called White Paper published by the Romanian Ministry of Foreign Affairs, the rights of minorities granted to them by the Romanian legislation are explicitly enumerated.[48] The Romanian move was a response to criticism in international bodies and more specifically from official circles in Hungary. Among these rights a special emphasis is put on a principle incorporated in the election laws of 1990 and 1992 and in the new constitution, according to which national minorities are entitled to representation in the Chamber of Deputies even if the number of votes is not sufficient to win representation through the regular electoral process. The provision in the constitution, however, stipulates that "citizens of a national minority are entitled to be represented by one organization only," which creates a background for rivalries and contradictions between different organizations within one and the same ethnic group. Since there is no legal mechanism to define which one organization is to be represented in the chamber, some conditions for conformity with the official attitudes on minorities have been created.

The HDFR (or, as it is also known, the Hungarian Democratic Union of Romania), which existed for some time after World War II, was reestablished at the outbreak of the Romanian revolution with the aim of representing the interests of the Hungarian minority in the country. In its first official statements, it appealed to ethnic Hungarians to form branches of the HDFR at local and county levels. While it declared that it would respect the territorial integrity of Romania, the HDFR demanded proportional representation in the legislature and equal educational opportunities in the native language of the minorities.[49]

HDFR membership (reportedly over 500,000 paying members) is organized in a loose structure of local chapters grouped into autonomous county branches. The autonomy enjoyed by local organizations reflects the diversity of interests of different Hungarian communities living in Romania and of their local or professional organizations. For this reason the HDFR also has the features of an umbrella organization covering a number of smaller political parties and other professional and civic groups of the Hungarian minority. The federation executive body is a presidium of 11 members, while the main policy-making body is the Council of Delegates. Attached to it are groups of experts to advise the leadership on policy issues. The HDFR publishes in

Hungarian the daily *Romaniai Magyar Szo* (The Hungarian Word in Romania).[50]

In the first postcommunist elections in May 1990, the HDFR won 7% of the votes and emerged as the number two political force in Parliament after the NSF, and the largest opposition party, with 41 seats in the two chambers of the 515-member Parliament, outstripping the so-called historical parties—the National Liberal Party and the National Peasants Party, which claim to be of pan-national importance.[51] As a result, a number of HDFR senators and deputies were elected chairmen, vice-chairmen, secretaries, and members of different commissions in the Senate and Chamber of Deputies. Also, in the countryside, two prefects, four vice-prefects, and 18 members of prefect offices were appointed—altogether, 6% of the overall number.[52]

Defending the view that the future of the Hungarian minority in Romania is bound up with the democratization of Romanian society, the HDFR actively supported the Romanian democratic opposition. It became a member of the Convention for the Establishment of Democracy and of the Democratic Antitotalitarian Forum, an organization set up to strengthen the influence of the opposition parties on national and local levels.

The political activity of the HDFR, however, was strongly impeded by Romanian nationalists and by extremists within its own ranks. A serious incident occurred in October 1991, when an alleged "political group of the HDFR" demanded a referendum with the aim of the establishment of an "autonomous territory" comprising all the areas inhabited by the Szeklers (Hungarians from the Szekler region). The issue was debated in the Romanian Parliament and contributed significantly to the further deterioration of Romanian-Hungarian inter-ethnic relations.[53]

In this case, as well as in the campaign to depict the HDFR as a security risk to Romania, demands have repeatedly been made for the HDFR to be banned and for a judicial investigation on those of its leaders who are accused of "irredentist" and "separatist" designs. In response, the HDFR leadership declared it was reconsidering its participation in the Parliament in view of the obvious anti-Hungarian bias. The HDFR went further in expressing the dissatisfaction of the Hungarian minority over the fact that Hungarian-language programs on Romanian television had been reduced by more than half and transferred to a channel that cannot be received in most parts of Transylvania.[54] Serious concern was also expressed about the shortage of Hungarian-language schools and teachers, and demands were reiterated for the reestablishment of Hungarian-language instruction at all educational levels and for the restoration of the Hungarian Bolyai University in Cluj and of the former Hungarian research institute in Transylvania.

Within the HDFR, two groups can be discerned, suggesting two different approaches for its political activity. The first one believes that "small steps" can be achieved by working with President Iliescu and the government. The other, represented mainly by younger members, stresses the need "for a conceptual breakthrough" in codifying the legal status of the Hungarian nationality in Romania. At its congress in May 1991, the HDFR reached a consensus that minority rights requiring codification "include the free use of the mother tongue in the administration and the judicial system in minority-inhabited areas; the restoration of the educational system in the mother tongue from kindergarten to university; and proportional minority representation at all levels of administration." The congress also adopted a resolution demanding that both Romanians and Hungarians should be considered "state-building" nations, a status that is seen "as a consequence of the historic fact that both nations are indigenous to Transylvania."[55]

Within the already established political pattern in Romania, these demands gave rise to further accusations from the nationalist camp. Thus, what the HDFR saw as legitimate defense of the collective rights of the Hungarian minority was perceived by Romanian nationalists as a part of "territorial irredentism" supported by Budapest. In response, the HDFR repeatedly has stated its position on the problem of autonomy. While it opposes the pursuit of "territorial autonomy," the HDFR has supported demands for different types of "cultural," "functional," and "local" autonomy. However, in the process of defending its policies against the attacks of Romanian nationalists, the HDFR itself has been undergoing a process of radicalization.

The dimensions of inter-ethnic tension clearly appeared in the parliamentary elections of September 1992. While the HDFR increased its vote marginally, it dropped to being the fifth-strongest faction after the nationalist PRNU in an increasingly nationalistic Parliament. In the absence of a clear-cut working majority and in a situation of general political fluidity, the forces most opposed to change (also known for their extreme nationalism) improved their leverage to dictate the views of the new executive.[56]

4. THE BALANCE SHEET SO FAR

Issues connected with the granting of rights to minorities in Bulgaria and Romania became a priority problem in the process of transformation from totalitarian to civil societies. Former communists were the first to grasp the considerable importance of this set of problems for their survival on the political scene. They actively played the nationalist card for their own political ends, although the rest of the newly emerging political players were not immune to the same kind of temptation. To a different extent, permanently or only in specific cases, all political parties, ethnic ones included, used nationalism to their political advantage. New democratic parties and formations, though much more sympathetic and liberal about minority rights, have so far not been able to develop a coherent policy towards this many-sided issue, mainly because of the immensity of the tasks they have faced in other areas and because of the necessity to comply with the sentiments of their own voters.

These observations are true to a much different extent for Bulgaria and for Romania, because these two countries have chosen two diametrically opposite roads for handling minority issues. While in Romania there has been an escalation of mutual fears, accusations, and overall tension between the ethnic Romanians and the Hungarian minority, Bulgaria started a pragmatic, step-by-step solution to the most explosive issues. The different historical and social backgrounds are only part of the explanation. A very significant role was played also by the substantively different approaches and behavior of the authorities and the representatives of the ethnic parties.

In Romania, the authorities did not clearly distance themselves from ultra-nationalist reactions and activism, nor were there any visible efforts to deter such activities. Minority problems were transferred to a parliamentary commission instead of to a reestablished Ministry for Minorities (such a ministry had existed for several years after 1949), as had been promised at the outset of the revolution. In this way, minority issues were pushed to the periphery and made dependent on complicated parliamentary procedures. On the other hand, Hungarian activists clearly expressed their sympathy towards Budapest, thus increasing the suspicions of Romanian politicians that there is a strong link between the HDFR and Hungary. In addition, the HDFR's demands for autonomy did not contribute to moderation in disputes or to the solution of the problems of the Hungarian minority; quite the opposite, such demands only dramatically increased the tension. The most recent evidence of this was the October 1992 HDFR declaration on local autonomy, which prompted a stormy debate in the Romanian Parliament.

In Bulgaria, the Movement for Rights and Freedoms developed its activities on an entirely different platform. It started a patient, long-term policy of defense of human and minority rights based on strict loyalty to the national sovereignty of Bulgaria. This approach was stimulated by the fact that Turks who returned to Bulgaria from Turkey between 1989 and 1990 tended to associate themselves more closely with the Bulgarian state than with Turkey.[57] In the opinion of Mehmed Hogha, a leading member of the MRF and a chairman of the Commission on Human Rights in the Bulgarian Parliament, the key to the MRF's political success is rooted in the fact that its leaders never forgot that they had to pursue their political purposes in the Balkan area, where ethnic and national consciousness is heavily burdened with prejudices and hostilities. For this reason, any workable policy has to be constructive without any hint of extremism, separatism, or bias in favor of some neighboring country. It should be a policy that "in behavior and action" provides convincing evidence that the struggle for minority rights can be achieved only by peaceful means, and must manifest a genuine concern for the nonviolation of the rights of the main ethnos in the country. Hogha pointed out that the fear of pan-Islamism is common to Bulgaria and Turkey. Thus a mechanism has to be built to check any tendency in this direction. In Bulgaria, this is a manageable task because the role of religious fanaticism is quite limited.[58] Following this line of behavior, the MRF isolated and dissassociated itself from the legally unrecognized Turkish Democratic Party, known for its extremism and pan-Turkism.

Another specific feature of the MRF's concept and political practice was its endeavors to overcome the limitations of an ethnic party by diversifying its ethnic membership. Declaring that it is an open organization, the MRF was able to attract some groups of Roma and Pomaks and a certain number of ethnic Bulgarians. The latter played an important role in the realization of MRF policies. Two out of three chairmen of commissions and also the deputy-chairman of the Commission for National Security in the National Assembly who are members of the MRF are ethnic Bulgarians. Also, the deputy prime minister in the present government of Lyuben Berov, a member of the MRF, is an ethnic Bulgarian.

On the other hand, the Bulgarian authorities, especially President Zhelev, have managed to play an impartial mediating role between nationalists and ethnic Turks. They pursued a well-balanced and realistic policy based on strong political will for an objective evaluation of internal minority issues and for finding a reasonable solution, so that the preservation of the unity and integrity of the state can go hand-in-hand with the creation of opportunities for the development of ethnic, cultural, and religious diversities.

Easing ethnic tension was helped when Bulgarian Turks were given the right to travel to Turkey and to practice Islam. Another important and quite specific factor conducive to ethnic reconciliation in Bulgaria that is absent in countries such as Romania and the Republic of Macedonia, is the shared understanding between Bulgarian authorities and MRF leaders of the concept of a "nation" as a political entity, that is, a community of people with different ethnic, religious, and linguistic backgrounds united by the idea of a common state.[59] As a result, the image of the Turkish minority as a threat and potential enemy has been surmounted to a great extent.[60] Gradually, Bulgarian public opinion has begun to see the MRF as a normal and accountable factor on the Bulgarian political scene and not as a Turkish fifth column in Bulgaria. All this made possible the functioning of the present government, which was formed through the MRF's right to nominate the prime minister.

These positive trends do not, however, mean that inter-ethnic harmony has been established in Bulgaria. Persistent views and opposing interests continue to attract public attention and drain political energies needed for other pressing problems. Recently, disputes on ethnic issues have been strongly intensified by the draft European Convention for the Protection of Minorities, which touches the highly controversial issue of individual versus collective rights. In Romania, the polarized views on this document are presented in the most confrontational way. From an international perspective, the dispute exacerbated relations between Romania and Hungary, since the latter is a very active member of the Council of Europe on issues of minority rights and has been deeply involved in the drafting of this document. In Bulgaria, some representatives of the MRF enthusiastically supported its approval by the Parliamentary Assembly of the Council of Europe on February 1, 1993, pointing out that it gives a definition of a minority unique in the framework of international law. They expressed hope that Bulgaria will be among the first countries to sign it and, with this, "all contradictions between the text on minority rights in the Bulgarian constitution and in the European Convention will automatically disappear."[61] The BSP's opinion was that "Europe is offering inadequate prescriptions to domestic illnesses."[62] Some UDF supporters suggested that the European Convention will be helpful to the Bulgarian population in other countries and that it can be accepted on condition that specific Bulgarian conditions are taken into account.[63] The opinion of the presidency was that there cannot be a universal definition of the notion of "national minority," that the Convention in its present form does not correspond to the conditions in the country and this is antithetic to the "Bulgarian model" of solving ethnic problems. Also, fears were expressed that "instead of solving problems the Convention may give rise to new ones" in Bulgaria.[64]

While this dispute is of a more or less theoretical nature, the problem of self-identification of Bulgarian Pomaks has touched even more sensitive and explosive issues. During the last year or so, allegations have increased that under MRF pressure Pomaks (Bulgarian Slavs converted to Islam in the 17th-19th centuries and who still speak Bulgarian) are giving their children Turkish names and sending them to Turkish-language classes. MRF activists also involved them in a school boycott of Turkish children, demanding that Turkish be included in the regular curriculum. The problem was further exacerbated during the December 1992 census when irregularities occurred in connection with answers to questions about the mother tongue of the population. In some municipalities in the Rhodope Mountains inhabited by Pomaks, it was registered that their mother tongue was Turkish even though they were ignorant of the language. In this connection, the BSP daily *Duma* suggested that the census results might have to be invalidated for the municipalities of Yakoruda, Satovcha, Garmen, and Gotse Delchev.[65] Two inquiry commissions and a parliamentary commission were sent in December 1993 to these municipalities, while the Mayor of Satovcha (MRF) was charged with forcible Turkification of the population there.[66] In response, the MRF declared that it "will not permit either the Turkification or the Christianization of the population in western and central Rhodopes" and it will not permit the legal persecution of Satovcha's mayor.[67] In an official document, presidential advisor Mihail Ivanov suggested that, since there are only several isolated cases that do not put into question the census results, an additional check of data on this specific point has to be carried out.[68]

Behind the dispute over census data it is not difficult to discern the struggle for political influence over the Pomaks. They are a peculiar group, among whom three trends of self-identification are visible. Some of these people consider themselves Bulgarians; others, with the development of democratic processes, have begun to identify themselves as Turks. There is also a third subgroup willing to strengthen their Bulgarian Muslim identity as separate from the other two. The reasons for this diversity are many. They are rooted in the continuous alienation of this population from the Bulgarian ethnos, which was stimulated by attempts towards forcible Bulgarization (the last ones being in 1971 and 1973), and by the fact that these people were not accepted as equal by Bulgarians. A significant role was played by deteriorating economic conditions that doomed the regions inhabited by Pomaks to poverty and social tension. The MRF, which is experiencing a substantial drain of its electorate because of the mass emigration of ethnic Turks to Turkey, needs the support of the Pomaks and is seeking to increase its following among them. Bulgarian politicians find this unacceptable and are trying by different means to stop the trends of Pomak self-identification as Turks in the western Rhodopes that developed only recently.

This brief outline of the most recent trends in inter-ethnic relations in Romania and Bulgaria indicates that the prospects facing the HDFR and the MRF are quite different. Because of severe contradictions and Romanian ultranationalism, the HDFR has been notable for defending the rights of the Hungarian minority, as is envisaged in its program. Minority problems in this country continue to impede the processes of democratization, deflecting national attention from the critical economic issues. In this atmosphere of political stagnation, the HDFR has not yet faced the dilemma of what will be its platform and future after basic minority rights are safeguarded. The MRF's role as a critical player in contemporary Bulgarian politics (together with the evolving process of codifying minority rights), coupled with the severe economic problems experienced by the majority of its voters, forced it to face squarely the question of its evolution. Although today the administrative and political power in southeast Bulgaria is almost entirely in the hands of the MRF, it has not been able to find a solution to the desperate economic situation there. The decline of local industries and of the tobacco market have led to the almost total collapse of tobacco-growing, the region's main agricultural activity, and to unemployment, whose rate is among the highest in the country.[69] Whether the MRF will be able to become a pan-national political party is unclear, but it is already obvious that pressing economic problems and its own economic incompetence have provoked strong disappointment among its core voters. Economic factors have also changed its political orientation and priorities. Looking for ways to hold back the new wave of ethnic Turks emigrating to Turkey, the MRF is more active in attempts to amend the new Land Law, pass a law on preferential economic development in mountainous and semi-mountainous regions, and obtain credit from Turkey to these regions. The MRF also came to the conclusion that, since most of its voters are landless and socially weak, it has to pursue a centrist, socially oriented policy line.

The most important minority issues facing Bulgaria and Romania in the process of their democratization show that each case is unique and has to be handled with extreme political caution. For the West, this supports the argument that both countries need "maximum international help and understanding and the more they get of both, the more they can get on with the kind of change that may avert disaster and secure the future."[70]

Minority problems in Bulgaria and in Romania have specific

quality and contents, while the difference in the way ethnic problems are approached in each country are well seen in attitudes of the Council of Europe. Bulgaria was offered full membership in May 1992, but the Council in its eagerness to deal with the minority rights issue has still not welcomed Romania.[71] It is also accepted in the West that the trend in Bulgaria is toward decreasing ethnic tension, and that the ultranationalist forces that took hold of Romanian politics after the September 1992 elections have been voicing their hard-line policy toward the Hungarian minority and Budapest ever louder. These differences may also be seen in the character and the contents of Bulgarian-Turkish and Romanian-Hungarian relations. Bulgaria and Turkey have found a way to solve a number of issues, and cooperation in the economic and military spheres is intensifying, while the problem of the Hungarian minority in Romania makes the signing of a bilateral treaty with Hungary problematic as relations remain tense.

Given this background, West European institutions can do a lot to promote the easing of inter-ethnic tensions and expansion of the process of democratization. The desire of these two countries to be integrated into Europe has already been a powerful lever in the hands of the West. The Council of Europe has taken a very active role in encouraging both governments to introduce democratic reforms and respect human rights. The West should continue condemning nationalist excesses, and should carefully watch developments in these countries in order to be able to play the role of mediator and objective advisor if and when both governments and the minorities accept such a role. To this end, it will be probably useful if some more diversified and flexible international structures are created to deal with minority groups, offering forums where it will be possible for representatives of national majorities, ethnic minorities, and the West to discuss the emerging problems, search for solutions, and learn from the experience of countries that have successfully solved similar problems. Another long-term form of Western aid can be education of individuals involved in ethnic issues.

The problem of whether a minority feels at home within the national state depends not only on legislative guarantees but also on the political and psychological climate among the different parts of the population. This climate has to be regulated through education and exchange of information. It is time for people in Bulgaria and Romania to stop fighting "historical wars" with each other and to look for means of reconciliation through education. The media in both countries, though to a different extent, have played a negative role in increasing the ethnic tensions; mechanisms have to be found to curtail this specific phenomenon. In addition, the principle of the freedom of the press must be strengthened.

The strongest guarantees for minorities are to be found in civic culture and governmental behavior that safeguards their identity. Both Bulgaria and Romania have to find their own ways to balance individual rights with the collective rights of minorities. For example, the article in the Bulgarian constitution prohibiting political parties on ethnic grounds is obsolete and has to be removed.

For both Bulgaria and Romania, incorporating minorities within their political systems and achieving societal harmony will be a long and thorny process and will depend on the overall democratization and economic recovery. Greater understanding and cooperation between the national majorities and the ethnic minorities, together with strict enforcement of human and civil rights legislation, are the only proper approaches.

Minority Population Estimates

	1	2	3	4
Bulgaria*				
(Total population: 8,472,727)				
Turks	700,000	822,253	900,000	1,250,000
Roma	450,000	287,732	800,000	1,000,000
Pomaks	170,000	143,788	300,000	
Romania**				
(Total population: 22,760,449)				
Hungarians		1,619,368		2,500,000
Germans	30,000	111,301		200,000
Roma	200,000	409,723	760,000	7,000,000

1. Lowest available figure; generally not credible.
2. Official or semiofficial figure; of variable credibility.
3. Highest credible figure.
4. Highest available figure; generally not credible.

Sources: Media reports and official publications:
*For Bulgaria the preliminary results of the December 1992 census are from 24 classes, April 4, 1993, and *Demokratsiya*, April 21, 1993.
**For Romania the preliminary results of the January 1992 census are from Romania, Ministry of Foreign Affairs, *White Paper on the Rights of Persons Belonging to National Ethnic, Linguistic or Religious Minorities in Romania* (June 1992), p. 1.

NOTES

1. Since there is no terminological and conceptual precision in the usage of such key notions as ethnicity and minority and because of the controversies these notions arouse between opposing parties, in this chapter *ethnic* and *minority* are used as synonyms. See Sreča Perunović, "Ethnicity as a Theoretical Category," *Europa Ethnica* 49, no. 3 (1992), pp. 134-40; and F. Capotorti, *Study on the Rights of Persons Belonging to Ethnic, Religious and Linguistic Minorities* (New York: United Nations, 1979).

2. Good information and analysis on the overall picture of minorities in Bulgaria and Romania in the 1990s can be found in the works of Hugh Poulton, e.g., *The Balkans: Minorities and States in Conflict* (London: Minority Rights Group, 1991); Duncan Perry, "Minorities and Bulgarian Nationalism," *RFE/RL Report on Eastern Europe*, no. 50 (Dec. 13, 1991), pp. 5–8; Richard Wagner, "Homogenisierung und Selbstbestimmung, Zur Situation der Minderheiten in Rumänien," *Europaeische Rundschau*, no. 2 (1992), pp. 51–61; and Michael Shafir and Dan Ionescu, "Romania—The Minorities in 1991: Mutual Distrust, Social Problems and Disillusion," *RFE/RL Report on Eastern Europe*, no. 50 (Dec. 13, 1991), pp. 24–28.

3. Andre Liebich, "Minorities in Eastern Europe: Obstacles to a Reliable Count," *RFE/RL Research Report*, no. 20 (May 15, 1992), p. 38.

4. For more details, see Judith Pataki, "Free Hungarians in a Free Romania: Dream or Reality?" *RFE/RL Report on Eastern Europe*, no. 8 (Feb. 23, 1990), pp. 20–21.

5. *Darzhaven Vestnik*, no. 6 (1990). See also Stephen Ashley, "Ethnic Unrest During January," *RFE/RL Report on Eastern Europe*, no. 6 (Feb. 9, 1990), pp. 4–11.

6. J.F. Brown, "Crisis and Conflict in Eastern Europe," *RFE/RL Research Report*, no. 22 (May 29, 1992), pp. 7–8.

7. J.F. Brown, "The Resurgence of Nationalism," *RFE/RL Report on Eastern Europe*, no. 24 (June 14, 1991), p. 36.

8. Reportedly 75% of the Roma in Bulgarian are Muslim (Poulton, *The Balkans*, p. 10).

9. For more information, see Georgi Vassilev, "A Real Historical Product" (in Bulgarian), *Pik*, no. 18 (May 5–12, 1993), pp. 14–26; and Ivan Ilchev and Duncan Perry, "Bulgarian Ethnic Groups: Politics and Perceptions," *RFE/RL Research Report*, no. 12 (March 19, 1993), pp. 36–37.

10. *Demokratsiya*, Oct. 22, 1991.

11. For more details about the BSP's use of nationalism, see Kjell Engelbrekt, "Nationalism Reviving," *RFE/RL Report on Eastern Europe*, no. 48 (Nov. 29, 1991), pp. 1–5; Stefan Troebst, "Nationalismus als Demokratisierung-hemmnis in Bulgarien (May 1991-January 1992)," *Südost-Europa* 41, no. 3–4 (1992), pp. 188-227. The latter article, however, mixes up anticommunist rhetoric with anti-Bulgarism and does not give an answer on how a sensible policy on minorities can be achieved with a highly unstable and controversial situation in the country.

12. "Romanian-American Symposium on Inter-Ethnic Relations," Bucharest, June 17–18, 1991, Meeting Report, Project of Ethnic Relations (P.E.R.), pp. 3–5.

13. Wagner, "Homogenisierung und Selbstbestimmung."

14. See G. Georgescu, V. Maciu, D. Tudor, and M. Roller, *Romania intre 1918–1923* (Editura de stat, 1948), p. 557; Krassimira Naumova, *National*

Question, Minorities Problem and Ethnic Conflicts in Romania of Today (1990–1992) (Sofia: Center for the Study of Democracy, 1993), pp. 8–9.

15. Wagner, "Homogenisierung und Selbstbestimmung," p. 57.

16. Gh. Gheorghe, *Tratatele internationale ale Romaniei, 1939-1965* (Bucharest, 1983), p. 100.

17. For more detailed information, see Bennett Kovrig, "The Magyars in Romania: Problems of a Cohabiting Nationality," *Südost-Europa* 35, no. 9 (1986); Aurel Braun, "Structural Changes and Consequences for the Nationalities in Romania," *Südost-Europa* 35, no. 7–8 (1986); and G. Panayotov, *Contemporary Aspects of the National Problem in Romania in National Problems in the Balkans: History and Contemporary Developments* (Sofia, 1992), pp. 233–46.

18. Michael Shafir, "Romania's Tortuous Road to Reform," *RFE/RL Research Report*, no. 1 (Jan. 3, 1992), p. 96.

19. See Michael Shafir, "Promises and Reality," *RFE/RL Report on Eastern Europe*, no. 1 (Jan. 4, 1991), p. 36; and Dennis Deletant, "The Role of Vatra Romaneasca in Transylvania," *RFE/RL Report on Eastern Europe*, no. 5 (Feb. 1, 1991), pp. 28–37.

20. Matei Calinescu and Vladimir Tismaneanu, "The 1989 Revolution and Romania's Future," *Problems of Communism* (January-April 1991), p. 59.

21. For more detail see Michael Shafir, "The Greater Romania Party," *RFE/RL Report on Eastern Europe*, no. 46 (Nov. 15, 1991), pp. 25–30.

22. See Tom Gallagher, "Ultranationalists Take Charge of Transylvania's Capital," *RFE/RL Research Report*, no. 13 (March 27, 1992), pp. 23–30.

23. See Michael Shafir, "Romania: National Liberal Party Quits Democratic Convention," *RFE/RL Research Report*, no. 24 (June 12, 1992), pp. 25–30.

24. See Michael Shafir, "The Movement for Romania: A Party of Radical Return," *RFE/RL Research Report*, no. 29 (July 17, 1992), pp. 16–20.

25. Robert Boute-Friedheim, "Hungarians Abroad: Next Up for Ethnic Cleansing?," *Freedom Review* 24, no. 2 (March-April 1993), p. 22.

26. *Darzhaven Vestnik*, no. 20 (1990).

27. Mihail Ivanov, *Statement, 1991 CSCE Meeting of Experts on National Minorities Subsidiary Working Body "A"* (Geneva: July 4, 1991).

28. Author's interview with President Zhelev's advisor on ethnic and religious matters Mihail Ivanov, April 1993.

29. A good example of this way of thinking is the article of E. Konstantinov in *Aspects of the Ethno-Cultural Situation in Bulgaria and in the Balkans* [vol. 2] (Sofia, 1992), pp. 9–20 (in Bulgarian).

30. *Konstitutziya na Republika Balgaria* (Sofia Press, 1991).

31. Author's interview with President Zhelev's advisors Mihail Ivanov and Plamen Bogoev (legal advisor), April 1993.

32. *Darzhaven Vestnik*, no. 86 (1991).

33. *Prava i Svobodi*, Jan. 8, 1993.

34. Program Declaration of the MRF, unpublished, p. 4 (in Bulgarian).

35. Ilyana Benovska Interviewing Ahmed Dogan, *Who's Who* (Sofia, 1992), pp. 63, 68 (in Bulgarian).

36. For more information, see *Standart*, June 5, 1993, p. 4–5; Kjell Engelbrekt, "The Movement for Rights and Freedoms," *RFE/RL Report on Eastern Europe*, no. 22 (May 31, 1991), p. 58.

37. For more information see Kjell Engelbrekt, "Movement for Rights

and Freedoms to Compete in Elections," *RFE/RL Report on Eastern Europe*, no. 40 (Oct. 4, 1991), pp. 1–5.

38. *Duma*, May 5, 1991.

39. See Eugenii Dainov, "Bulgaria: Politics after the October 1991 Elections," *RFE/RL Research Report*, no. 2 (Jan. 10, 1992), p. 14.

40. Author's interview with Mihail Ivanov, January 1993. To this, some MRF leaders add that for them this is a way to diminish the sharp political confrontation in the country. See *Standart*, June 5, 1993, p. 5.

41. *Otechestven Vestnik*, Oct. 12 1992.

42. *Otechestven Vestnik* and *Demokratsiya*, Dec. 31, 1992; see also Kjell Engelbrekt, "Technocrats Dominate New Bulgarian Government," *RFE/RL Research Report*, no. 4 (Jan. 22, 1993), pp. 1–5.

43. Plamen Tzvetkov, "The Politics of Transition in Bulgaria," *Problems of Communism* (May-June 1992), p. 41.

44. Dainov, "Bulgaria: Politics after the October 1991 Elections," p. 16.

45. *Trud*, Jan. 4, 1993.

46. Heinz Jurgen Axt, "Der 'Islamische Bogen' vom Balkan bis nach Zentralasien. Die Türkei als neue Regionalmacht?" *Südost-Europa* 41, no. 9 (1992), p. 565.

47. *Constitution of Romania* (Bucharest, 1991).

48. Romania Ministry of Foreign Affairs, *White Paper on the Rights of Persons Belonging to National Ethnic, Linguistic or Religious Minorities in Romania* (June 1991).

49. Pataki, "Free Hungarians in a Free Romania," p. 21.

50. Edith Oltay, "The Hungarian Democratic Federation of Romania: Structure, Agenda, Alliances," *RFE/RL Report on Eastern Europe*, no. 29 (July 19, 1991), pp. 29–30.

51. See Romania, *White Paper*, pp. 15–16.

52. Ibid., pp. 16–17.

53. Shafir and Ionescu, "Romania—The Minorities in 1991," p. 26.

54. Stefanescu, "Disputes over Control of Romanian Television," *RFE/RL Report on Eastern Europe*, no. 8 (Feb. 22, 1991).

55. Oltay, "The Hungarian Democratic Federation of Romania," pp. 32–33.

56. Michael Shafir, "Romania's Elections: More Change Than Meets the Eye," *RFE/RL Research Report*, no. 44 (Nov. 6, 1992), pp. 4, 8.

57. Ilchev and Perry, "Bulgarian Ethnic Groups," p. 37.

58. Author's interview with Mehmed Hogha, April 1993.

59. Such an understanding has been stated repeatedly by MRF leaders. It is pointed out also in its Program Declaration. A similar view has been expressed by Mihail Ivanov in the Bulgarian newspaper *Makedonia*, March 25, 1993, p. 3.

60. In the opinion of Catherine Lalumière, Secretary-General of the Council of Europe, "Bulgaria, in an entirely empirical way, is finding the right solutions and can serve as a model" (*Pik*, no. 18 [May 5–12, 1992], p. 22). The same view about the rational way in which Bulgaria is solving the minority issue was expressed by US politicians during the visit of Bulgarian Prime Minister Filip Dimitrov to the United States, March 1992.

61. This is the opinion of Junal Lutvi, *Prava i Svobodi*, Feb. 12, 1993; see also *Prava i Svobodi*, Feb. 5, 1993.

62. This is the opinion of Jurii Borissov, *Duma*, Feb. 26, 1993.

63. Such a view has been expressed by Valentin Dobrev, Deputy Minister for Foreign Affairs, in the newspaper *Standart* and in *Prava i Svobodi*, Feb. 26, 1993.

64. Mihail Ivanov, *Standart*, Feb. 2, 1993, *Makedonia*, March 25, 1993.

65. *Duma*, Dec. 15, 1992.

66. For more information, see *Debati*, Feb. 16, 1993.

67. *Demokratsiya*, April 28, 1993.

68. Republic of Bulgaria: Office of the President, *Document n.02-00–11* (March 17, 1993) (in Bulgarian); see also the interview with Mihail Ivanov in *Kontinent* (April 14, 1993).

69. For more information on these problems, see the chapter "Ethnic Relations and Economics," in *Aspects of the Ethnocultural Situation in Bulgaria*, vol. 1 (Sofia, 1992), pp. 187–279.

70. J.F. Brown, "Eastern Europe: The Revolution So Far," *RFE/RL Research Report*, no. 1 (Jan. 1, 1993), p. 74.

71. For an interesting analysis see Aurel Zidaru-Barbulescu, "Romania Seeks Admission to the Council of Europe," *RFE/RL Research Report*, no. 2 (Jan. 8, 1993), pp. 11–16.

5

The Problem of Ethnic Minority Rights Protection in the Newly Independent States

ALEXANDER A. KONOVALOV
DMITRI EVSTAFIEV

The importance of minority rights protection is demonstrated to a large extent by current developments in Europe, especially the rise of aggressive nationalist movements in a number of states. While it is a significant item of the human rights agenda, ethnic minority rights protection also has substantial strategic importance for international stability in Europe, as ethnic tensions have proved to be a perfect catalyst for major conflicts: the events in the former Yugoslavia represent perhaps the greatest military threat now facing the continent.

All the instruments, institutions, and strategic concepts developed during the years of the Cold War under the conditions of bipolar confrontation have been inefficient and inapplicable in preventing or settling ethnic, national, or religious conflicts. Nuclear deterrence strategy, huge armies, and military alliances conceived to prevent or stop massive invasions have been impotent and meaningless in the face of bloodshed in the Balkan peninsula. This means that the international community must focus on ethnic problems in developing the key foundations of any future international security system; nowhere is this task more urgent than in the former Soviet Union.

SURMOUNTING THE SOVIET LEGACY

The chaotic disintegration of the Soviet Union has critically affected "traditional" security considerations in Europe, such as those concerning nuclear weapons and installations and the dismantling of conventional military structures. But there are some aspects of the process that have even greater importance for the future of stability and democracy on the Eurasian landmass. One is the issue of the Soviet legacy in the ethnic minority area.

The importance of the issue is underlined by some negative tendencies witnessed recently in most (if not all) of the Newly

Independent States (NIS) emerging on the territory of the former Soviet Union; among them are trends particularly linked to the issue of ethnic problems and ethnic minorities:

1. Increased fragmentation of the new countries, given the absence of firm central authority. Such processes are ongoing in most of the NIS, demonstrating that the Eurasian instability started by the disintegration of the USSR is not over. Separatist tendencies of an ethnic, economic, and tribal nature now can be found in all the NIS.

2. Intensification of both internal and inter-republican low-level violence that seems to be paradigmatic of political life in the new states.

3. Overlapping ethnic conflict across borders, which has produced massive flows of refugees—for example, in Russia's North Caucasus, which has sustained a flow of refugees, armed formations, and criminal elements resulting from conflicts in the immediate area (South Ossetia, Chechnya, Ingushetiya, Kabarda, Kharabakh, Abkhazia, and Georgia).

According to a study published in July 1991 by the Center of Political and Geographic Research, on the territory of the then USSR there were 79 areas of ethnic conflicts (not counting variations), which had been prompted by changes of borders, forced or sponsored migration of the population, changes in the status of some areas or state jurisdiction, suppression of national feelings, or interrelationships between ethnic groups or regions.

Not all of these trouble points witnessed escalation to the level of military action, but one should remember that the potential for crisis still remains. Such an overview of ethnic-related instability can provide us with a framework for the further analysis of minority problems.

The specific origins of each situation can often be traced to the mostly negative influence of the Soviet legacy. Among the most important and troubling aspects of that legacy, one can list the following three:

First, most of the republics have fallen victim to the old communist practice of state-sponsored migration for economic purposes. Such migration was intended to aid the economic development of certain regions by forcing large quantities of identifiable ethnic populations to migrate to more actively developing regions. Thus, substantial groups of ethnic Russians and other Slavs were brought to Central Asia, where they formed the bulk of those who worked at industrial enterprises. This process can be characterized as the introduction of an ethnically alien element into specific (and highly delicate) ethnic, cultural, and religious areas. In this regard, we are facing contradictory trends. On the one hand, it seems probable that most of these migrants will gradually leave these areas in the years to come. On the other hand, however, the issue of preserving the economic stability in those states (in most of the Central Asian states, Slavs and other migrants constitute 80%–90% of those working in industry) remains unsolved, which could lead the national leadership to provide incentives for groups of non-native population to continue to stay in the places where they migrated, in some cases several generations ago.

Second, all the parties operating on the territory of the former USSR should focus their attention on overcoming the problems of the Stalin-era deportations of some ethnic groups and whole nations, which created in some places (especially in the Northern Caucasus) highly unstable situations. So far, it seems that no one in the NIS (and in Russia in particular) has proposed relevant solutions to these problems. The Russian experience has demonstrated that one can only hope to "freeze" the situation without truly resolving it. One should also note that partial (politically motivated) deportations of some ethnic and sub-ethnic groups (such as those experienced by Lithuanians, Estonians, Latvians, and Western Ukrainians), while not creating equally dangerous conflict situations, substantially damaged inter-ethnic and interstate relations.

The third and probably most disturbing negative element of the Soviet legacy in the field of ethnic problems is the correlation between ethnic instabilities and the absence of commonly accepted legitimate borders. Under communist rule, most internal borders were considered simply administrative, and thus were subject to easy changes due to political or economic reasons, without much attention to the ethnic ramifications. Such a situation occurred when some areas of Russia with dominant Russian population were transferred to Kazakhstan. Not surprisingly, those areas (in North Kazakhstan) currently represent the most troubling factors for the Kazakh leadership. The other classic example of actions that have caused extensive ethnic violence is Nagorno-Karabakh. These fundamental difficulties are reinforced by the ongoing economic crisis throughout the Newly Independent States.

Such a complex situation makes it clear that the vital task for settlement of the ethnic minorities issues is the elaboration of a collaborative mechanism for managing the Soviet legacy. This mechanism should be truly collaborative, and in addition must involve both the states where the ethnic minorities live and the "mother-states," as well as international institutions.

It is also quite clear that the basic approach to the issue must be "multi-dimensional." All parties must understand that *stability is indivisible* (especially with regard to countries that for prolonged periods of time constituted one state and despite political proclamations remain highly interconnected), i.e., it is impossible to attain stability and prosperity for one nation or ethnic group at the expense of others.

Most of the parties concerned are trying to manage the past; no one (except maybe Kazakhstan President Nursultan Nazarbaev) is trying to prepare for the future. And it should be properly understood that historical problems and negative experiences cannot justify ethnic minority rights violations from either a moral or a *realpolitik* point of view.

The involvement of international and nongovernmental organizations in the process of elaborating the collaborative mechanism can be of particular help for several reasons. First of all, international organizations have accumulated valuable experience in the field of human rights protection in general, and ethnic minorities in particular, including their activities in the former Soviet Union.

Second, and perhaps the most important aspect, is that only the involvement of international bodies in the process of discussion of the matter can provide the necessary objectivity for assessments. It is quite clear that because of the historical issues, Russia cannot solely address the problem of ethnic minorities, since it is perceived by many others (especially the Baltic states and Ukraine) to be the main heir of the imperial past and the main source of totalitarian practice in inter-ethnic relations. This is not the forum to discuss whether this is true; but we must admit that the perception in such issues is perhaps more important than reality.

Thus international bodies, especially the UN, the European Community, and the Council of Europe, are the parties capable of providing mediation and independent analysis functions.

Management of the Soviet legacy can be of considerable importance to "outside" parties. Nonviolent and gradual solutions to the ethnic minorities issues that can avoid aggressive nationalism and further fragmentation of the new states under the pressure of minorities can create highly important precedents for the future of human and ethnic minority rights protection all over the world.

In addition, the situation in the NIS gives the international community a unique opportunity to demonstrate its capabilities in resolving the problem of ethnic minority rights protection as the major issue of international security. Unfortunately, it seems that after the end of the Cold War, the human rights issues that were widely used in the 1970s and 1980s for rhetoric purposes in East-West confrontation were relegated to the bottom of the list of priorities.

It also should be noted that a highly specific correlation exists between ethnic minority rights and responsibilities. This issue has not been developed properly, since most of the attention was paid to protection of the rights of ethnic minorities. Nevertheless, it seems that the Soviet legacy can be managed only on the basis of reciprocity. Among such responsibilities one can list:

1. Respect for the territorial integrity of the state. This perhaps can be addressed as the basic principle (for the NIS) and the most complicated one. Such respect is possible only if citizenship rights are granted to all residents. In the NIS, however, the citizenship issue is complicated by the above-mentioned problem of the legitimacy of borders in certain areas that witnessed transfers from one republic to another during communist rule. Moreover, the implementation of such a principle clearly demands some steps on behalf of the motherstate, including the refusal to create new national autonomies within new states, which would be especially difficult in areas where ethnic tension has already occurred.

2. Accepting that employment rights can be predicated on the knowledge of a particular language. Despite the fact that this kind of limitation is often used for "squeezing" ethnic minorities from some countries (especially the Baltic states), such steps may be legitimate. The negative response it received from most of the "Russian-language" communities was provoked by the fact that perhaps the only real result of the often-discussed "russification" was the introduction of the Russian language into the routine life of these states, creating an environment of artificial comfort for Russian communities.

3. Loyalty to the state of residence. The need for this responsibility is quite clear. The possibility of "double citizenship," which of course is highly acceptable politically and thus promoted by the Russian political leadership, should be given serious consideration by the states of the former Soviet Union.

SITUATION ANALYSIS

In speaking about the problem of minority rights in Russia and other countries of the NIS, one faces a dramatic challenge: which dimension of the subject to focus on? Practically speaking, each nation that formed the Russian Empire (and the Soviet Union later on) has a long history of suppression of its national rights. But this study intentionally concentrates on one new aspect of the national minorities problem that resulted from the Soviet breakup. The disintegration of the USSR transferred more than 20 million ethnic Russians, as well as Russian-speaking citizens of the USSR who identified themselves with Russia despite their wish, into residents of foreign states. Moreover, in many autonomous regions of Russia itself, Russians have started to be treated as national minority representatives.

The problem of Russian minority rights in the NIS is one of the key issues of the internal political struggles in Russia. Negative developments with regard to these rights would ruin the prospects for democratic change in Russia as well as in much of the NIS. That is why this part of the study gives the main priority to the problem of Russian minorities, either in the NIS or in Russia itself.

Russians and Other Ethnic Minorities in the Former Soviet Republics

Before dealing with the specific issues of what can be done by the international community and international bodies, one should properly understand the specifics of the situation in different independent states of the former Soviet Union. The entire issue of minority rights protection in Russia is ultimately related to the fate of the Russian communities in the states of the former USSR; therefore, the importance of this issue necessitates separate treatment.

Table 1 (at the end of the chapter) shows the number of Russians in the former Soviet republics, according to official 1989 statistics. There should be some remarks made with regard to this table. First, in some cases the official data presented there is criticized by some specialists as being skewed for political reasons. In some cases, such as Kazakhstan, Estonia, and Latvia, there are clear grounds for such allegations.

Second, due to changes in the political landscape since 1989, the ethnic situation has changed significantly. It is extremely difficult to assess the current situation, but we can outline some trends. On the one hand, the number of Russians and the percentage they constitute in the republics of Central Asia has significantly decreased, due to the migration resulting from civil war and ethnic instability in the region. According to data provided by the Federal Migration Service of Russia, during the period 1989–1992, Russia accepted 480,000 refugees and 80,000 migrants, most of whom were from the Central Asian region.

According to unofficial data published in spring 1993, of the 388,000 Slavs (most of them Russians) who lived in Tajikistan before the civil war, more than 300,000 have already emigrated. In other Central Asian republics, the rate of migration varies from 4% to 5% of the Russian population.

At the same time, substantial numbers of Russian refugees settled not in Russia but in Kazakhstan for economic reasons, thus increasing the Russian community there. In the Baltic states, especially in Estonia, the percentage of Russians essentially grew due to the higher birth rate in Russian families.

One can clearly see that the issue of protecting the political, economic, and cultural rights of the Russians and Russian-speaking minorities will unequivocally dominate the CIS and Baltic policy agenda of any Russian Federation administration. The Russian leadership, however, has not yet worked out a comprehensive policy and efficient approaches to this issue, although there is clear recognition that military means cannot ensure Russian minority rights. For example, Sergei Filatov, currently the chief of President Yeltsin's administration and one of Yeltsin's most active supporters as First Deputy Chairman of the Supreme Soviet of the Russian Federation, has argued that political instruments should be found to protect minority rights in the former USSR.

But the lack of concrete actions by Yeltsin's administration essentially gives the initiative in this sphere to the communists, who are perceived by many as the only protectors of Russians; and the nationalistic forces of some countries, especially in the Baltics, continue along their anti-Russian course, thus generating possible major instability. It should be well remembered that the lack of a clear-cut position by the Russian leadership towards the conflict in the Trans-Dniestr region in fact led to the eruption of military conflict that resulted in thousands dead there on both sides. Only later on, after the protection of Russians became one of the leading issues on the domestic agenda and a cause of public criticism of the Yeltsin administration, did Foreign Minister Andrei Kozyrev finally conclude that moral influence is not sufficient for reaching this objective.

This chapter will focus on the situation in the Baltic states, Ukraine, and Kazakhstan, which reflect different aspects of the problem that exists in all the areas of the former Soviet Union.

The Baltic States

The situation in the sphere of ethnic minority rights protection in the three Baltic states is definitely one of the most threatening in the former USSR. Most of the discussion of this problem is in fact concentrated on "the Baltic issue." This is largely a result of discriminatory citizenship laws adopted by the legislative bodies of Latvia and Estonia.

Violations there of ethnic minority rights are targeted mostly against Russians, who constitute in Latvia and Estonia 34% and 30.3% of the population, respectively; no other substantial ethnic minority is present in those republics. It is quite clear that there is some basis for the animosity of political leaders and the native population towards those who settled there in substantial numbers after the 1940 occupation by the Stalin regime: first, negative historic analogies; second, the unfavorable demographic situation for Latvians and Estonians that occurred as a result of the forced migration of other ethnic groups during the postwar period; and third, the presence of the Russian (former Soviet) armed forces, which played a highly negative role during the Baltic struggle for independence.

It should be noted, however, that the Latvian and Estonian leadership declined to participate in the process of collaborative management of the Soviet legacy on the basis of universal human rights principles and a gradual and selective approach, while embarking on the path of unilateral and voluntaristic actions.

The basic principle of the citizenship laws adopted in Latvia and Estonia surprisingly resembled the charter of the Palestine Liberation Organization, which grants the opportunity to live in Palestine after Israel is exterminated only to those who lived there before 1948 (i.e., the creation of Israel). In Latvia the idea of the "zero variant" in the citizenship laws was abandoned from the very beginning, and legal limitations on citizenship rights were instituted. Thus a significant part of the population of the country was denied citizenship rights.

In addition to the legal violations of the legitimate rights of ethnic minorities in Latvia, we have witnessed an extensive process of "squeezing out" Russians from economic activity, thus forcing their emigration from the republic. Many specialists predict the possibility of a social crisis with clear divisions along national lines in Latvia. According to Nelli Yakimenko, secretary of the Committee on Human Rights Protection of the Russian Congress, the Latvian leadership did not respond to a Russian proposal at the bilateral negotiations on the issues of protection of the rights of the non-native population, thus demonstrating its lack of desire to settle the issues politically.

One of the latest steps launched by the Latvian leadership was an attempt to issue so-called provisional residence documents, valid only for a year, to all those who live in Latvia due to service in the armed forces of the former Soviet Union. That decision affected a significant portion of the population of the country (between 75,000 and 250,000 people, according to some estimates) and was perceived in Russia as preparation for ethnic cleansing. It provoked a strong response from Russian President Boris Yeltsin and further deteriorated relations between the two countries. The Latvian authorities ultimately changed their decision, but a dangerous coloring to the issue continues to exist.

One of the strangest citizenship documents adopted in Latvia, and one that should be at least briefly mentioned, is the provisional legislation on abandoning citizenship. It states that all those who have citizenship rights in the Latvian Republic but do not want them must report in writing to the Department on Citizenship and Emigration, which would study each case separately. But only those who had already served their term in the armed forces would be given the opportunity to reject Latvian citizenship. This ridiculous rule illustrates the general situation of citizenship rights in Latvia.

In Estonia the rights of citizenship were granted to all Estonians and also to those non-Estonians and their descendants who had lived in the country before 1940 (i.e., prior to Stalin's occupation). For the rest of those who were not granted citizenship rights automatically, a special procedure was proposed that included a language exam, security investigation, and finally an oath of loyalty.

The Estonian law on citizenship contradicts the country's constitution, which gives citizenship rights to those whose mother or father were Estonians; the new law recognizes only the father's lineage. In practice, the results of such procedures largely depend on the decision of the official bodies, which are openly anti-Russian. Thus the possibility of a non-Estonian receiving citizenship is minimal.

The Latvian Foreign Office, in response to Russian criticism, accused Moscow of violating the rights of those Latvians who live in Russia. Violations mentioned included the practice of collecting taxes in hard currency and the absence of Latvian-language schools in Russia. This action was clearly a political one and even the liberally-oriented Russian Foreign Ministry totally rejected the accusation, indicating the real reason for the emergence of such a problem as the absence of interstate agreements on the rights of ethnic minorities and the refusal of Latvian officials to adopt the principle of "double citizenship."

The Estonian Foreign Ministry also accused Russia of rights violations, pointing to the situation of the Estonian and Setu communities that live in the Pskov area of Russia near the border with Estonia. This accusation was regarded as cynical even by the leading liberal mass media in Russia. The Estonians and Setu (who comprise 4% of the population of the district and enjoy all political rights; this is not equally so with regard to Russians, who constitute 30% of the population of the state of Estonia) were granted all rights of cultural development. For example, there is only a single Estonian-language school, not because of any political reasons but rather because of the lack of pupils—in some classes, there are only two or three. In the town's library there are more than 10,000 Estonian books. The only fact that could be regarded as a violation of rights was the absence of an Estonian-language newspaper.

Such openly cynical and discriminatory policies of the Baltic states towards the Russian and Russian-speaking communities were strongly criticized by President Yeltsin in his letter to UN Secretary-General Boutros-Ghali, in which he proposed including the issue of human rights violations in the agenda of the 47th session of the UN General Assembly.

At the same time, the strong response of the Russian president to human rights violations in the Baltics produced some positive results. For example, Estonian President Lennart Meri declared that language exams had become substantially easier in order to give more non-Estonians opportunity for citizenship.

Nevertheless, it seems that the attempts of the Russian government and in particular the Defense Ministry to link the issue of minority rights violations to the withdrawal of Russian armed forces from the Baltic states as an instrument of pressure upon the leaders of Latvia and Estonia proved to be unfruitful and counterproductive, creating additional points of international tension.

On the other hand, one should clearly note that the behavior of the other side in the political turmoil in the Baltic states—the Russian community—is not quite acceptable at the moment. Given the fact that the Russian community participated actively (directly and indirectly) in the anti-independence movements in the Baltic states, it is clear why Estonian and Latvian officials envisage Russians as a threat to the independence and territorial integrity of their states.

The other specific issue is the problem of former Soviet military who after retirement settled in the Baltic states. We should admit that their presence in the Baltic states became possible only as a result of the 1940 occupation and clearly provokes sensitive questions.

Generally speaking, the Russian community (or at least a substantial part of it), while it wants to stay in Latvia and Estonia (mainly for economic reasons) and enjoy all political rights, does not have an idea of the responsibilities that it should assume in this case.

The lack of mutual understanding, and the non-acceptance of the idea of the indivisibility of security and stability, as well as anti-Russian policies in the Baltic states, have resulted in the radicalization of the position of the Russian communities there. Most of the relatively moderate organizations, such as the Russian Democratic Movement of

Estonia, lost public support, while hard-line national groups, for example, the Russian Community of Estonia, Russian Sobor, and the Cossack Community in Estonia, enjoy wide political support among Russians, who perceive them to be the only protectors of their interests.

Such developments produced a situation where the idea of a Russian republic of Estland in the regions of Estonia with predominantly Russian population is regarded quite seriously. Essentially the situation in Estonia resembles the situation in Moldova on the eve of the war in the Trans-Dniestr region, which demonstrated that attempts to create an ethnically "clean" state can produce substantially higher political costs than peaceful integration of other ethnic groups into the newborn independent state's political and social system.

The Lithuanian example, on the other hand, can serve as a model for the settlement of ethnic issues using normal legal mechanisms and principles, thus securing proper stability and interaction between different ethnic groups while essentially enhancing internal stability. Some significant problems exist, however, despite the fact that according to the citizenship laws in Lithuania all those people who were permanently settled in the republic up to the date of independence were granted full citizenship rights.

Among these problems, we can list the issues related to the cultural development and religious freedom of the Polish community (which, together with the Jewish community, constitutes one-fourth of Lithuania's population). After independence, the Polish autonomous districts formed in Vilnius and Shaltchininks (where most of the Polish community has lived for centuries) were disbanded, and direct supervision was transferred to the Vilnius government. There were highly dangerous tendencies in the "Sajudis" establishment, where some politicians claim that there are no Poles on the territory of Lithuania, but only Polish-speaking Lithuanians, and thus a special policy towards this ethnic minority is not needed.

There are also some problems with education in the Polish language, since the Polish University is not officially recognized. Most surprisingly, the use of the Polish language is banned at the services in the Polish Cathedral of St. Stanislav. At the same time, even the communist mass media in Russia acknowledged that ethnic rights violations in Lithuania cannot be compared to those in Latvia and Estonia.

Ukraine

The situation in Ukraine is of special importance, for two basic reasons. First, it provides a valuable demonstration of how issues of ethnic minorities can be settled with positive results in a large but multinational state where the native nationality (Ukrainians) constitutes the dominant majority (and except for Russia, Ukraine is one of a kind in the NIS).

The second reason is that in Ukraine, despite a situation of full official legal protection of ethnic minorities, some points of tension still exist, not only with regard to the Russian community (which can be explained by the controversial interstate relations) but also to the other ethnic minorities. Such problems have resulted from actions by the various political groups and political leaders that are oriented towards aggressive nationalism.

The problem lies in the preservation of opportunities for cultural development of the Russian community. According to the Department of Education of the city of Kiev administration (where the Russian community was traditionally large), in 1992 only 47 Kiev schools still have a Russian education process, while 119 formerly "Russian" schools were transformed to educate in the Ukrainian language.

On November 29, 1992, a new nationalistic organization, the Ukrainian Anti-Communist Anti-Empire Front, was organized, adding to the fears of the eruption of aggressive xenophobic nationalism because the organization declared its aim as the struggle against "separatism and federalism." This formula is clearly aimed against the Russian communities.

As the result of such developments, the issue of ethnic minority rights became a part of the political struggle in Ukraine. For example, the political opponents of RUKH and Anti-Empire Front—the Movement for Rebirth of Donbass—issued a declaration in protest against "artificial transfer of the education in some schools in the Donbass into the Ukrainian language." Many other organizations and parties demanded that Russian be given the status of the second official language of the country.

There are also some ethnic problems in the Trans-Carpathian region with regard to the Hungarian community. Despite the fact that the Kiev leadership understood the political vitality of the issue and adopted decisions that granted the right to education in the native language, the demands escalated to creation of territorial autonomy, which, according to Mikhail Tovt, head of the administration of the Beregovski district (where Hungarians comprise 70% of the population), can solve some of the Hungarians' problems, including "limitation of the migration of Ukrainians to the region."

In addition to the issues related to ethnic minorities in Ukraine, there is also a wide spectrum of problems concerning specific religious groups, for example, those who belong to the Ukrainian Orthodox

Church, which is part of the Russian Orthodox Church. It should be well understood that this religious community includes not only ethnic Russians but also most of the Orthodox Ukrainians and is currently the subject of intense attacks by some regional power bodies, especially in the west of the country and in the Ukrainian armed forces. Violations of the rights of some religious denominations have been acknowledged by the Christian-Democratic Party of the Ukraine and the Ukrainian Legal Foundation. For example, in the town of Lvov, the new Cathedral of the Greco-Catholics is planned to be the only religious institution for the military of all three Christian churches in Ukraine, thus demonstrating the favored position of one denomination over the others. This means that the basis for further violation of religious freedoms has been already created.

Kazakhstan

The peculiarity of the situation in Kazakhstan is determined by the fact that Kazakhs constitute less than 40% of the population of the republic. In addition to the Russian community, which according to official 1989 data constituted 37.8% of the population, there are substantial communities of Germans, Ukrainians, Koreans, Uzbeks, and Kyrgyz. All these ethnic groups (except the Koreans and Germans, who were exiled to Kazakhstan in the Stalin years) had begun settling in the area prior to the Russian Revolution, jeopardizing the ability of the leadership of the state to build a classic nation-state.

One of the most critical problems in this area was the constitutional discussion of the problem of the state language in Kazakhstan's Parliament. Some radical nationalist elements demanded adoption of the Kazakh language (which is used by less than 50% of the population) and that the Russian language should not be used at all. The position of President Nazarbaev has remained vague.

At the same time, the republic's Council of Ministers issued rules that limit the opportunities of those who are not speakers of the Kazakh language for government service, in essence a "kazakhification" of the government bodies. In addition, some regional power bodies— for example, the Aktiubinsk regional Council of Deputies—adopted decisions that were aimed at limiting the use of the Russian language. This produced massive public response and ethnic tensions, especially in the northern regions of the republic with predominantly non-Kazakh (Russian, Ukrainian, German, and Korean) population. The final result of the rise of the aggressive nationalistic trends in the leadership of Kazakhstan was the conflict that emerged after the dismissal of the chairman of the Karaganda television and radio broadcast service, Budihzhan Mukushev, who openly countered the nationalistic line of some representatives of the Nazarbaev team. Being afraid of the political-ethnic turmoil, President Nazarbaev and the Parliament adopted a compromise formula, which proclaimed Kazakh the official language of the country, while Russian retained its role as the "language of inter-ethnical communication." At the same time, the constitution stressed that no discrimination or limitation of human rights should occur due to language differences. In addition, the Kazakh leadership even agreed to a "double citizenship" formula that creates the situation in which at least one-third (and, by some assessments, one-half) of the citizens of Kazakhstan will be at the same time citizens of the Russian Federation.

Nevertheless it seems significant that the change in the position of President Nazarbaev occurred not because of his adherence to the protection of ethnic minorities (though in the case of Kazakhstan it is not clear who should be considered a "minority") but rather for realpolitik reasons. This leaves substantial space for violations in the future if the political environment changes.

RUSSIAN MINORITIES IN RUSSIA

Another important issue is the protection of the rights of ethnic Russians on the territory of Russia itself, especially on the territories of the so-called national autonomies.

The number of ethnic Russians in the autonomous republics, districts, and regions of Russia is given in tables 2 and 3. As one can see, Russians constitute the dominant majority in seven out of 21 autonomous republics, the marginal majority in another three republics, and more than 40% of the population in three others. At the same time, it would be a great mistake to think that the rest of the population represents the "native" population. For example, in most of the republics there are substantial communities of Ukrainians.

In some republics—Tuva, Kalmykiya, Buryatiya, and Yakutiya—only the native population is proclaimed to have the right of self-determination. In Yakutiya, non-natives also cannot occupy the positions of president and vice-president of the republic. In some other republics—in Karelia, for example—nationalist pressure groups demand that the authorities introduce some limitation on the rights of non-natives. Such a situation to a large extent influenced the tensions around creation of the German autonomic republic. Many Russians, frightened by the discriminatory practices adopted in "national" autonomies, took a negative stance towards the idea.

Ethnic conflicts in the former Soviet Union have resulted in the other specific type of Russian minority in Russia—those ethnic Russians who were forced to come back to Russia from the republics of the former USSR. Traditionally, the very term "refugee" means a person who had to leave his own country, but in that case the situation more likely looks like the state left its own citizens. As was stated by Mr. Arutjunov, the chairman of the Subcommittee on the Rights of Refugees of the Russian Supreme Soviet's Committee on Human Rights,

> Usually refugees make claims on the country that threw them away, but in this situation all the claims are addressed to Russia. This country is too weak to protect their rights in the former Soviet republics and simultaneously cannot provide them even with minimal living standards inside. These difficulties are actively used by the national patriotic movements. And if they manage to convince millions of oppressed Russians from the former Soviet republics to share such ideas, it would clear a path to power for the right-wing patriots and stop for an indefinite time the democratic reforms in Russia.

But indifference and the incompetence of authorities have compounded the already negative attitudes of local Russians towards those who came from the republics. There were several reasons for such a phenomenon. The economies of the former Soviet republics were constructed on so-called complementary bases, i.e., modern industrial growth was not the product of internal development but rather of imposed socioeconomic structures. In the social structures of these republics, Russians occupied positions that appeared only because of industrial development. They provided the core elements as qualified workers, managers, and intelligentsia. As such, industrialization in these republics was based on technologies and equipment brought from outside, and often more sophisticated than the local population was trained to use.

The native population was, and to a very large extent continues to be, oriented toward non-industrial types of jobs. The industrial enterprises were not the result of natural development of the national republics but resulted from the unpredictable activities of the "planned economy," which damaged traditional styles of life and often caused serious ecological damage. The death of the Aral Sea or the devastated Semipalatinsk nuclear test site are obvious examples of the negative consequences of Moscow-imposed development.

When coming back to Russia due to fears for personal safety and uncertain prospects, the former "expatriates" find themselves in the same position that the native population occupied in the republics they came from. All the prestigious social niches are occupied already, the shameful system requiring administrative permits to live in the big cities still exists, and what jobs exist are usually found in low qualified, dirty, and non-prestigious agricultural work outside big urban centers. As a result of this senseless policy, the Russian leadership is trying to channel the growing flow of highly qualified refugees from republics to the rural areas of Russia, where they hardly manage to utilize their skills and potential.

The other root of discord between the "Russian" Russians and those who came from the republics of the former USSR is defined by the substantial differences in sub-ethnic cultures. The Russians in the republics took a lot from the cultural traditions of ethnic groups they lived among for several generations. It is well known, for instance, that alcohol consumption in the Russian families who lived in the Central Asian republics is substantially lower than those who remained in Russia itself, while the birth rate is much higher. The newcomers are also shocked by the poverty, disorder, and low living standards they encounter in the rural areas of Russia. Polarization is not unimaginable as a result.

REFUGEES AND OTHER GROUPS

The General Staff of the Armed Forces of the Russian Federation estimates that some 30 armed conflicts are going on or coming to a head on the territory of the former USSR; this number could grow to 70. One of the most serious and growing problems directly linked with the minority rights issue is a massive flow of refugees. In the autumn of 1992 there were 1.2 million to 1.5 million refugees in the CIS states, 500,000 of them in Russia.

According to official UN statistics, the total number of refugees in the world was assessed at 17 million. But by the end of the current century the number on the territory of the former USSR could reach 20 million. This might seem an unrealistic forecast, but do not forget that there are already 1.5 million refugees on the territory of the former Yugoslavia, which had a population 15 times smaller than Russia's. It is evident that such a situation would be a complete disaster for Russia, the other CIS states, and the rest of the world. Under such conditions, one should forget all plans for democratic reforms and concentrate instead on physical survivability of the population.

On the one hand, the refugees are recognized in the public mind as the victims of ethnic violence, and that is correct. But there is the other side of the coin—situations where the refugees themselves become an active component in the violence. Some who were victims of the "primary" ethnic violence and who lost everything see revenge (military conflict) rather than political compromise as the only way to get back at least a part of their losses or to be partially compensated. In other words, the "Palestinian paradigm" is appearing in the former USSR. Refugees who initially were the victims of ethnic conflicts are becoming sources of violence.

This explosive situation is actively used by local political elites. For instance, Armenian refugees from the villages seized by the Azerbaijanis provided the core of Armenian formations in Karabakh, while refugees from South Ossetia are actively involved in Abkhazian forces fighting Georgia. Georgian refugees, in turn, are well represented in the numerous armed formations in Georgia. It was reported in December 1992 that the Georgian political leadership tried to invite Meskhetian Turks to come to their historical motherland to participate in the war against Abkhazia. Previously, they had objected to their return from Central Asia, where this people was deported by Stalin's decree; now, the Georgians promised to give houses to those who could win this right in combat actions. In turn, Abkhazian leaders promise Cossack volunteers fighting with Georgia grants of land and houses left by the Georgian refugees, as well as the right to own armaments. These desperate diasporas represent highly explosive material in the skilled hands of radical policy makers.

Ethnic conflicts in the former Soviet Union have another dangerous dimension. They directly engage the units of the former Soviet Army deployed in the areas. The disintegration of the USSR resulted in the division of a huge military machine. The troops deployed in Ukraine and Belarus provided the cores of national armed forces in these countries, but those deployed in the other Soviet republics have a clear sense that they have no national identity and that no one is going to take care of their destiny. While Soviet Army units deployed outside Russian territory (besides Ukraine and Belarus) were taken under Russian jurisdiction by a decree from President Yeltsin, these troops had been closely linked to and dependent for everyday life on local civil authorities. Generals and officers serving formally in the Russian armed forces cannot oppose the local national civil authorities for many reasons, chiefly their fear of dramatic cuts in their living standards, which are dependent much more on local good will than on the Defense Ministry in Moscow. Moreover, their family members would automatically become hostages in conflict situations.

That is why the compromises of the Soviet, and later on Russian, generals with local authorities resulted in the use of Soviet and then Russian troops in ethnic conflicts aimed at suppressing minority rights. Some examples are well known. The Fourth Army, based in Azerbaijan for nearly 20 years, acted against the Armenian villages in Kharabakh (May 1991). On the other side, helicopters of the Seventh Guard Army, based in Armenia, attacked positions of the Azerbaijani Army. But the far more usual forms of Russian armed forces engagement in ethnic conflicts that violate minority rights are arms transfers and mercenaries. It is hardly possible to distinguish now which part of weapons in the hands of numerous paramilitary formations, national armies, or criminal gangs was seized in combat actions, lost by the Soviet forces during chaotic evacuations, or illegally sold by local military commanders in accord with agreements with national leaders.

For instance, after the quick evacuation from Chechnya, the Russian units left 165 modern tanks and 25 aircraft. Only well-trained specialists can operate modern tanks, helicopters, or aircraft, making it evident that such specialists were hired by local authorities from the Russian armed forces. Under such conditions, ethnic clashes, once unleashed, quickly escalate and become more difficult to peacefully settle.

FRAMEWORK FOR ACTION
BY THE INTERNATIONAL COMMUNITY

In order to analyze the mechanisms and possible ways of enforcement of the basic rights of ethnic minorities, we should first deal with some important theoretical problems that have arisen from this brief analysis of the situation.

First of all, one should address the issue of how to identify an ethnic minority. This is not only a factor of definition, but rather a political question, especially in the case of some newly forged post-Soviet states, such as Kazakhstan (where Kazakhs comprise less than 40% of the population), Latvia (where the quantitative superiority of the natives is only marginal), or most of the "national autonomies" of the Russian Federation (in which the "title nationality," i.e., that nationality that gives its name to the official title of the autonomous area, comprises in some cases less than 25% of the total population). In such cases, it seems more relevant to substitute the term *title nationality* (which is widely used now in the CIS) for *ethnic majority* and the term *non-title nationality* for *ethnic minority*.

The analysis of the situation also demonstrates that the attention of the international community should not be limited to ethnic minorities. In some republics, the question is the issue of specific sub-ethnic group rights, protection, and respect. This term is usually used for specific groups that substantially differ from the rest of the population (while being an inalienable part of the nation) in historic, cultural, linguistic, and religious aspects or from a tribal point of view; examples of such sub-ethnic groups include Cossacks, Siberians, and Pomors in Russia, Junior, Senior, and Middle Juzes in Kazakhstan, and Western Ukrainians. This aspect of the problem is especially important in those states where ongoing events have demonstrated deep fragmentations of society along traditional regional/clan divisions.

Tajikistan serves as a classic example of a state where the conflict of different political powers was sharpened by the lack of respect for sub-ethnic groups. The forces representing the old authoritarian political regime effectively used traditional confrontations of regional clans, essentially fomenting a civil war. During its initial stages, the Pamir group was dominant and openly violated the rights of others; when the Kulyab group gained the upper hand, it responded with violent "sub-ethnic cleansing" in the Gorni Badahshan area.

It should also be well understood that the case of the conflict between the Trans-Dniestr region and the Kishinev leadership resulted initially not from political demands (which were often perceived in the West to be communist ones) but rather from the inability of the Moldovian leadership to abandon the path of forcible "Romanization," which denigrated the rights of the ethnic and sub-ethnic minorities that essentially constituted the majority in the region. Thus there is a clear relationship between the issue of ethnic minority rights protection and ethnic conflict prevention.

We have to agree with the opinion of one of the leading experts on the ethnic situation in the former Soviet Union, Ludvig Karapetian, that the policy adopted in some republics, "based upon not only ignoring international documents but also on the false idea that territory belongs only to one . . . title nation, but not to the all peoples that live there" can lead to ethnic conflicts.

We should not forget that a similar potential for sub-ethnic conflicts exists even in Ukraine, where the traditional regional fragmentation of the Ukrainians has deep roots and is reinforced by language and religious differences. Indeed, the international community's efforts should not ignore protection of the rights of religious minorities and specific religious groups.

Finally, the issue of the protection of ethnic minority rights cannot be studied without addressing a wider spectrum of problems concerning inter-republican relations and ethnic conflicts.

Based on the experience of the past two years, we can list the following types of ethnic minority rights violations:

1. Direct violations of the basic human rights of ethnic minorities, such as refusal to grant the rights of citizenship that are officially adopted by the state bodies of the countries.
2. Violations of economic and political rights, based on officially adopted decisions on the superiority of the "title" nationality to occupy official positions or enjoy economic and political benefits.
3. Violations of ethnic minority rights related to the sphere of cultural development.
4. State-sponsored activity of nationalistic organizations that openly manifest their objective as limitations on the human rights of ethnic minorities.
5. Ethnic minority rights violations that result from ethnic or sub-ethnic conflicts.

In this regard, one should clearly understand that only few states have dared to embark on the path of the open and legal violation of ethnic minority rights, such as adoption by legislative bodies of discriminatory citizenship laws, such as in Latvia and Estonia. On the other hand, it is quite clear that such laws could only be adopted if there is a total assurance that the international community would take no action against such violations.

One should pay attention also to the activity of the state-sponsored nongovernmental organizations such as the Fund for the Decolonization of Estonia. The activity of this organization is aimed at the deportation of Russians from the territory of the Estonian Republic and enjoys wide official support, a fact underlined by Russian Foreign Minister Kozyrev. But the fund's nongovernmental status gives the Estonian government the opportunity to deny all connection with it.

Thus most of the attention should be paid to "tacit" (non-official) violations of ethnic minority rights. Among such violations we can list the following:

- Adoption of legal documents that grant the "title" nationality superiority in ownership of land and other resources of the country or region. This issue is especially important in the republics with limited resources. Among the countries with such violations are Kyrgyzstan (where 50% of the land resources were transferred to the national land fund) and some "national autonomies" of Russia.
- Discriminatory practices in employment in state bodies or organizations. In addition to the Baltic states, this practice exists in Kazakhstan, Tataria, and Yakutiya.

- Artificial limitation of the use of the Russian language in regions with a predominantly Russian population.
- Official or officially sponsored harassment of cultural, religious, and political organizations of ethnic minorities.
- Disbanding of the territorial autonomies established prior to the independence of the state, such as has been employed in Georgia, Lithuania, and Azerbaijan.
- Denial of claims to true nationality. This practice was widely used during the Soviet period in Uzbekistan and Kirghizia and does not seem to have been abandoned since. Similar violations occurred in Ukraine, Lithuania, and Georgia (with regard to the Abkhaz and Ossetian ethnic groups).
- False statistics on various ethnic and sub-ethnic groups, which seems to be rather routine practice in Kazakhstan.
- Artificial limitation of religious activity of non-title nationalities.

These aspects of the problem in fact constitute some kind of framework for possible actions by international organizations in this field as well as points of special attention. Meanwhile, remedies include:

- "Zero variant" on citizenship, which means that citizenship rights should be granted to all those who permanently lived on the territory of the state at the moment of independence. That seems to be the inalienable and non-debatable part of an ethnic minority rights protection agenda.
- Opportunities for further cultural development, including education in the native language. At the same time, the necessity to know the native language of the title nationality as a condition for occupying official positions seems normal. Moreover, in some cases where artificial russification occurred (Ukraine, Belarus, Kazakhstan), it seems natural that the number of schools offering education in the native language will increase at the expense of the "Russian" ones, but at the same time there should be an opportunity to preserve several of the existing Russian schools if the local population expresses such a will, or even to keep the status quo (in areas like the Donbass, the Crimea, Odessa, Ukraine, the northern areas of Kazakhstan, and national autonomies in Russia). The specific problem is preservation of the opportunity for higher education in the non-native language that demands the establishment of special higher education institutions in regions where the ethnic minorities settle in concentrations.

- The granting of full economic rights, including equal rights of property in natural resources and land to all.
- Religious freedoms should be secured. Despite the fact that up to now no significant problems have occurred in this sphere, such a situation is potentially important in case of adoption of a state religion in multireligious and multi-confessional countries, e.g., Kazakhstan, and those specific cases when the leadership of the country and most of the population belong to different religious denominations (Belarus, Ukraine).

We should also pay some attention to politically sensitive issues that demand further study, such as the question of federalization of some countries that emerged from the territory of the former USSR. In some cases, it is quite clear that an absolutely natural process of federalization in accordance with traditional ethnic or sub-ethnic differences can lead to the weakening of the central authority beyond the limits acceptable to the political elite of the country, and thus to the disintegration of the country, demonstrating the absence of true determination in nation-state building. Such a situation clearly exists in Ukraine and Belarus and is potentially emerging in Kazakhstan.

Early recognition of some states in the former USSR without linkage to their adherence to human rights principles proved to be a mistake made for realpolitik reasons that left the international community with no working leverage. On the other hand, in some cases there are no opportunities for positive influence. This is mainly so in cases of ongoing ethnic conflicts.

Nevertheless, we would like to advance five specific recommendations concerning this issue:

First of all, the international community should act on the basis of total and unequivocal rejection of the "double standards" practice that in fact greatly contributed to the tremendous human rights violations in the Baltic states, since the governments of these states would never dare to embark on the path of open violations of basic human rights without counting on the support of some international bodies. The idea of international involvement has been to a large extent compromised by this double standard on the part of some officials. For example, Max van der Stoel, CSCE High Commissioner on National Minorities, in his mission to the Baltic states, did not notice any ethnic minority violations; this should be remembered as an example of the kind of approach that produced internal turmoil in the Russian political establishment.

Second, international bodies and organizations should operate on the basis of true and full information about the processes unfolding in the former USSR. Independent sources of information are critical. Thus the idea of stationing permanent UN fact-finding missions in the former Soviet Union seems relevant. In addition, taking into consideration the importance of the problem, it seems sensible to establish within the organizational framework of the United Nations a special agency dealing with the rights of ethnic minorities in the former USSR.

A third recommendation is that employment of special instruments of influence, such as economic and political sanctions or expulsions from the international organizations, should be given credence. In fact, the experience of their use against South Africa because of its practice of apartheid—i.e., violations of the rights of the ethnic *majority*—creates a highly specific precedent for the future. On the other hand, such steps can be used only against those states that embark on the path of open violations of internationally accepted principles of human rights. We cannot neglect also the deterrent capability of such sanctions against potential violators, but their effectiveness against tacit or unofficial violations is doubtful. In any case, with regard to the former Soviet Union, only two states—Latvia and Estonia—can be regarded as candidates for such sanctions.

Fourth, it should be recognized that the problem of the Russian minorities in the former USSR has become a key factor of international security and stability. After the breakup of the Soviet Union, this is a multi-dimensional threat that includes Russian minorities in the former Soviet republics, Russian minorities in autonomies in the Russian Federation, and finally relations between the "Russian" Russians in the Russian Federation and the Russian newcomers, i.e., refugees who came to Russia from all over the former USSR. The Russian leadership must do its best to help them settle in Russia and to integrate them into the market economy, but at the same time one has to admit that under the current economic circumstances no leadership in Russia will manage to resolve this problem if massive flows of Russian refugees start.

This is why the international community should focus on the issue of creating incentives for ethnic Russians to stay in the republics where they have lived for several generations. It is evident that quick integration into the market economy of the huge quantities of newcomers is impossible due to economic crises, corruption, and the incompetence of local authorities. At the same time, a massive withdrawal of Russian specialists will damage the economies of the former Soviet republics. We must not forget that wars often start with massive deportations of population. For instance, the war between

Armenia and Azerbaijan started with massive mutual evictions of "hostile" national representatives.

Studying the factors that have provoked Russians to leave the republics of the former USSR, we have concluded that difficulties in obtaining citizenship in the newly established state should be considered the number one problem. The public associates lack of citizenship with restrictions on buying houses and on getting jobs, unemployment assistance, and social security. That is why the efforts of international institutions and organizations should concentrate on assistance to the Russian minorities in getting citizenship in the countries where they live. Double citizenship for ethnic Russians and Russian-speaking minorities would play a positive role. If getting local or double citizenship seems unlikely, Russia has to provide all these persons with Russian citizenship and to take them under its jurisdiction.

The other area of international community engagement in solution of ethnic minority rights in the NIS is linked with the problem of peacekeeping. It is well known that the Russian armed forces are widely involved in peacekeeping missions all over the territory of the former USSR. The units of the Russian armed forces are ensuring peace in South Ossetia and in the Trans-Dniestr area of Moldova. The 201st Division of the Russian armed forces is an important factor in the internal situation in Tajikistan. Many peacekeeping actions of the Russian armed forces in the NIS elicit positive response in the United Nations.

At the same time, these actions need to be given more credibility from the international community. It is evident that Russia will have to accept the main burden of peacekeeping in the NIS because of its strategic interests in keeping stability in neighboring states and traditional geostrategic and historical factors. But such actions should not be perceived as another form of imperial policy. To avoid this impression—and this is the fifth recommendation—international organizations should be engaged in these activities as well. This does not mean that large contingents of international forces should be sent to the various Newly Independent States, but in each case the decision about peacekeeping actions should define the mandate for Russian forces and send some observers and liaison officers to support the success of the missions.

CONCLUSION

The situation of ethnic Russians in the NIS is not unique; it has parallels in other parts of Europe, and solutions to this problem that have been successful elsewhere should be reexamined to judge their usefulness and applicability to conditions in the former Soviet Union. One thing is certain—just solutions must be found to address the concerns and perceptions of ethnic Russians who have suddenly become foreigners in new countries. The number of ethnic Russians involved also suggests that any such solution must be applied *in situ*, as Russia itself is highly unlikely to be able to effectively absorb any mass influx of ethnic Russian refugees. This stark reality should solve as a catalyst in the search for practical steps to address these issues.

Table 1
Russians in the Former Soviet Republics (millions)

Republic	Total Population	Number of Russians	%
Ukraine	51,452	11,356	22.1
Belarus	10,152	1,342	13.2
Uzbekistan	19,810	1,653	8.3
Kazakhstan	16,463	6,228	37.8
Georgia	5,401	341	6.3
Azerbaijan	7,021	392	5.6
Lithuania	3,675	344	9.4
Moldova	4,335	562	13.0
Latvia	2,667	906	34.0
Kyrgyzstan	4,258	917	21.5
Tajikistan	5,093	388	7.6
Armenia	3,305	51	1.6
Turkmenistan	3,523	334	9.5
Estonia	1,565	465	30.3

Source: Data of the Federal Migration Service of Russia, published in *Ogonyok*, no. 7, 1993.

Table 2
Ethnic Russians in the Automous Republics of Russia

Republic	Total Population	Number of Russians	%
Buryatiya	1,038,252	726,165	70
Dagestan	1,802,188	165,940	9
Checheno-Ingushetiya*	1,270,429	293,771	23
Chuvashiya	1,338,023	357,120	26
Kabardino-Balkariya	753,531	240,750	32
Kalmykiya	322,579	121,531	38
Karelia	790,150	581,571	73
Komi	1,250,847	721,780	58
Mari-El	749,332	355,973	47
Mordoviya	963,504	586,147	60
North Ossetia	632,428	189,159	29
Tataria	3,641,742	1,575,361	42
Tuva	308,557	98,831	30
Udmurtiya	1,605,663	945,216	56
Yakutiya	1,094,065	550,263	50

*This republic dissolved in 1992, when its constituent parts disintegrated into the Republic of Chechnya (which seceded from Russia and is not recognized) and the Republic of Ingushetiya (within the Russian Federation).

Source: Data of the Federal Migration Service of Russia, published in *Ogonyok*, no. 7, 1993.

Table 3
Ethnic Russians in the Autonomous Regions and Districts of Russia

Autonomous Regions and Districts	Total Population	Number of Russians	%
Adigeya	432,046	293,640	67
Gorno-Altai	190,831	115,188	63
Jewish	214,085	178,087	80
Karachai-Cherkess	414,970	175,931	41
Khakassiya	566,861	450,430	80

Source: Data of the Federal Migration Service of Russia, published in *Ogonyok*, no. 7, 1993.

6

Can Decentralization
Solve Russia's Ethnic Problems?

NICOLAI N. PETRO

Will Russia hold together? The question seems to mesmerize both Russian and Western analysts. Many have reached the conclusion that Russia cannot simultaneously pursue democracy and decentralization, for while democracy presumes a decentralization of political authority, decentralization in turn can lead to demands for complete independence and hence to the disintegration of the state. No less a political luminary than John Stuart Mill was stymied by this contradiction and concluded that democracy is "next to impossible in a country made up of different nationalities."[1]

Not surprisingly, therefore, today's ethnic, political, and economic turmoil has been compared to one of the darkest intervals in Russian history—the period from 1598 to 1613 know as the "Time of Troubles."[2] When the last descendant of the Ryurik dynasty died leaving no heir, the Poles took advantage of the ensuing power struggle and occupied Moscow. Russia's many disparate regions seemed incapable of uniting to mount an effective opposition, and it seemed that Russia's brief history as an independent state might be at an end.

But the analogy to the present should not end there. It is worth remembering that national unity was eventually restored—not by central authorities, however, but by a broad-based popular movement that emerged from the provinces. After liberating Moscow, its leaders convened a national assembly (the *Zemsky sobor* of 1613) to elect a new Russian leader. The assembly then arranged a popular referendum on their candidate by sending emissaries to every major locality to confirm the acceptability of the new tsar to the people.[3] Russia was saved by a rather unusual (for the 17th century) combination of popular democracy and decentralization. Can these two principles save what is left of the Russian Federation today?

1. NATIONALISM, DEMOCRACY, AND THE LEGACY OF SOVIET FEDERALISM

Although the USSR and the Russian Soviet Federated Socialist Republic (RSFSR) both claimed to be federations, they were ruled as unitary states. As Lenin frequently reminded his Bolshevik colleagues, "The entire legal and actual constitution of the Soviet republic is built on the basis of the Party's correcting, determining and building everything according to a single principle."[4] Attempts at secession were forcibly suppressed so that, in fact, Soviet federalism became nothing more than an administrative convenience that allowed the CPSU to rule the country more effectively.

The resulting system did little to relieve ethnic discontent and indeed often exacerbated it. By the late 1970s, ethnic and linguistic issues had become rallying points for popular discontent with communist rule in a number of different republics. At the subrepublican level, Volga Germans, Crimean Tatars, and Koreans demanded administrative autonomy. Modelling themselves on the dissident movement, these ethnic constituencies appealed to the Soviet leadership to respect its own constitution, generally with little result.

Repressed national consciousness thus came to play an important role in the ultimate unraveling of the USSR. In the Baltic states, where the generation approaching 60 could still recall independence, the political process was quickly "nationalized." Based on the early successes of the Baltic leaders in obtaining greater autonomy, opposition groups in Belorussia, Georgia, Armenia, and even Central Asia adopted the same strategy—encouraging nationalism in order to more quickly and decisively sever ties with Moscow.

In 1989, however, few of these emerging political leaders actually expected to achieve independence quickly. In the short term, for example, many Baltic representatives were notably reluctant to undermine Gorbachev and sought to preserve the USSR as a voluntary confederation. Prominent political figures like Romuald Ozolas, Heinz Valk, and Marjiu Lauristen foresaw a prolonged period of affiliation with Russia before actual independence.

The August 1991 coup attempt, however, offered these ambitious new political leaders a unique opportunity. The collapse of effective levers of control spawned a flurry of sovereignty declarations that have redefined relations between the constituent elements of the Union and of the Russian Federation. The reliance of regional political elites on nationalism produced some unintended consequences for local populations. A particular form of nationalistic democracy emerged that has generally failed to enhance either human rights or ethnic tranquillity. In some regions, indeed, independence has throttled nascent pluralism. Sergo Mikoyan has aptly characterized the process of secession as the transfer of an "imperial mentality" from the center to the outlying regions—in Georgia, Moldova, Tajikistan, and the Caucasus, new regimes have moved quickly to squelch dissidents and separatists.

In many regions of Russia (and the other former republics), separatism is fueled not by local ethnic minorities but by the greed of local party bosses who demand independence in order to maintain a discreet distance from reformers in Moscow. In Yakutiya (Sakha), Karelia, and North Ossetia, where the Russian population outnumbers the historical natives by as much as ten to one, it is clear that the sudden interest in accommodating ethnic diversity is merely a ruse.[5]

In light of these disappointing results, the new nationalist political elites often continue to rely on the trump card of "Russian imperialism" to rally public support. But for Moscow's reluctance to recognize their independence, they argue, the economy would be in much better shape. Increasingly, however, people are tired of excuses and long for pragmatic, effective government capable of producing results, even if it means accommodating Russian interests. The recent Lithuanian and Latvian election results show that the plausibility of this argument is weakening.

Perhaps the most unexpected consequence of the emergence of nationalist democracy has been the rise of a distinctly Russian national consciousness, which had been diffused and submerged within the context of multinational Soviet institutions. As other ethnic groups have sharpened their differences with the Great Russians, the latter have in turn begun to redefine their own interests. New political leaders have emerged in Russia proper who argue that all of Russia's difficulties stem from an excessively hasty embrace of Western-style democracy. They call for a re-centralization of political authority, economic planning, increased subsidies of major industries, and a "gathering of Russian lands." Nor are these appeals limited to the conservative right—many democratic reformers have reached the conclusion that Russian democracy can survive only if it is imposed from the top down. In order to do so, they say, it may be necessary to temporarily suspend the current Congress and constitution and rule by presidential decree.

The failure of nationalism to foster democracy and human rights has done much to fuel separatism inside the Commonwealth of Independent States (CIS) and the Russian Federation. The creation of defensive political alliances among former party bosses, nationalist leaders, and wealthy young entrepreneurs, all intent on keeping as much distance between themselves and Moscow as possible, highlights the Russian government's failure to forge a postcommunist concept of Russian governance (*Rossiiskaia gosudarstvennost'*). The result has been a prolonged crisis of political authority, continued economic deterioration, and open talk of separatism as the only way to break the impasse.

2. THE FEDERATION TREATY
OF 1992: A STRATEGY FOR RUSSIAN UNITY

Still, the prospects for Russian unity are far from hopeless. Some important steps have been taken to halt the fragmentation of the Russian Federation, the most important being the signing of the so-called Federation Treaty on March 31, 1992. Actually this is not one treaty but three agreements in which representatives of the various autonomous republics, provinces, and cities, and autonomous oblasts and districts within the Russian Federation agree to define a new relationship with federal authorities.

Under this treaty, the Russian Federation comprises three distinct federal entities. First are the national states (republics), successors to the Autonomous Soviet Socialist Republics of the former RSFSR. Each contains a substantial minority population, though only three have minorities that account for more than half of the population. Of 20 republics, only Tatarstan and the Chechen Republic have not signed the treaty. Second are national-territories, formed from existing autonomous oblasts and regions. All 11 of these regions have signed the Federation Treaty. Finally, there are the 57 administrative units comprising the remainder of the Russian Federation. Many of these contain small, dispersed ethnic constituencies that have no formal administrative representation.

For all its complexity, the triune treaty structure is based on a simple premise: only by encouraging the devolution of administrative authority from the center can the territorial integrity and historical unity of Russia be preserved. The treaty begins with the significant assertion that the signatories are all components of the Russian Federation and "recognize their responsibility for the preservation of the historical state unity [*istoricheski slozhivshegosia gosudarstvennogo edinstva*] of the peoples of the Russian Federation."[6] The signatories thus acknowledge that they are not constituting a new federation but redefining their membership in an existing one.

The treaty stipulates the sovereignty of the republics, but in a number of crucial points they clearly defer to the supremacy of the federation. There is no provision in the treaties, for example, for secession from the Russian Federation. The treaty stipulates that republican authorities have complete authority to determine and execute laws on their own territories (art. 3, para. 1), and that their authority in these matters cannot be changed. Yet, upon closer examination, federal law will continue to be a constraint even in those areas that are defined as being within the exclusive jurisdiction of the republics. Thus, for example, the treaty gives republics the right to enter into independent negotiations with foreign powers and businesses (art. 3, para. 2), but says that these relations must be coordinated with federal authorities. On the controversial issue of mineral rights and usage of land and water resources, the treaty stipulates that all resources belong to the peoples of that republic, but that ownership (*vladenie*) and usage (*pol'zovanie i rasporiazhenie*) are to be determined jointly according to the laws of the republic and the laws of the Russian Federation. The same is also true of federal resources (art. 3, para. 3).

Finally, a state of emergency may be declared in a republic only with the agreement of the local government, yet even if the emergency is entirely contained within one republic local authorities must inform the president of Russia and the Supreme Soviet of the Russian Federation and conduct themselves in accordance with federal laws during the state of emergency (art. 3, para. 4).

The Federation Treaty is clearly an evolving document, designed to accommodate widely differing regional circumstances. By avoiding specific enumeration of the rights of the republics (and other "subjects of the federation"), the document is designed to allow for the growth of powers of local government, a process President Yeltsin favors. At the same time, however, the signatories pledge to strive for the continued territorial, cultural, linguistic, and historical integrity of Russia. To reinforce this pledge, the treaty stipulates that federal laws and local laws must be guided by "mutual respect and mutual sense of responsibility." Substantive conflicts between the two are to be resolved by binding arbitration procedures to be set down in the new Russian constitution. Conflicts over jurisdiction are to be resolved by the Constitutional Court of the Russian Federation (art. 4, para. 3).

It is fair to say that the treaty requires consultation with federal authorities on virtually every important decision made by a republic. Why then did these "sovereign" republics agree to such constraints? One important consideration is the havoc that the disintegration of central lines of economic distribution has wreaked on their standard of living. While some regions have prospered relative to central Russia and Moscow, no region is yet close to pre-1985 levels of industrial production. Mineral-rich regions such as Yakutiya (Sakha) and Sakhalin would seem to have considerable leverage, but they are constrained by the fact that the personnel, the technology, and the manufacturing industry to utilize those resources are largely in the hands of their Russian population, or lie outside their territories. The prospect of foreigners investing enough in those regions to provide an alternative infrastructure is still many years away—for now, these regions must deal with Moscow if they are to survive.

There is also the appeal of having close ties with a European culture. For many smaller nationalities, Russian culture has been their vehicle into Europe. At a time when these republics and regions wish desperately to expand their contacts with other nations, their knowledge of the Russian language is an important facilitator of contacts with an outside world where there are few speakers of Evenki or Mansi.

Finally, having benefitted from the weakening of Soviet central authority, these regimes now face the prospect of being engulfed in ethnic turmoil or in a separatist conflict themselves. Emphasizing their separation from Russia would drive away precisely the technically skilled population those regions need for their economic survival. On the other hand, appearing to accommodate ethnic Russian interests might encourage militancy among other ethnic groups. Political accommodation with Moscow thus provides a useful cover for both federal authorities and local governments.

As important as this treaty is as a standing document, however, it serves just as importantly to establish a framework within which to resolve future ethnic and administrative conflicts. It does so by emphasizing the priority of universal human and civic rights over territorial and ethnic sovereignty. This is done by making the "defense" of these rights (for both individuals and national minorities) the obligation of government authorities at every level, but the "regulation and defense" of such rights the specific obligation of federal authorities. The emphasis on universal rights, as law professor Boris Krylov has correctly noted, shifts the emphasis of the federation away from ethnic demands and rights and toward the rights of individual citizens of any nationality wherever they may reside within the Russian Federation.[7]

Does the Federation Treaty provide sufficient protection for ethnic minorities inside Russia? It is too early to say for certain, but its authors clearly believe that they have found a means to balance individual rights against the collective rights of ethnic minorities. The solution provided by the treaty is to emphasize federal jurisdiction in issues defining the rights of ethnic minorities, while making the sovereign republics and the Russian Federation co-responsible for the protection of these rights. While both the Russian Federation and the republics must protect these rights, only the federation may "regulate" them (art. 1, para. 1). The federal level thus becomes an arbiter of last resort for ethnic minorities, providing an important level of protection against local authorities.

At the same time, however, by encouraging regional self-administration and regional approaches to conflict resolution, federal authorities wish to put in place mechanisms that would make such appeals unnecessary. To assist in this process, the Council of Nationalities of the Supreme Soviet of the Russian Federation and the State Committee on Nationalities (recently renamed State Committee for the Affairs of the Federation and Nationalities) have agreed to establish regional centers to assist in the development of programs in multiethnic regions. The first such center will be established in Samara.[8]

The Federation Treaty is an important first step in halting the slide toward disintegration, but it leaves many issues unresolved. There is no mention, for example, of how taxes are to be apportioned and collected. It is expected that these will be regulated by bilateral treaties between federal authorities and the republics, as in the case of Yakutiya (Sakha), which recently negotiated the right to keep 20% of minerals gathered on its territory and 45% of hard-currency earning from foreign diamond sales. Still, the absence of agreed-upon principles to guide budget and tax policy opens the door to endless conflict over apportionments.[9] Also, the structures for resolving jurisdictional conflicts have not yet been tested or, in some cases, have not yet even been created, because the proposed Russian Federation constitution has not yet been ratified. Until these structures are in place their efficacy will be in doubt.

But the broader problem plaguing the Russian Federation is that its cohesiveness is directly proportional to Moscow's ability to improve the quality of life in the country. The vast majority of people in the Russian Federation wish to preserve Russia's territorial and cultural unity, but local fears for the prospects for democracy in Moscow and the slow pace of economic revival have fueled speculation regarding Russia's disintegration. The key to Russian unity therefore lies in speeding its economic recovery and reassuring the constituents of the federation that federal authorities are indeed capable of pursuing democratic reforms and decentralization simultaneously. Any movement away from these two goals encourages secessionist sentiment, regardless of ethnicity. Conversely, visible economic progress and a resolution of the crisis of power at the federal level will just as quickly dampen any desire for independence. Both issues, however, are so intertwined that they must be resolved simultaneously.

Before turning to a long-range strategy for the evolution of Russian federalism, two crises that were festering before the Federation Treaty was signed must be addressed—relations with Tatarstan and the Chechen Republic. While many regions have declared their sovereignty, what makes the examples of Tatarstan and the Chechen Republic unique is that they alone of all the territories and peoples of the Russian Federation have refused to sign the Federation Treaty. Since only the Chechen Republic and Tatarstan have interpreted sovereignty to mean separation from the Russian Federation, normalizing relations with these two republics has become a test of Russia's worst-case scenario. If Moscow can establish harmonious relations with these two breakaway republics, then it should not be difficult to accommodate the needs of those regions that have not demanded separation from the federation.

3. TATARSTAN

The situation of the Tatars was an anomaly under the Soviet federal system: Tatars, who rank sixth among Soviet nationalities in total population, were never given their own republic. The obvious slighting of the Tatar national identity no doubt affected the region's decision on August 30, 1990, to be the only region of the Russian Federation to declare its intention to separate from the Russian Republic and to join the Commonwealth of Independent States.

Tensions between Russia and Tatarstan were further exacerbated when the parliament in Kazan announced in February 1992 that it would hold a referendum on the status of the republic. This move, violating a one-year moratorium on referendums declared by the Russian Congress just three months earlier, was declared unconstitutional by the Russian Constitutional Court. The ambiguously worded referendum passed with just 61% in favor of independence. In June 1992, however, a survey conducted by the Supreme Soviet of Tatarstan showed that only 22% of the population supported Tatarstan sovereignty outside the Russian Federation.[10]

Both Moscow and Kazan profess their desire for a federal union, but they have very different interpretations of what this means. The position of the government in Kazan is that the current Russian Federation must be reconstituted. Tatarstan is willing to join as a creator of a new federation, but will not be a party to the current Federation Treaty, which, it says, treats the constituents of the federation as mere administrative subdivisions. Most damning in the Federation Treaty is its failure to provide for secession. Secession, says Tatar presidential adviser Rafael Khakimov, is the only guarantee Tatarstan has against the resurgence of dictatorship in Moscow.[11]

Despite these differences, considerable progress toward an accommodation between the two has been achieved since December 1992. Tatar President Maminter Shaimiyev has acknowledged two important principles: the desirability of preserving the Russian Federation's territorial integrity and the desirability of a federal association with the Russian republic.

In 1993, a number of important results have been achieved. Both sides have agreed on a division of revenues from oil production and export quotas. Tatarstan will receive the revenues from its quota, in return for which Russia will not tax oil shipments through its territory and Tatarstan will contribute two million tons of oil this year to the payment of Russia's external debt.[12] Tatarstan has also agreed to the opening of offices of the Russian Ministry of Foreign Affairs and the Russian State Committee on Nationalities Policy in Kazan. These offices will facilitate the process of obtaining visas and travel documents and also function as a coordinating center for foreign economic activities in Tatarstan. According to a Tatar spokesperson, the opening of these offices "does not represent recognition of the independence of Tatarstan, since it does not aspire to leave the federation." A compromise of sorts thus appears to have been reached whereby Tatarstan's separate status is tacitly recognized, while at the same time it is being drawn into the coordinating structures and processes of the existing Federation Treaty. The Russian government has announced plans to open similar offices in distant regions such as Yakutiya, further diminishing differences between the status of Tatarstan and the other members of the Russian Federation.

The progress made in Tatarstan-Russian relations indicates that the Federation Treaty is indeed flexible enough to accommodate extensive autonomy of different regions. While Tatarstan aspires to "associate" status within the federation (similar to that of Puerto Rico in the United States or West Berlin in the pre-1989 Federal Republic of Germany), the ultimate definition of the status of Tatarstan has been put off for the time being as not essential to the negotiation of specific agreements.[13] Unless the current Russian government is replaced by a significantly more authoritarian one, however, there do not appear to be any insurmountable obstacles to the normalization of relations between Kazan and Moscow.

4. THE CHECHEN REPUBLIC

Russia's conflict with the other nonsignatory of the Federation Treaty, the Chechen Republic, must be seen in the context of the fragile ethnic mosaic of the Caucasus region. It cannot be resolved without addressing the broader issue of Russia's mission in the region. The Caucasus has long been the object of conflict between Russia, Turkey, and Iran. In 1864, Russia succeeded in pacifying the area only by exterminating tens of thousands of hill people in the western Caucasus and deporting many more to Turkey. The Soviet period saw the further deportation of Cossacks, Chechens, Ingush, Karachaevans, and Balkarians.

In the spring of 1991, in an attempt to redress past injustices, the

Congress of People's Deputies passed a decree on the "Rehabilitation of Repressed Peoples." This well-intentioned document sought to restore the national boundaries that had existed in the region before they had been "forcefully changed," but in doing so it set off a powderkeg. The formerly unified administrative units of Chechnya and Ingushetiya separated, as has Kabardino-Balkariya. The ensuing territorial disputes have led to well over 100 deaths and numerous assaults on Russian peacekeeping forces detached to the region. At least two wars of secession involving Georgia have spilled over into Russia, and this may be just the beginning. The entire region contains nearly 17 million people and 80 major ethnic groups spread over seven territorial jurisdictions within the Russian Federation alone.

It was clearly a mistake for the Supreme Soviet to try to resolve the historical injustices done in the region by stressing national and ethnic rights, rather than territorial stability and individual rights. The second mistake was to decree a change in boundaries without first establishing a mechanism through which these changes could be reviewed and, if necessary, amended by the local populations. The bloodshed in the region thus stands as a sharp indictment of the very concept of a centrally administered unitary state. Had lawmakers in Moscow had any sense of the real grievances in the region, they doubtless would have hesitated to grant these populations such a painful measure of "justice."

The declaration of independence by the Chechen Republic and its refusal to sign the Federation Treaty are consequences of the hardening of ethnic self-perceptions in the region. Like the Tatars, the Chechens have a long history of military conflict with Russia. Many modern cities of the Caucasus region, such as Vladikavkaz, Nazran, and Grozny (the capital of the Chechen Republic) are former Cossack outposts. Thus, when former Soviet General Dzhokhar Dudaev assumed power in the region in November 1991 and defied central authorities in Moscow, it caused a first test of wills between President Yeltsin and the Congress over the use of military force. This crisis was ultimately resolved in favor of a negotiated solution, but the instability of Dudaev's government has hampered negotiations and tempted Russian authorities to pressure the region into adhering to the Federation Treaty. At the time of this writing (April 1993), President Dudaev appears increasingly isolated. The Congress, with the support of the trade unions, has moved to impeach him. Meanwhile, Vice-Premier Yaragi Mamadaev has proposed an administrative division of responsibilities between Russia and the Chechen Republic while keeping the republic within the Russian Federation.

Taking advantage of Dudaev's weakness, Russian Vice-Premier

Sergei Shakhrai flew to Grozny in January 1993 and signed a ten-year protocol that, again, follows the pattern established by the Federation Treaty. Although Mamadaev did not formally participate in this agreement, he had previously prepared a draft based on the recent accord negotiated between the Russian Federation and Tatarstan.[14]

The principle guiding the Federation Treaty—local self-rule in exchange for a pledge to preserve the territorial and cultural integrity of the Russian Federation—lies at the heart of both this accord and the Federation Treaty. In point two of the agreement, both sides agree to set up working groups to determine a division of jurisdiction and mutual delegation of authority between the Russian Federation and the Chechen Republic. This division is to occur on three levels: those functions to be administered by the Russian Federation; those to be administered by the Chechen Republic; and those to be administered jointly. Working groups are to meet regularly and to prepare acceptable texts before the end of 1993.

As in the case of Tatarstan, both sides appear to be well on the way to an accommodation. The Chechen delegation sees official Russian participation in the negotiations as *de jure* recognition of Chechen independence. The Russian side in turn has gotten the Chechens to recognize the desirability of membership in the federation and of working toward a resolution of difficulties within the framework of the Federation Treaty. It is even possible that a new government in Grozny will simply sign the Federation Treaty.[15]

5. THE COSSACKS

But while this crisis may be dissipating, another is just emerging—the resurgence of Cossack identity. Cossacks are a distinctive social group whose main characteristics have been 1) a sense of service to the Russian Empire, 2) fierce independence of small, rural communities, and 3) defense of the Russian Orthodox faith. Historically, the Cossacks have carried Russian government authority and Russian traditions into the northern Caucasus. Just before the Bolshevik revolution, Cossacks were heavily concentrated in the lower Don region, numbering over 1.5 million, or 42% of the local population. Smaller Cossack self-governing entities existed throughout the southern border of the Russian Empire and into Siberia. A survey conducted by the Russian government in 1991 shows that in the Don region (Rostov oblast) today some 28% of the population still identify themselves as Cossacks.[16] On June 15, 1992, the president and the Supreme Soviet passed decrees on "The Rehabilitation of the Cossacks," recognizing the Cossacks as a distinct minority. Some Cossack leaders now demand a "return" of certain autonomous regions to their control and reparations for the loss of nearly one-third of their population under the Soviet terror.

The Cossack revival offers both problems and opportunities for the resolution of ethnic/territorial conflicts in the region. On the one hand, most established Cossack hierarchies support strengthening central authority in Moscow. Despite their dislike for communism, they credit Soviet institutions with maintaining law and order and defending Russia's borders. Many see this as the main historical mission of the Cossacks.

Other Cossacks, however, emphasize the tradition of freedom and independence of spirit as the most important facet of Cossack rebirth. In the tense early days of the March 1993 crisis between the president and the Congress of People's Deputies, Cossack leaders were among the first to pledge their support to Yeltsin. They hope that the decrees on rehabilitation will lead to the formation of small, autonomous economic/governmental structures in local villages throughout Cossack territories, and speed the process of private land usage and agricultural revival. This latter aspect is also attractive to many of their neighbors who generally view the restoration of traditional Cossack autonomy favorably.

Russia thus has a potent ally in the Caucasus that favors regional decentralization while maintaining a strong cultural and political orientation toward Moscow. The trick will be accommodating their peculiar brand of self-identity within the context of the federation. In the United States, for example, groups such as the Amish and the Native Americans have been accorded special status to preserve their distinctive heritage. A similar solution might be tried in Russia.

6. SOLUTIONS TO THE CAUCASUS CAULDRON

So complex is the ethnic mosaic in the Caucasus region that some Russian officials have suggested that this region of perennial conflict be cordoned off from the rest of the federation. Such a non-solution, however, would not resolve the current crises. It is impossible to draw an imaginary border in the region that would not either leave millions of Russians stranded or incorporate widely disparate ethnic groups into the federation. Moreover, there is the strategic interest that the area poses to the other powers of the region, Turkey and Iran. The latter would surely view Russia's withdrawal from the region as an opportunity to expand ties to Islamic minorities, a move that would threaten the position of Christian Armenia and Georgia and force the other members of the CIS to be more actively involved in the region. A religious confrontation in which the Christian and Islamic populations would be forced to take sides would seriously split the already fragile alliance among members of the commonwealth.

Efforts at negotiating a permanent solution have been unsuccessful so far because there seems to be no concerted Russian strategy for the region as a whole. The Russian Foreign Ministry seems primarily concerned with not undermining the internal stability of Georgia, now led by former Soviet Foreign Minister Eduard Shevardnadze. Conservative parliamentarians worry about the loss of Russian territories. The Ministry of Defense worries about getting bogged down in another Afghanistan. In response, three types of solutions have been advanced to help pacify the region.

The first, proposed by a group of experts of the Main Directorate for the Preparation of Cadres for Government Service (Roskadrov) of the Russian government, urges the Russian government to openly become the arbiter of the region's ethnic and territorial disputes. They recommend that disputed territories be put under direct presidential administration; that all ground transportation between North and South Ossetia be controlled by Russian forces; that the federation assist in the development of distinct Ingush government structures and the Ingush constitution; that Russian forces adopt a much wider peacekeeping and disarmament role; and lastly, that a state of emergency be decreed to allow for restrictions on the local press.[17]

This approach might temporarily pacify the region, but it will not resolve the conflicts there. Russian arbitration would be perceived as favoring the Ingush at the expense of the Chechens. The objective of this proposal is to tranquilize the region by administering a strong dose of law and order, but the history of similar pacification measures in the past suggests that tensions will continue to simmer below the surface and erupt again as soon as peacekeeping forces withdraw.

Another approach is being recommended by the head of the Council of Nationalities of the Supreme Soviet of the Russian Federation, Ramazan Abdulatipov, and the head of the State Committee for the Affairs of the Federation and Nationalities of the Russian government, Vice-Premier Sergei Shakhrai. In mid-January 1993, along with a local group, the Senezh Forum, they convened a three-day roundtable of major political parties and public organizations of the region. The gathering, which included parties from different ends of the political spectrum, succeeded in reaching agreement on several statements of principle and established a set of standing organizations through which to continue their dialogue.[18]

In the "Declaration of Principles Guiding Relations Among Nationalities," the participants agreed that the Northern Caucasus forms a single "historico-cultural unit and a part of the Russian Federation." Future negotiations among the groups would therefore be based on the constitution of the Russian Federation, the constitution of the various republics of the region, and the principles of the Federation Treaty. The participants also agreed to organize a council of the heads of government and administration at the level of oblast and krai that would meet regularly. Finally, a Northern Caucasus Democratic Congress would coordinate the efforts of groups in the region that support decentralization and peaceful, democratic solutions to territorial conflicts. Although the delegates were not able to agree on all points in the various working groups set up by the organizers, the possibility of appealing to the Russian Constitutional Court for the resolution of certain issues was frequently cited.

A third proposal has been to resurrect the Transcaucasian Confederation, which existed briefly in the USSR in 1918 and then again from 1922 to 1937. The confederation would be modeled on the Swiss confederation; i.e., the smallest administrative regions would become almost mini-states and be given complete administrative autonomy. If they desired, they could delegate certain powers to larger administrative units. The idea is to decentralize power in the region to such a degree that local borders and ethnic claims become politically irrelevant.[19]

The Russian government seems to have adopted elements of all three proposals. First, it recognizes that Russian armed forces are the only ones capable of putting an end to the fighting in the region and of supporting an overarching governmental authority that would encompass the entire region. It is in this vein that President Yeltsin's remarks of February 28, 1993, that Russia should have "special powers to guarantee peace and stability in the former Union," should be understood.[20] In this role, Russia can rely on the support of local Cossack forces.[21] Indeed, utilizing the Cossacks would give authorities in Moscow a chance to exert some restraint over the Cossacks, who have at times taken it upon themselves to offer military support for the cause of Russian unity.

Beyond the immediate imposition of a ceasefire, however, the government seems to have embraced the idea of a regional confederation composed of smaller ethnic/territorial enclaves. This proposal could work, however, only if these enclaves were essentially micro-states, each with a separate administration, each regulating its ethnic relations individually. The guiding principle of such a Transcaucasian Confederation would be the supremacy of individual human rights over ethnic rights in adherence to the principles of the Federation Treaty. The Russian government's decision to emphasize local self-government is a welcome departure from a centralized approach used in the past. It resembles the concept of European federal subsidiarity proposed by former German Foreign Minister Hans-Dietrich Genscher, which also seeks to encourage localities and regions to use their diversity to common advantage.[22]

Russia will be taking a considerable risk if it intervenes decisively to end fighting in the region, but if the groundwork for such intervention is laid carefully there is a possibility of achieving long-term stability for the region. What is especially important is that Russia obtain international support for this effort. To allay fears among CIS states, Russia has requested United Nations assistance in peacekeeping and administration, and has sought to coordinate efforts with other CIS countries.

Alternatively, a multilateral CIS force might serve as a valid peace broker, especially with United Nations assistance and coordination. Utilizing CIS institutions would be a logical choice, given the extensive ties forged under the former Soviet regime. Indeed, it may be one of the most important functions that such a multilateral force, which now lacks any clearly defined mission, could serve. The recent joint peacekeeping effort in Tajikistan, involving Kazakh, Uzbek, Kyrgyz, and Russian forces, might well serve as a model.[23]

7. LONGER-TERM SOLUTIONS:
GUIDED DECENTRALIZATION AND WESTERN ASSISTANCE

The prospects for Russian unity remain greater than in many other regions of the former Soviet Union because calls for regional autonomy inside Russia have nearly always proved to be aspects of a struggle for power among elites, not a struggle over national identity. We are not, therefore, witnessing a conflict of nation-building aspirations and governmental institutions making mutually exclusive claims to political sovereignty. Cultural and national identification with Russia remains strong throughout the federation, as shown by the evolution of regional politics. While the nomenklatura in these regions initially saw only the need to hold on to power, today they find that they must respond to the demands of the local population. Demands for greater autonomy in order to stabilize prices and expand trade with other regions is a direct result.

The greatest desire of these regional political leaders is for clear lines of authority. This message came through again at the March 1993 Congress of People's Deputies, where regional and republican leaders consistently opposed any further disintegration of central authority. Clearly designated authority would allow regional leaders to know where to appeal for assistance at the federal level. This explains their preference for stronger presidential rather than parliamentary rule and their support for President Yeltsin in the March 1993 constitutional struggle. Only in the absence of clear authority do republican and subrepublican leaders reluctantly prefer to be left alone.

The success of the Federation Treaty shows, ultimately, that the Russian government can accommodate demands for decentralization and counter the disintegrative tendencies that led to the demise of the USSR. As a result, Russia does not face the prospect of imminent disintegration, or of serious ethnic explosions outside the Caucasus. The prospect of disintegration and ethnic upheaval will rise sharply, however, if the economic situation does not improve or if Moscow's commitment to decentralization and democracy appear in danger.

To prevent disintegration, therefore, the Russian government must pursue a difficult strategy: to simultaneously strengthen democratic institutions, further the process of regional decentralization, and improve the economy. Such a strategy, which I term "guided decentralization," can reverse the centrifugal forces that the demise of the USSR has unleashed by making Russia as desirable a partner politically and economically as it is culturally.

Guided decentralization must begin with the recognition that a democratic government must be authoritative to be effective. Further progress toward federal decentralization in Russia thus requires, paradoxically, a central government in Moscow with more—not less—political authority. The present weakness of the government, partly the result of the absence of new structures and concepts of government to replace old Soviet ones and partly the result of political in-fighting, has encouraged the uncontrolled diffusion of power to various regions of the country. Unfortunately, the weakening of authority at the center has not generally been accompanied by greater democracy at the local level, because elites have been far too willing to manipulate the grievances of local populations, both Russian and minority, in order to preserve their personal freedoms. Unless this process is reversed, the rationale for regions to join the center will eventually disappear. Today, a strong center is the best guarantee that civic and minority rights will be protected against local dictators.

One body recently formed to help strengthen the authority of the center is the Council of Heads of the Republics (Sovet glav respublik). It serves to coordinate economic, political, social, and foreign policy among the various republics of the federation. Just as importantly, it strengthens the president in his power struggle with the Supreme Soviet by institutionally linking him and the heads of the different republics. They in turn rely on him and on the apparatus of the Russian Security Council to help maintain authority within their own republics. Yeltsin has stated his desire to see more actual authority transferred to these regions. In turn, the heads of the republics have sided with him on the need for a stronger presidential authority in the country.[24]

Another essential prerequisite for the preservation of the Russian Federation is the adoption of a new constitution that better defines the mutual jurisdictions of the executive and legislative branches. The Federation Treaty is an important step in resolving political disputes between the center and outlying regions, but the treaty is part of a new constitution that has yet to be adopted. The new Russian constitution should embody the assumptions underlying the nationalities policy being pursued (with striking accord) by the Russian government and the Supreme Soviet.

A third component of guided decentralization is a policy of economic revitalization, which should begin not at the center but in each of Russia's already distinct economic regions. The process of economic regionalism is already well underway—numerous economic agreements have been signed between regions, between cities, between oblasts. They are made necessary by the disintegration of old economic and political ties. At the same time, however, they feed a reconceptualization of center-periphery relations that has already found concrete expression in the Federation Treaty and in bilateral negotiations.

A regional reorientation of investment and economic development is thus the logical extension of the political and administrative decentralization envisioned by the Federation Treaty. Rather than fight this trend, the center would do far better to recognize its benefits and channel it to support the federal structure. Expanded privatization, for example, will encourage economic integration as investors seek larger and more profitable outlets for their goods and services. As regions on the periphery gain control of their natural resources, they will want to improve ties to Russia's large population centers and to the commodities markets and exchanges in Moscow and St. Petersburg that are their link to the West. Tatarstan, for example, is currently looking for investments in its Elabuga car manufacturing plant and its oil refineries and sees Russia as its primary partner in doing so. As its Prime Minister, Muhammad Sabirov, has remarked, "We are not interested in distancing ourselves from Russia. Tatarstan is interested in the economic strengthening of Russia."[25]

Some will say that regionalizing economic policy undercuts the center. But as economic consultant Leonid Grebnev has shown, the many regions of the Russian Federation have natural resources and industrial capabilities that complement each other.[26] Hence they naturally desire not economic autarky, but further economic integration with the regions of the Russian Federation and the CIS. Such integration cannot proceed from the top down by decree, but will develop only as the needs of local manufacturers develop. The most effective means to encourage these centripetal tendencies is to enact a comprehensive packet of legislation aimed at fostering an internal common market. As the economic situation improves, so will the ability of the federation to stimulate regional development in underdeveloped regions and bind them even more firmly to the center (a process that has worked with Sicily and the Basque lands).

Similar centripetal economic forces already appear to be at work in the CIS. A core group of states, including Belarus, Kazakhstan, Russia, and Uzbekistan, seem inclined to strengthen their cooperation within the "ruble zone." The eastern regions of Ukraine may well follow suit if granted the regional autonomy they desire. While these economies will need to develop regionally, the fact that such an overwhelming percentage of intellectual, financial, and telecommunications resources are located in Moscow makes it indispensable to integrating economic ties between CIS states and between regions of the CIS and foreign economic partners.

Western economic and technical assistance can be decisive here if disbursed wisely. The quickest way to encourage economic rebirth is to invest not in the center but in regional and local business ventures. Regional economic investment will bring quicker results, be more visible to the population, encourage local entrepreneurs, and encourage horizontal ties across regions rather than vertical economic centralization.

Guided decentralization also requires a more authoritative Constitutional Court. In most successful federal systems, it has been the courts that have asserted the affirmative duty of members of the federation to cooperation and self-restraint (what the Germans, for example, call *Bundestreue* or federal comity). It is fervently to be hoped that the Russian Constitutional Court evolves in this direction, but as of yet there is no body of federal constitutional law to rely on because there is no new constitution.

Russia will survive this critical period if it can make secession a more costly option than integration. It will fail, however, if the West rewards secession with economic investment and diplomatic recognition. While it may be tempting to cut deals with certain resource-rich regions, such a policy is ultimately self-defeating, for it is sure to alienate the great majority of the Russian population. It is in the best interests of the West, therefore, to state a clear preference for a unified Russian Federation, and even to support efforts by federal authorities, in conjunction with other CIS states, to impose order in regions of the country prone to turmoil and ethnic strife.

Concerns are often raised in the West about the revival of Russian nationalism. Could it not impede the progress toward federalism? Today, there are many political forms that Russian nationalism takes.[27] Some "patriotic" groups, like the Christian Democratic Movement and the Constitutional Democratic Party, combine a revival of Russian national consciousness with strong commitments to political pluralism, private property, and national self-determination. We should therefore be wary of confusing appeals to Russian nationalism with outright chauvinism.

By and large, the conservative wing of the Russian political spectrum appeals not to narrow nationalism but to the public's concern for domestic tranquility and social equity. As a result, the concerns of most mainstream conservative political forces in Russia (usually labeled "nationalists" in the West) can be accommodated by the framework of the Federation Treaty, which seeks to encourage an orderly transition to local self-government and the preservation of Russia's cultural and territorial integrity. Those few who advocate a communist-inspired form of recentralization are not really nationalists at all but neo-Bolsheviks. As the latest referendum results again show, they are a very small minority with almost no popular backing in Russia today. They may lament the loss of former Soviet territories, but they have few alternatives to offer.

Beyond distinguishing more carefully among political groupings inside Russia, the West might also look for ways of assisting political groupings like the Senezh Forum that strive to diminish ethnic tensions in the region. Private foundations might assist moderate conservative groups like the Suzdal Initiative, organized by the 29-year-old leader of the Constitutional Democratic Party, Dmitri Rogozin, with the support of Russian Vice-President Aleksandr Rutskoi and Mikhail Gorbachev. This group, which represents a wide spectrum of business and political leaders from all CIS states, seeks to establish a "laboratory" for working out new forms of relations within the CIS.[28] It is especially important to include moderate conservatives in the resolution of these issues so that they do not feel isolated from the political process. The striking success of Ramazan Abdulatipov and Sergei Shakhrai, each from "opposing" branches of the government, in designing and implementing the Federation Treaty, shows what can be accomplished.

The West can offer assistance but, ultimately, Russia must develop its own distinctive model of decentralized government. Fortunately, there are a variety of models it can choose from in its own historical past. The experience of Russian administrative decentralization and self-government in the zemstvo unions during the latter half of the 19th and early 20th centuries belies the notion that stability and prosperity can be achieved only through centralization.[29] Adopting some modern variant of this past experience might be preferable to importing a foreign model that has no roots in Russia's historical experience.

In the final analysis, the success of any federal union rests on the desire of its members to pursue a common destiny. So far, this desire has not been tapped sufficiently by the federal government, which is still bogged down in internecine struggles. But if Russia can resolve its constitutional crisis this year, then its prospects for forging a successful federation appear very good.

With the convening of the Constitutional Assembly in June 1993, the debilitating controversy over the status of the subjects of the Russian Federation has entered its final stages. To be sure, the detail of the federal arrangement will take years to work out, but the ultimate objective—maximum regional autonomy within a loosely governed federal structure—has apparently been embraced by all key players.

Skeptics will question whether such a loose federation can hold, given Russia's historical propensity for centralized control. Only time will tell, of course, but it is worth noting that Russia only achieved its high degree of centralization during the last three centuries—and then only superficially (recall Pitirim Sorokin's famous comment that "under the iron roof of an autocratic monarchy there lived a hundred thousand peasant republics").[30] The prospect of regionalization of Russian politics, therefore, need not foreshadow the collapse of the Russian Federation. While some regions may wish to follow the path of Tatarstan, others will not, particularly if they are granted extensive local administrative and economic autonomy.

The current desire to equalize the status of all the subjects of the federation (cities, regions, and republics) is a perfectly predictable response to the overcentralization of administrative control in Moscow. It reflects a deep-seated understanding that true federalism can emerge only after the grip of central authorities over people's everyday lives has been broken. Whether or not the Federation Treaty is ultimately incorporated in the new constitution, it has already served its purpose in smoothing Russia's transition from a centrally administered state toward a new system of regionally based government.

NOTES

1. "Considerations on Representative Government" in J.S. Mill, *Utilitarianism, Liberty and Representative Government* (New York: E.P. Dutton, 1951), p. 486.

2. "Dezintegratsiia Rossii: Tezisy doklada Soveta po vneshnei i oboronoi politike," *Nezavisimaia gazeta*, no. 238 (Dec. 10, 1992). This gathering of influential Russian political analysts mentions the periods of feudal principalities, and turmoil of the 17th and early 20th centuries as justifying "the most decisive measures to prevent the disintegration of the state."

3. Sergei Pushkarev, *Self-Government and Freedom in Russia* (Boulder, CO: Westview, 1988), pp. 8–13.

4. Sergei Maksudov, "Prospects for the Development of the USSR's Nationalities," in Alexander Shtromas and Morton A. Kaplan, eds., *The Soviet Union and the Challenge of the Future*, vol. 3 (New York: Paragon House, 1989), p. 331.

5. Robert J. Osborn, "Russia: Federalism, Regionalism and Nationality Claims," paper presented at a conference on "Russia and America: From Rivalry to Reconciliation," University of Pennsylvania, Philadelphia, February 1993, p. 18.

6. Supreme Soviet of the Russian Federation, Preamble, para. 3, *Dogovor, Konstitutsiia* (Moscow: Izvestiia, 1992), p. 81.

7. B. Krylov, "Federativnyi dogovor zakliuchen," *Narodnyi deputat*, no. 16, 1992, pp. 63–64.

8. Sergei Zhigalov and Sergei Chugaev, "Povolzh'e i Ural podderzhivaiut novuiu gosudarstvennuiu natsional'nuiu politiku Rossii," *Izvestiia*, March 2, 1993, p. 2.

9. Osborn, "Russia," p. 33.

10. Iurii Reshetov, "Mozhet li Tatarstan skazat' 'Da', esli Kazan' govorit 'Net'," *Rossiiskaia gazeta*, March 4, 1993, p. 6.

11. Rafael Khakimov, "Reintegratsiia Rossii?" *Nezavisimaia gazeta*, Jan. 5, 1993, p. 2

12. "Kazan' i Moskva dogovorilis' po voprosu o razdele tatarskoi nefti," *Rossiiskie vesti*, Feb. 2, 1993, p. 1.

13. The Spanish name for the Commonwealth of Puerto Rico is "Estado Libre Asociado." Today, the only US government body that can interfere in Puerto Rican legislation is the US Supreme Court. In the case of West Berlin, while it is treated like any other Land, its occupied status requires that federal legislation be re-enacted through its own legislative body, the Berlin Senate.

14. R. Akhmedov, " . . . a drugie ofitsial'nye litsa ChR dumaut inache," *Severnyi kavkaz*, Jan. 23, 1993, p. 6.

15. See the remarks by the state secretary of the Cabinet of Ministers, Shepa Gadaev, "'Narod progolosuet za dogovor s Rossiei,'" *Severnyi kavkaz* (Nal'chik), March 6, 1993, p. 1.

16. Igor' Iakovenko, "Donskie Kazaki," *Gospodin narod*, no. 12, 1992, p. 3.

17. Sergei Modestov, Boris Mozdukhov, Aleksandra Rabysheva, "Osetino-Ingushskii konflikt: Vykhod iz tupika," *Izvestiia* (Moscow evening ed.), Jan. 13, 1993, p. 4

18. Evgenii Bobrin, "Put' viden. Kremnistyi," *Rossiiskaia gazeta*, Jan. 20, 1993, p. 2; V. Grigoryev, "Poisk putei soglasiia," *Vesti gorodov yuga Rossii*, Jan. 25–31, 1993, pp. 1–3.

19. Suren Zolian, "Imia shansa—Zakavkazkaia federatsiia, *Moskovskie novosti*, Jan. 10, 1993, p. 2.

20. Although certain CIS neighbors professed alarm at his remarks, the Russian government clarified that Yeltsin was referring specifically to its peacekeeping efforts in the Caucasus and Moldova. Daniel Schneider and Chrystyna Lapychak, "Russia, Ukraine Stalemated in Arms Talks," *Christian Science Monitor*, March 8, 1993, p. 6.

21. Plans are already underway to incorporate Cossacks into the border patrols. Daniel Schneider, "Amid New Security Effort, Russia Moves to Secure Ex-Soviet Borders," *Christian Science Monitor*, March 8, 1993, p. 6.

22. "The Future of Europe," speech by Hans-Dietrich Genscher, delivered at the Palacio das Necessidades, Lisbon, Portugal, July 12, 1991.

23. Aleksandr Karpov, "V Tadzhikistane pribyvaiut mirotvorcheskie sily," *Izvestiia*, March 5, 1993, p. 1.

24. Vasilii Kononenko, "Glavy respublik: svoe otnoshenie k referendumu poka ne opredelili," *Izvestiia*, Feb. 10, 1993, p. 1

25. Radik Batyrshin, "Kazan' zakliuchit soglashenie so vsemi gosudarstvami SNG," *Nezavisimaia gazeta*, Feb. 25, 1993, p. 1.

26. Vladimir Kucherenko, "Budushchaia Rossiia: Soiuz svobodnykh regionov," *Megalopolis-Ekspress*, no. 23, 1992, p. 12.

27. See Nicolai N. Petro, "Conservative Politics in Russia: Implications for U.S.-Russian Relations," in Alvin Z. Rubinstein, Oles Smolansky, and George Ginsburgs, eds., *Russia and America: From Rivalry to Reconciliation* (New York: M.E. Sharpe, 1993).

28. Anna Ostapchuk, "S molodymi politikami poobshchalis' mnogie," *Nezavisimaia gazeta*, Oct. 3, 1992, p. 2.

29. Among the notable Western works on this subject are T.J. Polner, et al., *Russian Local Government During the War and the Union of Zemstvos* (New Haven: Yale, 1930); S. Frederick Starr, *Decentralization and Self-Government in Russia, 1830–1870* (Princeton: Princeton U. Press, 1972); Sergei Pushkarev, *Self-Government and Freedom in Russia* (see note 3); and Jacob Walkin, *The Rise of Democracy in Pre-Revolutionary Russia* (New York: Praeger, 1962). Two interesting recent Russian publications in this area are Aleksandr Solzhenitsyn's *Rebuilding Russia* (New York: Farrar, Straus and Giroux, 1991); and R. R. Abdulatipov, L.F. Boltenkova, and Iu. F. Iarov, *Federalizm v istorii Rossii* (Moscow: Respublika, 1992). This last volume is the first in a new series of books whose editors include the chairman of the Council of Nationalities of the Supreme Soviet of the Russian Federation.

30. Pushkarev, *Self-Government and Freedom in Russia*.

Part III
The Role of Confidence- and Security-Building Measures

7

A Call for Confidence-Building Measures for Minorities in Eastern Europe

ANDRZEJ KARKOSZKA

1. INTRODUCTION

The largely peaceful disintegration of the Soviet type of government in Eastern Europe and the subsequent liquidation of the communist bloc of states dramatically changed the entire international system. The disappearance of the Soviet Union and the Warsaw Pact marked the end of the Cold War. This represents the end of a period of the 20th century that shaped relations among nations to a degree comparable only with that of the two World Wars and the decolonization process. In the aftermath of the 1989 revolutions in Eastern Europe, a profound ideological divide and an all-encompassing power rivalry between East and West vanished. The change in the international situation can be characterized as a shift from one that involved a high degree of military insecurity for states in a paradoxically stable international environment to one that involves low military insecurity, but in conditions of great instability. From a structural point of view, the international system looks similar to that of the 19th century, with clear multipolarity, fluidity, and considerable uncertainty as to its future shape. However, all aspects of international life, at least in Europe—economics, technology, ecology, social mobility, and hundreds of other aspects—are vastly different from those of the 19th century. We are thus entering a *terra incognita* in international relations. The new, post-Cold War pattern of relationships between states will probably give rise to new paradigms and norms for their analysis; one of the most visible differences in approach may be seen in the area of international security.

It is hard to overestimate the traumatic effect of such changes, particularly in Eastern Europe. Not only did the changes come with an unexpected rapidity, they also surpassed all the assumptions we may have held as to their scope and depth. The political, social, and economic systems of the eastern and southern part of Europe have been turned upside down, all in the name of freedom, reform, and modernization. This has caused social and economic dislocation on a vast scale, as well as the political and economic polarization of these societies. In the turmoil, and with the rise of a freer media and free political expression in many of these countries, the ghosts of extreme nationalism and chauvinism on the one hand and old grievances of ethnic deprivations on the other have risen to the surface of the political scene as powerful forces. One after another, multinational states have broken down, sometimes peacefully, but more often violently, under the pressure of these forces, shattering hopes for a stable and peaceful post-Cold War Europe.

2. THE SALIENCE OF THE NONMILITARY ASPECTS OF SECURITY

In the past, security concerns in Europe largely focused on military aspects, mainly on offensive versus defensive potential of the armed forces of states or alliances and on their mutual perceptions of each other's intentions. The ultimate concern was the preservation of a second nuclear strike capability and, through that, deterrence of a suicidal first nuclear strike. In today's world, the danger of a widespread nuclear conflagration has subsided to a minimum. In Europe, partially due to the treaties on Conventional Forces in Europe (CFE) and Confidence- and Security-Building Measures (CSBMs) introduced as part of the CSCE process, the conventional military capabilities in Europe have been drawn down into a situation of generally stable equilibrium. The military confrontation between the former adversaries of NATO and the Warsaw Pact has been transformed into open, friendly and—in some cases—even quasi-alliance relations. Most of the postcommunist states of East Central Europe espouse the same basic values of democracy, free enterprise, and market economies as their West European or North American cousins. In such a context, all of the states of Europe and their citizens could feel quite secure—if only the military aspects of security were of concern. Unfortunately, reality intrudes.

What is apparent from even a cursory examination of today's European scene is that at best a mixed picture exists. The fact is that it is not the unquestionably positive aspects of the end of the Cold War that shape prevailing perceptions of European and, particularly, East European security, but rather unforeseen negative internal and international outcomes of the ongoing transformation to democracy and market economies. The "peace dividend" from the end of the Cold War never materialized. Hopes for quick economic progress on the part of East Europeans seem to have been postponed for some considerable time to come; instead, a deep recession, growing unemployment, social sacrifice, and internal strife are the order of the day.

Growing economic polarization among various social groups, typical of the early stages of building market economies, creates a fertile ground for the polarization of political parties and the growth of "popular" movements. Some of these find that ethnic and nationalist themes best serve their purposes. A free mass media, released from the bounds of censorship, has been used to promote both just and unjust causes. Newly introduced democracy permits bringing into the open long-suppressed grievances and hopes for political, religious, ethnic, and economic equity. Ethnic clashes, fomented by both political and economic changes, abound, involving a range of social and ethnic groups, often even the state apparatus itself. It is clear that the security perceptions of people living in this part of Europe are based on feelings of insecurity despite the fact that purely military conditions around them seem, generally speaking, to be satisfactory. In their turn, the instabilities of Eastern Europe influence, in many ways, perceptions of security on the entire continent.

It is thus the nonmilitary aspects of security—political, economic, ecological, and societal (the latter embracing cultural, religious, and ethnic issues)—that take a front seat in the evolving international security arena, placing them ahead of, for the first time, traditional political-military concerns. But nonmilitary issues can always transform themselves into military ones, should they become internally politicized; or begin to operate in conjunction if belittled, dismissed, or not fully satisfied; or start to involve neighboring states and, thus, assume an international character. We are currently witnessing this phenomenon in the Balkans, Georgia, Moldova, and Azerbaijan. Because of the growing interdependence of nations and states, this process of internationalization of internal societal/economic, demographic, ethnic, and religious tensions and dislocations seems to be much more rapid than ever before. If this observation is true, then the readiness of the international community, in terms of possessing the appropriate reactive and regulatory mechanisms for avoiding the transformation of internal and local tension into international political-military conflict, is of crucial importance.

3. THE GRAVITY OF THE ETHNIC CONFLICTS

This level of readiness on the part of the international system already, to a large extent, exists. A multitude of organizations and institutions, a great number of legal international instruments, political movements, and international humanitarian associations work intensively in a plethora of social, economic, and political areas, all seeking to exert a positive influence on the stability of international relations.

This influence is exerted in both direct and indirect ways: by setting general and specific legal and moral standards, developing legal and institutional structures, establishing a code of operation for bureaucracies, creating implementation mechanisms, ensuring an effective international response to the misconduct of states, and forming various institutions and organizations to deal with individual and group human rights. However, extensive and constantly expanding as it is, the international legal and organizational response nevertheless often lags behind the dynamics of societal changes in the world. This is partly the result of a well-justified preoccupation with the political-military aspects of security during the last half century.

So far, in speaking about the relative importance of the various nonmilitary aspects of security, there has been no particular emphasis on any specific category—economic, ecological, cultural, religious, or ethnic. It is clear, however, that prevailing opinion considers the last one, the ethnic minorities issue, to be the main cause of the ongoing hot conflicts in Europe, and it is thus elevated above all others. It was in many cases national aspirations for independence, the struggle of ethnic minorities for equal rights and freedoms, or desires to protect the supremacy of a national majority or protect ethnic kin in a neighboring state that shattered the map of Europe after 1989. As state borders in many regions of the continent do not dovetail with ethnic borders, and as the cultural advancement of many peoples continues to serve to awaken their national awareness and aspirations, the situation in this regard may continue to bring to the fore ever new ethnic conflicts. Such phenomena belong to a well-known cultural pattern. With unclear inter-ethnic boundaries, such a well-developed self-awareness leads ethnic groups to assert their distinctive character through, among other things, the possession of their own territory. This in turn leads to hostility towards those who seem to stand in the way of such aspirations.

Thus, instead of enjoying its new-found unity and working together to speed up the economic and social recovery of its Eastern half, Europe finds itself racked by numerous ethnically based inter-state, inter-ethnic, and religious conflicts. The intensity, cruelty, and destructiveness of these clashes have been unknown in Europe for five decades. Seeing the ruins of former Yugoslavia, Nagorno-Karabakh, Trans-Dniester, or Abkhazia, knowing that many more dormant and smoldering ethnic controversies exist in several corners of the continent and, moreover, knowing that massive migrations into and within Europe may exacerbate such controversies even further, one can justifiably consider ethnic relations to be the most prominent security issue in Europe for the foreseeable future. Ethnic conflicts threaten to stay with us for a long time and, as a result of increasing mass ethnic migrations, their cultural and economic accommodation will be difficult; such conflicts may become even more intense and frequent. However, it should be underlined that this is not an exhaustive list of the probable nonmilitary security concerns of the future. It is sufficient to mention the prospects of an eventual scarcity of natural resources, such as energy and water, or the serious threat of environmental degradation of some regions, to know that there are many other problems in Europe that may cause regional or global instability in the future.

The gravity of both the existing and potential ethnic conflicts in Europe is unquestionable. However, it must be noted that ethnic or ethno-territorial conflicts in Eastern Europe are centuries old and have long been subject to ebbs and flows. Over the last 50 years, decolonization, the globalization of international norms on human rights, and the creation of various institutions concerned with individual and minority rights have brought about an unprecedented improvement in the status of many peoples, nations, and ethnic minorities. Despite the ethnic conflagrations now raging throughout Eastern Europe, the fact remains that the past four years in Europe still constitute an enormous improvement in both individual and group human rights.

The ongoing ethnic conflict in Eastern Europe seems, at present, to be getting out of hand and it may soon threaten the stability of the entire continent. However, Europe has a unique chance among the other regions of the world to moderate the menace of ethnic strife and even to regulate it. Much depends on a proper understanding of the problem, which is often connected with emotions and prejudices.

The sudden awakening of ethnic/national awareness and a renewal of the search for protection of minority rights is primarily a constructive phenomenon, associated with the implementation of basic individual human rights (which are often cited as an example in arguments for collective minority rights). It is a reaction to the often long, vicious persecution and subjugation that took place under totalitarian regimes, and it has been viewed by many as being a natural outcome of the end of these regimes.

The revival of ethnic consciousness and ethnic demands that followed were all a byproduct or a consequence of the democracy introduced by the 1989 revolutions. Democracy permitted these demands to surface but, being young and fragile, it is not yet able to manage them properly. Nevertheless, as long as democracy flourishes, it creates the best and only guarantee of a proper solution to ethnic problems.

Ethnic conflicts are also often a byproduct of economic crisis. The political and economic transformation of Eastern Europe, where such conflicts abound, temporarily added new hardships to already handicapped social groups. But, again, the transformation creates a basis for future affluence in the states in question, and hence for an improvement in the economic standing of minority groups. This observation does not ignore the experience of Western Europe, where ethnic problems persist despite overall affluence.

4. ETHNIC CONFLICT AND THE INTERNATIONAL NORMATIVE SYSTEM

The ongoing political and ethnic conflicts in Europe exist on a continent governed by a stringent network of rules for military and political behavior. There exists, for the continent as a whole, a set of agreements that stabilize the quantitative parameters of armed forces, constrain military activities, and make such activities transparent to all states of the continent. This positive situation may, of course, be undermined by interstate conflicts generated by ethnic or other problems. However, the existence of such agreements exerts a restraining influence on states' actions. The extensive institutional structure of European relations—from the UN, the CSCE, the EC, and the Council of Europe to NATO—enables better than ever, though not necessarily effective, international reaction to any instability and open conflict on the continent, including instabilities caused by ethnic disputes. It is essential to Europe's well-being that this structure be made still more responsive and more efficient in handling nonmilitary, at present predominantly ethnic, instabilities and conflicts.

To amend the weakness of existing international mechanisms dealing with nonmilitary aspects of security, particularly its societal aspects, a two-pronged approach can be applied. One would be a reevaluation, consolidation, and further development of the existing legal standards concerned with ethnic minorities. This "normative" approach would have to take into consideration the general normative and organizational mechanisms of the UN, the CSCE, the EC, the Council of Europe, and existing subregional and local/bilateral/multilateral arrangements between states, as well as the internal laws and practices of individual countries that have bearing upon the issues in question. The second, "functional" approach, which will be considered in the next section, would concentrate on possible improvements or enhancements of implementation procedures already established by various political and legal instruments, which help to protect and execute the rights of ethnic minorities at the different levels of state bureaucracy.

The international community does not lack normative standards for the protection of human rights and, more specifically, of the rights of persons belonging to a minority. These were developed over a number of years, building on the experience and efforts of the League of Nations and the UN, as well as such regional organizations as the CSCE, the Organization of American States (OAS), the Organization of African Unity (OAU), and the Council of Europe. Notwithstanding the differences in specific formulations and the description of evolutionary development of such norms, the results of the process can generally be summarized as follows.

First, the norm established by article 27 of the International Covenant on Civil and Political Rights, namely, that the rights of individual members of a minority group are protected but not those of the group *qua* group, has gained international acceptance. However, the CSCE's Copenhagen Document indicates that while the existence of collective minority rights is rejected by most states, the specific concerns of minorities that are not adequately ensured through the protection of individual rights, such as the availability of education in their native language, also have to be recognized. This added dimension to the understanding of the scope of minority rights may be helpful in specific cases, but it raises a disturbing conceptual problem of how this relates to the universality and equality of human rights.

Second, the duty of states to protect the ethnic and other identities of their minority groups has become an internationally recognized obligation. If and when this duty is universalized, this standard of behavior will make it mandatory to protect a minority even when it is not formally recognized by a state, as long as the minority actually exists. This is no small achievement, given the undeniable fact that many contemporary states with multicultural social structures strive for the strongest possible integration based on democracy, freedom of individual choice, loyalty and patriotism of citizens, and the neutrality of the state's bureaucratic apparatus. Assimilation and integration are thus often the final tacit goals of the state, not the preservation of social and ethnic divisions.

Third, it is already well recognized that the protection of minority rights has to be in full agreement with the norms of international law. It thus excludes protection of any activity by the minority that may jeopardize the sovereignty, territorial integrity, or political independence of a state in which the minority exists. In other words, as embodied with particular clarity in all the documents of the Council of Europe, a generally accepted condition for obtaining protection under state law is satisfaction of the so-called state loyalty clause. These issues are clearly connected to the thorny question of national self-determination. The essential issue in the protection of minorities, and in ethnic conflicts, is the ability of a minority to preserve itself in a manner of its own choice, that is, "self-determination" in terms of cultural, religious, and ethnic affiliation. The problem is that national self-determination is usually associated with independence, and sometimes even secession. While nothing in the existing body of international norms on the rights of minorities suggests such a far-reaching interpretation, it cannot be denied that there exists a logical continuum from minorities to peoples and nations, the last two having no difficulty in justifying their quest for independence. There is always a latent threat that an ethnic group will re-examine its self-definition and seek independence or, even more dangerously, unification with a neighboring mother-state. Hence the need for extreme caution in raising ethnic issues between neighboring states and the importance of a psychological and political basis for mutual trust while such issues are being resolved.

Fourth, there is a long-lasting dilemma of how to respect the sovereignty of states and the rule of noninterference in their internal affairs in view of the clear need for international control over states' legal and bureaucratic treatment of minorities. This seems to have been solved decisively in favor of treating the protection of the rights of persons belonging to ethnic and other minorities as a factor of international concern and thus not an issue that belongs solely to the internal jurisdiction of individual states. On the political plane, this new approach resulted in the general international approval of a juncture between the level of compliance with a country's internal law on minorities and the acceptance of a given state's "right" to equal participation in international relations. This conditional admittance of states in organizations such as the Council of Europe or the European Community creates an incentive for the spread and consolidation of widely recognized norms. The acceptance of the supremacy of generally accepted individual and minority rights opens the way to international control and implementation procedures that involve intrusive methods of verification as well as direct appeals for assistance of abused individuals and social groups to international organizations.

The growing maturity of international standards for minority rights, despite the continued general nature of their character, has served to facilitate the development of specific internal rules and laws in individual states. Increasingly, the normative system for the protection of minority rights is evolving from a mixture of political and legal norms into predominantly legal ones. The result is that the execution of these norms for the protection of minorities has become less susceptible to political shifts within a state, and their overall implementation has become more effective. These commonly accepted norms in turn permit better international oversight and serve to simplify decisions by the international community for intervention on behalf of the oppressed and disenfranchised.

These few general observations about the state of affairs in the normative system concerning protection of minorities should not be taken as a indication of finality to the process. In spite of the achievements embodied in particular in the documents prepared by the series of CSCE meetings and conferences devoted to human rights, national minorities, and the "human dimension," the process of definition of legal standards on minorities is still far from its conclusion. What has been achieved is only what was possible given the current stage of interstate relations. Further progress is needed and will largely depend on the subsequent evolution of European relations in all its dimensions. In particular, progress will be determined by the nature and promptness with which ongoing ethnic conflicts are resolved. Another factor bearing on the development of a complex system of protection of minorities is the future of the state as a subject, or an actor, in the international political and legal system and its relative position to substate "actors," in this case organized ethnic groups.

The most important postulate emanating from these general observations concerns the need for the universalization of the new standards and regimes being created for the management of minority issues. Thanks to the political transformation under way in recent years in most of the states of Eastern Europe, such an outcome can at last be seen to be within the realm of possibility. However, this universalization does not mean the establishment of a single rigid, global, and precise constitution on minorities that could respond to all of the possible nuances of their actual situations and conditions. This seems neither necessary nor possible. Instead of seeking the universality of detailed norms at the state level, the best solution appears to be rather an application of generally recognized principles through specific state-wide legal norms that are flexible enough to respond to local circumstances, long-standing established habits, and the expectations of particular minorities and majorities. Thus, within the framework of general standards on minorities, various specific solutions can be established at a regional, multilateral, bilateral, national, and local trans-border levels.

5. IMPLEMENTATION OF
LEGAL NORMS ON ETHNIC MINORITIES

There is no single predetermined set of norms or standards that guarantees the best protection of minority rights. In real life, it is the mixture of all levels of normative activity, from local to universal, from specific to general, that may provide the proper framework for success. However, even the best normative arrangements mean nothing to the individuals and social groups that will be affected by them if the norms are not implemented, that is, if they remain only on paper. The Soviet Union's internal laws on ethnic minority rights were relatively progressive and comprehensive, while their interpretation and implementation were dismal. The opposite applies to Switzerland, where few formal norms on minority rights exist, but their actual enforcement (the term *implementation* does not apply here) is full and complete.

The UN's competence in ethnic and other minority rights is predominantly linked to the sphere of basic individual human rights. UN documents set a very wide spectrum of such rights. Neither the UN Charter nor the Universal Declaration on Human Rights, however, contains any mention of minority rights. It is only article 27 of the 1966 Covenant on Civil and Political Rights that recognizes, though does not define, the rights of "ethnic, religious or linguistic minorities." In theory, several UN bodies and organs are involved in the implementation and enforcement of human rights. In practice, these matters are focused in the Human Rights Commission of the Economic and Social Council (ECOSOC) and in the Human Rights Committee working as part of the International Covenant on Civil and Political Rights. It was only in 1991 that the creation of the UN Working Group on the Rights of Persons Belonging to National, Ethnic, Religious and Linguistic Minorities indicated a shift in the normative treatment of ethnic group rights within the UN system.

The UN-sponsored system of implementation of these rights envisages, in principle, several methods: obligatory reports on abuses of human rights; factual review of information provided by states or of complaints and petitions by individuals; public debate of the issues; NGO reports; conciliation services provided by the Human Rights Commission; complaints from states against other states; *ex officio* investigations; economic sanctions; and compensation for damages to the victims of human rights abuse. The ECOSOC can employ special procedures in response to reports of massive violations of human rights that do not even require a formal complaint from a state or an individual. These include appeals, good offices investigations, and public condemnation. Thus UN procedures involve a range of responses including prevention, appeals, mitigation, complaints, investigations, visits, good offices, and compensation.

This quite impressive list of theoretical implementation procedures pales, however, when confronted with the reality of their practice. In short, UN procedures are not widely known to the public, and they are slow in action and excessively formalized. But the major hindrance lies in the unfortunate fact that only about half of the UN's members are party to the International Covenant on Civil and Political Rights, barely one-third have recognized the competence of the Human Rights Committee, and even fewer have ratified the Optional Protocol to the Covenant. Taken together, these circumstances have rendered these important benchmark-setting international instruments largely ineffective.

The regional European efforts to provide for the effective implementation of minority rights, worked out within the framework of the Council of Europe and the CSCE, set out substantially more elaborate mechanisms than those of the UN. The basic documents associated with the Council of Europe are the Convention on the Protection of Human Rights and Fundamental Freedoms (with additional protocols) and the European Social Charter. Among the implementation measures envisaged in these instruments are complaints by states and complaints and accusations against states by individuals, NGOs, and citizens groups, which, when lodged with the Secretary General of the Council, obligate the latter to deliver such complaints to the European Commission on Human Rights for its consideration. Additionally, the European Court on Human Rights and the Committee of Ministers are involved in the process. The procedures of the Council of Europe are considered the most effective yet developed among the international mechanisms of protection of human rights. However, it should be noted that the members of the Council of Europe represent a relatively homogeneous group of states. Among members of the COE, the protection of human rights is treated as a critical element of the Council's integrative policy, an element considered to be as decisive for the future integration of new members as their economic performance. Positive as they are, the implementation mechanisms functioning under the aegis of the Council of Europe have a limited value for Europe as a whole. They may serve as precedent-setting or as a model, but their influence is circumscribed by the fact that they effectively apply to only those states that are already in full compliance with minority rights, not to those in which implementation is most needed. This leaves a large number of East European states outside the scope of such implementation mechanisms.

The other and most comprehensive European setting in which

the protection of minority rights is a priority issue is the CSCE. The implementation procedures designed at this forum were developed over a long period of time, beginning with the 1975 CSCE I conference in Helsinki. Among the milestones in this process were the 1985 Ottawa and 1986 Bern meetings of experts on human rights and on human contacts, respectively, the 1986–1989 Vienna follow-up conference, the 1989 Paris human dimension meeting, the 1990 Copenhagen conference on the human dimension, the 1991 Geneva meeting of experts on national minorities, and, finally, the 1991 Moscow meeting on the human dimension. These deliberations and their ensuing documents have initiated an extensive machinery of implementation for minority rights, particularly through information gathering and consultation.

Under these CSCE provisions, states are obliged to respond to requests for information and complaints and, subsequently, to agree to bilateral meetings with a complaining state. Interestingly, the information exchanges are not to be confidential. The right to request information is also given to individuals. Another formal procedure, already applied on several occasions, is the provision for an invitation of ad hoc groups with special investigative tasks and the use of rapporteurs on specific matters of concern. Additionally, expert missions can be organized. The result of all of these endeavors, in the form of reports, are to be considered by the Committee of Senior Officials, meeting in either routine or emergency session.

Although the CSCE mechanisms, particularly in information gathering, seem quite extensive, their practical value from the point of view of the protection of ethnic minorities is limited. The decision to utilize ad hoc investigative groups, rapporteurs, or expert missions is difficult to obtain under those CSCE rules that still require consensus for decisions. Requests for information regarding ethnic conflicts in other states are rarely put forward because of the political consequences of such a step. Most of the CSCE actions undertaken so far have been launched only in response to ethnic conflicts already underway. They thus represent not so much actions to enforce an implementation of minority rights as a reaction to an emergency situation caused by an open military conflict. The international political and moral pressures on parties involved are the only direct instruments of coercion, given the right of veto that may block any concrete action. In the case of the use of the emergency CSCE mechanism, which might be invoked in response to the danger of an ethnic conflict, there are no enforcement provisions short of calling on the UN Security Council for action.

A major breakthrough has been achieved in the CSCE context by the creation at the 1992 Helsinki II conference of the office of a High Commissioner on National Minorities (see chapter 11). The Commissioner is entitled to collect and receive information regarding the situation of national minorities from any source, including the media and NGOs. The Commissioner is also able to receive reports from states regarding developments concerning national minority issues. In the execution of his mandate, the Commissioner is entitled to communicate with governments, regional and local authorities, and representatives of associations, NGOs, religious and other groups of national minorities.

With the establishment of the office of the High Commissioner, the CSCE mechanism was given a tool to provide early warning of minority issues that might develop into conflicts. The Commissioner will be free to report on any minority issue causing concern, and it is not necessary for the state in which the minority lives to agree that a report is necessary. States are expected to allow the Commissioner to visit and work according to this mandate. Moreover, the Commissioner can, at an early stage of tension, "promote dialogue, confidence and cooperation between parties." Thus for the first time, albeit on a limited scale, ethnically based tensions inside states can be managed and prevented without recourse to the cumbersome CSCE procedures. If it is considered that there is a risk of conflict, a report can be made by the Commissioner to the Chairman-in-Office and to the Committee of Senior Officials. The Commissioner may be given a mandate for further action to find a remedy or, if these efforts fail, the matter can again be placed on the Committee agenda. Once again, the CSCE mechanisms for consultation and fact finding would apply.

There are several possible ways to consolidate the existing international implementation mechanisms in the field of minority rights. Among them, enumerated only as examples, the following could be considered: a Special Rapporteur on Minorities mandated to investigate minority abuses and entitled to report to the UN Secretary-General or UN Security Council directly; a new understanding of the gravity of ethnic issues, which should, logically, make it easier for direct access of the Human Rights Commission to the Security Council; spot and routine inspections of the execution of human and minority rights, activated on an automatic basis in the case of a state's or an individual's warning of an imminent conflict; the creation of a register of minorities as a basis for the work of protective mechanisms on a regional or global basis; a court of conciliation and arbitration empowered to investigate ethnic disputes; and the establishment of permanent contact with minorities' representation by the CSCE's Office for Democratic Institutions and Human Rights. And sooner or later the operating procedures of the CSCE, effective as long as they are not vetoed by a participating state, will have to be amended in line with the concept of "directed conciliation" and the principle of "consensus minus one" adopted to permit prompt preventive action and the subsequent implementation of remedial action when European peace and stability are jeopardized by an ethnic conflict.

The existing international normative system of protection of the rights of ethnic minorities and formal implementation mechanisms seem quite extensive but, in practical terms, they are not very efficient. States tend to offer lip service to minority rights but remain reluctant to internationalize their internal problems with ethnic groups. These minorities have rather limited means for raising their grievances in international forums, which, under the current international system, means that states are protected from outside intrusion into their internal affairs. Only recently has this situation begun to change. It is thus reasonable to expect little practical improvement in the existing international and national systems for the protection of minority rights. One possible way of searching for real improvements could be by looking for more practical procedures, adapted to specific regional, national, or local conditions, and having a legal, administrative, or political character, which might lead to ethnic confidence building.

6. IMPROVEMENT OF THE PROTECTION OF MINORITY RIGHTS BY CONFIDENCE BUILDING

In view of the difficulties confronted by the formal implementation of investigative and protective mechanisms in the field of minority rights, particularly in Eastern Europe, other ways should be tested that could squarely fall under the rubric of confidence building. It is because of a lack of trust, because of psychological and cultural prejudices based on historically shaped stereotypes, that the classic normative approach to ethnic conflict resolution is often not successful. Breaking down entrenched hostilities and prejudices can perhaps best be achieved at specific and targeted levels and in the way most appropriate to a given situation. Thus some measures can be applied at a national, others at a subregional (trans-border) or local level in ways that involve various approaches in the spheres that define ethnicity: history, language, culture, religion, territorial location, and/or economic conditions.

One way of seeing ethnic confidence-building measures (ECBMs) would be by the adaptation of the basic rules on the subject from the area of arms control and military security, where the notion was applied with great success. It would be the purpose of ECBMs to promote mutual understanding, tolerance, and confidence in intentions among different ethnic groups. While in the military and security CBMs it was first about elite (government) perceptions and only later about the common public opinion (beliefs), in the ECBMs it is this latter group, i.e., the widespread social beliefs and stereotypes, that are crucial and of primary importance. As in CBMs and CSBMs, the target is "threat perception" and "lack of confidence," but in ECBMs the actual threats and suspicions are often intangible, historically rooted beliefs. Thus the ECBMs task seems to be much more difficult.

ECBMs should be based on the fact that European societies are ethnically diverse and multicultural. Their *modus operandi* should be the establishment of direct contact between persons and groups concerned. They should thus involve social, cultural, sport, youth, religious, and educational groups and organizations, NGOs, schools, and mass media, as well as local, regional, and governmental forms of cooperation. The rules that need to be applied in these interactions are openness, advanced information, and acting against the "enemy image" that exists between different groups through an intercultural learning process. ECBMs would work, therefore, on the *source* of conflict and not so much on its *course*, although they may also be highly beneficial in the post-conflict social recovery.

ECBMs are applicable to the all states in Europe, though their role would be of particular value in the East, where the domestic legal context for minority protection is less developed and deep ethno-territorial disputes exist. ECBMs could not substitute for the existing normative processes; rather, they would be designed to facilitate their establishment or implementation. The functioning of ECBMs may help to overcome the pain of some of the intrusive implementation of existing legal measures.

ECBMs could consist of pragmatic political and administrative acts, as well as legal arrangements on different organizational levels of a government. They could be interstate and intra-state measures, the latter ones subregional, local, and municipal.

Bilateral interstate arrangements may respond to characteristic interstate concerns, such as fear of aggrandizement, annexation, or irredentism. They may be oriented towards mutually agreed measures aimed at helping to manage relations between the host-state and the ethnic mother-state to ensure that actual or potential ethnically based frictions between them do not endanger good neighborly interactions. In this way, the influence of a mother-state may be altered from a negative or, at least, suspicious one into a positive role, benefitting the minority but with the host-state's blessing. In such a situation, minorities may act not as a vehicle of friction, but as cultural and linguistic bridges between the states concerned. Such a constructive mechanism is particularly advantageous when the arrangement is reciprocal though not necessarily symmetric.

National constitutions and regulations in a state need to correspond closely to the unique socioeconomic problems of minorities, to the realities of minority-majority relations, and to the dangers of racial xenophobia or chauvinistic nationalism. It is at this level that ethnic and other minorities can obtain political representation, in whatever legal or political way it may be realized. It is at this level where funds for special minority needs are controlled and distributed, education programs launched, laws on the media and the spread of information established, regulations on travel and various forms of links with the mother-state issued, and the level of participation of a given minority in a state's administration decided.

It is also in the nation-state setting that the protection of rights of dispersed or nomadic minorities without a mother-state, such as the Roma, can best be assured. No other level creates an institutional entity that is able to originate legally binding regulations for such minorities, although international organizations and international public opinion can address issues in order to exert pressure directed at the preservation of the rights of such people. Protection of these rights would, however, require not only national legislation, which is lacking in most European (not only East European) states, but also simultaneously entrusting to existing international organizations the special task of overseeing the implementation of the rights of such minorities. The nominated organization would thus serve as a "surrogate mother-state" for such minorities.

Local interactions, that is, those geographically restricted in their application but erected on the larger foundation of a state's law, conform, in turn, to the day-to-day interactions at the grassroots social level. They may be established in the form of rights to a local cultural, linguistic, religious, or administrative autonomy, and as such they may possibly constitute a high degree of ethnic freedom. This solution to the issue of minority protection is, however, not free from potential drawbacks. It may fortify the distinction between the minority and majority and may be conducive to separatism and irredentism. A more readily acceptable form of local mechanisms for promoting, if not protecting, the rights of ethnic minorities could be trans-border cooperation, often through the creation of special zones. Of particular utility here may be the concept of Euroregions, of which several are currently being created in Eastern Europe. Economic or ecological motivations notwithstanding, trans-border cooperation may help in a number of ways to meet the interests of local ethnic communities in, for example, the preservation of their cultural heritage, the teaching of native languages, and the provision of religious services.

Momentum is building for real progress on these issues. As part of the Central European Initiative, a meeting of the Foreign Ministers of Austria, Hungary, Bosnia-Herzegovina, Croatia, Italy, Poland, Macedonia, Slovakia, and Slovenia, along with a Deputy Foreign Minister of the Czech Republic, was held on November 19–20, 1993 at Debrocen, Hungary. In a communique issued at the end of the meeting, the group declared that minorities should be granted the right to self-government in areas where they form a majority, and cultural autonomy in regions where they are a minority. If implemented, such an approach would go a long way towards solving many of the problems faced today. ECBMs are a viable first step in implementing this type of practical undertaking. It only requires good-will and courage to take that first step.

8

The Failure to Recognize Minority Rights and Claims: Political Violence/ Terrorism in the East and West

RICHARD ALLAN

We must learn to compose our differences, not with arms, but with intelligence and decent purposes.
D.D. Eisenhower

INTRODUCTION

Historical analogies can often mislead and confuse the moral choices posed by claims of popular justice and equality. If, indeed, in the decision-making process the mistakes of the past are ignored, minorities will have fewer and fewer ways to channel their frustrated desires to participate in the political process, seek economic achievement, and attain social integration and acceptance. If segregation and other forms of discrimination are mandated by any method—official or popular—then those who are truly oppressed, or who perceive themselves to be oppressed, will in time express their displeasure in a violent manner. When violence occurs—and it will—no stranger to the incident can ignore the event.

Articulating the official US position on the former Yugoslavia, a high-ranking member of the Bush administration said, "It's Serbs, it's Croats, it's Bosnian Muslims, the whole panorama. If you're intent on killing each other, don't blame it on somebody else. We'll do what we can to help, but in the end, you've got to have some sense that there are limits to your insanity."[1] As a statement of national or international policy—whether on behalf of a nation or a group of nations—this is a woefully insufficient response to the senseless killings in Yugoslavia or anywhere else and a failure of international responsibility.

International law, incorporating common law and property rights, protects the national/geographic borders of a sovereign nation and holds them impenetrable by a foreign power. But must those borders always remain inviolable? What happens when territorial greed, genetic cleansing, religious, racial, or ethnic routing place a minority group in physical danger or subject to intolerable, nondemocratic conditions, without redress to a governing sovereign?

Anticipating the tenor and international style of communication during the balance of this decade, and considering all the weapons that have been internationally produced, stockpiled, secreted, or in active or contemplated development, an observer must come to the conclusion that the true danger to our life today and tomorrow will not be generated by a clash between democracy and communism or by inflammatory economic competition among aggressive industrial nations, but from uncontrolled local or regional wildfires provoked at a time when a government can no longer govern or no longer wishes to control certain activity. When a nation can no longer "interpret for itself the requirements of justice,"[2] then any conflagration within its domain can have an impact far beyond any imaginable distance. The dismantling of the Soviet Union, the "death" of communism, or the reach toward democracy in the republics of the former Soviet Union and Central and Eastern Europe does not necessarily guarantee the birth of democracy. The East must address the issues of minority rights and violence. If it fails to do so, internal and regional conflict will spread far beyond local borders, inciting disparate groups across the East and West seeking satisfaction for their own claims. Violence will follow violence.

I

Although as noted above, historical analogies can often mislead or confuse present questions of claim or right, a short detour to the past is appropriate. The disintegration of the Habsburg Empire may be assigned, albeit simplistically, to either the political activities of those in exile or to those domestic nationalistic groups unhappy with its endemic problems. Those who adopt the first causal explanation will "glorify the empire" as a model of how different nationalities could remain together within one environment and be both at peace and prosper as long as "they are not misled by agitators."[3] The second view is that the empire self-destructed because it failed to recognize the need for intrinsic social changes—its domestic inadequacies—and additionally rushed into a costly war. Accepting either event as the primary cause of its extinction, internal violence was one important byproduct when the empire began to unravel.

In one presently familiar segment of the empire, a sizable number of rightist Croatians and Slovenes attacked individual Serbs and wrecked as much Serb property as they could. One may excuse this violence as merely a mob reaction during difficult times. But once the empire lost its cohesive power to control or bend the actions of its population to its own will or agenda, nationalistic popular feelings had no physical or psychological rein. Consensus no longer existed. Individuals, submerging themselves as part of larger groups, believed they could express their own hatred without fear of interdiction. Perceiving injustice, they gave vent to their own concept of popular justice as they saw fit. The weakness of the Hapsburg forces of repression meant there were no barriers to physically violent expression.

The Ottoman Empire was a far-flung realm that reached its peak in the late 16th and 17th centuries, stretching northwest from Asia Minor to the Danube. It ultimately collapsed under the weight of nationalism from within and from without by its defeat in World War I. However, unlike the Hapsburg Empire, the Ottoman demise was due in part to the nationalist aspirations of its dominant population, the Turks. Yet prior to its demise, a writer in the second half of the 19th century, attempting to comfort his Turkish readers, maintained the belief that the empire was bound to survive because the populations in the Balkans were so diversified that no one segment could withdraw and freely form or sustain an independent state. It is only when there is a nation "numbering many millions, with a common identity and a common language such as the Arabs"[4] that there can be a danger to the empire. Here, too, he cautioned his readers— incorrectly—that there was no danger from this quarter because the Arabs were bound to the whole of the empire by their "Islamic brotherhood."

Whether one examines the notion of patriotism in the Ottoman Empire adopted by the Turks, the separatist aspirations of the Egyptians, the influx of the Russian Tatars, the treatment of the Albanians at the hands of the Turks, or the plight of the Kurds, the belief expressed in that vast empire was that if a person adopted Islam and spoke Turkish, that would be sufficient as an "entrance fee" into the ruling class or at least entrance into the administrative strata. Clearly history proved that wrong. Once the Ottoman Empire began to unravel, violence erupted, spurred in part by the failure to recognize minority aspirations and exasperated by extreme nationalistic desires.

II

The movement toward a democracy is accomplished by physical force or by the force of a popular demand for open elections, or by merging the energy of both. History provides sufficient evidence that when the consensus that is the basis for a movement toward a democratic form of government falters or fails, then the driving force for the protection of all people, and especially minorities, is placed in great jeopardy. Equally disturbing is the history of political violence or terrorism initiated by minorities either in search of their own "place" in the infrastructure and to correct present inequality or as a "pay-back" for real or perceived past injustices. When it is the latter, there is little a government can do to alleviate the pain of the past or to prevent the violence.

Domestic terrorism often springs from historical grievances based on economic discrimination or deprivation by those who control wealth, conflict between competing group rights, or minority domination by those in power. In addition, the degree of concern for minority rights decreases in inverse correlation as the distance from the seat of power increases. Consequently, when a government surrenders or fails to retain control of any element of governance or consensus, the consequences are somewhat predictable. But when a group of people, in an attempt to develop a democratic political culture, has no historical basis for its development, then the equation for success becomes more complex, perplexing, and dangerous. Whether political stability can be sustained during the initial stages of creation or formation of basic democratic principles for the governance of *all* people will depend in great part on whether all the people have the basic opportunity to eat and a place to sleep.

After the initial stages of democratic development, the political, industrial, and military leadership of a nation must forge a working alliance to protect equally the rights of all of those who reside within their geographic borders. The right to state protection and equality cannot be premised upon language, religion, or ethnicity. State-supported terrorism does not evaporate with the first step toward democratic reform and government. And terrorism is not the first victim of democracy. Minorities know that they need not rejoice with the "proclamation" of democracy. Early disillusionments during the building of a democratic infrastructure, coupled with nostalgia for the familiarity of what once was, are not prime building blocks for the future.

In Spain during the transition years from Fascism to democracy in 1975 to 1978, 205 violent deaths could be attributed to the movement toward democracy. Five polls taken between 1977 and 1983 indicated there was substantial support for the democratic process. In the early 1950s, "over a third of Germans indicated that they would support or be indifferent to an attempt by a new Nazi party to seize power and just under a third supported restoration of the monarchy."[5] Twenty years later, 90% of the population accepted, approved, and believed that democracy was the "best form of government for Germany."[6] What happened in these two countries? Why is the democratic evolution in Germany being challenged today with violent racist attacks against minorities, Roma, and others?

One theory holds that democracy can flourish only in those areas of the world that have had either a long or intense influence or relationship with Western culture.[7] It is argued that there must be some predetermined crucible that permits democracy to flourish within a non-homogeneous population. If one accepts this geopolitical approach to the viability of democratic reform in the area of the world most immediately affected by the Soviet Union's implosion, the prognosis is not promising for either the area, its minorities, or the West. The efforts in reaching consensus must be redoubled and settlement of minority issues cannot be postponed for a calmer day.

Given the unpromising background of the situation in the former Soviet Union—minority clashes, organized crime, a situation close to economic collapse, the proliferation of weapons in the hands of individuals and readily available for purchase—or the extreme minority tensions in Central and Eastern Europe, it is readily understood that a country reaching for democracy must, by necessity, resolve long-standing minority issues, whether they be demands for a separate territorial identity or internal equality. To complicate the issue, the line between the two is often obfuscated. Therefore, the legitimacy of a claim for rights cannot be dismissed because a long passage of time has somehow canceled its validity. The emotions of history will not accept that logic. On the other hand, if there is any claimed validity—time-barred or not—the stability of a democracy is only protected by the political elite who recognize the claim and can marshal the consensus necessary to address the issues. To address a concern for minority rights does not mean capitulation. In the same vein, the petitioner with the grievance or claim must understand that time changes, erodes, and builds. A century ago, the great majority of Native Americans lost most of their land to the white settlers. Clearly, today that land cannot be returned to them for a multiple of valid and logical reasons. But a compromise is sought that will provide economic security and stability to the future of those whose heritage was lost. Majority does not mean "right," and minority need not be equated with "persecution."

On both side of the Atlantic Ocean, the West is not now and will never be free of terrorism and political violence. The West, notwithstanding its role as the bastion of democratic principles, is not free of random violence in the name of religious, political, or ethnic rights. The West—where the debate for minority rights does from time to time take center stage in the public arena—has not defeated the use of violence as a weapon for recognition.

There are lessons to be learned by the governments of Eastern and Central Europe and the NIS, because to forget is to invite the repetition of violence. The members of the international community must initially understand that there is no model of a human rights program the West has constructed with total success for replication. Second, it must be accepted that terrorism can and does become a way of life, a means of existence, or a method to retain the power realized through confrontation and terrorism. For some, there can be a point of no return from violence; for others, conflicting objectives and splintering within a terrorist group may make the movement toward resolution impossible. Last, the West must accept, intellectually and emotionally, that it cannot demand of foreign governments that they provide more protection for their minorities than it has provided to its own disadvantaged. To do otherwise is to invite ridicule, loss of credibility, and a turning away from the path of reform and transition.

One of the rare moments of success that came to a minority employing political violence or terrorism, although admittedly not on the scale or intensity found in France, Northern Ireland, or Italy, was that of the Flemish movement in Belgium. After the revolution in the 1830s gave Belgium its freedom from the Netherlands, the new government ordered that French would be the only official language for the new nation. This left most of the population, which was then illiterate and spoke "low German" rather than French, with a "second class" language that not only prohibited them from participating in the legislature, judiciary, military, and secondary and higher education, but also disadvantaged them socioeconomically and politically. Time moved slowly in the new country, and eventually 30,000 Flemings, prodded by Flemish intellectuals, submitted what was to become a famous petition for the "restoration" of their language. And although collective measures were growing, the Belgian government ignored the petition for almost half a century, and viewed the demands as "useless" or "dangerous," creating a general discrimination based on the use of language. The emancipation movement of Dutch- or low German-speaking Belgians produced friction and sometimes violence between the French-speaking and Dutch-speaking population. Yet at no time was there a demand for either separation or a federalist reorganization to provide the Flemings with an autonomous region, although many Flemings regarded the Belgian state with sufficient hostility that they considered it their "enemy."[8] It was through this struggle that a de facto Flemish state was born within the country, and was thought by many French-speaking Belgians to betray the nation's well-being. Flemish "nationalism of language"[9] not only survived but flourished after the national Parliament was worn down by time with persistent demands and a minimum of violence. In this study the key to understanding the success of the movement was that the Flemish did not initially seek the annulment of the French language, but only the bilingual recognition of Flemish as another official language in what was to become "their region."[10]

The Flemish use of violence as a method to achieve their goal was never a prime tool for radical political or territorial change, and, more importantly, its intensity was never sufficiently grievous or barbaric that it would marshal the opposition necessary to demand a counterattack to destroy the movement. Decades, though, have brought about a change in the historical balance of the country. The Flemings had sought equality of opportunity and language, not separation. They now represent three-fourths of the population and occupy an economically stronger portion of the country than those French-speaking Walloons who once controlled the infrastructure. The change in the population and economic structure of Belgium has infected the Flemings with the "demon of separatism," and they now seek to chart their own course of independence and government.[11]

Another conflict, but one that had existed in the West for centuries, was caused by a Germanic movement aimed at acquiring possession of an Alpine region called Alto Adige or South Tyrol. Its initial military value gave the Hapsburg monarchy a pretext to annex it, following annexation by the kingdom of Italy, then finally by the Emperor of Austria. These events exerted considerable influence on the area's language and demography. The urban middle class, predominantly Italian, found itself in open conflict with the German-speaking peasantry. During their reign, the Austrian authorities "induced" a substantial portion of the Italian population to leave the region. After the outbreak of World War I, Italy, as an Entente partner, sought award of the area. It was the hope of US President Wilson that Italy could occupy the region for military purposes, but would not govern the cultural life of the "alien" population.[12] By 1919, however, the Italian population comprised 70% of the total population. The 200,000 minority inhabitants of German origin were not considered a matter of any great significance when the area was eventually ceded to Italy. Although Italy had not signed any treaty for the protection of its own minorities it nevertheless gave its assurances to the international community that it would provide and did in time grant wide-ranging concessions to its German-speaking minority in the Alto Adige.[13] Although Austria protested the Italian moves for annexation, the delegation representing the German-speaking Tyrolese population conceded that Italy should control the foreign policy, finance, justice, defense, and communication needs for the area. Despite the apparent movement toward protection of German-speaking Tyrolese, separatist violence began.

In 1933, Hitler "temporarily" abandoned the Tyrolese, who had been pursuing a separate German-speaking state, for the purposes of reaching a rapprochement with Italy, but in 1943 the Third Reich annexed the area with no complaint from those seeking to move away from Italian control.

At the end of World War II, the Austrian government, with the support of the Tyrolese, argued that even in pre-Fascist Italy the democratic government had pursued a policy of oppression toward the German-speaking minority in the Alto Adige and that history would not support any claims that postwar anti-Fascist Italy could make.[14] The Italian and Austrian governments moved toward reconciliation of the Alto Adige minority problem, entering into a bilateral treaty that would grant the German-speaking inhabitants far-reaching equality of rights with the Italian-speaking population in the region. This treaty included a special provision that would allow the German-speaking inhabitants to maintain their particular culture and traditions. Austria pledged to recognize Italy's free exercise of sovereign rights over the territory and withdrew its demand for a plebiscite. Unfortunately, the implementation of the terms of the treaty or the "settlement of the Alto Adige question" occupied the efforts of both governments for decades thereafter, with claims that the Austrian government attempted to exceed the terms of the treaty or that it would no longer consider itself bound by its terms if its new demands were not met. The Italian government protested that a violent anti-Italian campaign was being orchestrated in Austria. The Austrian government, in turn, alleged that the Italian military police had mistreated political detainees from the Alto Adige and had behaved in a manner that exceeded all bounds of reasonable conduct toward the German-speaking population. As the governments accused each other, it was clear that extremist elements had gained the upper hand with a minimal use of terrorism. In this position of power, they could prevent any reconciliation and accord between the two governments and create a totally autonomous area. To the international community, Austria was not as vigorous as it might have been in its interdiction of these terrorist elements, which had utilized Austria as a safe-haven for their attacks in the Alto Adige. Only after a series of events that included a biased television program in Austria that appeared to justify the recourse to violence, the killing of four Italian soldiers, and the acquittal of a group of self-confessed terrorists did the Alto Adige question reach true international proportions. These events prompted serious cooperation between the two governments, and the Italian government for its part followed a consistent policy of "not permitting terrorist activities to block the search for a solution of the Alto Adige question, the very thing the terrorists were trying to do."[15] As both countries redoubled their efforts and moved toward full implementation of all the elements necessary for the protection of the minority German-speaking population, there was a gradual disappearance of terrorist activities.

Another interesting case is Switzerland, a small, unusually weak country measured in terms of its limited size, state expenditures, and gross national product, but strong with respect to its long history of democratic traditions, including use of public referendums to build governance by consensus. With its federalism, fragmented party system, and self-regulating society, political power in Switzerland is highly diffused. Employing the process of direct democracy, it permits a portion of the decision-making process to be directly controlled by the people. Consequently, the system allows the democratic process the room and flexibility to attempt to protect the rights of all persons. Although the process is evolutionary and may at times appear to be too slow in moving toward a particular solution (such as the belated recognition of women's right to vote), a person within the community can observe the process. But even this small democratic country—which was founded after a short burst of political violence[16] by the radical element of the day—witnessed the beginning of 1993 with a bomb blast that killed a person linked to separatism in Switzerland's most rebellious canton.

Notwithstanding the consensus-building process and disregarding the presence of a voiceless minority of foreign workers without any rights of Swiss citizenship, the country faces a contemporary problem that is rooted in the confusion left by Napoleon's New Order.[17] In an un-Swiss swing of ultranationalism and ethnic confrontation, there is a movement afoot to reunite areas of a mainly German-speaking canton of Bern with the French-speaking canton of Jura into what is seen as the historic Jura region. Because the Swiss have the tendency to view the political process as a logical method to develop common-sense solutions, how well the government reacts to the violence and the manner in which the general public responds to the nationalistic demands will determine the extent of continued violence.

In Ireland, there are some who had advocated uniting all people of that island simply because of language; there were others who attempted to equate conditions there with the strong role the Roman Catholic religion played in nationalistic movements of the Basques in

Spain and France and the Bretons in France. For these groups, the supporting role of the Catholic priest in the early stages of these movements was quite formidable. The same is not true in Northern Ireland.

The current Irish nationalist movement traces its roots back to 1902 after decades of a marginal role in the Parliament in London. Its aim was securing political and economic independence from Britain by peaceful means. While a disaffected element in Northern Ireland is Roman Catholic, and the supporters of Sinn Fein and the Provisional Irish Republican Army (PIRA) in Ulster are found among the Catholics, neither group is motivated by "religious tenets."[18] Nor is there support from the Catholic Church; on the contrary, it has condemned their violence.

Ulster, or Northern Ireland, comprises six of the original 32 counties of Ireland; the other 26 now form the Republic of Ireland. Ulster is part of the United Kingdom. Protestants, who make up the majority, form 62% of the population.[19] The Protestant Loyalists want to remain part of the United Kingdom, while the Catholic Republican minority seeks to unite with the Irish Republic in the south to establish one sovereignty over the entire island. Contrary to public conception, the militant Protestants have killed as many Catholics as Catholic militants have killed Protestants.[20]

It is important to appreciate that democracy does not guarantee the absence of terrorism. One form of terrorism is violence aimed at a symbol of government. In this context, terrorism is neither a new phenomenon nor will it ever disappear. It may be contained, and there are lessons that can be learned from the West. But can the present debate, turned violent, be resolved by limiting the choice of options to territorial sovereignty or the status quo? Clearly neither answer is acceptable to all the people. The United Kingdom—a democracy with a long history, with multi-party elections and Western standards of human and civil rights and conduct—suffers from a strain of the virus of communal nationalism that has permitted fewer than 200 terrorists to occupy the time and attention of 20,000 British soldiers and impede a reconciliation.

It cannot be claimed that the present *raison d'être* for the senseless violence aimed at individuals, not merely symbols of government, is based upon centuries of abuse of Catholics by the Protestant majority, or by the government in London being a taxing, subjugating, absent authority. But because of a religious delineation, the right to vote by the minority has not provided a true admission to the privileges of full citizenship. What does exist today in Ireland has been described as a "synthetic combination" of a real and imagined past, present and potential fears of suppression of rights and opportunities in a region with a poor economic base and record for growth.[21]

As a lesson for the East and as a guide for the West, the government in London seeks to find a solution through peace talks in Northern Ireland. Despite the fact that it supports a democratic philosophy, that it is the birthplace of the common law, and that it is a symbol of democratic process, London must overcome a long history of hostility and violence.

As a general formula for determining the true presence of a democracy, it has been proposed that one examine the existence of the right of the adult population to vote. For the first half of the test, one must accept the premise that a minority candidate or party may never obtain a plurality of votes. The test continues: do these same persons have access to the courts of their region and do these courts legitimately review each individual's claim or defense? If the two elements are present, then a democracy exits both in theory and practice.[22] The "Lebanon formula" of shared political power, which is being suggested for solving the Northern Ireland conflict, mandates political representation based on the ethnic or religious affiliations that comprise the entire population, as distinguished from a geographic distribution. The solution of shared power is workable, but only so long as the consensus to maintain this type of fixed formula exists. The formula must also be protected by enforceable judicial and constitutional safeguards.[23] Additionally, it is more difficult to maintain the fixed formula for a society that is mobile. If identifiable ethnic or religious groups are represented instead of all the people domiciled within a particular geographic region, then what happens to the interests of the region itself with mobility and population mixing in a nonhomogeneous society?

In Northern Ireland, a province within a democratic nation, terrorism will continue by both sides until the minority feels protected, if not accepted, by the majority, and the majority no longer fears the advent of reverse discrimination.

In other parts of Western Europe, terrorism within the last three decades was motivated by a mixture of desires and causes, from time to time either supported or encouraged by an external patron in the form of a foreign state or foreign subnational entity. The objectives of this "transnational terrorism" are more diffuse and are generally attempts to carry the message of external difficulty to the host nation.

With the demise of communism and its intense regional control and international designs, it is believed that the "quartermaster" of international terrorism has shrunk its support of terrorism in the West. But clearly this has not solved the indigenous problems of terrorist attacks. As noted later in this chapter, both the East and West will face a new form of terrorism that will seep out of the East, which can be described as tribal, based upon collective memory of tribal grievances.

Italy does not have the long modern history of democracy that the United States, United Kingdom, or France do, but it is viewed politically and ethnically as part of the democratic West. It has been the victim of indigenous terrorism (in addition to an enormous volume of violence generated by organized crime), as an outgrowth of disparate goals that have degenerated into violence. With shortages in housing, hospitals, schools, and employment coexisting with continuing nonfeasance and severe political and governmental corruption,[24] a cadre of recruits has always been readily available to those who moved outside acceptable political methods of change. Each end of the spectrum has had its share of recruits: the Marxist-Leninist and the neo-fascist and Nazi.

Over the last 25 years, statistics show that the great majority of acts of domestic terrorism and political violence far exceeded those of transnational terrorism on Italian territory. The terrorist group most widely known outside of Italy was conceived in Milan in 1970—the Red Brigades. They moved from minor acts of brutality to kidnapping and murder of those persons who symbolized the establishment, namely the "imperialist state of multinationals": business executives, judges, prosecutors, and members of the majority political party. In 1978, the brigatisti kidnapped and murdered the president of the Christian Democratic Party, Aldo Moro. At year-end 1981, this group also carried out four abductions in various areas of the country, including the kidnapping of the senior United States staff member of NATO's Southern European land forces. This was their first occasion to move outside their domestic targets. In 1984, they specifically aimed at the United States and murdered one of it diplomats, Leamon Hunt, who was then director-general of the Multinational Forces and Observers.

In France, separatist violence forms the core of indigenous terrorism. But today, an additional element has been introduced. In some cases, racist attitudes have become part of the motivating force of terrorism, with anti-Semitism presently on a rapid and incendiary increase. National outcry has not diminished the volume of anti-Semitism. Whether it be the separatist Corsican National Liberation Front (FLNC)—which since 1976 has been seeking the restoration of their national language and distribution of colonial lands to the Corsican peasants—or the Marxist-Leninist group known as Direct Action with its two principal tracts: "For a Communist Plan" and "On

American Imperialism," the violence continues. Direct Action's targets were representative of the domestic (as well as foreign) "bourgeois, capitalist, racists and imperialists" and included not only the killing of a senior French Defense Ministry official but also the chairman of the Renault motor company, Georges Besse, both in 1985.

Terrorism in Spain is the outgrowth of its Civil War, the subsequent long rule of Generalissimo Francisco Franco, and then its transition to democracy under King Juan Carlos. In 1959, during Franco's rule, a terrorist organization called Basque Fatherland and Liberty (ETA) became an offshoot of the Basque government in exile in France. Since the restoration of democracy in Spain, its 2.6 million Basques fully participate in the democratic process and take refuge under the nation's constitutionally protected political and civil rights agenda. Notwithstanding the democratic thrust of Spain's 1978 constitution and the country's strong connections to democratic principles, several thousand ETA Basques continue violent action in support of the unification of seven provinces (four of which are located in Spain, three in France) under one independent and sovereign Basque state. ETA's acts of violence help define its target of terrorism: representatives of the Spanish military and police, Spanish business aligned with Basque interests, and tourism to damage the Spanish economy and international image.

In the United States, transnational terrorism has not been nearly as successful as in the Middle East or Western Europe. In the 1960s and 1970s, Croatian terrorists succeeded in attacking Yugoslav immigrants. Armenians attacked Turks. In 1954, Puerto Rican nationalists shot and wounded five members of Congress on the floor of the House of Representatives.[25] Black terrorism in the United States took the form of three prominent groups: the Black Panther Party, the Black Liberation Army, and the Republic of New Africa. Each of these groups represented changes in the attitude of the black community campaigning for socioeconomic change in the United States with the advent of an aggressive civil rights movement. The violence of these three groups was largely aimed at law enforcement officials and the "establishment." At the same time black nationalist violence found willing headlines in the United States press, white-led terrorism from the left was forming under the name Students for a Democratic Society (SDS). Its movement from nonviolence to terrorism can be traced from student unrest with the advent of the United States' involvement in the Vietnam War. But a faction of the SDS became dissatisfied with the aims of the organization and broke away, calling itself initially the Weathermen and then the Weather Underground Organization. The path it defined for itself was as a white movement for the support of civil rights for blacks; Latin American revolutionary Che Guevara became the group's martyr symbol. In October 1981, in a particularly violent attempt to obtain sufficient funds to continue its terrorist activities and purchase additional weapons, a small group of both black and white activists coordinated their activities and attacked an armored car service transporting a large amount of money.

A greater understanding (though not necessarily with equal acceptance) of the civil rights movement, coupled with police interdiction, led to the demise of groups such as the SDS and the Black Panthers. But with the downturn of the US economy and the recession/depression of the early 1990s the country has seen a dramatic rise in the numbers of skinheads and neo-Nazi organizations and the expansion of the KKK, with a rise also in the amount of violence aimed at minority groups. Domestic terrorism in the United States has a clear causal connection to current domestic issues, but these issues are usually addressed in some fashion (actively or passively by law enforcement and through increased popular media awareness and education that often leads to legislation), which diffuses the injustice complained of to a degree necessary that a "violent" minority group can no longer control a magnet for popular support with majority sympathies.

The United States had its share of good luck and been unusually successful in its campaign of terrorist interdiction until the massive explosion that rocked the World Trade Center in New York City on February 26, 1993.[26] In 1988, a member of the Japanese Red Army was fortuitously stopped by a member of the New Jersey State Police while operating his automobile at a rest stop on the New Jersey Turnpike. An examination of the car revealed several home-made bombs capable of both serious property and personal injury. His destination with the bombs is pure speculation, but his intent was not.

The mood has changed in the United States with the beginning of 1993. The British, Egyptian, and Israeli governments have claimed that the United States has become a safe training ground for terrorist groups seeking either to collect funds for terrorist activities abroad or (to some, more important) a safe haven for terrorist groups that direct, plan, and orchestrate their violent operational efforts in the US against targets in Egypt and Israel.[27] Britain claims that in seeking "charitable contributions" in the United States, the IRA raises funds that are then released to support acts of terrorism. It is claimed of Omar Abdel-Rahman, an Islamic fundamentalist, that not only is he the driving force behind terrorist acts in Egypt,[28] but that his mosque in New Jersey may have been used as the headquarters for the attack on the

World Trade Center. Has the *jihad* or holy war been brought to the United States? Israel claims that the Hamas, a Palestinian terrorist group, has its headquarters in suburban Virginia.[29] These three nations claim that the accused groups have been identified as participating in criminal activity in their countries but are protected by United States criminal and civil rights laws that place an individual's rights superior to that of a state's. Good police work and due process do not prevent violence; the innocents of our society become victims despite the constitutional guarantees.

In the preceding examination of the West (omitting Germany in this analysis because of the complexity of its place in history since the late 1930s), one is struck by the enormity of the impact of domestic terrorism. Each of these countries has either been reunited with its past connections to democracy or is a continuum of its democratic principles. On most occasions, each act of terrorism was addressed by the government as a separate incident of lawlessness and political violence, but the issues presented by the petitioners for change or redress were ignored. In a small number of instances, the claims of minority recognition were fully addressed, if not completely resolved. In all instances, the major principles of democratic conduct were not abandoned by the government. The right to vote was not suspended; access to the courts was not denied.[30] There were, however, important moments when individual "civil rights" were violated in pursuit of the domestic terrorist, and that cannot be denied.

The argument for or against the right of a government to breach the civil rights of any one individual in the name of a war against terrorism has its own shades of philosophy. That one person should go free then to breach the rights afforded all cannot be an open-ended rule. The West has grappled with that issue from the beginning of its own domestic dialogue to determine the meaning and breadth and dimensions of the civil rights it affords all its citizens. That debate continues—and so does the violence. But in attempting to transpose the scope of minority problems and the efforts at reaching solutions in the West to minority issues in the emerging democracies, one must recognize that an important difference exists: the historical structure of Central and Eastern Europe and the NIS presents its own unique problems. This apparent difference should not be cause for an excuse or an interpretation that the experiences of the West have no bearing on the issues facing the East. To ignore the long Western experience is to virtually guarantee recurrence of the mistakes and disasters encountered on the extended path to resolving minority claims and rights.

III

In the East, minority rights and violations are the focus of the Western press. In Poland, in 1991, the number one bestselling nonfiction paperback book was *Mein Kampf*. In 1993, the Polish government adopted a program to bring the Polish legal system into conformity with EC norms. None of the programs adopted addressed civil or human rights. And while it is believed by some that Poland is a decade slower in the development of a youth culture, strong and undiminished anti-Jewish feelings still persist, even though only a few thousand Jews remain in that country.

An example of one direction taken in that country is the Polish National Community Party platform—"God, Nation and Family are the sources of supreme value," and the platform adds that Saddam Hussein is a world leader to be admired, that capitalism is evil, and that Solidarity is a tool for Jewish nationalism.

When reform or transition is generated from within the power structure, both sides of the power equation normally see little use for violence. The exception, of course, was and is in those parts of the world that refuse to actively move toward the democratic process—China, Burma, and, earlier, South Africa and Chile. Although Romania could easily have been on that list, its election in 1992 aided in stabilizing the country; but it is still a country with no democratic history. In Romania, after the fall of communism in the rest of Eastern Europe, the armed forces seemed to stand ready to suppress the freedom movement. But when the order came, some army units refused to fire on demonstrators. The army then suppressed the Securitate, which had remained loyal to Ceauşescu. In its struggle toward democracy, there remains a significant number of people who favor an "iron-handed dictatorial leadership."[31] In Leipzig (East Germany) in October 1989, both the communist authorities and the opposition leader recognized the need to avoid another Tiananmen Square massacre. In East Germany, Poland, and Czechoslovakia, the communist governments had never shied away from violence; but at the moment of decision in 1988 and 1989, they refrained. The conclusion seems to be that violence without a viable state to initiate and support it has little utility.

Fifteen "countries" were created by the implosion of the Soviet Union. The focus of the implosion, Russia, is attempting to develop a viable economy and democratic institutions and to understand and build the foundations for multi-religious/ethnic minority freedom. But a series of disturbing questions suggest unsettling conclusions: Are democratic goals attainable without a truly strong leader in a country with intense political divisions, a soaring crime rate,[32] a military in free-falling decay,[33] and (as of May 1, 1993) no postcommunist constitution? In a country without a history rooted in the democratic process—open elections or referendum—how is a consensus for the protection of all its citizens built? In turn, without a consensus or with a succession of weak governments, how will minorities not only in the Russian Republic but in all the republics of the former Soviet Union be protected and thrive? Disregarding whatever public justice may be offered by the majority, what will be the response of the minority? Has Russian "nationalism" overpowered democratic evolution, and does nationalism prevent rational economic policy that will support not only the entire population but a program to protect the civil and human rights of all people?

A draft of the Russian military doctrine plan[34] released in May 1992 is a gloomy portent if the movement toward democratization in the entire region fails or falters and violence by and against minorities is the response, as with continued ethnic cleansing in such places as Tajikistan.[35] The Russian armed forces believe that "violations of the rights of Russian citizens and of persons who identify themselves with Russia ethnically and culturally in the former USSR republics" may be a source of conflict. Therefore, it was determined, a mission of the Russian armed forces must be dispatched to protect those rights and interests. Among those persons to be protected are those who are Russian citizens and those unidentified "persons abroad" connected ethnically and culturally with the "USSR." The source of power to protect those rights is the one-quarter million Russian troops stationed outside of Russia.

One assumption that has developed is that a conservative element of the military has created a scenario that will provide political justification for forceful intervention, and thereby control any evolution of the democratic process in the new sovereign states.[36] The consequences of any such act will create "a potential Yugoslavia on a larger scale" for the West for a number of reasons. The draft military doctrine plan holds that Russia will view the introduction of foreign troops in contiguous states as a direct military threat. And although minorities in contiguous states or nations may seek the help of Western resources, and although the immediate threat of a nuclear confrontation has been vastly reduced, if the desires of the minority in any portion of that world are not addressed or, conversely, if the majority deals harshly with the minority, then with the enormous weapon proliferation, with mismanagement of their control, and with open supermarkets for their sale, terrorist wars and political violence will spread beyond "Yugoslavia." Acts of terrorism in the guise of a war of independence to correct history will not be confined to the region.

One need only understand the full meaning of the systematic use of rape of men and women as a conscious weapon of terrorism.

The United Nations had 60,000 peacekeeping troops in the field by the end of 1992, compared with 10,000 at the start of 1993, and the demand for troops is ever increasing. The threat of instability and the spread of war in the Balkans would further endanger stability. Hungary may well become more prominent in the picture because of the number of ethnic Hungarians living on the other side of its borders in Romania and Slovakia. The number of Hungarians living in these contiguous regions is actually a third of Hungary's actual population. No one could doubt for a moment that a sitting government in Budapest would be permitted by its population to "allow" any hint of ethnic cleansing in those areas.[37] The Hungarian government has created an Office for Hungarians Abroad as an agency to protect its "citizens" living in Romania. The Romanian government, in turn, seeks assurance that Hungary will make no territorial demands on behalf of its minority. And the general staff of the Bosnian Serb Army had warned Hungary against interfering in areas of conflict within the former Yugoslavia long before a community of Hungarians complained of psychological warfare conducted by the Serbian leadership against them in three communities where they seek to establish territorial, cultural, and personal autonomy.

Poland, without a civil or human rights law, is and has been uneasy about German rightist claims to Silesia, as the Czechs are about the Sudetenland. An opinion poll conducted at the beginning of February 1993 revealed that a slight majority of the Czech citizens believe the split of Czechoslovakia was unnecessary. The poll conflicts with the Czech government's seeking to tighten its common border with Slovakia. Bulgaria is restricting transit immigration in an attempt to prevent the settlement of any minority group that cannot make its way to the West. In addition, several public statements by Romanian intelligence have revealed that it is working toward advancing Romanian-Moldovan unification. This has prompted sharp protest from Russia and a demand for an open investigation.

What the emerging picture reveals is that the East and West can expect that practically every nation/state/sovereign from the Rhine River east will be peering across its borders either in fear of its neighbor or in fear of the minority within its own borders seeking "yet another" demand. Does a host government, with its historical paranoia, resort to the suppression of minority rights as a method to contain assumed terrorism before it becomes a reality? In turn, each member of a minority group must wonder when its turn for cleansing—for whatever reason—may begin or when its historical claims will be "unfairly" denied.[38] If, in seeking to accommodate and resolve the issues embracing religious and ethnic confrontation, the decision makers move toward politicizing the obstacles that will define the methods to conclude these problems, then solutions will never be attainable and terrorism will be the response.

IV

The East must understand and implement a democratic model that knowingly accepts a method of consensus government that permits minorities inclusion in governance and access to individual economic growth and social integration. Simultaneously, it must maintain a broad range of ties and formulate methods of cooperation with the West so that it may make the necessary economic and social transitions and to find support for these transitions from its population. Economic stability is a natural suppressor, albeit not eliminator, of the germ that supplies the pretext to express frustrated nationalism in the form of violence toward minorities. In the case of Eastern and Central Europe and the NIS, that violence will be a new form of terrorism—new in the sense that terrorism in modern times has been generally viewed and partially defined either as state-directed or state-targeted, namely as violence directed at a state by attacking its population, property, and installations. The new terrorism that will emerge from the East is group or tribal violence directed at people because of who they are or who they once were and wherever they may be presently located. This type of violence will move across borders into the West.[39]

For self-protection and the protection of a growing movement toward democracy and minority rights, the West must implement policies to support the emerging democracies, and must employ its diplomatic and economic resources and prestige to insure and maintain progress towards those goals. The concerted effort of the West must be just that—concerted. Without a consensus by the West as to minimum standards of human and civil rights and without a unified approach to their implementation, loopholes will be found in the protection and verification mechanism. The consequence would be a program of rights that will lack true force. Bilateral and multilateral treaties to create the web necessary to assure compliance are cumbersome and too time-consuming in the ratification process. It has been said in multiple ways that civil and human rights are developed by consensus and protected by concessions. But the power of unanimity, settlement, understanding can either protect or destroy. Equally true, without consensus there is only destruction.

The brand of nationalism flowing though Central and Eastern

Europe and the NIS is not short-lived and, with few exceptions, has a long history of germination. The West cannot afford to permit the direct or indirect effects of continuing and expanding violence in the East that is attributable to ethnonationalism or, for that matter, any form of nationalism. If the West fails to be an active force in the East for the protection of minorities and the promotion of democratic reform, then, for example, the Muslim nations of the world[40] will move to fill some of the political void with their own concepts of individual rights.[41]

To support the development and success of a civil and human rights program, a European agency or council without the participation of the United States and Canada will lack the force of their economic powers and democratic traditions. The solution therefore lies within the CSCE, but with a mandate that contains enforcement procedures. The foundation to proceed further is there: the Helsinki process created the "vision" for the common aspirations of all people, and although it has failed in the former Yugoslavia, the process connects 53 countries as both a preventative and crisis management tool.[42] Although political accommodation among so many countries does create difficult obstacles, its consensus-driven work has been credited with the wave of change in Eastern Europe at the turn of the decade. Its bonding ability can provide the entire agenda for implementation of civil rights and minority protection programs:

- the *conduit* for development of minority rights;
- *procedures* to implement its concepts and philosophy;
- *verification* of implementation;
- a *mechanism* that would remove one claim for the necessity for terrorism, namely a procedure for the public review of minority grievances;
- *mediation* of issues *before* they develop.

If the West does not act, its failure will create a power vacuum that may prove unacceptable and more dangerous to Western democratic consensus.

As was noted earlier in this chapter, the debate in the West continues: how wide and forceful a circle should the arms of civil rights embrace? Yet violence continues in the West despite the long historical evolution of its civil rights movements, its accommodationist patterns, and the capacity and good will of the elites. The East must understand, as it watches the West, that the debate never ends; its minorities, borders, and terrorism are but one link in a chain in a continuing formation of a democratic society that is struggling for identity and strength.

The East must permit and encourage a method that allows an open and free arena for competing ideas. The knowledge so gained creates the basis for popular rejection or support for a particular cause. As in the West, with dialogue and information between and among the media and the population, the effect upon opinion formers often produces a movement toward compromise and rectification of past and present ills. In this manner, the democratic format has been fairly successful at interdiction and reduction in the intensity of minority terrorism responses.

Minorities in the East—examining the phenomena in the West—must accept that they too have responsibilities and accept the axiom that to achieve their goals the historical clock cannot be turned back on all claims, that terrorism cannot be the first method of response, and that a compromise that recognizes the integrity of minority civil rights must be addressed as they relate to the whole of society. Last, there must be within the East a judiciary, independent from the ruling majority and powerful enough to enforce individual rights and protect minority interest from popular emotions. The long history of anger by minority groups must cease, and the old blanket of dealing with minority rights must be rejected. To create a patchwork quilt of the old ignores the diversity of the present. An entirely new approach must be adopted toward individual rights and terrorism. The most important concept, not thought of by most in the West, is that "civil rights" were not created as a special privilege constructed or fashioned for an elite minority, but were human rights thought important for all people. The issue through time has been who are "the people." The East has the opportunity, with its unprecedented and massive reach toward democratic principles, to sweep all its people toward the 21st century.

CONCLUSION

In 1940, the lost battle to save Paris lasted 32 days. On the 31st day, Mussolini declared war on France. The French Premier, Paul Reynaud, noting the timing and manner of the attack, said, "The watching world will judge." Today, the watching world will also be judged.

Time is no longer a luxury for any part of the world; it has been spent. Minority rights cannot be contained as if they were a criminal activity or a legitimate claim without popular support. Those persons—from the East and West—who decide our future must acknowledge that the demands of minorities and stateless persons will continue to escalate and, if not addressed, will produce terrorism that will continue to plague future generations. Further, they must accept a difficult negotiating principle: violence attributable to minority unrest cannot be the sole reason to terminate a dialogue toward a peaceful resolution of conflict.

Vaclav Havel, decrying the continuation of crimes against human rights, said "None of us is just its victim; we are all responsible for it."

NOTES

1. *The New York Times*, Jan. 10, 1993.

2. Norman Cousins, *The Pathology of Power* (New York and London: W.W. Norton, 1987), p. 191.

3. Robert A. Kann, *History of the Hapsburg Empire* (University of California-Berkeley Press, 1974), p. 517.

4. Namik Kemal, quoted in *Nationalism and Modernity*, ed. Joseph Alpher (University of Haifa Press, 1986), p. 39.

5. Samuel P. Huntington, *The Third Wave* (London: University of Oklahoma Press, 1991), p. 264.

6. Ibid.

7. The 58 democratic countries in 1990 include 37 West European, European-settled, and Latin American countries, six East European countries, nine former British, US, and Australian colonies, and six other countries (Japan, Turkey, South Korea, Mongolia, Namibia, and Senegal) (Huntington, *The Third Wave*).

8. Arend Lijphart, ed., *Conflict and Coexistence in Belgium*, Institute of International Studies (University of California Press, 1981), p. 58.

9. With the rise of a nationalism of language, the Flemish "national consciousness . . . grew stronger and stronger" (Lijphart, *Conflict and Coexistence in Belgium*, p. 58).

10. Unlike the United States, it is believed that the melting pot mentality does not exist in Belgium, but in truth it does exist in places such as Brussels, where one worker in three is a foreigner, and where one resident in five is a foreigner.

11. *The Economist* (April 17, 1993).

12. Mario Toscano, *Alto Adige—South Tyrol* (Johns Hopkins University Press, 1975), p. 7.

13. In contrast, Poland, Czechoslovakia, Romania, and Greece had signed a treaties for the protection of minorities within their borders (Ibid., p. 12).

14. Ibid., p. 15. It has to be recognized that during the period of Mussolini's control of Italy, the German-speaking minority was treated harshly by the Italian government: the Italian language was declared obligatory in government and schools (private and public), family names were Italianized, German newspapers were suppressed, and the creation of Italian settlements in the area was planned.

15. Ibid., p. 110.

16. Jane Eve Hilowitz, ed., *Switzerland in Perspective* (New York: Greenwood Press, 1990), p. 35.

17. Carol L. Schmid, *Conflict and Consensus in Switzerland* (Berkeley: University of California Press, 1981), p. 134.

18. To be technically accurate, the terrorist arm of the IRA that executes the violence is the Provisional Irish Republican Army (PIRA).

19. There are 950,000 Protestants and 650,000 Roman Catholics in Northern Ireland.

20. In 23 years of violence, 3,023 people have been killed, about one-half of them by each side. The PIRA has killed about 900 security force members, at the same time losing about 300 of their own number—some by their own bombs (*The New York Times*, Dec. 13, 1992).

21. The British government has steadily increased its economic contributions to Northern Ireland to help alleviate the sectarian friction where financial deprivation exists.

22. For a fuller discussion of this issue, see Richard Allan, *Terrorism: Pragmatic International Deterrence and Cooperation*, Institute for East-West Studies Occasional Paper Series, no. 19 (New York, 1990), p. 11.

23. In January 1993 in south Belfast a man was shot to death by two masked men who burst into his home in a mixed Protestant-Catholic area. Two other men sitting in the same room were ignored. Earlier that same evening a Protestant member of the Ulster Volunteer Forces was shot but survived this third attempt on his life. Both attacks occurred at almost the same moment as PIRA mortar attacked a security base in West Belfast. This kind of violence is inconsistent with, and makes a mockery of, such nominal safeguards.

24. Milan magistrates continue to deal further blows to the political control of the country by adding to the growing number of Italy's business and political elite in jail.

25. In New York alone from 1974 to 1983, bombings attributable to the Armed Forces of National Liberation, also known as FALN, a Puerto Rican independence group, killed many people at various sites, including a restaurant where George Washington had made his farewell address to his troops, an airline terminal, and a Mobil Oil Company building.

26. The timing of terrorist attacks in the week after the explosion beneath New York's World Trade Center indicates that it may not have been an isolated event: in Warrington, England, a gasworks bomb exploded, as did a department store bomb in London; an embassy bomb in Belgrade; a train bomb in the Georgian Republic; a train bomb in Russia; a coffee house bomb in Cairo; a tax-office bomb in Athens; and three downtown bombs in Madrid.

27. *The New York Times*, Feb. 21, 1993.

28. *The New York Times*, Jan. 7, 1993.

29. The US government has admitted that its overseas missions have been in contact with Hamas groups and has ordered that activity to stop (*Wall Street Journal*, March 3, 1993).

30. In England, lack of access to the courts for the PIRA members has been decried by many international organizations investigating the denial of due process accorded those who had been arrested as suspected members of this terrorist group.

31. An opinion poll released March 16, 1993 by the Romanian Institute for Public Opinion Surveys (IRSOP) indicates more than one in four Romanians (27%) were in favor of a dictatorship.

32. "Moscow is now patrolled by the official militia, local and municipal militia, Interior Ministry troops, paratroops, riot police, volunteer auxiliaries, private police forces, and cossack vigilantes." All to no avail (*Jane's Intelligence Review* 15, no. 5, [May 1993]).

33. *RFE/RL Daily Report*, March 16, 1993. A recent issue of *Nedelya* (no.

10) carries a wealth of statistical data, which, if accurate, provides disturbing evidence of conditions in the Russian army.

34. *Jane's Intelligence Review* 4, no. 12 (December 1992).

35. Three hundred thousand persons who had become refugees during the Tajik civil war are reported to have returned home. But thousands of supporters of the Islamic opponents of the conservative forces remain in Afghanistan.

36. In a long interview published by the Spanish newspaper *El País*, the head of the militant Officers Union predicted that a coup launched by the army would find considerable support within the officers corps (*RFE/RL Daily Report*, March 16, 1993).

37. On March 11, 1993, the six parliamentary parties of Hungary reached a much-desired consensus that may lead to the adoption of the country's first law on domestic national and ethnic minorities. The law, discussed since 1991, is expected to set a pattern that its neighbors will follow in their own treatment of ethnic minorities, especially the Magyars.

38. The war and terrorism in Bosnia is about religious difference as well as territory and politics. The West has been unwilling to intervene with force; between May 1992 and March 1993, 130,000 people were killed, 20,000 raped, 70,000 placed in detention camps, 740,000 made refugees within Bosnia, and 1 million made refugees elsewhere (*Time*, March 15, 1993, p. 40).

39. "Europe will be confronted by the same problems in Bosnia as the world has had with the Palestinian question, but the bombs will not be exploding in Cyprus or Jerusalem, but in London and Paris" (*Security Intelligence*, Jan. 25, 1993, p. 1).

40. "Turkey is under internal pressure to aid Muslims in Bosnia. Many Turks feel the Greeks are openly aiding the Serbs and if Turkey does not help the Muslims it will signal weakness." The conflict in Turkey that has inhibited its immediate involvement in the Balkan upheaval is between the Turkish military, "which wants no part of the Balkan war," and religious fundamentalists. One element in Turkey's internal conflict is its concern in building a trade relationship with former Soviet republics in Central Asia (*Security Intelligence*, Jan. 25, 1993).

41. As an example of this situation let me quote from a Muslim publication, *Khilatah Magazine*, exhorting its readers: "Finally, our work as Muslims in the West [is that we must] tell someone that Islam provides the best way of life. . . . [What] we have to offer is a glorious history of glorious achievements. This means that we should address much of our activity to assist in the work to *establish an Islamic society* in Muslim countries. The Muslim community must address this central issues *in all their dealings as inhabitants of the West*—in the schools, shops, colleges, work place, recreation centers, and media" (emphasis added) (Farid Kassim, "Capital: It's a Crime," *Khilatah Magazine*).

42. Ian M. Cuthbertson, ed., *Redefining the CSCE: Challenges and Opportunities in the New Europe*, Institute for EastWest Studies Special Report (New York, 1992), p. ix.

Part IV

International Norms and
Responses to the Minority Question

9

The International Community
and Forms of Intervention
in the Field of Minority Rights Protection

KOEN KOCH

1. HIGH TIDE OR LOW TIDE
FOR THE RIGHTS OF MINORITIES?

At first glance, it is not unreasonable to describe the present period as high tide for the promotion and protection of minority rights. At the universal as well as the regional levels, we see the adoption of an impressive set of normative commitments. In the autumn of 1992, during its 47th session, the United Nations General Assembly accepted a declaration, submitted by the Commission on Human Rights through the Economic and Social Council, on the rights of persons belonging to cultural, national or ethnic, religious, and linguistic minorities. This can be considered the culmination of the process that started in 1966 with the adoption of the International Covenant on Civil and Political Rights, which held that "In those States in which ethnic, religious or linguistic minorities exist, persons belonging to such minorities shall not be denied the right, in community with other members of their group, to enjoy their own culture, to profess and practice their own religion, or to use their own language" (article 27). Article 1 of the nonbinding 1992 declaration stipulates: "States shall protect the existence and the national or ethnic, cultural, religious and linguistic identity of minorities within their respective territories, and shall encourage conditions for the promotion of that identity." Indeed, there is an enormous gap between the rather negative "shall not be denied" and the positive "shall protect and encourage."

The Parliamentary Assembly of the Council of Europe followed suit. In February 1993, it adopted Recommendation 1201 on an additional protocol on the rights of minorities to the European Convention for the Protection of Human Rights and Fundamental Freedoms. The Assembly expressed the hope that the Committee of Ministers would speed up its work so that the meeting of Heads of State and Government in Vienna (October 8–9, 1993) would be able to adopt such a protocol and open it for signature, precisely because "this matter is extremely urgent and one of the most important activities currently under way at the Council of Europe."[1]

This urgency has of course to do with the actual political situation in former Yugoslavia and in other parts of Europe where the rights of minorities are being trampled on. The deep concern of the Assembly is epitomized by the fact that the protocol does not fail to ban the practice of "ethnic cleansing." In June 1993, a European Charter for Regional or Minority Languages was adopted, as a convention, by the Committee of Ministers.

In the framework of the Conference on Security and Cooperation in Europe (CSCE), the Document of the Copenhagen Meeting of the Conference on the Human Dimension, the Report of the July 1991 CSCE Meeting of Experts on National Minorities in Geneva, and the 1992 Helsinki Document "The Challenges of Change" have to be mentioned as milestones in the progress towards a comprehensive instrument of minority rights. This last document also contains a reference to "ethnic cleansing," in the sense that participating states pledge to "refrain from resettling and condemn all attempts, by the threat or use of force, to resettle persons with the aim of changing the ethnic composition of areas within their territories."[2] The participating states also decided to establish a High Commissioner on National Minorities. His task, however, will be to act as an "instrument of conflict prevention at the earliest possible stage," rather than to promote the protection of minority rights per se. The High Commissioner is dealt with in chapter 11 in this volume.

Recent developments in the field of minority rights protection at the universal and regional levels appear impressive indeed. A rather comprehensive set of instruments to protect minority rights seems to have been constructed, or, at least, seems to be under construction by the international community. This positive picture is enhanced by developments in the thinking about the legitimacy of intervention by the international community in case of gross and systematic violation of human rights. The actions in Iraq to help the Kurds and in Somalia under the aegis of the UN gave practical relevance to this development. As the UN Secretary-General noted in his 1991 report to the General Assembly:

> It is now increasingly felt that the principle of non-interference with the essential domestic jurisdiction of States cannot be regarded as a protective barrier behind which human rights could be massively or systematically violated with impunity. . . . The case for not impinging on the sovereignty, territorial integrity and political independence

of States is by itself indubitably strong. But it would only be weakened if it were to carry the implication that sovereignty, even in this day and age, includes the right of mass slaughter or of launching systematic campaigns of decimation or forced exodus of civilian populations in the name of controlling civil strife or insurrection.[3]

What is at issue here is not the unilateral right of intervention in the defense of human rights. This would result in chaos or anarchy, or, perhaps more probably, in inactivity and impotence. The principal issue is collective action, based on a decision in accordance with the UN Charter, which must be applied equally in similar cases and respect the principle of proportionality. This last stipulation is especially interesting because the idea that collective action "must be applied indiscriminately in similar cases" hints at the possibility of the development not of a right, but of an *obligation*, of the international community to intervene when human rights are grossly and systematically violated.[4]

Indeed, there seems to be developing something of an international human rights regime with specific reference to the rights of persons belonging to some kind of minority, i.e., an international body of rights and normative commitments, implementation and monitoring mechanisms, and the possibility of intervention by the international community when these rights are grossly and systematically violated. Unfortunately, however, there is more reason to be pessimistic than optimistic. One has to acknowledge the gap between the rosy "reality" of the politicians, diplomats, and legal experts hammering out codes or charters of minority rights in conference rooms in New York, Geneva, or Strasbourg and the grimmer one of people living in Sebrenica, Tuzla, Vitez or, for that matter, in Nagorno-Karabakh. These people are precisely the victims of the "ethnic cleansing" so forcefully condemned by the UN Secretary-General and the Parliamentary Assembly of the Council of Europe, and in the Helsinki II document, but they are confronted with the shocking unwillingness and inability of the international community to intervene effectively to put an end to the "ethnic cleansing." In April 1993, officials of the United Nations High Commission for Refugees (UNHCR) no longer refused to assist in the evacuation of Muslim inhabitants of besieged cities and villages. They admitted that by so doing they unwittingly condoned and even contributed to the practice of "ethnic cleansing," but they thought this was the only alternative left to ameliorate the massive human suffering.

Indeed, there seems to exist a glaring contradiction between theory and practice when it comes to protecting minorities. In theory, the international community has made normative commitments, embodied in universal and regional minority rights instruments and the general discussions about the legitimacy of intervention in case of gross violation of these rights. In practice, however, we see the impotence of the international community in protecting the rights of minorities when they are violated. This contradiction breeds cynicism among the general public and encourages those who ridicule the efforts of diplomats negotiating minority rights catalogues without providing adequate mechanisms for implementation, monitoring, and intervention in case of violations. To a disturbing extent, the international community seems to excel in "declaratory" diplomacy and "symbolic politics" but to fail in executing practical policies, which puts its credibility at stake.

The actual performance of the international community in this field forces us into an agonizing reappraisal. In such an analysis, at least two sets of questions should be dealt with. In the first place, we have to question the robustness of the body of international normative commitments in the field of minority rights. Does the international community really care? Which factors determine the relative strength or weakness of these normative commitments? What are the prospects of broadening and strengthening them? What is the point of this when the international community falls short in implementing its commitments and defending these rights? Will not this declaratory and symbolic policy encourage on the one hand cynicism, despondency, or apathy, and on the other aggression and violence in respect to all those whose rights are not guaranteed or protected by the international community? This leads to the second set of questions. When we take for granted, for the sake of argument, the existence of a body of minority rights, under what conditions will the international community, i.e., the collectivity of states, be prepared to uphold these rights if need be?

I will try to answers these questions as follows. In section 2, I will analyze what can be called the Copenhagen-Geneva Standards: what is the specific nature of the normative commitments, to what extent are measures taken to implement these commitments, and what are possible forms of intervention? This analysis will be summarized in a tentative balance sheet. Section 3 will dwell on the nature and the root causes of the minority question. This analysis will provide some explanation for the state of affairs summarized in section 2 and will provide some background for the development of some policy guidelines on the basis of the Copenhagen-Geneva Standards, the topic of sections 4 and 5.

2. THE COPENHAGEN-GENEVA STANDARDS

In the first years after World War II, attention to the problem of minority rights was very limited, especially in comparison with the abundant attention given to the minority question after World War I. In the Universal Declaration of Human Rights, no reference was made to minority rights. During the process that led up to Charter of the United Nations, one diplomat remarked, "What the world needs now, is not protection for minorities, but protection from minorities." The reason for this attitude, of course, was Hitler's abuse of the protection of the rights of minorities (see Helgesen 1992, 159).

From what was said in section 1, it has become clear that attention to minority rights grew very slowly indeed. After the rather modest start in the 1950s and 1960s with article 14 of the European Convention and article 27 of the International Covenant on Civil and Political Rights, real progress only began in the 1980s and 1990s, epitomized by the CSCE Copenhagen Document (1990) and the CSCE Experts Meeting on National Minorities in Geneva (1991). The momentum spilled over to the United Nations (the 1992 Declaration) and the Council of Europe. This is, of course, a rather logical succession, as the history of the human rights crusade shows that it is, tactically speaking, fruitful to open the battle in the political (e.g., the CSCE) arena, before moving into the legal field (Helgesen 1992, 185).

This is not the place to analyze in depth the development and the content of the various minority rights instruments. This is done very competently elsewhere (e.g., Barcz 1992; Helgesen 1992; Heraclides 1992). It is important to note that there is some consensus about the fact that after Copenhagen and Geneva the high point for new and more specific normative commitments had passed. Some governments, indeed, initially opposed the idea of the Geneva meeting because they thought that after Copenhagen it could only bring disappointment. Fortunately, this fear did not materialize.

Of course, the Copenhagen-Geneva Standards (which regard the rights of minorities, for instance, to use their mother tongue, to establish and maintain their educational, cultural, and religious institutions, and to participate in decision-making procedures concerning minority issues, among others, as well as the obligations of the states to protect the ethnic, cultural, linguistic, and religious identity of national minorities and to create conditions for the promotion of that identity) can be criticized because of the fact that

> the most controversial issues could be solved only by compromising on carefully formulated clauses. This resulted in the insertion of a great number of escape clauses which highly

affect the obligatory character of the provisions concerned. Often the CSCE States only pledge to "endeavor" or to "consider" and in one case they only were prepared to "note" [the very sensitive issue of possible autonomous administration of minorities, para. 35 of the Copenhagen Document]. Moreover, they could achieve agreement often only by referring to "national legislation" as another escape clause. (Bloed 1990, 41)

This, of course, diminishes the strength of the normative commitments, as can be illustrated by the way the question of language rights, an essential element of minority identity, is dealt with. It is enlightening to compare sections 32.3 and 34 of the Copenhagen Document. Section 32.3 reads: [minorities have the right] "to use freely their mother tongue in private as well as in public" and section 34 reads: "The participating States will endeavor to ensure that persons belonging to national minorities, notwithstanding the need to learn the official language or languages of the State concerned, have adequate opportunities for instruction of their mother or in their mother tongue, as well as, wherever possible and necessary, for its use before public authorities, in conformity with applicable national legislation." Clearly, the tension between minority rights and the claims of the unitary or national state is here illustrated. It is also clear that the balance is tilted toward the interests of the state. There is a vast difference between instruction *in* or *of* the mother tongue. The phrases "wherever possible and necessary" and "in conformity with applicable national legislation" provide states with considerable leeway to follow their specific policies.[5] The clause "wherever possible and necessary" could even give governments the opportunity to obstruct the use of minority languages before the courts, because, for instance, bilingual judges are not available, the cost of interpreters is prohibitive, and, given the obligation on the part of the minorities to learn the "official" language, why bother anyway? In other words, it would be very difficult to designate some practices as *prima facie* violations of the language rights of minorities. The same goes for other important minority rights.

The Copenhagen-Geneva Standards have the character of a political commitment. The position of minorities would improve dramatically if states would faithfully implement their commitments. The standards, however, do not provide a strong legal basis for intervention, by economic or military means, when minority rights are violated. In terms of obligation, the normative commitment to these rights is rather weak, and the rights are rather ambiguously formulated, as exemplified above. There is another aspect we have to acknowledge. Although the international community has admitted the importance of minority rights, the international community does not consider these rights important enough to consider forceful intervention when these rights are violated.

Only in two cases will intervention on behalf of persons belonging to some minority be possibly considered: when the treatment of minorities provides a serious threat to the international peace and security and/or when the *basic* human rights, the so-called integrity rights, of persons belonging to minorities are grossly violated. Even then, we have to admit that the international community is very slow in accepting its responsibilities and duties. This reluctance is even greater than its reluctance to accept its obligations under the collective security regime, the backbone of the UN Charter.

Inis Claude, Jr. provided a classic treatment of the reasons for the failure of a collective security regime in his book *Swords into Plowshares: The Problems and Progress of International Organization* (1956). Joffe summarizes the argument aptly:

> A key conceptual weakness of collective security is that the principle requires . . . all members of the system, or at least the great powers, to treat aggression or the threat of aggression as the supreme evil, against which all other values are dwarfed. States, however, follow their own interests; they do not elevate the punishment of wrong-doers above all other values and they are loath to sacrifice their particular interests on the altar of abstract justice. . . . Collective security presupposes, rather than creates, its own necessary condition: common commitment to peace. (Joffe 1992, 39, 44)

Unfortunately, this argument applies a fortiori when human rights are grossly and systematically violated.[6] In the international community, the question "Am I my brother's keeper?" is not answered in the affirmative, yet. This boils down to the following conclusion: intervention, by economic sanctions or military means, on behalf of persons belonging to national, ethnic, or linguistic minorities, will in principle take place only when the maltreatment of minorities is a threat to international peace and security and/or when their basic human rights are grossly violated, *not because their specific rights as persons belonging to a minority are violated*. And the probability that this intervention will be executed, even if legitimized under the UN Charter and authorized by the Security Council, is rather small. This is a sad conclusion, but it would be irresponsible to draw a more agreeable picture and take pious wishes as a point of departure for future policies.

The corollary of this is that the promotion and protection of minority rights has to start, so to speak, at the "other end," with programs of assistance and cooperation in this field among governments of good will. This, of course, limits the possible forms of intervention by the international community. Emphasis must be placed on implementation, on cooperation and assistance; it is only realistic to exclude more coercive forms of intervention by economic or military means as far as the protection of minority rights is concerned.

The emphasis on implementation is not a "soft" option, and should not be considered an easy way out; it requires unremitting attention and investment of massive material and intellectual resources. I would argue that it is easier to indulge in discussions about more normative commitments than to find ways and means of implementing already existing ones; nevertheless, in the end the self-gratifying habit of hammering out ingenuous but rather ambiguously formulated compromises on normative commitments will be counterproductive.

In many cases, the violation of minority rights is the harbinger of the massive violation of basic human rights and outright violence and aggression, as is exemplified by Serbian maltreatment of the Albanians in Kosovo, most notoriously in the late 1980s. The international community did not pay much attention to the fate of the Kosovars, and can now be only ashamed about its prolonged inability to intervene effectively to protect basic human rights in former Yugoslavia. The international community can possibly break out of the deathtrap of inertia before and paralysis after the fact when priorities are changed: from codification of still more and more specific rights to collective endeavors to implement codified rights.

Barcz concluded rightly that "the level of national minority protection as laid down in the Copenhagen Document constitutes the utmost of what can be achieved between the European States at this moment. . . . In the near future the development of standards within the European framework will not go beyond what has already been agreed upon in the Copenhagen Document" (Barcz 1992, 92, 98). Heraclides correctly described the post-1991 period as a "saturation phase (commitment-wise)" (Heraclides 1992, 17).

The formulation and adoption of new normative commitments are not necessary, useful, or realistic. Not necessary, because even when we acknowledge the above criticism, the Copenhagen-Geneva Standards, if only they were faithfully implemented by the participating states, would mean a dramatic improvement in the position of minorities. Not useful, or even detrimental for the credibility of the international community, because the gap between commitment and implementation of rights would become still greater, breeding cynicism and apathy on the one hand and aggression and violence on the other. Not realistic, because it has become clear that the political limits for reaching consensus seem to have been reached.

At the end of the 1980s, the political situation provided a window of opportunity that was happily and productively used. But precisely because of this use and because of the fact that the traditional East-West divide no longer obscured political disagreements, the political nature of the minority question became clear. Moreover, it became clear that there exists a fundamental philosophical and political difference between two dominant approaches to the rights of minorities. Some states, such as the United States, the United Kingdom, France, Greece, Spain, Bulgaria, and Romania, see the matter from a nondiscrimination/equality/individual rights angle; others states, such as Hungary, Austria, Italy, and the Nordic countries, are in favor of a positive measure/group rights/participation *qua* group/autonomous rule (see Heraclides 1992, 17). Of course, some common ground can be and has been found between these two approaches, as the Copenhagen-Geneva Standards have shown. But it is only fair to admit that in the last instance these two approaches are mutually exclusive.

The same political divide plays a role in the discussion about implementation. Generally, the new emphasis on implementation is applauded, but Helsinki II did not bring us the required adaptation and amendment of the existing human dimension institutions and instruments. Some states were wary of any institutional changes. As a second line of defense, they laid emphasis on procedures and institutions rather than on the substance of problem solving (see Zaagman 1992, 60). In view of the urgency of the minority question, it is rather disappointing to note that the only initiative Helsinki II produced in this field was the organization of *one* CSCE seminar (a one-week meeting of field experts) on "successfully resolved minority problems."

In any case, the political limit of consensus has been reached in the Copenhagen-Geneva Standards. We have to appreciate that within the international community the consensus possible in the field of minority protection is rather limited. In other words, there is no such thing as an international community united in a philosophical and normative approach towards minority questions, prepared to uphold minority rights effectively and forcefully if need be; instead there is a quarrelsome collection of states, fundamentally differing in approaches and policies, prepared to accept compromises only to a certain extent, reluctant to implement commitments, and a fortiori reluctant to intervene to protect minority rights.

Commitment-wise, implementation-wise as well as intervention-wise, the margins in the field of minority protection are very narrow. These margins are essentially of a political nature; they have to be understood when we try to find ways and means to protect minority rights.

3. THE POLITICAL-IDEOLOGICAL NATURE OF THE MINORITY QUESTION

Minority questions are politically sensitive indeed, not so much because these questions are very complicated (which they really are), but because in a very direct and dangerous way they touch upon our ideas about the ideal model of the state, about the relationship between state and nation, and about the relationship between state, nation, and citizen. In many cases, a minority problem is essentially not so much a minority problem per se, but a state problem, i.e., a problem caused by the way the state thinks it appropriate to handle cultural, linguistic, ethnic, religious, or national diversity. In numerous cases, states, or rather their policies, are the causes of minority problems. The paradoxical character of the issue of protection of minority rights becomes apparent: on the one hand, the state has to be considered a threat to the identity and rights of minorities; on the other hand, the state, and the collectivity of states, is called upon to protect that identity and these rights. In this sense, the description of the international community, i.e., the collectivity of states, as a deus ex machina protecting minority rights is rather misleading, because this suggests incorrectly that these rights are threatened by some unknown third party. The Baron von Münchhausen analogy is much more adequate, pinpointing the fact that as far as the international protection of minority rights is concerned, the collectivity of states or individual states are called upon to undo what some of them or they themselves are doing wrong.

The relationship between states and minorities is a precarious one indeed. The precariousness of this relationship is exemplified by the common emphasis on the necessity of protecting minorities and on the indispensability of states, and the collectivity of states, as protecting agencies. In the field of protection of minority rights, at least in the case of the more serious violations, "violating" states are, however, opposed to other states who are prepared to defend minority rights. The more necessary it is, in view of the character of the violation of these rights, to intervene forcefully, the higher the probability of international conflict. The "defending" states have to weigh their own national interests, the lives of their citizens, against the value of guaranteeing, for instance, the cultural and language rights of "people in a far away country of whom they know nothing," to paraphrase the infamous words of Chamberlain in 1938. The more minority rights are violated, the less other states will be prepared to intervene. The possibility of intervention in case of gross violation of basic human rights of persons belonging to a minority is already discussed above.

The von Münchhausen analogy—states must undo what they themselves do wrong—can be illustrated by two examples. As one of the guiding principles of the emerging European states system in the 17th century, the relationship between state and religion was organized on the principle of *cuius regio, eius religio*. All people belonging to a religion other than the ruler's became members of a religious minority, although in another country adherents to the same belief belonged to a majority religion. It is, then, very interesting to note that the Treaty of Westphalia of 1648, which established the legal framework of the European state system, contained some stipulations to protect (religious) minorities.

The reconstruction of the map of Europe in the period after World War I, presumably according to the principles of self-determination and the nation-state and resulting in the establishment of a number of new "nation-states" in East Central Europe, is another case in point. Precisely because this region is characterized by considerable cultural, linguistic, ethnic, and national heterogeneity and by the intermingling of these different groups as oil and water, as Renan said, the establishment of a number of would-be nation-states in East Central Europe as the successors of the defunct multinational Austro-Hungarian and Ottoman Empires immediately produced a number of formidable minority problems. And again, it is noteworthy that this was accompanied by the organization of an intricate system of treaties aiming at the protection of minorities within the League of Nations framework. Unfortunately, this system was not altogether successful, to put it mildly. Even in 1917, Brailsford already foresaw that each of these new little states "with their minorities within minorities would reproduce the hatreds and confusions of Europe" (cited in Howard 1981, 79). The tragic history of this region after World War I was characterized by the rapid succession of changes of state borders, changing majorities into minorities and back again, causing discrimination, hatred, and violence.

These two examples illustrate the political "construction" of majorities and minorities. Minority or majority status, then, does not depend on some inherent quality of the group of people in question, but on the socio-political environment. The "constructional" aspect emphasizes that there is nothing inevitable in the fate of majorities and minorities, but that the issue of majorities and minorities is amenable to political manipulation and change, by the way state boundaries are drawn and redrawn.

This may seem to suggest that the existence of the state system and the existence of the minority question inevitably go together. This, however, is not necessarily true. Of course, in most cases, state boundaries do not coincide with cultural, linguistic, religious, ethnic, or "national" divisions. In this sense, the nation-state, conceived of as an entity characterized by the congruence of the political and the "national" unit (see Gellner 1983, 1), is a rare breed indeed.[7] Apart from those who hold the nationalist ideology about the necessity of the congruence of the political and the national unit as scientific truth, this is almost self-evident. State boundaries reflect, in the last instance, the relations of power between states, demarcating their respective spheres of sovereignty. The specific territorial patterns of cultural, linguistic, or ethnic divisions and the intermingling of linguistic and ethnic groups are the outcome of past migration movements and of demographic developments, processes determined not only by political, but also, for instance, by economic and ecological factors. It would have been very accidental indeed had the interplay between political, demographic, migrational, and economic factors produced a perfect "fit" between state boundaries and cultural, linguistic, religious, or ethnic divisions.

The fact of cultural, linguistic, religious, or ethnic diversity within specific state borders, however, does not produce in itself the so-called minority question. Nor does the root of the minority question lie in this diversity as such, but rather in the deep-seated and long-standing ideas politicians and citizens, philosophers and ideologues have about this diversity. Cultural, linguistic, religious, and ethnic diversity touches upon the central strands of our thoughts about state, nation, society, and individual. It has to do with our opinion about the ideal character of the state, its duties and functions; the essence of what makes nations and of what makes people feel that they belong to a certain nation; the moral and cultural fabric of society; the necessary conditions for its coherence and survivability; and the desired relationships among citizens and between citizens and their state and nation.

The specific content of these ideas can transform the fact of diversity into an issue of majorities and minorities, the latter posing a "problem" to be dealt with, threatened, tolerated, or respected by the former. It is equally important to note that the specific content of these ideas, designating the criteria for deciding the specific pattern of majorities and minorities and who belongs to the one or the other, changes according to time and place. The corollary of this is that majorities or minorities are not to be considered "natural" entities, but in the end as politico-ideological, socio-historical constructs. These constructs, of course, are very real in the political and social effects they have on the lives of the people belonging to them.

The most detrimental construct in this sense, of course, is the ideology of nationalism, holding that every nation, conceived of as a specific group of human beings distinguishing themselves by some cultural, linguistic, or ethnic characteristics from all other human beings, has an exclusive right to its "own" state, and that this state can function only when its citizens belong to that same nation. Indeed, the sheer existence of a minority, then, can be perceived as a threat to the survival of the state and the "state-forming" nation. Programs of (forced) assimilation, (forced) deportation, outright liquidation, and violent change of borders—the comprehensive concept that is today called "ethnic cleansing"—are traditional and, unfortunately, much-tried ways of providing final solutions for "minority problems." The ideology of nationalism, as far as it is embraced by governments and states, is a universal threat to minorities. But when minorities take refuge in the same ideology, the conflict will only be exacerbated and, in a paradoxical way, the legitimacy of the nationalist ideology will be strengthened. In any case, a minority protection regime, meant to protect nationalist minorities from nationalist governments, will be of no avail. In other words, the success of a minority protection regime depends on the political and ideological attitude towards cultural, linguistic, or ethnic diversity.

Pluralism is an alternative to the ideology of nationalism. Pluralism accepts the fact of diversity, even "fosters the rich contribution of national minorities to the life of our societies," according to the CSCE document "Guidelines for the Future," and sets out to guarantee each individual the right to enjoy his own culture and religion and to use his own language, regardless of which side of a state border he lives on. Pluralism entails a specific vision about the relationship between state and citizen. It assumes, so to speak, a "non-national" state, a political structure that is neutral, "non-national" in the sense that it guarantees all its citizens regardless of their national background the same cultural, linguistic, and religious rights. The state then is seen as an instrument to realize human rights and aspirations; the nation is conceived of as the commonwealth of citizens sharing the same democratic rights and duties, united in a common political project.

A key concept in this pluralism is the idea of nonterritorial, functional autonomy in the sphere of culture, language, and religion. Every cultural, linguistic, religious, or ethnic group could have its own school system, or more generally put, its own cultural "infrastructure," subsidized on an equal basis by the state, provided that the instruction given is adequate and does not prevent participation in society. On the one hand, this idea is based on the premise that the problems of multicultural, multiethnic, or multi-linguistic society cannot be solved in a territorial manner, precisely because there are no culturally, ethnically, or linguistically homogeneous regions. Every new territorial division would entail the production of new majorities and minorities. On the other hand, the idea is premised on the democratic values of self-organization, participation in relevant decision-making processes, and self-management precisely in this sphere.

The idea of nonterritorial, functional autonomy was first explored by the Austro-Marxists Otto Bauer and Karl Renner as a solution for multinational empires in East Central Europe before World War I. They considered the carving up of these empires into smaller states rather impractical, because economic development called for greater rather than smaller decision-making units. In order to guarantee the cultural, linguistic, and ethnic identity of all groups in these greater units, they proposed the idea of cultural self-administration. Their ideas were not put to the test.

In some countries, however, the practice of consociationalism, resembling the idea of nonterritorial, functional autonomy, developed as the result of the political conflict between religious and linguistic groups. Accepting that in a multi-religious or multi-linguistic country the enjoyment of their own religious and linguistic rights implied respect for the same rights of others, some groups came to the acceptance of the fact and the value of a multicultural society. A further exploration of the idea of nonterritorial, functional autonomy in its theoretical as well as its practical aspects could contribute to the solution of the minority question.

Pluralism rejects on principle and for practical reasons territorial solutions to the problems of multinational, multicultural, or multiethnic societies. This implies acceptance of the territorial status quo, not because actual borders are "just," but because every change to them substitutes new problems and injustices for old ones. On the basis of the mutual acceptance of the territorial status quo, governments could embark on common programs for the mutual protection of the identity and cultural rights of one another's minorities. As Barcz rightly remarked, states will not agree to develop minority protection standards without a guarantee that their political independence and territorial integrity will not be threatened (Barcz 1992, 95–96).

Because of the acceptance of the status quo, governments need no longer perceive a specific minority as a "fifth column," as the instrument with which neighboring states could try to endanger their territorial integrity. "Endangered" governments feel free to harass these minorities, interpreting endeavors of other states to protect the threatened groups as proof of the aggressive intentions of the other states concerned. In these circumstances, a mutually enforcing process of recrimination, discrimination, hatred, and violence can easily be set in motion, with the threatened minority footing the dreadful bill first and foremost.

This analysis leads to the conclusion that the rejection of the nationalist ideology by majorities *as well as* minorities and the acceptance of the territorial status quo are necessary prerequisites for the promotion and protection of the identity and the cultural and language rights of minorities. We now return to the Copenhagen-Geneva Standards to analyze the political parameters for minority protection agreed on by the participating states.

4. STATE RIGHTS AND MINORITY RIGHTS

The minority rights summarized in the Copenhagen-Geneva Standards are conditional in two respects at least. Paragraph 37 of the Copenhagen Document reads: "None of these commitments may be interpreted as any rights to engage in any activity or perform any action in contravention of the purposes and principles of the Charter of the United Nations, other obligations under international law or the provisions of the Final Act, including the principle of territorial integrity of States."[8] Apart from this, the so-called citizenship clause needs to be mentioned. The Geneva Report proclaims: "The participating States affirm that persons belonging to a national minority will enjoy the same rights and have the same duties of citizenship as the rest of the population." One could say that the interests of the state (guarantee of territorial integrity and political independence) are well taken care of.

The imbalance between state rights and minority rights is epitomized by the fact that the duties of the citizens belonging to some minority are spelled out, but that states are not obliged to recognize the existence of a minority when people choose to belong to a minority and express the will to protect their minority identity.[9] The essential weakness of the CSCE minority rights protection regime is thus emphasized. The application of minority rights standards is fundamentally dependent on the recognition by the state concerned of the existence of a minority. Simply by denying the existence of a minority, states can absolve themselves of their normative commitments towards minority protection. In other words, the application of standards concerning minorities requires a provision making the existence of a minority *independent* of its recognition by the state in question. Precisely because of its political explosiveness, states have not been able and will not be able in the future to come up with a universally applicable definition of what a minority is. Nevertheless, minorities do exist, and their protection needs first and foremost the recognition of their existence. If a universally applicable definition adopted by all states is impossible, a second-best option, perhaps, is the possibility of a group of authoritative, neutral experts drawing up a list of minorities that deserve international recognition and protection. To enhance the moral and political impact of this list, it is better to proceed in a minimalist and non-exhaustive rather than a maximalist manner. Especially here, the better is the enemy of the good.

In section 2, it was concluded that commitment-wise, implementation-wise and intervention-wise the political limits of consensus seem to have been reached. The above-mentioned imbalance between state rights and minority rights is another illustration of this fact. Where to go in this situation? As the road towards more normative commitments and more institutionalized implementation mechanisms seems to be rather unpromising at the pan-European level, attention may be directed at the regional and bilateral level, at least for two reasons. At that level, the regional specificity of minority questions can be better dealt with, and the chances for a common political understanding of the minority question are greater, especially when the relationship between the countries concerned are good (acceptance of the territorial status quo, etc.). The activity in this field, e.g., the treaty between the Republic of Poland and the Federal Republic of Germany (see Jasudowicz 1992) and the treaty system Hungary is developing with its neighbors in the field of minority protection is really encouraging. The study of the results of these treaties could provide important incentives for others to follow suit.

As was described above, the implementation of normative commitments depends not so much on the obligatory character of these commitments, but on the good will of governments. Even if this good will is present, we have to acknowledge that the implementation of minority rights, for instance following the concept of nonterritorial, functional autonomy in education and culture, is a very costly affair. Especially in the new democracies in East Central Europe, the shortage of material resources can frustrate the implementation of programs. It would be advisable that third countries and nongovernmental organizations (schools, churches, cultural organizations) be prepared to provide material assistance. The more support is provided on a project basis, the more effective it will be.

5. BY WAY OF A CONCLUSION: MODESTY, "CONSTRUCTIVE PATIENCE," AND PERSEVERANCE

The above analysis can only lead to a few sobering conclusions and policy recommendations. Necessary conditions for the protection of minority rights are the acceptance of the territorial status quo and, more generally, the rejection of the ideology of nationalism by states and minorities as well; international stability is also critical. Respect for minority rights depends on the political maturation of a pluralist and democratic society. In many cases, this requires a Copernican turnaround. It is rather impossible to *force* people to such a mental turnaround; people can learn to appreciate the value of pluralism, for instance, only by accepting that the tragedy of 20th-century European history, the sad story of discrimination, forced assimilation, deportation, liquidation, aggression, and war, has been brought about to a considerable extent by the ideology of extremist nationalism. Our concept of European history has to be changed from national or nationalist histories into the history of the common fate of people. Scientific as well as educational programs to develop such a common European history must be organized and funded. In this way, the dreadful self-fulfilling process of recollection and anticipation, the bitter fruit of the propagation of nationalist histories (*we know what they did to us, they know what we did to them; so we'd better prepare ourselves for another round of fighting and better still we will strike first*), can be avoided. On this basis, mutual respect can grow. At the very least, this idea of a common European history could be recommended as a topic for a CSCE seminar.

The same goes for another aspect of pluralism as a basis for the protection of minority rights, the key concept of nonterritorial, functional autonomy. A study of this concept is the more interesting because the concept of nonterritoriality provides the possibility of political and administrative participation of minorities and of self-management and self-organization *without* the danger of territorial autonomy so feared by states, the danger of creeping secession and irredentism.

As a third topic for such a CSCE seminar, the question of a list of internationally recognized minorities, described above, could be recommended. Such a list could break the deadlock of states denying the existence within their borders of minorities and thus absolving themselves of their normative commitments towards minorities.

The international community faces a lack of credibility because of the gap between normative commitments and implementation, between declaratory politics and actual behavior; witness the performance of the international community in former Yugoslavia. The adoption of new normative commitments and faithful implementation should go hand in hand. The latter is a more difficult thing to ascertain than the former. It is necessary that implementation now catch up with the level of normative commitments. A moratorium on new normative commitments is called for; all energy must be invested in the process of implementation. The material aspect of the implementation of minority rights must be emphasized. Common programs and specific projects must be developed. The more well-to-do countries have a special responsibility here, as do some nongovernmental organizations.

While it is true that in the CSCE framework commitment-wise and implementation-wise the political limits of consensus are more or less reached, it is advisable to concentrate on the regional and bilateral level. Bilateral treaties, such as mentioned above and based on the Copenhagen-Geneva Standards, should be recommended. Third countries should be called upon to provide material assistance, if necessary. At the least, the study of the results, problems, and possibilities of these treaties should be the topic of another CSCE seminar.

These recommendations are modest indeed. Nevertheless, they are not easy to implement. Their implementation requires constructive patience[10] and perseverance, precisely because they are not spectacular. In the end, however, these small practical steps will turn out to be more productive than the great symbolic strides forward.

NOTES

1. It is appropriate to note here that with regard to the protection of minorities, article 14 of the European Convention is the only international human rights instrument that contains a legally binding obligation: "The enjoyment of the rights and freedoms set forth in this Convention shall be secured without discrimination on any ground such as sex, race, color, language, religion, political or other opinion, national or social origin, *association with a national minority* [emphasis added], property, birth or other status." This article, however, can only be invoked in conjunction with the violation of another article of the European Convention. The Strassbourg jurisprudence does not provide persons belonging to minorities with possibilities for enforcement of protection of their specific minority rights.

2. The Helsinki Document directed the organization, in spring 1993 of a CSCE Human Dimension Seminar entitled "Case Studies on National Minorities Issues: Positive Results."

3. Report of the Secretary-General on the Work of the Organization, UN Doc. GAOR, 46th Sess., Supplement no. 1 (A/46/1) at 5.

4. Only, of course, when such an obligation to intervene is in place can we say that some sort of international rule of law exists. Under national rule of law, the state has both the right and the obligation to prosecute perpetrators of crimes.

5. The European Charter for Regional or Minority Languages is characterized by more or less the same imbalance. Protection and encouragement of regional or minority languages could be to the detriment of the official languages and the need to learn them. States themselves specify the minority languages to which the Charter shall apply, and the supervision of the implementation of the Charter is mostly in the hands of the states themselves.

A comparable ambiguity can be found in the UN 1992 Declaration, article 2.1: "[Persons belonging to minorities] have the right . . . to use their own language, in private and in public, freely and without interference or any form of discrimination" and article 4.3: "States should take appropriate measures so that, wherever possible, persons belonging to minorities have adequate opportunities to learn their mother tongue or to have instruction in their mother tongue."

6. It is useful to emphasize that collective action, with respect to collective security or the protection of basic human rights, will never take place without the consent of the permanent members of the Security Council, and never against one of them. The limitations of a *universal* regime for the protection of minority rights thus are very clear.

7. See, for instance, Fred Halliday's remark: "The term 'nation-state,' based as it is on the assumption of ethnic homogeneity and political representativity, is, in empirical terms, inappropriate to the modern world" (Halliday 1989, 47). Oakeshott notes: "All European states began as mixed and miscellaneous collections of human beings precariously held together . . . no European state (let alone an imitation European state elsewhere in the world) has ever come within measurable distance of being a 'nation-state' " (Oakeshott 1975, 188). Nielsson's research indicates that only a quarter of the states in existence can be described as real nation-states (Nielsson 1985, 32). Smith's estimate is about 10% (Smith 1986, 229). Most states, then, are to be considered multicultural, multinational, multi-linguistic, or multi-religious entities. This fact is obscured by the indiscriminate use of the concepts of the (national) state, nation, and nation-state, especially in English.

8. Article 8.4 of the 1992 UN Declaration is even stronger in this respect: "Nothing in this Declaration may be construed as permitting any activity contrary to the purposes and principles of the United Nations, including sovereign equality, territorial integrity and political independence of States."

9. The first sentence of paragraph 32 of the Copenhagen Document reads: "To belong to a national minority is a matter of a person's individual choice and no disadvantage may arise from the existence of such choice."

10. The apt phrase "constructive patience" was coined by Jan Helgesen (1992, 185).

REFERENCES

Barcz, Jan. 1992. European Standards for the Protection of National Minorities with Special Regard to the CSCE. Present State and Conditions of Development. In *Legal Aspects of a New European Infrastructure*, ed. Arie Bloed and Wilco de Jonge. Utrecht: NHC.

Bloed, Arie. 1990. A New CSCE Human Rights "Catalogue": A Critical Analysis. *Helsinki Monitor* 1, no. 3, pp. 36–43.

Claude, Inis L., Jr. 1956. *Swords into Plowshares: The Problems and Progress of International Organization*. New York: Random House.

Gellner, Ernest. 1983. *Nations and Nationalism*. Oxford: Basil Blackwell.

Halliday, Fred. 1989. State and Society in International Relations: A Second Agenda. In *The Study of International Relations: The State of the Art*, ed. Hugh C. Dyer and Leon Mangasarian. London: MacMillan, pp. 40–59.

Helgesen, Jan. 1992. Protecting Minorities in the Conference on Security and Co-operation in Europe (CSCE) Process. In *The Strength of Diversity: Human Rights and Pluralist Democracy*, ed. A. Rosas and J. Helgesen. Dordrecht: Njhoff.

Heraclides, Alexis. 1992. The CSCE and Minorities: The Negotiations Behind the Commitments, 1972–1992. *Helsinki Monitor* 3, no. 3, pp. 5–18.

Howard, Michael. 1981. *War and the Liberal Conscience*. Oxford: Oxford University Press.

Jasudowicz, Tadeus. 1992. Some Legal Aspects of the Protection of Minority Rights in Europe. In *Legal Aspects of a New European Infrastructure*. See Barcz 1992.

Joffe, Josef. 1992. Collective Security and the Future of Europe: Failed Dreams and Dead Ends. *Survival*, Spring, pp. 36–50.

Nielsson, Gunnar P. 1985. States and "Nation-Groups": A Global Taxonomy. In *New Nationalisms of the Developed West*, ed. Edward A. Tiryakian and Ronald Rogowski. Boston: Allen and Unwin, pp. 27–56.

Oakeshott, Michael. 1975. *On Human Conduct*. Oxford: Clarendon Press.

Smith, Anthony D. 1986. State-Making and Nation-Building. In *States in History*, ed. John A. Hall. London: Basil Blackwell, pp. 228–63.

Zaagman, Rob. 1992. Helsinki-II and the Human Dimension: Institutional Aspects. *Helsinki Monitor* 3, no. 4, pp. 52–64.

10

Codification of Minority Rights

ISTVÁN ÍJGYÁRTÓ

One glance at the ethnic map of the world is enough to convince us that ethnic conflict is not unique to East Central Europe. Moreover, it is erroneous to unequivocally state that communism stifled national consciousness, its internationalist ideology extinguishing national affiliation from the soul of the people. Though the above-mentioned view may be valid in the case of Hungary, current ethnicity-related events certainly do have a tradition in those states that confront us with the phenomenon known as national communism. For example, in Romania, where the orthodox national communism of Ceauşescu survived the shock of December 1989, the representatives of the fallen system continue to occupy their seats in the Bucharest Parliament. In other countries, such as the former Soviet republics, where the tradition of national communism is negligible, society has called for a new legitimacy to fill the power vacuum and resolve the political, ideological, and moral crisis. Only the concept of the nation could provide an immediate and effective foundation for this legitimacy.

We are faced with a global phenomenon, as the examples of Canada, India, and numerous developing countries demonstrate. The so-called theory of nation building has been unsuccessful. In fact, today we are faced with the full force of the harmful effects of this concept and its political manifestations.

1. THE BACKGROUND OF CURRENT
ETHNIC PROBLEMS IN EAST CENTRAL EUROPE

East Central Europe, the field of the paradigmatic changes of the 20th century, is a focal point of ethnic conflict. Disintegration in this region is unique for a number of reasons. First, it does not follow economic or geopolitical rifts, but primarily and—at the moment—exclusively, the ethnic principle.

The second characteristic that distinguishes the ethnic problems in East Central Europe from those in other regions is that in this part of the continent, we are talking about native ethnic communities that were formed prior to states, not groups that more recently settled the territory of an existing state, who raise the question of relations between the rights of immigrants and native minority communities, that is, are minority rights applicable to immigrants? This creates difficulties primarily for the universal codification of minority rights in Western states.

Last but not least, we must consider the fact that in the region, state borders do not coincide with ethnic borders. The consequences of the post-World War I peace are well known, particularly the fact that it is all but impossible to draw equitable borders in the region of Central and Eastern Europe. As a result, we must recognize that by acquiring territories inhabited by homogeneous minority communities, successor states have embraced ethnic groups for whom the new organizing principles of ethnic or historical community are only newly permissible. For example, as a result of such border changes, there are an estimated 2 million Hungarians in Romania, 600,000 in Slovakia, 400,000 in Serbia, 200,000 in Ukraine, 40,000 in Croatia, 16,000 in Austria, and 10,000 in Slovenia.

2. COLLECTIVE RIGHTS AND SELF-DETERMINATION

Beginning in the 1980s, minority issues and guarantees of minority rights became increasingly frequent in political declarations and international political documents (primarily the Copenhagen Document,[1] the Geneva Report,[2] and the Paris Charter[3]). Nevertheless, these cannot be considered legally binding documents; they merely express the intentions of the signatory states. The UN Charter and the Universal Declaration of Human Rights[4] do not deal specifically with the issue of minorities. The rights contained in the UN documents can be safeguarded only inasmuch as they are considered the *human rights of persons belonging to a minority*. Thus we arrive at one of the most sensitive questions: Should national minorities be granted collective rights or not?

The International Covenant on Civil and Political Rights[5] is at this time the only legally binding document that provides rights for persons belonging to ethnic, religious, and linguistic minorities. This document establishes the "non-discriminatory treatment of individuals," which guarantees equal treatment by the state to persons belonging to both the minority and state-forming majority community. This means, however, that persons belonging to ethnic, religious, and linguistic minorities whose human right to education is recognized are, in practice, subject to the education system of the majority. This example illustrates that those who reject separate collective rights assume the ideal existence of a "benign state" and a "generous majority."

For the specific purpose of this chapter, we can distinguish two constitutional and state models. The first is the French-style liberal nation-state developed after the French Revolution. Here, the sovereign state is constituted by the citizens who renounce their natural rights for the benefit of the community. Thus, in fact, the state becomes the sole representative of national sovereignty. The sovereign nation-state is indivisible; it does not recognize intermediary formations or autonomies.

Another model is based on a complex system of self-governing bodies in which the individuals establish and transfer their rights to specific public entities; among them, the state is the most competent. Because the state is not the proprietor of national sovereignty, this allows for the formation of local and autonomous public entities. The United States is the classic case demonstrating the viability of this model.

The functional problems of the existing Central and East European states based on the liberal nation-state model are attributed precisely to the presence of ethnic groups who are not culturally and politically assimilated and as a result are unable to adapt to the basic criterion of nation-state: the existence of the homogeneous nation. In these states, members of the minority can become genuine citizens only when they specifically renounce their particular ethnic identity. Inasmuch as they are unwilling to do so, they become—according to the opinion of the majority—a source of danger to state sovereignty. Under certain historical conditions, nation-states that reject the collective rights of minorities have not hesitated to declare minority populations to be collectively guilty of disloyalty or treason.

The legal concept of nation-state and the corresponding ideology of the homogeneous nation, combined with the principle of democratic national self-determination, indirectly determined the post-World War I peace treaties, including those on the protection of national minorities.

In the 1980s, the principle of the democratic self-determination of peoples was the only acceptable principle for the peoples of Central and Eastern Europe who strove for independence and unity. If the principle of self-determination had been properly realized after World War I, the victors could have avoided the creation of such a large number of minority ethnic groups (thus also avoiding the resulting tensions). However, the realization of the rights of the victors, the establishment of spheres of influence, and the results of the diplomacy culminating at Yalta and Potsdam restricted the implementation of the principle of self-determination. At the same time, the new borders provided the basis for the new European status quo.

Renewed attempts to implement the principle of self-determination arose only after World War II. At that time, the major powers selectively applied the principle in the granting of independence to colonial peoples through the United Nations.[6] The letter and the spirit of the UN Declaration reflect this standpoint. The weaknesses of the nation-state model, which was nonetheless partially accommodated, were once again revealed: the principle was applied only to so-called political nations, which, in fact, were communities that had reached a particular level of political organization; it was not applied to peoples or ethnic groups. As a result of this approach, in some cases ethnic groups that represented a numerical minority became the politically dominant groups of society.

3. THE PRINCIPLE OF
SELF-GOVERNMENT AS A POSSIBLE SOLUTION

According to István Bibó, only democratic, stable, and mature social and political communities that have a mission surpassing their mere physical existence are willing to initiate a dialogue with their state concerning their claims to self-determination. The most important lesson of post-1945 European ethnic conflicts—specifically those in Belgium, South Tyrol, and the Spanish Basque territories—was that concrete solutions to the problems of ethnic communities must be found before the state or its regions are threatened with disintegration. In Belgium, the separation/integration problem of the Flemish and Walloon populations involved a lengthy and complex 20-year legal and political process. In another example, in addition to the Italian peace treaty and constitution, an agreement between the Austrian and Italian governments also provided a legal basis for guarantees for a certain level of autonomy for the German-speaking population in South Tyrol (the most important condition was that which secured the status of Austria as a protective power).

In the above cases, recognition of the sovereignty and particular identity of the respective national communities or minorities was the first necessary step. Consequently, the principle of "limited sovereignty" was also implemented. According to this principle, the state renounces parts of its sovereignty, while the national community living in numerical minority in turn limits its claim to self-determination in order not to damage the territorial integrity of the state and the vital interest of the majority. Such application of "limited sovereignty/ limited self-determination" clears the path for establishing intermediary bodies and various types of self-governments and autonomies. National minority institutions required to preserve national identity include 1) cultural autonomy, serving the interests of geographically dispersed minorities; 2) territorial autonomy, serving the interests of minorities that live in compact communities; and 3) a combination of cultural and territorial autonomy, accommodating minorities that are spread out across the administrative borders of a territorial autonomy. Inasmuch as this model can be implemented in Eastern Europe, minorities and minority institutions must be granted particular rights, which involve, *inter alia*, increased (but legally regulated) access to funds.

4. POSSIBILITIES FOR THE CODIFICATION OF MINORITY RIGHTS IN EAST CENTRAL EUROPE

In recent years, international forums have paid increased attention to the need to resolve minority problems. The most recent results include the UN Declaration on the Rights of Persons Belonging to National or Ethnic, Religious and Linguistic Minorities adopted by the General Assembly in December 1992, the European Charter for Regional or Minority Languages open to signature by the Council of Europe in 1992, and the CSCE institution of the High Commissioner for National Minorities. Parallel to these developments, there have also been initiatives in the Central and East European region regarding the establishment and implementation of the principles guiding minority policy. These principles and their bilateral and regional codification are based on specific conditions and experience and must be carried out in light of existing international norms. Special attention must be paid to the fact that new independent countries have proved to be the most cooperative regarding minority issues. As part of their stabilization processes, and motivated by their responsibility toward their co-nationals forced to live in numerical minority outside their own state borders, these new states have found it necessary to resolve their own minority problems. In the following paragraphs, I will discuss the Hungarian-Ukrainian Declaration (later joined by Croatia and Slovenia),[7] the Hungarian-Slovenian Agreement on the special rights of minorities,[8] and the Hungarian-Russian Mutual Declaration on the treatment of minorities.[9] I will also discuss their effects on the codification processes of each country.

Paragraph 68 (sections 1–5) of the Hungarian constitution modified in 1989 and 1990 deals with minorities. According to its text, national and ethnic minorities are state-forming factors. The Republic of Hungary protects the minorities living on its territory and secures their collective participation in public matters, the fostering of their particular culture, the use of their native language, their native language education, and the right to use their names according to their own language. Hungarian laws guarantee minority representation. National and ethnic minorities may establish self-governments at the local and national levels.

Both a special codification committee and a "roundtable" composed of the minority representatives living in Hungary participated in the preparation of the law on the rights of national minorities, the adoption of which requires a two-thirds majority in the Parliament. The draft law elaborates the following: fundamental principles; individual minority rights; minority communal-group rights; regulations on minority self-rule; the role of the ombudsman, and the legal status and activities of ethnic minorities; the cultural autonomy of national and ethnic minorities; use of the native language of the minority; and the regulations regarding support, financing, and assets of minorities. The draft establishes the right to identity and the right to free choice of identity as the exclusive and inalienable right of the individual (thereby defining individuals as legal subjects); the right to a homeland; the right to freely use the native language; and other related liberties.[10] It allows persons belonging to minorities and their institutions to freely maintain relations with their native country and other countries. The draft law defines the right to parliamentary representation and the right to minority self-identity also as a community right.

The draft law also allows a minority group to establish its own self-governing body, which would enjoy legal license to establish cultural autonomy and its own internal organization and administration. The draft law is currently pending in Parliament, and a political consensus has been achieved regarding the codification of its fundamental principles. The adoption of the draft law is likely to be forthcoming.

Even before Ukraine declared its sovereignty, one of its initial autonomous diplomatic acts was the signing of a declaration establishing the principles of cooperation in the field of national minority rights guarantees with Hungary. One of its main sources was the CSCE Copenhagen Concluding Document. The declaration grants national minorities adequate rights, both on the individual and community levels. Both countries agreed to respect their citizens' right to decide to which national community they belonged and to promote the preservation of their minorities' ethnic, cultural, linguistic, and religious identity. The parties encourage the establishment of a national minority status that guarantees their right to effective participation in public matters, including the making and implementation of decisions that affect their place of residence. State authorities must function with the participation of all minorities living on their territory, taking account of particular minority interests. National minorities have a right to education in their native language at every level of instruction, and a joint Hungarian-Ukrainian committee is to be set up to coordinate the concrete tasks involved. In the spirit of the Hungarian-Ukrainian Declaration, the Declaration of the Kiev Supreme Council was drawn up on the eve of Ukrainian independence in November 1991 as the preliminary document for a future minority law. The minority law was adopted on June 25, 1992.

The Ukrainian minority law contains 19 articles that establish the structures of the Ministry for Nationality Affairs and the Council of Minority Representatives. It also allows for the functioning of similar bodies on lower administrative levels. It guarantees the right to cultural autonomy, the right to use the native language and native language education, and the right to use national symbols. It also promises to meet the literary, artistic, and mass media demands of national minorities and to establish nationality, cultural, and educational institutions. Where the national minority comprises a majority of the population, the law allows for the use of the native language in public affairs. The law contains measures regarding the use of names according to native language rules, and the free maintenance of relations with other members and institutions of the nation living in other states.

Thus, the principles underlying the Hungarian-Ukrainian Declaration were effectively realized in the development of the Ukrainian Minority Law. In interstate relations, a regularly functioning joint committee, in which seats are also provided for minority representatives, guarantees the coordination of minority activities. The role of these joint committees is to oversee the interim minority policies of each state and to make suggestions regarding their improvement. Such suggestions may deal with culture, education, trans-frontier cooperation, and finance.[11]

As a result of being in agreement with its fundamental principles, Croatia and Slovenia also signed the declaration, which thus provides a framework for regional cooperation regarding minority protection.

In Slovenia, the constitution of 1974 already defined the native Hungarian and Italian minorities to be state-forming factors. It guaranteed special rights not only to their members, but also to their communities, primarily in the field of native language use, culture, education, and use of national symbols. A new constitution was adopted in December 1991, when Slovenia became an independent state. The new constitution introduces the concept of "national community" and extends the rights of minorities even further (including direct representation on local and state levels, and a veto right regarding those legal proposals that regulate minority rights). Hungary and Slovenia signed a bilateral agreement on November 6, 1992, in which they guaranteed special rights to Slovenian national communities living in Hungary and Hungarian national communities living in Slovenia.

The agreement goes beyond the mere declaration of various rights; above all, it concretely establishes the mechanisms for the protection and development of the identities of Hungarian and Slovenian communities living as part of a minority. These include

- a native language education network;
- minority cultural institutions;
- native language use in all spheres of public life;
- native language mass media;
- trans-state cooperation;
- involvement of minorities in decisions affecting their community;
- informing the majority about the nature of minority culture.

Similar to the Ukrainian-Hungarian example, a joint committee also functions in the Slovenian case.

Finally, it is useful to briefly describe the recently signed "Declaration on the principles of cooperation between the Republic of Hungary and the Russian Federation regarding the guarantee of the rights of national or ethnic, religious and linguistic minorities." Before doing so, however, it is necessary to discuss briefly the new (large) minority communities of Russians living outside the borders of Russia and their relationship with the mother country.

5. THE RUSSIAN MINORITY

With the establishment of the Commonwealth of Independent States (CIS), Russia's extension into Europe has been restricted to an extent unknown since its rise to superpower status. As a result, Russians who had migrated for centuries throughout the empire found themselves in an unfamiliar minority situation. Moreover, numerous groups that are not Russian either linguistically or ethnically, but that have been assimilated as a result of Soviet "modernization," now also voice their claim to Russian support in the event they are threatened with discrimination by a majority.

The Russians and Russian-speaking peoples now living outside of Russian state borders are currently struggling with problems of self-definition; the nascent organizations designed to defend their interests have not yet gained full legitimacy. Meanwhile, by comparison, Hungarian national communities living outside the borders of Hungary have in the last two years taken advantage of processes within their respective states and have not only identified themselves with the entire Hungarian nation linguistically and culturally, but have also defined themselves as political communities. This means that their representatives, who express the interests of the Hungarian communities and have gained legitimacy through the electoral process in each state, can participate in the politics of their given state within its institutional structures. In this sense, such communities come close to the level of organization that we refer to as a characteristic of a majority nation.

Thus, the main concern of the Hungarian government is to keep in touch with and maintain partner relations—in an open and controllable fashion—with these autonomous, self-defining Hungarian national communities. Russian politics, however, face the double challenge posed by the ethnic factor on the one hand and the continued dominance of the previous power structure on the other. The two dimensions of the challenge are the following: while Hungarian and Russian politicians try to convince their neighbors that the solution to the national question can only be sought according to the democratic rules of the game, the affected neighbors argue that precisely that approach will undermine the developing democracies. While in Western Europe inter-ethnic group contrasts do not fundamentally threaten the existing democratic institutions, in the East, the ethnic challenge radically questions democracy itself. This dilemma is, of course, false, and the theoretical counter-argument can be made only with reference to the relevant existing international standards and the need for new international norms.

The declaration between Russia and Hungary—in contrast to the previously mentioned similar documents—establishes the principles of cooperation between two non-neighbor states. Already the terminology used by the UN (the rights of national or ethnic, religious, and linguistic minorities) in itself implies that the document primarily refers to cooperation in the international arena. The points of the declaration repeatedly refer to the need for such cooperation (e.g., the possibilities for the development of new international standards, unified interpretation of already existing rights, and the perfection and most effective utilization of developing institutions and mechanisms). Such bilateral and regional agreements promote international legal codification of minority rights. The most significant institutions include the United Nations and the CSCE. The declaration establishes the following fundamental minority rights:

- equality of rights and the prohibition of discrimination;
- protection of minority identity;
- the principle of free choice of identity;
- free use of the native language both in the private and public spheres, including use of names according to native-language rules;
- access to and dissemination and exchange of information in the native language;
- the right of minorities to establish their own religious institutions;
- the right to the native land;
- the minorities' right to their own education network.

In the spirit of the proposals of the CSCE concluding document of Geneva in 1991, the document establishes that possibilities for minority self-rule, including territorial autonomy, are necessary for the preservation of their identity.

With regard to the declaration, it is important to remember that Russia has no new constitution and it has not adopted a minority law. Thus, beyond declaratory statements by government officials and politicians, the Hungarian-Russian agreement represents the only concrete point of reference regarding the goals of Russian politics for non-Russians living within its borders, Russians living outside the borders who seek the support of the Russian state, and international public opinion. For this reason, it is especially important for Moscow to declare its respect for international standards in this regard as well as its consideration of the above-mentioned principles both in the international arena and in its internal legislative process.

6. CONCLUSION

First, for those national minority communities that are not able or do not wish to define themselves politically, the implementation of so-called positive discrimination is satisfactory. In the case of national minorities who are politically active, it seems necessary to raise the possibility of developing a political dialogue between certain governments and the legitimate representatives of the respective communities in order to discover the common domains shared by both majority and minority as well as the mutual interest of minorities that are related to the protection, promotion, and transmission of community identity.

Second, the international community can play the role of mediator by developing a code of conduct that consists of the principles underlying the dialogue. The CSCE and the Council of Europe are two already existing international institution that may take such a role. The consequences of this process could provide the foundation for internal codification, bilateral and regional agreements and treaties, and international standards.

The situation of national minorities in Central and Eastern Europe necessitates an urgent, effective, and essential solution. Persons belonging to minorities are not second-class citizens. They have the same right to democracy as members of any given national majority. A democracy that does not allow members of the minority to make their own decisions regarding their identity is neither effective nor stable. The particular characteristics of communities living in numerical minority differ from those of similar groups in Western Europe. In many cases, the latter have their own interest representation and encompassing political platforms whose realization they would like to achieve within the constitutional limits of the state they reside in. At the same time, some states in the region continue to relate to minorities according to their old reflexes.

Some Central and East European states, recognizing that the resolution of the problem must begin from within the region, have taken important steps in securing minority rights. At the same time, the minority question has provided a basis for cooperation. The elimination of suspicions between minority and majority and between neighboring states in the region was a prerequisite for this cooperation. Indeed, existing documents indicate that a positive approach to the question is possible.

NOTES

1. Document of the Copenhagen Meeting of the Conference on the Human Dimension of the CSCE, 1990.

2. Report on the CSCE Meeting of Experts on National Minorities, Geneva, 1991.

3. CSCE Charter of Paris for a New Europe, 1990.

4. Universal Declaration of Human Rights, adopted by the UN General Assembly in December 1948.

5. International Covenant on Civil and Political Rights, adopted by the UN General Assembly and opened for signature in December 1966.

6. Declaration on the Granting of Independence to Colonial Territories and Countries, adopted by the UN General Assembly, 1960.

7. Declaration on the principles of cooperation between the Republic of Hungary and the Ukrainian Soviet Socialist Republic in guaranteeing the rights of the national minorities, signed in Budapest on May 31, 1991. Croatia and Slovenia joined also in 1991.

8. Agreement on the insurance of special rights of the Slovenian minority living in the Republic of Hungary and the Hungarian national community living in the Republic of Slovenia, signed in Ljubljana on November 6, 1992.

9. Declaration on the principles guiding the cooperation between the Republic of Hungary and the Russian Federation regarding the guarantee of the rights of national minorities, signed in Budapest on November 11, 1992.

10. The concept of a homeland formulated in paragraph 1 is differentiated from the concept of birthplace. The right to a homeland involves the recognition and protection of an individual's tie to his or her parents, and ancestral home. The birthplace only partially and in specific cases coincides with the homeland. The legal formulation is thus more comprehensive.

11. Since the declaration was signed, the Hungarian-Ukrainian joint committees has had three sessions, in the course of which they debated issues such as joint financing of a Hungarian theater in sub-Carpathia, the establishment of a Ukrainian school in Budapest, etc.

REFERENCES

Alen, André. *Belgium: Bipolar and Centrifugal Federalism*. Brussels, 1990.

Bibó, István. *The Paralysis of International Institutions and the Remedies. A Study of Self-Determination, Concord among the Major Powers and Political Arbitration*. Hassocks: The Harvester Press, 1976.

Bíró, Gáspár. "Autodétermination, liberté individuelle, liberté nationale." In *L'Europe centrale et ses minorités: vers une solution européenne?*, ed. André Liebich and André Reszler. Paris: Presses Universitaires de France, 1993.

———. "Kisebbségek és kollektív jogok" (Minorities and collective rights). *Régio*, no. 2, 1991.

Héraud, Guy. "Népek és régiók Europája" (The Europe of peoples and regions). *Régio*, no. 2, 1991.

Liebich, André. "Minorities in Eastern Europe: Obstacles to a Reliable Count." *RFE/RL Research Report*, no. 20, May 15, 1992.

Reisch, Alfred A. "Hungary Intensifies Bilateral Ties with Ukraine." *Südost-Europa*, no. 6, 1991.

11

Preventing Ethnic Conflict in the New Europe: The CSCE High Commissioner on National Minorities

KONRAD J. HUBER

1. INTRODUCTION

Faced with the threat of inter-ethnic conflicts throughout East Central Europe and the former Soviet Union, the Conference on Security and Cooperation in Europe (CSCE) may have decided that an ounce of prevention is worth a pound of cure.

At their 1992 summit meeting in Helsinki, CSCE's 51 participating states[1] agreed on the creation of a High Commissioner on National Minorities as an instrument for the early identification and possible resolution of potentially destabilizing ethnic tensions. Max van der Stoel, a former Dutch foreign minister and representative to the United Nations, was named to the new post at the Stockholm meeting of CSCE foreign ministers in December 1992.

These developments recognized two important suppositions. First, one of the greatest dangers to security in post-Cold War Europe may result less from disputes between countries and more from conflicts involving—or appearing to involve—national minority issues[2] within a country. Second, an independent and objective outsider who has both an international mandate and the confidence of all parties may be able to play a valuable role in the early resolution of inter-ethnic troubles.

Modern-day Europe, it seems, is being consumed by the flames of allegedly "age-old" hatreds. Conflagrations have erupted from the Caucasus Mountains to the Dniester River, and the devastation of the former Yugoslavia continues to rage. As the Yugoslav crisis has revealed, the international community was ill-prepared for these new "ethnic" conflicts. The CSCE was no exception. Started in 1972 to facilitate East-West dialogue during the Cold War, the CSCE had no institutional capacity for dealing with inter-ethnic conflict when large-scale violence in Yugoslavia first erupted in 1991.[3] (Though its name suggests a potential role in such issues, the CSCE's Conflict Prevention Center, which did exist at the time, is primarily dedicated to reducing the danger of inter*state* warfare through procedures that,

among other things, encourage the open exchange of military information between states.)

In light of this difficult experience with the Yugoslav and other
crises, creating the office of High Commissioner on National Minorities (HCNM)[4] represents a pragmatic step toward the prevention of
inter-ethnic conflicts by the CSCE. Not intended as an "ombudsman"
for national minorities nor as an investigator of individual violations of
CSCE human rights standards, the High Commissioner instead
provides the CSCE with "early warning" and "early action" on ethnic
tensions that might develop into a conflict endangering peace, stability, or relations between CSCE participating states. In consultation
with the CSCE's political authorities, and with the cooperation of the
state(s) involved, the High Commissioner attempts, at the earliest
possible stages, to give an objective evaluation of brewing strife, as well
as constructive recommendations for its resolution. In the course of
fact-finding missions to the state(s) concerned, the High Commissioner may promote dialogue, confidence, and cooperation between
disputing parties.

When tensions threaten to develop into violent conflict, the High
Commissioner can issue an "early warning" to the CSCE, formally
calling attention to the seriousness of the situation. In certain situations, the CSCE may also authorize the High Commissioner to
undertake "early action": a formal program of further contact and
closer consultations with the parties in order to explore possible
solutions to underlying tensions.

Backed by the participating states' consensus on the mandate of
the office, the High Commissioner can address growing problems with
both the full prestige of the CSCE and considerable flexibility in
response. The goal of this response is to identify the nature of, and to
contain, de-escalate, and resolve tensions before the need to issue an
"early warning" actually arises. It is hoped that an "early warning," as
defined in the High Commissioner's mandate, will be issued only
rarely: when ethnic tensions surpass preliminary attempts at containment and indeed threaten to erupt into open violence. Before such a
dangerous stage is reached, the High Commissioner may be able to
catalyze a process of dialogue and cooperation, possibly leading to the
resolution of underlying issues of contention. In addition, this mechanism may encourage the CSCE, informed impartially by HCNM
investigations, to involve itself promptly in potential conflicts that the
participating states might otherwise (prefer to) overlook.

As an instrument for the early identification and possible resolution of ethnic tensions, the High Commissioner adds to the CSCE's
growing complex of functionally differentiated yet interrelated institu-

tions for conflict response. In its assumption of greater conflict-management responsibilities within the region, the CSCE, which is nominally dedicated to promoting "security and cooperation in Europe," is attempting both to respond constructively to recent developments and to define an ambitious role in the vastly altered geopolitical landscape of the new Europe. It remains to be seen, however, how effective the efforts of the "new" CSCE will be in this realm, as indeed the functioning of all multilateral organizations, including Europe's other regional structures and the United Nations itself, are profoundly shaped by the intergovernmental nature of their decision-making processes. Potentially destabilizing conflicts of an apparently inter-ethnic character may have their root more in the internal conditions, exacerbated by the opportunistic policies of leaders, within a country. International response, particularly without the implicit but convincing threat of effective sanctions (including military action) as eventual options, may have limited impact on the resolution of such violent conflicts, especially the more the fighting escalates. Thus, early identification of potential conflicts, with an emphasis on exploring options for the possible resolution of underlying tensions, may help prevent escalation beyond the point of effective and relatively painless engagement by the international community.

Such is the context in which this chapter reviews the mandate, history, and initial experience of the newly created post of High Commissioner. In particular, the background to its establishment will be considered, specifically in terms of developing consensus within the CSCE both on national minority issues and on the proactive response to potential conflicts. The High Commissioner's function is then analyzed within the CSCE's increasingly institutionalized approach to conflict response. By way of conclusion, this chapter examines the role of the CSCE vis-à-vis other intergovernmental efforts to promote security in the new Europe.

2. THE HIGH COMMISSIONER'S MANDATE

In the decisions of the 1992 Follow-up Meeting in Helsinki, the CSCE clearly identified the High Commissioner as a device for providing " 'early warning' and, as appropriate, 'early action' at the earliest possible stage in regard to tensions involving national minority issues that have the potential to develop into a conflict within the CSCE area, affecting peace, stability, or relations between participating States" (para. 23).[5] In subsequent sections, the Helsinki Document specified procedural and organizational guidelines for the functioning of the High Commissioner.

Most significantly, the High Commissioner is granted considerable latitude in identifying situations for potential involvement, while
maintaining accountability with the CSCE through the Committee of
Senior Officials (CSO), the CSCE's political body, and through the
Chairman-in-Office, the foreign minister chairing the Council of
Ministers for Foreign Affairs (the CSCE's central decision-making and
governing body). For example, the High Commissioner consults with
the Chairman-in-Office prior to an on-site visit and reports confiden-
tially to the Chairman-in-Office on findings and overall progress in a
situation. Through the Chairman-in-Office and the CSO, the High
Commissioner can inform the CSCE directly of situations that may
require "the attention of and action by" the Council of Ministers for
Foreign Affairs or the CSO. An "early warning," when necessary, is
issued to the CSO, and authorization for "early action," a more
extensive program of mediation, is sought from the CSO as well.
Otherwise, the High Commissioner is required to work in confidence
and to act independently of all parties to the tensions.

Broadly speaking, the High Commissioner may become engaged
in situations in which ethnic tensions could develop into a conflict
threatening peace, stability, and relations between participating states.
The mandate, however, attaches a few important prohibitions for the
High Commissioner's involvement. First, according to paragraph 5(b),
the High Commissioner is precluded from engagement in situations in
which organized acts of terrorism are involved. Second, according to
the following sentence, paragraph 5(c), the High Commissioner will
also not consider violations of CSCE commitments pertaining to the
human rights of individuals belonging to a national minority, thus
effectively preventing the High Commissioner from acting as a human
rights "investigator" or as an "ombudsman" for national minorities.
The emphasis is clearly to be maintained on conflict prevention, not on
investigating alleged cases of human rights abuses.

The mandate also stipulates cases in which the High
Commissioner's involvement is to be conditional on CSO authorization. Such cases would be those in which tensions have developed
"beyond an early warning stage" (para. 3), or in which the CSO is
already involved (para. 7, 21). In these situations, a special mandate
for High Commissioner engagement could be provided by the CSO.

Aside from these qualifications, the decision on the High
Commissioner's engagement in a situation is understood to be a
matter of his or her discretion. Primary emphasis of HCNM engagement, however, is to be as early as possible, *before* ethnic tensions have
reached such a critical stage that an "early warning" must be issued. In
this period before the issuance of an "early warning," the High

Commissioner may undertake the following activities, according to paragraphs 11–12 of the mandate:

1. Collecting and receiving information regarding national minority issues.
2. Assessing situations for the potential threat to peace and stability in the CSCE area.
3. Obtaining firsthand information about the situations of national minorities through on-site visits and personal meetings with all parties directly concerned with the tensions.
4. Promoting dialogue, confidence, and cooperation between parties involved in the tensions during the course of the missions.

The role of the High Commissioner in this period is that of an impartial third party whose objective assessment of the situation and low-key efforts at preventive mediation might contribute constructively to the early resolution of tensions. The High Commissioner is considered to have a reasonably flexible role at this stage, while at the same time maintaining accountability through the Chairman-in-Office, as detailed in paragraphs 17–18. The Chairman-in-Office is to be consulted prior to on-site visits and to be provided strictly confidential reports on missions' findings and overall progress in the situations.[6]

In the event that a situation requires the urgent attention of the CSO, the High Commissioner can issue an "early warning," thereby putting the issue to the CSO at their next meeting, as provided for under paragraphs 13–15.[7] The High Commissioner may also propose to the CSO that "early action" be carried out, although the mandate does not make it clear whether the issuance of an "early warning" is a necessary precondition. Such a program of "early action" is defined to include further contact and closer consultations with the parties concerned in order to explore possible solutions (para. 16).

Otherwise, under paragraphs 23–26, the High Commissioner is given considerable discretion in monitoring national minority issues and carrying out missions. He or she is authorized to receive information on national minority issues from any source, although communications from entities that practice or publicly condone violence or terrorism may not be acknowledged. During on-site missions, contact may be sought with "all parties directly concerned," which are defined to include not only the national, regional, and local governments of participating states but also nongovernmental and religious representatives of national minorities (as long as they do not employ or openly sanction the use of violence or terrorism). At any given time, the High

Commissioner may also enlist the services of up to three experts (from an official CSCE roster), who may provide "brief, specialized investigation and advice" and accompany the High Commissioner on visits.

Clearly there are, and will be, numerous situations involving "ethnic tensions" that could threaten peace, stability, or relations between CSCE participating states. In their earlier stages, many if not most of these situations will also meet the criteria for High Commissioner action. More problematic, however, are potential "gray areas" in the mandate. The current formulation, under which the High Commissioner is active primarily before and through the time that an "early warning" might be issued, does not greatly elaborate guidelines for potentially constructive efforts at conflict mediation and resolution that an impartial third party, such as the High Commissioner, could carry out during this period.[8] Though an initial on-site visit is indispensable for fact-finding and confidence-building purposes, "ethnic tensions" are rarely one-time events that can be understood and addressed satisfactorily through a single mission. The current formulation may also assume, somewhat uncritically, that conflicts develop only from "potential" to "actual," after which point the CSO takes over responsibility for conflict management. Real-life conflicts may not correspond so neatly to bureaucratically convenient formulations, leaving some unanswered questions: When have ethnic tensions developed "beyond an early warning stage"? For how long, and in what ways, would the High Commissioner continue to be involved in a situation that never develops beyond such a stage? When does the High Commissioner's involvement "terminate," and could the CSO in fact request High Commissioner assistance in promoting dialogue, confidence, and cooperation *after* open conflict has subsided?

Other definitional issues may have direct bearing on the very question of HCNM involvement in a particular situation. For example, what sorts of violence constitute organized terrorism, or conflict beyond the point of mere "tensions," thus disqualifying further High Commissioner action? When is the CSO "already involved" in a situation, thus conditioning High Commissioner involvement? The lack of clear criteria—or a clearly defined authority—for evaluating these last questions leaves open the possibility that a participating state could attempt to block or circumscribe HCNM activity in a situation that should otherwise merit his or her full attention.

Finally, there are some unanswered questions related to the long-term functioning of the position, including the means for considering whether an appointee's performance has been "impartial" (the expectation expressed in paragraph 8 of the mandate), again leaving the High Commissioner open to unilateral attempts to impugn his or her credibility, but also providing the CSCE with no objective guidelines for dealing with a High Commissioner whose performance is generally considered to be problematic. There are also no stated procedures for revising the mandate's provisions, which after all reflect consensus at a specific moment in both the region's and the CSCE's history. (Currently any changes would require a new consensus among participating states at the level of foreign ministers or heads of state or government; "consensus" is defined in the CSCE as the absence of formal opposition by any state to a specific proposal.)

These questions notwithstanding, it is clear that the High Commissioner is a new and promising institution, the establishment of which was a milestone in itself, and many of these issues will be resolved during its organizational development. It should be emphasized, however, that the key to the effectiveness of a preventive instrument such as the High Commissioner derives from flexible, independent discretion to devise an appropriate role for ongoing involvement in a given situation.

3. DEVELOPING CSCE CONSENSUS ON NATIONAL MINORITY ISSUES

Seen as a whole, the creation of a High Commissioner on National Minorities represents remarkable consensus in the CSCE, not only on the importance of national minorities issues, but also on the need for an instrument of conflict prevention at the earliest stages. Originally proposed by the Dutch at the Prague Council of Ministers Meeting in January 1992, the idea for the High Commissioner quickly gathered wide support at the Helsinki II meeting, for two reasons. Historically, there has been increasing attention paid to, and agreement expressed on, national minority issues within the CSCE at the level of normative commitments.[9] At the practical level, the Yugoslav crisis and numerous other conflicts, both actual and potential, have galvanized the CSCE to respond proactively to incipient hostilities that (may) have an ethnic dimension. These two factors culminated in the 1992 decision to establish the High Commissioner, the deliberations on which are also reviewed below.

As has been noted elsewhere,[10] scant agreement was reached on national minority issues within the CSCE from 1972 through 1985, during which time it was the former Yugoslavia, ironically, that often championed the most ambitious formulations for the protection of minority rights. Such issues began receiving greater attention at successive meetings after 1985, including the Ottawa Meeting of Experts on Human Rights of that year and the Bern Meeting of

Experts on Human Contacts of 1986. At the 1986–1989 Vienna
Follow-up Meeting, "a qualitative jump" was made in terms of
commitments on national minorities, according to one analyst.[11] In
particular, "conditions for the promotion of the ethnic, cultural,
linguistic and religious identity of national minorities" were to be
created and protected,[12] thus laying the foundation for the 1990
Copenhagen Document.

At the Copenhagen Meeting of the Conference on the Human
Dimension,[13] the CSCE adopted the farthest-reaching commitments
to date on minority rights, a "pinnacle" for normative language on this
issue[14] (and for language on many other human rights issues as well).
An entire chapter of the Copenhagen Document was devoted to
national minority issues, and important formulations were devised for
the following items, among others: the relationship between the
protection of minority rights and the functioning of democracy and
the rule of law; the basic ethnic, linguistic, cultural, and religious rights
of national minorities; the possibility of local or autonomous administrations for national minorities (in accordance with state policy); and
the need for adequate opportunities for instruction in a mother
tongue, as well as in the official language(s) of the state.[15] The 1991
Geneva Meeting of Experts on National Minorities added various
provisions to the growing body of texts on national minority issues
and, perhaps most notably, stated explicitly that such issues are of
"legitimate international concern and consequently do not constitute
exclusively an internal affair of the respective state."[16] At the level of
normative language, the 1991 Moscow Meeting of the Conference on
the Human Dimension merely affirmed the observance and promotion of earlier commitments.

4. CSCE RESPONSE TO THE NEW "ETHNIC" CONFLICTS

The Moscow meeting, however, was noteworthy in adding the possibility of on-site investigative missions as a means for responding to
alarming developments in the human rights situation of a participating state.[17] In this regard, the so-called Moscow mechanism supple-
ments a procedure established at the Vienna Follow-up Meeting for
more "intrusive" CSCE monitoring of a state's human rights conditions, which hitherto had been considered by a number of participating states as a purely internal affair and thus off-limits for international
scrutiny.[18] Though strictly speaking not instruments of conflict response, these mechanisms embodied a new approach that relies on
notification and clarification of human rights problems within the
CSCE framework, at the same time involving "third party" actors as

investigators (and, potentially, mediators). Significantly, such procedures can be initiated without the consensus of the full CSCE.[19] This is a substantial step forward in that obtaining full consensus of all participating states is unwieldy, if not impossible, to secure for every CSCE action, particularly for timely and effective response to unfolding violence.

As the Yugoslav fighting clearly showed, the early identification, investigation, and resolution of political crises and armed conflicts arising (or seeming to arise) from national minority issues may now be crucial to preserving stability in post-Cold War Europe. Without the weight of communist rule, long-repressed ethnic and national identities have once again risen to the fore. Some leaders may now see the chance for the legitimate self-determination of oppressed groups, while others may be opportunistically garnering political advantage through the "rehearsal" of ethnic hatreds. By no means mutually exclusive, both approaches may be finding fertile ground in the widely-felt scarcity and uncertainty of postcommunist life. To shore up waning political support, moderate leaders may be inclined to make concessions to nationalistic forces, thus polarizing the situation even further. In the absence of effective institutions for democratic decision making and for the impartial protection of basic rights, such inter-ethnic dynamics can readily lead to armed action, particularly given the proliferation of military forces in many areas.

Indeed, during the two and a half years between the Vienna and Helsinki Follow-up Meetings, the CSCE was confronted with a mushrooming of conflicts that involve, or appear to involve, inter-ethnic strife within and between numerous participating states, most notably the Yugoslav successor states, Armenia and Azerbaijan (Nagorno-Karabakh), Georgia (Southern Ossetia), and Moldova (Trans-Dniestria).[20] With the signing of the November 1990 Charter of Paris for a New Europe by the heads of state or government, the CSCE established an institutional framework of decision-making and executive organs, without which flexible response to the latest developments in such conflicts would have been unthinkable. Through such bodies as the Council of Ministers and the CSO, moreover, the CSCE began calling for cease-fires, censuring both states and irregular military forces involved in the fighting, and even suspending a participating state (the Serbian-Montenegrin "Yugoslavia") for continuing to foment hostilities. Under the new mechanisms and procedures developed for greater CSCE response to such hostilities, high-profile missions were launched to gather firsthand information and to promote dialogue and reconciliation in these conflicts. With regard to Nagorno-Karabakh, the CSCE took the unprecedented step of convening a multilateral conference, still ongoing, to negotiate a peaceful resolution to the status of the predominantly Armenian enclave within Azerbaijan.

Such efforts have contributed to the understanding, containment, and future resolution of these conflicts. To be sure, the CSCE's response has been noteworthy given the dramatic eclipsing of its original Cold War functions, the lack of appropriate institutional capacity, and the cumbersome process of securing consensus (not merely majority) approval for any action. Within the CSCE, however, there was also growing recognition that its efforts at ethnic conflict resolution were perhaps "too little, too late." The CSCE was responding reactively, not *proactively*, to embryonic trouble spots. Full-blown conflicts were not only more complicated but also more costly to resolve. Early resolution could save lives, preserve stability in the region, and strengthen the multilateral system of peace and cooperation among nations.

As a pragmatic response to the changing conditions "on the ground," both in former Yugoslavia and elsewhere, Helsinki II thus extended CSCE "intrusiveness" in states' internal affairs, not only with the establishment of the High Commissioner on National Minorities, but also with the elaboration of other CSCE measures toward conflict prevention, crisis management, and peacekeeping. Indeed, CSCE efforts in this field have now developed from devising a necessary (i.e., unavoidable) response to a conflict already underway, to focusing on "early warning" and conflict prevention at the earliest stages of tensions as well. The High Commissioner is thus a logical supplement to—and an important new development for—CSCE's approach to crisis management, which had been largely reactive to date.[21]

5. HELSINKI II DELIBERATIONS ON THE HIGH COMMISSIONER

At Helsinki II, the Dutch High Commissioner proposal was seen as a significant step towards ethnic conflict prevention within the CSCE, and it readily attracted 25 co-sponsors.[22] Emerging from the Netherlands' experience as European Community (EC) president during the initial Yugoslav conflagration, then Foreign Minister Hans van den Broek put forth the idea of the High Commissioner, first in Prague in January 1992 and then in Helsinki later that year. Revised to take into account the reservations of various participating states, the final mandate is remarkable both for its innovation and for its detail (although, as noted above, some ambiguities remain, largely because of the consensus-derived nature of the text). For the first time, a CSCE representative may respond promptly to a potential conflict without the specifically expressed consent of the full CSCE (or even the CSO). Instead, the High Commissioner has the broadly granted authority to engage in early warning and preliminary conflict prevention.

Initial opposition to the High Commissioner proposal centered around concerns that the functioning—and even mere existence—of the High Commissioner might create or exacerbate violent inter-ethnic conflicts, as well as some questions about the accountability of the institution of the High Commissioner. Compromise language was eventually devised to address these and other points of contention: Except in cases clearly excluded by the mandate, it is left to the High Commissioner to decide the nature of his or her involvement in a situation where improper outside attention could worsen tensions. In terms of the accountability of the office, a formula was devised both to maintain the independence of the High Commissioner and to create guidelines for consulting and communicating with the CSCE's political organs (as well as for securing authorization to engage in more extensive mediatory activities under the "early action" rubric). In response to the reservations of a number of states, particularly those with ongoing concerns about armed separatist movements on their territories, the mandate includes explicit restrictions on HCNM engagement in situations involving terrorism or organized acts of violence and on HCNM acknowledgement of communications from entities using or espousing the use of violence or terrorism.

Thus, while reflecting the major concerns of participating states at a historically specific moment in the CSCE process, the decision at Helsinki II preserved the essential elements of the Dutch proposal: the High Commissioner is to be an independent and impartial instrument for the early investigation and resolution of ethnic tensions through quiet and flexible means.

6. OPERATIONALIZING THE HIGH COMMISSIONER

Former Dutch Foreign Minister Max van der Stoel[23] was speedily nominated in September and confirmed in December of 1992 as the first High Commissioner. He assumed the post in January 1993 and immediately started the work of the High Commissioner along three main dimensions: initiating on-site missions, establishing relations with CSCE institutions and other entities, and setting up an office in The Hague.

A. Missions

By the end of April 1993, van der Stoel had conducted on-site visits to investigate the situation of the Russian populations in the Baltic states[24] and that of the Hungarian population in Slovakia. These missions were undertaken on the basis of strong evidence of troubling ethnic tensions that were considered potentially threatening to peace, stability, or relations between CSCE participating states, and it was thought that in both situations the High Commissioner's involvement would contribute constructively toward the early and apparently achievable resolution of the tensions. (There were also no circumstances that would have disqualified the High Commissioner from initial attention to these situations.)

In both situations, the participating states directly concerned with the tensions provided ample assistance to the High Commissioner's visits, and appropriate government ministers and officials were available to meet with him. Contacts with nongovernmental entities were also sought, and the services of an expert were employed on one of the visits. Confidential reports on these missions, including recommendations for further action by all parties concerned, were submitted to the Chairman-in-Office, Swedish Foreign Minister Margaretha af Ugglas, who was also consulted throughout the process.

While it is perhaps too early to evaluate the High Commissioner's preliminary efforts in these situations, it is important to note the apparent readiness of various parties, particularly participating states, the Chairman-in-Office, and the CSO, to consider the High Commissioner's involvement a potentially constructive contribution to the understanding and resolution of the underlying tensions. Certain HCNM recommendations have served as the basis for further discussion and exchange among the parties in each situation, and as of late April 1993, the High Commissioner's findings and recommendations had also been reflected in support by the CSO and the Chairman-in-Office of High Commissioner efforts. As a means of containing tensions through the clarification of alleged violations, these CSCE representatives have sought to underscore the HCNM assessments, through both public and official channels, to the states concerned.

In both cases, the High Commissioner is also to maintain an ongoing role in monitoring the situations and in pursuing options for possible resolution with the parties concerned. In the Hungarian-Slovak situation, the governments of Slovakia and Hungary have given their approval, in principle, to the HCNM proposal to establish a small team of neutral experts who would investigate minority rights questions in both countries through short-term, semi-annual visits over a two-year period. With the endorsement of the CSO, this proposal now requires only the elaboration of components related to its implementation. In the Baltic states, initial response has been given by the governments to the High Commissioner's recommendations on citizenship and language issues, specifically in Latvia and Estonia, and on the establishment of national institutions with competence in human rights and minority questions in all three countries.

B. INTRA-CSCE AND EXTERNAL RELATIONS

In addition to regular contact with the CSO and the Chairman-in-Office, the High Commissioner has an ongoing relationship with the CSCE Office on Democratic Institutions and Human Rights (ODIHR) in Warsaw. ODIHR is authorized by Helsinki II to administer the High Commissioner budget and to provide logistical support for travel and communication.[25] The resource list from which the High Commissioner may draw experts to assist in his or her activities is also maintained at the Warsaw office. In addition, the basis for potential coordination with the Conflict Prevention Center, though principally charged with military security issues between states, will also be explored. On a more informal basis, the High Commissioner has begun to develop contacts with appropriate intergovernmental organizations, such as the United Nations, the Council of Europe, NATO, and the Council of Baltic Sea States, to improve coordination of efforts aimed at the early resolution of ethnic tensions.

C. THE HAGUE OFFICE

In January, van der Stoel also began setting up an office in The Hague. The Dutch government donated the use of office space and equipment, in addition to supplies and services. With the High Commissioner's salary the only one covered by the budget, van der Stoel has secured the assistance of professional and administrative staff seconded by the foreign ministries of the Netherlands, Poland, and Sweden, as well as the services of a US human rights specialist. However, as the High Commissioner becomes engaged in more situations, the workload will continue to mount considerably for the staff, which is responsible for monitoring national minority issues throughout the CSCE region, supporting the High Commissioner during missions, and assisting in follow-up activities and relations with other institutions. Future consideration may have to be given to augmenting the resources, both financial and professional, available for High Commissioner work, if demands on the office continue to expand.

7. THE ROLE OF THE
HIGH COMMISSIONER IN THE NEW CSCE

Since the dissipation of the Cold War, the CSCE has moved increasingly towards monitoring, responding to, and now preventing potential inter-communal conflicts through formal procedures and institutions. In broad terms, Vienna established the principle of more "intrusive" human rights monitoring, Paris laid the foundation for the necessary political and executive institutions, and Helsinki II expanded this new approach and at the same time attempted to develop it into a more coherent whole. Since 1990, diminished East-West confrontation along ideological lines has transformed the CSCE's historic functions as a forum for discussing human rights issues and as a mechanism for monitoring military security. With new possibilities for East-West consensus on issues across the board, practical and concrete cooperation among CSCE states has become the new emphasis, particularly on "human dimension" issues and conflict response.

The creation of the High Commissioner follows this trend towards conflict response through formal mechanisms and institutionalized procedures. At the same time, there still is considerable momentum behind the CSCE's interim approach to inter-communal conflicts, a sort of ad hoc pragmatism reflected in the patchwork of missions throughout the region. Care will have to be taken that responsibilities are clearly differentiated, and efforts not duplicated between CSCE organs. One formulation would be for the High Commissioner to be active while an "early warning" has not yet been issued. This period may include a program of "early action," authorized by the CSO, to move disputants closer to a resolution of differences. In addition to the High Commissioner's crucial role before an "early warning" is formally registered, serious consideration should be given to flexible authority and adequate resources for the High Commissioner to engage in "early action" or similar activities, where quiet efforts at preventive diplomacy may contribute invaluably to the early resolution of ethnic tensions.

Should tensions surpass the High Commissioner's capacity for useful mediation, it would become the CSO's task to craft effective measures for conflict resolution, taking into account the recommendations of the High Commissioner. HCNM input would probably be important in the initial organization of any longer-term monitoring or confidence-building missions authorized by the CSO, and ongoing contact with the High Commissioner might profitably be maintained in such situations, as well as in cases of separate negotiation processes or peacekeeping efforts approved by the CSO. (Of course, an appropriate role for other CSCE organs, such as the ODIHR, should also be devised in such instances.)

Fundamentally, the High Commissioner should continue to act as a device for warning and mediation at the earliest stages of potential conflicts involving national minority issues. To maximize the potential value of such a device, the CSCE needs to continue to evaluate and to strengthen the means for coordinating and implementing effective policy, which currently involves formulation through a complex array of decision-making bodies, consultative meetings, and executive institutions.

8. THE CSCE'S ROLE IN MULTILATERAL EFFORTS AT CONFLICT RESPONSE

The CSCE's recent emphasis on conflict *prevention*, as opposed to merely "conflict resolution" or "conflict management," reflects the new realities of a multipolar world in which intergovernmental structures, as opposed to superpowers, are expected to assume responsibility for issues of war and peace. Within East Central Europe and the former Soviet Union, these very issues of regional security now have new dynamics, propelled largely by internal factors, but with potentially international implications nonetheless. Under circumstances that vastly differ from those surrounding its first 18 years, the CSCE is attempting to providing "frontline" response to real and likely challenges to security in a newly volatile realm. This role is all the more necessary—and daunting—in light of the United Nations' extensive and complicated interventions in war zones around the globe.[26] It remains to be seen, however, whether the CSCE's unique characteristics offer the possibility of success, and not failure, in its self-appointed tasks of crisis management and conflict prevention.

Fundamentally, the CSCE's effectiveness in conflict response may be limited by a number of factors that derive primarily from its character as an inter*state* process among *governmental* representatives. Sovereign states not only cooperate, but also compete, with one another in this arena. Decision making among governments with concerns about domestic politics can at times advantage "painless" solutions over more costly ones. Process may be valued over product, and the easiest response to public outcry over massive human suffering may be rhetorical rather than substantive. True political will can thus become difficult to generate in a timely and coherent fashion among the participating states, many of which may also fear that overly forceful CSCE "instrusiveness" may one day be angled in their direction.

This CSCE decision-making process has affected not just the formulation of policy for the region, but also the course and nature of the CSCE's institutional development. For example, CSCE institutionalization, characterized by the centralization of decision-making power in the CSO and the delegation of more limited functions to separate offices throughout Europe, has been shaped largely by states' interest in maintaining control of the CSCE through a strong political organ, as well as some states' concerns that the CSCE would develop too readily into an overly bureaucratic "mini-UN" (or even usurp NATO's role in military matters).[27] Institutional initiatives, moreover, have been pursued in response to historically specific circumstances, at times without critical regard for how an existing institution might be revamped or expanded to encompass a new function, once its need has been conclusively determined. (This proliferation of institutions, both a reflection and a result of the multifaceted and inherently political nature of the CSCE process, can lead to what sometimes appears to be overlapping or redundant structures, although they do all have functionally differentiated roles.) The intergovernmental nature of the decision-making process has also encouraged the CSCE to undertake initial institutionalization through the secondment of diplomats from participating states, an approach that is not very likely to be sustainable in the long run (although it has been fiscally, and thus politically, more palatable in the short term). Once established, a new structure clearly needs proper resources, both human and financial, to fulfill its mandated task, and participating states will soon have to reckon with this growing need, particularly as demands on the CSCE in the area of conflict prevention continue to rise.

Ultimately, though, the lack of clearly elaborated recourse to more stringent sanctions, including the possibility of military action, may constrain the effectiveness of the CSCE in the area of conflict response. The CSCE needs to create a process for dealing with conflicts that get beyond the mediatory abilities of such instruments as the High Commissioner or a confidence-building mission authorized by the CSO. In this regard, formal linkages should be fully developed with intergovernmental organizations, primarily the UN (although the EC, the Western European Union, and NATO might also have roles), in the implementation of sanctions or the realization of military operations including humanitarian relief, peacekeeping, and "peacemaking."[28] Whether or not such linkages are achieved, there could certainly be improved coordination of efforts, even at earlier stages in growing crises, with Europe's other intergovernmental organizations, including the Council of Europe, in addition to the aforementioned EC and NATO and the UN operations throughout the entire CSCE region. Indeed, consultations need to be carried out, and decisions made, on a "hierarchy of response" in a given situation, perhaps with the CSCE taking the lead in evaluating an appropriate role for the international community in conflict prevention. (Such coordination would require a more open exchange of information among institutions, an openness that would have to be balanced against the need, in certain situations, for confidentiality in the work of an initial mediator.)[29]

These obstacles notwithstanding, the CSCE may be able to play a crucial role in intergovernmental efforts to prevent or resolve ethnic conflicts in Eastern Europe and the former Soviet Union. With each country as a participating state, the CSCE has great legitimacy as an actor in the region. Decisions, once reached through an often difficult process of consensus making, carry the full weight of the collectivity. Furthermore, through the High Commissioner and other mechanisms, the CSCE is beginning to develop the institutional capacity for early and effective response to inchoate "ethnic" conflicts. To maximize its effectiveness, the CSCE needs to consider institutionalizing not just a procedure for "early warning," the essence of which, after all, can be provided by nongovernmental monitors, the media, and even participating states; additional resources must be committed to conflict prevention, perhaps along the lines of "early action" or similar activities approved by the CSO and carried out by the High Commissioner. Furthermore, CSCE capacity for mediating full-blown conflicts, again under the supervision of the CSO, should also be enhanced.

Finally, as with the functioning of the High Commissioner, the CSCE needs to return to the beginning, to the source of potential conflicts. In cooperation with the Council of Europe, greater emphasis needs to be placed on strengthening the ability of individual states to protect basic rights, especially those related to minority issues, and to promote cooperation between ethnic communities. Within the CSCE, participating states should be encouraged to address national minority issues and growing inter-ethnic tensions rigorously through existing CSCE mechanisms and in the course of "review conferences" and "implementation meetings" to be held in alternating years, the post-Helsinki II approach to monitoring and promoting observance of human dimension commitments. Through the High Commissioner and ODIHR, the CSCE could also help provide expert assistance on improving safeguards for basic rights and on encouraging inter-ethnic cooperation before tensions develop and conflicts erupt.

Prevention, after all, is always the surest cure.

APPENDIX

from the Concluding Document of the Helsinki Follow-up Meeting (1992)

CSCE HIGH COMMISSIONER ON NATIONAL MINORITIES

1. The participating States decide to establish a High Commissioner on National Minorities.

MANDATE

2. The High Commissioner will act under the aegis of the CSO and will thus be an instrument of conflict prevention at the earliest possible stage.

3. The High Commissioner will provide "early warning" and, as appropriate, "early action" at the earliest possible stage in regard to tensions involving national minority issues which have not yet developed beyond an early warning stage, but, in the judgement of the High Commissioner, have the potential to develop into a conflict within the CSCE area, affecting peace, stability or relations between participating States, requiring the attention of and action by the Council or the CSO.

4. Within the mandate, based on CSCE principles and commitments, the High Commissioner will work in confidence and will act independently of all parties directly involved in the tensions.

5a. The High Commissioner will consider national minority issues occurring in the State of which the High Commissioner is a national or a resident, or involving a national minority to which the High Commissioner belongs, only if all parties directly involved agree, including the State concerned.

5b. The High Commissioner will not consider national minority issues in situations involving organized acts of terrorism.

5c. Nor will the High Commissioner consider violations of CSCE commitments with regard to an individual person belonging to a national minority.

6. In considering a situation, the High Commissioner will take fully into account the availability of democratic means and international instruments to respond to it, and their utilization by the parties involved.

7. When a particular national minority issue has been brought to the attention of the CSO, the involvement of the High Commissioner will require a request and a specific mandate from the CSO.

PROFILE, APPOINTMENT, SUPPORT

8. The High Commissioner will be an eminent international personality with long-standing relevant experience from whom an impartial performance of the function may be expected.

9. The High Commissioner will be appointed by the Council by consensus upon the recommendation of the CSO for a period of three years, which may be extended for one further term of three years only.

10. The High Commissioner will draw upon the facilities of the ODIHR in Warsaw, and in particular upon the information relevant to all aspects of national minority questions available at the ODIHR.

EARLY WARNING

11. The High Commissioner will:

11a. collect and receive information regarding national minority issues from sources described below (see Supplement paragraphs (23)–(25));

11b. assess at the earliest possible stage the role of the parties directly concerned, the nature of the tensions and recent developments therein and, where possible, the potential consequences for peace and stability within the CSCE area;

11c. to this end, be able to pay a visit, in accordance with paragraph (17) and Supplement paragraphs (27)–(30), to any participating State and communicate in person, subject to the provisions of paragraph (25), with parties directly concerned to obtain first-hand information about the situation of national minorities.

12. The High Commissioner may during a visit to a participating State, while obtaining first-hand information from all parties directly involved, discuss the questions with the parties, and where appropriate promote dialogue, confidence and co-operation between them.

PROVISION OF EARLY WARNING

13. If, on the basis of exchanges of communications and contacts with relevant parties, the High Commissioner concludes that there is a *prima facie* risk of potential conflict (as set out in paragraph (3)) he/she may issue an early warning, which will be communicated promptly by the Chairman-in-Office to the CSO.

14. The Chairman-in-Office will include this early warning in the agenda for the next meeting of the CSO. If a State believes that such an early warning merits prompt consultation, it may initiate the procedure set out in Annex 2 of the Summary of Conclusions of the Berlin Meeting of the Council ("Emergency Mechanism").

15. The High Commissioner will explain to the CSO the reasons for issuing the early warning.

EARLY ACTION

16. The High Commissioner may recommend that he/she be authorized to enter into further contact and closer consultations with the parties concerned with a view to possible solutions, according to a mandate to be decided by the CSO. The CSO may decide accordingly.

ACCOUNTABILITY

17. The High Commissioner will consult the Chairman-in-Office prior to a departure for a participating State to address a tension involving national minorities. The Chairman-in-Office will consult, in confidence, the participating State(s) concerned and may consult more widely.

18. After a visit to a participating State, the High Commissioner will provide strictly confidential reports to the Chairman-in-Office on the findings and progress of the High Commissioner's involvement in a particular question.

19. After termination of the involvement of the High Commissioner in a particular issue, the High Commissioner will report to the Chairman-in-Office on the findings, results and conclusions. Within a period of one month, the Chairman-in-Office will consult, in confidence, on the findings, results and conclusions the participating State(s) concerned and may consult more widely. Thereafter the report, together with possible comments, will be transmitted to the CSO.

20. Should the High Commissioner conclude that the situation is escalating into a conflict, or if the High Commissioner deems that the scope for action by the High Commissioner is exhausted, the High Commissioner shall, through the Chairman-in-Office, so inform the CSO.

21. Should the CSO become involved in a particular issue, the High Commissioner will provide information and, on request, advice to the CSO, or to any other institution or organization which the CSO may invite, in accordance with the provisions of Chapter III of this document, to take action with regard to the tensions or conflict.

22. The High Commissioner, if so requested by the CSO and with due regard to the requirement of confidentiality in his/her mandate, will provide information about his/her activities at CSCE implementation meetings on Human Dimension issues.

SUPPLEMENT

SOURCES OF INFORMATION ABOUT NATIONAL MINORITY ISSUES

23. The High Commissioner may:

23a. collect and receive information regarding the situation of national minorities and the role of parties involved therein from any source, including the media and non-governmental organizations with the exception referred to in paragraph (25);

23b. receive specific reports from parties directly involved regarding developments concerning national minority issues. These may include reports on violations of CSCE commitments with respect to national minorities as well as other violations in the context of national minority issues.

24. Such specific reports to the High Commissioner should meet the following requirements:

- they should be in writing, addressed to the High Commissioner as such and signed with full names and addresses;
- they should contain a factual account of the developments which are relevant to the situation of persons belonging to national minorities and the role of the parties involved therein, and which have taken place recently, in principle not more than 12 months previously. The reports should contain information which can be sufficiently substantiated.

25. The High Commissioner will not communicate with and will not acknowledge communications from any person or organization which practices or publicly condones terrorism or violence.

PARTIES DIRECTLY CONCERNED

26. Parties directly concerned in tensions who can provide specific reports to the High Commissioner and with whom the High Commissioner will seek to communicate in person during a visit to a participating State are the following:

26a. governments of participating States, including, if appropriate, regional and local authorities in areas in which national minorities reside;

26b. representatives of associations, non-governmental organizations, religious and other groups of national minorities directly concerned and in the area of tension, which are authorized by the persons belonging to those national minorities to represent them.

CONDITIONS FOR TRAVEL BY THE HIGH COMMISSIONER

27. Prior to an intended visit, the High Commissioner will submit to the participating State concerned specific information regarding the intended purpose of that visit. Within two weeks the State(s) concerned will consult with the High Commissioner on the objectives of the visit, which may include the promotion of dialogue, confidence and co-operation between the parties. After entry the State concerned will facilitate free travel and communication of the High Commissioner subject to the provisions of paragraph (25) above.

28. If the State concerned does not allow the High Commissioner to enter the country and to travel and communicate freely, the High Commissioner will so inform the CSO.

29. In the course of such a visit, subject to the provision of paragraph (25) the High Commissioner may consult the parties involved, and may receive information in confidence from any individual, group or organization directly concerned on questions the High Commissioner is addressing. The High Commissioner will respect the confidential nature of the information.

30. The participating States will refrain from taking any action against persons, organizations or institutions on account of their contact with the High Commissioner.

HIGH COMMISSIONER AND INVOLVEMENT OF EXPERTS

31. The High Commissioner may decide to request assistance from not more than three experts with relevant expertise in specific matters on which brief, specialized investigation and advice are required.

32. If the High Commissioner decides to call on experts, the High Commissioner will set a clearly defined mandate and time-frame for the activities of the experts.

33. Experts will only visit a participating State at the same time as the High Commissioner. Their mandate will be an integral part of the mandate of the High Commissioner and the same conditions for travel will apply.

34. The advice and recommendations requested from the experts will be submitted in confidence to the High Commissioner, who will be responsible for the activities and for the reports of the experts and who will decide whether and in what form the advice and recommendations will be communicated to

the parties concerned. They will be non-binding. If the High Commissioner decides to make the advice and recommendations available, the State(s) concerned will be given the opportunity to comment.

35. The experts will be selected by the High Commissioner with the assistance of the ODIHR from the resource list established at the ODIHR as laid down in the Document of the Moscow Meeting.

36. The experts will not include nationals or residents of the participating State concerned, or any person appointed by the State concerned, or any expert against whom the participating State has previously entered reservations. The experts will not include the participating State's own nationals or residents or any of the persons it appointed to the resource list, or more than one national or resident of any particular State.

BUDGET

37. A separate budget will be determined at the ODIHR, which will provide, as appropriate, logistical support for travel and communication. The budget will be funded by the participating States according to the established CSCE scale of distribution. Details will be worked out by the Financial Committee and approved by the CSO.

NOTES

1. The CSCE is an intergovernmental process that began in 1972 and reached its first landmark in 1975 with the signing of the Helsinki Final Act, under which participating states agree to observe and promote commitments on military security, economic cooperation, and human rights. Currently, there are 53 participating states, including all of the countries of Europe and the former Soviet Union, as well as the United States and Canada. At the time of the 1992 Follow-up Meeting in Helsinki, which is often called Helsinki II to avoid confusion with the first Helsinki summit of 1975, there were only 51 participating states involved in the decision-making process due to the suspension of the rump Yugoslavia (Serbia-Montenegro) and to the not-yet-completed separation of the Czech and Slovak Republics into sovereign states. For concise reviews of the CSCE process, see Arie Bloed, ed., *From Helsinki to Vienna: Basic Documents of the Helsinki Process* (Dordrecht: Njihoff, 1990); Erika Schlager, "The Procedural Framework of the CSCE: From the Helsinki Consultations to the Paris Charter, 1972–1990," *International Human Rights Law Journal* 12, no. 6–7 (1991), pp. 221–38; and Arie Bloed, ed., *The Conference on Security and Cooperation in Europe: Basic Documents* (forthcoming).

2. *National minority* has no normative definition within the Helsinki process. By convention the phrase is used to denote, in the most general terms, a non-dominant population that is a numerical minority within a state.

3. For analyses of the CSCE's initial response to the Yugoslav crisis, see a number of articles in *Helsinki Monitor* 3, no. 1 (1992). For a discussion of the impact of the Yugoslav crisis, as well as the war in Nagorno-Karabakh, on the development of the CSCE's conflict response mechanisms, see Norbert Ropers and Peter Schlotter, "CSCE: Multilateral Conflict Management in a Transforming World Order, Future Perspectives and New Impulses for Regional Peace Strategies," Foundation for Development and Peace and the Institute for Development and Peace, Paper series *Interdependence*, no. 14 (Bonn, 1993). Here it is also interesting to note that during the 1990 Copenhagen Meeting of the Conference on the Human Dimension, there was a Swedish proposal to recommend the establishment of a "CSCE Representative on National Minorities" at the Paris Summit Meeting later that year. It was proposed that such a representative would have "the mandate to study situations of national minorities which, in his opinion, could affect security in Europe" and to report on his (or her) findings and recommendations before the 1992 Follow-up Meeting. As a member of the delegation has noted, however, the CSCE lacked the institutional framework for such an idea to be realized, though it received favorable attention from other delegations at the time.

4. The term *High Commissioner* and the abbreviation *HCNM* are used interchangeably throughout the text according to readability.

5. See the Appendix to this chapter for the full text of the mandate.

6. The mandate does not specify what the Chairman-in-Office may then do with the mission report, but presumably it would be used as the basis for further consultations with the state(s) concerned and other participating states regarding possible solutions to the tensions.

7. The mandate does not make it clear what would happen if the CSO chose *not* to act on an "early warning" issued by the High Commissioner.

8. For a valuable discussion of the potential functioning of the High Commissioner, based on the mandate, see "Early Warning and Preventive Action in the CSCE," Report of the CSCE Devising Session, October 19, 1992,

prepared by Conflict Management Group and Harvard Negotiation Project (Cambridge, MA, 1993).

9. To be sure, the development of consensus on normative commitments regarding national minority issues has occurred at historically specific moments in the CSCE process. Progress toward common definitions of the principles guiding states' responsibilities in this realm may well have culminated with the Concluding Document of the Copenhagen Meeting of the Conference on the Human Dimension (1990). The unique characteristics of the CSCE decision-making process may also have masked significant differences in states' positions, differences that may have, and could continue to, become more evident again.

10. For more complete reviews of the history of the CSCE's normative commitments on national minorities, see Jan Helgesen, "Protecting Minorities in the CSCE Process," in *The Strength of Diversity: Human Rights and Pluralist Democracy*, ed. Allan Rosas and Jan Helgesen (Dordrecht: Njihoff, 1992), pp. 159–86; and Alexis Heraclides, "The CSCE and Minorities: The Negotiations Behind the Commitments, 1972–1992," *Helsinki Monitor* 3, no. 3 (1992), pp. 5–18. This section draws substantially on the latter article.

11. Heraclides, "The CSCE and Minorities," p. 8.

12. Concluding Document of the Vienna Follow-up Meeting (1989), Principles, para. 19.

13. "The human dimension" is a catch-all term for the CSCE's category of human rights issues, humanitarian affairs, and related concerns. There have been a number of CSCE meetings exclusively under this category, including the three meetings of the so-called Conference on the Human Dimension in Paris (1989), Copenhagen (1990), and Moscow (1991). In addition to the results of these meetings, the Concluding Document of the Vienna Follow-up Meeting (1989) and the Charter of Paris for a New Europe (1990) are generally understood to bear directly on the human dimension sphere. For a complete history of the human dimension, see Alexis Heraclides, *Conference on Security and Cooperation in Europe: The Human Dimension, 1972–1991* (forthcoming). For consideration of recent human dimension developments, as well as the future of the human dimension in the CSCE, see Alexis Heraclides, "The Human Dimension: Normative Commitments," pp. 65-76, and Rob Zaagman, "The Human Dimension: Institutional Aspects," pp. 52–64, in *Helsinki Monitor* 3, no. 4 (1992).

14. Heraclides, "The CSCE and Minorities," p. 9.

15. See the Document of the Copenhagen Meeting of the Conference on the Human Dimension (1990), chapter 4.

16. See the Report of the Geneva Meeting of Experts on National Minorities (1991).

17. For more information on the "Moscow mechanism" and indeed on the Moscow meeting in general, see Arie Bloed, "The Moscow Meeting of the Human Dimension," *Helsinki Monitor* 3, no. 1 (1992), pp. 4–16.

18. Time limits intended to speed up the execution of this procedure, known initially as the "human dimension mechanism" and now as the "Vienna mechanism," were introduced at the Copenhagen and Moscow Human Dimension Meetings. For more information on this mechanism, see Rachel Brett, "The Development of the Human Dimension Mechanism of the Conference on Security and Cooperation in Europe," University of Essex

Human Rights Centre, Papers in the Theory and Practice of Human Rights, no. 1 (1992).

19. In addition to these mechanisms in the human dimension sphere, a "Mechanism for Consultation and Cooperation with regard to Emergency Situations" was also adopted by the Council of Ministers at its first meeting in Berlin on June 19–20, 1991 to respond to alarming political crises, such as the one developing at that time in former Yugoslavia. To a great extent, these mechanisms for addressing human rights problems and political crises draw on the CSCE tradition of devising procedural approaches for reviewing the implementation of CSCE agreements, particularly in the realm of military activity, and for promoting greater confidence and security between participating states. For a more extensive discussion see Ropers and Schlotter, "CSCE: Multilateral Conflict Management."

20. Though often characterized by the media in terms of inter-ethnic strife, fighting in Trans-Dniestria has been understood by most serious analysts as more of a political conflict. Also, since mid-1992, the CSCE has become engaged in other actual and potential conflicts, as well as authorizing additional measures in response to the ongoing crises mentioned here. Most notably, on-site missions for different conflict-related purposes have been approved and, in some cases, already undertaken in Estonia, the Abkhazia region of Georgia, Macedonia, Tajikistan, and Kosovo, Sandjak, and Vojvodina (rump Yugoslavia).

21. For a more extensive treatment of the Helsinki Follow-up Meeting, see the special issue of *Helsinki Monitor* 3, no. 4 (1992).

22. For a more detailed discussion of the Helsinki II deliberations on the High Commissioner, see Hannie Zaal, "The CSCE High Commissioner on National Minorities," *Helsinki Monitor* 3, no. 4 (1992), upon which this section also relies.

23. Prior to his appointment as High Commissioner, van der Stoel held the following positions, among others: Dutch Minister for Foreign Affairs (1973–1977 and 1981–1982), Permanent Representative of the Netherlands to the UN (1983–1986), and Member of the Netherlands Council of State (1986–1992).

24. With regard to the Baltic region, there have been repeated allegations of discrimination, mostly in connection to legislation on citizenship and language issues, against Russian-speaking persons, particularly in Estonia and Latvia (which have a sizeable concentration of such populations); however, High Commissioner visits to the region in mid-January and early April 1993 revealed no evidence of persecution of national minorities in these situations.

25. The first-year budget covers the High Commissioner's salary as well as communication charges and mission expenses, including travel and the services of interpreters and experts.

26. For a blueprint for UN action in the realm of humanitarian intervention, see the report of Secretary-General Boutros Boutros-Ghali, "An Agenda for Peace," UN document A/47/277-S/24111, released June 17, 1992.

27. For one analysis of the dynamics and future of the overall process of CSCE institutionalization, see "Beyond Process: The CSCE's Institutional Development, 1990–92," Report of the US Commission on Security and Cooperation in Europe (Washington, DC, 1992).

28. Initial measures towards coordination with other intergovernmental organizations have been articulated in the Charter of Paris for a New Europe

(1990), the Prague Document on Further Development of CSCE Institutions and Structures (1992), and the Helsinki II Document (1992).

29. This point on openness was made by Arie Bloed in a conversation with the author.

About the Authors

Adam Smith Albion is a Research Associate at the IEWS European Studies Center at Štiřín, the Czech Republic. He previously was a researcher at the Historical Institute of the Czechoslovak Military Academy before joining the IEWS as a Research Associate in 1991. He specializes in East Central European security developments, especially Balkan issues.

Richard Allan, currently the American Scholar-in-Residence at the Institute for EastWest Studies, is a professor at the Brooklyn Law School. He is an expert on low intensity warfare, terrorism and criminal justice. His latest publication is "Terrorism, Extradition, and Sanctions," in the *Albany Law Journal of Science and Technology* 3, no. 2 (1993).

Ian M. Cuthbertson is the Vice President of Programs at the IEWS. A former Senior Research Officer in the Arms Control and Disarmament Research Unit of the Foreign and Commonwealth Office, he has published extensive works on security issues, including *The Guns Fall Silent: The End of the Cold War and the Future of Disarmament*, (with Peter Volten), *Enhancing European Security: Living in a Less Nuclear World*, and *Redefining the CSCE; Challenges and Opportunities in the New Europe.*

Dmitri Evstafiev is a Research Associate at the Institute for USA and Canada at the Russian Academy of Sciences in Moscow.

André W.M. Gerrits is a senior lecturer at the Institute for Russian and East European Studies at the University of Amsterdam. His recent publications include *The Failure of Authoritarian Change: Reform, Opposition, and Geopolitics in Poland in the 1980's* and *East European Studies and the End of Communism: Opportunities, Challenges, and Risks.*

Iván Gyurcsík, a lawyer based in Slovakia, was a parliamentary correspondent for *Szabad Ujsag* and for the past year has been a Fellow at the Hungarian Human Rights Foundation in New York. Mr. Gyurcsik is a co-founder of the Coexistence Political Movement, and is a Schumann Fellow at the IEWS.

Konrad J. Huber currently works as an advisor to the CSCE High Commissioner on National Minorities, former Dutch Minister of State

Max van der Stoel. Mr. Huber's professional experience in human rights and humanitarian affairs includes positions with nongovernmental organizations in the US and Latin America.

István Íjgyártó is the Head of Department for Political Analysis at the Hungarian Government Office for Hungarians Living Abroad, and is a specialist in the fields of minority problems in Central and Eastern Europe and the Newly Independent States, especially Russia and Ukraine. Formerly a research fellow with the Demographic Research Institute in Budapest, Hungary, Mr. Íjgyártó was a National Forum Foundation Visiting Fellow in 1991.

Andrzej Karkoszka is the Director of the Department of Strategic Planning at the Ministry of Defense of Poland. Before his current post, Dr. Karkoszka worked for many years as a senior researcher at the Polish Institute for International Affairs, and as a Senior Fellow of the IEWS.

Koen Koch is a professor of international relations at Leiden University, the Netherlands, and has written extensively on the role of international organizations in the emerging world order.

Alexander A. Konovalov is the Director of the Center for Military Policy and Systems Analysis at the Russian Academy of Sciences. His current research includes works on Russian-US relations in the military-political field; problems of civil-military relations inside Russia and the CIS; and foundations of the future Russian-US military strategic partnership.

Jane Leibowitz is a Senior Program Associate at the IEWS. In addition to working for the National Republican Institute in Washington, DC, Ms. Leibowitz was a researcher for the Sawyer/Miller Group and Amnesty International in New York City.

Robert W. Mickey is currently a Research Associate at the IEWS European Studies Center at Štiřín, the Czech Republic. He joined the IEWS as a Research Assistant in 1991, after serving as a Research Assistant for the European Security Project at the Center for Foreign Policy Development at Brown University.

Ivanka Neveda, a political scientist specializing in Balkan security issues, is a Senior Research Associate at the Free Initiative Foundation in Sofia. Previously she was the Vice Director of the Bulgarian

Institute of International Studies. Her fellowships have included the Wilson Center for International Scholars at the Smithsonian Institution and the University of Maryland.

Joseph S. Nye, Jr. is the former director of the Center for International Affairs at Harvard, and a Professor of International Affairs on leave from Harvard University. He was a Senior Fellow of the Aspen Institute, former director of the Aspen Strategy Group, and Deputy to the Undersecretary of State for Security Assistance, Science, and Technology; he also chaired the National Security Council Group on the Nonproliferation of Nuclear Weapons. Professor Nye's most recent publication is the book *Understanding International Conflicts*. He is currently Chairman of the National Intelligence Council at the Central Intelligence Agency.

Nicolai N. Petro was the founding director of the Center for Contemporary Russian Studies at the Monterey Institute of International Studies. He has taught at the University of Virginia, Sweet Briar College, and the University of Pennsylvania, and is presently teaching at the University of Rhode Island. Dr. Petro has also been an International Affairs Fellow of the Council on Foreign Relations, and has served in the Office of Soviet Union Affairs at the US Department of State, and as temporary political attache at the US Embassy in Moscow.